JUDGES

BERIT OLAM
Studies in Hebrew Narrative & Poetry

Judges

Tammi J. Schneider

David W. Cotter, O.S.B.
Editor

Jerome T. Walsh
Chris Franke
Associate Editors

A Michael Glazier Book

LITURGICAL PRESS
Collegeville, Minnesota

www.litpress.org

A Michael Glazier Book published by Liturgical Press.

Cover design by Ann Blattner.

ISBN 13: 978-0-8146-8845-8 (pbk)

1   2   3   4   5   6   7   8   9

Library of Congress Cataloging-in-Publication Data

Schneider, Tammi, 1962–
     Judges / Tammi J. Schneider.
          p.   cm. — (Berit olam)
     Includes bibliographical references and index.
     ISBN 0-8146-5050-3 (alk. paper)
     1. Bible.   O.T.   Judges—Criticism, Narrative.   2. Bible as literature.
I. Title.   II. Series.

BS1305.2.S36   1999
222'.32066—dc21
                                                            99-24445
                                                            CIP

For my Mother
Ruth Aaron

CONTENTS

ACKNOWLEDGMENTS

It is a great pleasure to acknowledge and thank those who have contributed to this volume in so many ways. In the past generation of scholarship, important trends were established introducing new ways of examining and understanding texts. I owe a great debt to these scholars for creating a strong base of scholarship from which to build.

This volume would not have happened without Marvin Sweeney. Marvin made the initial contact between the series and myself, discussed Judges and the Hebrew Bible with me constantly, and read versions of the manuscript. I cannot thank him enough for his insight, knowledge, and sense of humor. My students in Hebrew Bible at CGU, and all the students who participated in my seminar, "Women in the Book of Judges," continue to be a deep source of excitement, new ideas, and solid scholarship. The women of the Orange County Jewish Feminist Institute are my inspiration and my muses and this book belongs to them as much as anyone. Karen Torjesen and Lori Ann Ferell, who chaired the Religion Department at CGU while I wrote this book, are powerful role models who supported me through this process with their visionary leadership and ability to be scholars, teachers, mentors, friends, and good cooks all at the same time. Teresa Shaw was a source of encouragement through her own impressive scholarship and friendship.

A special thanks to David W. Cotter. I truly benefitted from his skill as an editor, the insight he has into texts, both mine and the Biblical text, the speed with which he worked on my manuscript, and his updates on Minnesota football.

I owe my family my deepest thanks. I cannot thank my siblings, parents, and step-parents enough for their help in planning my wedding while I wrote this book. My in-laws' warm acceptance of me into their family and their excitement for this project are more than anyone could ask. My husband's commitment to scholarly pursuits alleviated some of my guilt for spending most of our first month of marriage finishing this manuscript. His constant "musing" keeps my mind racing with new ideas influencing this project and everything I do. My mother's firm belief that there was nothing my siblings and I could not achieve if we set our minds to it is best represented in her repeated refrain to me, "Just finish the book." So to all who were part of this project, thank you, it is finished.

INTRODUCTION

The book of Judges is one of the best and least known of the books in the Hebrew Bible. The stories about Samson and Delilah, and Deborah and Baraq are some of the most loved in literature and Hollywood. Despite the popularity of some characters and the stories in which they play a role, others, such as Achsah, the unnamed raped *pîlegeš*, and the final story about the civil war among the tribes of Israel are virtually unknown to the average reader.[1] This situation results partially from the desire to treat the book of Judges as a collection of charming tales while at the same time denying the serious theological messages contained in the many heart-breaking accounts.

In most scholarly treatments, the book of Judges is considered to be a cycle of stories governed by a Deuteronomistic refrain; when the Israelites behave they prosper but when they stray hardship follows. In Judges the Israelites repeatedly stray from their deity's commandments. They then cry out to their deity, who raises a judge who helps them and rights things in their lifetimes.[2] Upon the judge's death the

---

[1] The name Achsah should be transliterated *ʿaksâ*. Because it is a character's name, and used so often, the author will not follow standard transliteration methods for it, nor for other personal names. The term *pîlegeš* will not be translated in this book because there are no good English translations. The traditional translation, "concubine," is problematic because of its precise English meaning and lack of evidence indicating that "concubine" coveys the salient elements of the Hebrew term, to be discussed in more detail below. Since the translation, and evaluation of someone who is a concubine, clouds the reader's impression of the various characters labeled with this term, the present author will transliterate the term rather than translate it.

[2] Throughout this book the God of Israel, YHWH, will be referred to as, "the deity," or, "the Israelite deity." The author's reason is that since this commentary will be distributed to a primarily monotheistic reading audience, the deity addressed

Israelites stray again, and the deity raises another judge to help them. The pattern continues until the end of the book, at which point the biblical author hints that Israel needs a king, preparing the reader for the books of Samuel through Kings which recount Israel's dynastic period.

Although the book of Judges is cyclical and does follow the aforementioned pattern, such a synopsis misses the critical point that the Israelites do not begin each cycle at the same place each time. The present study will argue that the book of Judges is organized to show a degenerative progression; each cycle shows a generation beginning yet lower on the scale of legitimate behavior regarding the Israelites' relationship to their deity than the previous generation had. The worsening situation is shown in the book through the actions of the judges and the Israelites in their relationships to each other, to the surrounding communities, and, most importantly, to their deity. The deterioration of Israel's relationship to its deity leads finally to the situation that, problematic as it was considered even then, kingship was the only answer to Israel's predicament. Judges' organizing principle is not related to historical chronology but reflects a worsening theological situation in Israel's relationship to its deity during the narrative time of the period of Judges. Israel's decline is revealed by the order of the stories, which are unified by thematic threads, the use of irony, and specialized terminology.

In modern scholarship the book of Judges is treated as an important historical source for the time period between the Exodus from Egypt and the beginning of the United Monarchy.[3] Scholars recognize that a theology strongly reflective of the Deuteronomistic Historian has been imposed upon the text and suggest that if this late theological imposition were removed, scholars would be left with stories reflecting historical events.[4] As a result, the book has become the domain of historians

---

in the biblical book is considered the same as that worshiped by the readers. This creates a situation where the most prominent character in the book is also one with whom the reader has a personal relationship and predetermined notions of who that character is, regardless of how the other characters in the text view the character. Referring to Israel's God as "the deity" will keep the reader's relationship with the characters as even as possible and remove the reader's personal religious theology from the text before considering it.

[3] In an effort to avoid lengthy and frequent footnotes the author will limit herself to specific general texts which contain longer bibliographies for those who are interested in further detail. A greater discussion of this appears later in the introduction. R. Boling, "Judges, Book of," *ABD* 3, ed. D. N. Freedman (New York: Doubleday, 1992) 1107–17.

[4] Ibid., 1107.

and an appreciation of the artistry of the narrative has fallen by the wayside.[5] More recently, partially because the book contains so many stories concerning women, feminists have rediscovered the book and focused on the literary construction of various individual stories or issues running throughout the narrative.[6] More recent scholarly trends, such as treating the Deuteronomistic History from a literary and historical perspective, place Judges within the Deuteronomistic History and contribute to understanding the book in its larger context.[7]

The present examination is interested in how the entire book of Judges functions as a unified literary document. The focus is on the major themes which run throughout the book: the search for, as well as an examination and critique of, differing forms of leadership, the role of women as the barometer of how society functions, the polemic regarding ongoing north/south tensions among the tribes of Israel as well as that related to David and Saul, and Israel's relationship to its deity. These themes are inherent in the narrative, as is made evident by the issues the book addresses, the amount of text dedicated to each topic, the terminology employed, transitions between the various units, and intertextual references tying Judges into the larger biblical corpus. The text of Judges expresses these concepts through the content, terminology, and structure of the individual narratives and also that of the book as a whole. Despite what are considered to be later Deuteronomistic additions at the beginning and end of the book, Judges is a well-integrated theological narrative which builds its story and supports its thesis until its conclusion.

---

[5] For example, in Boling's entry on Judges in *ABD*, one paragraph concerns the book of Judges as Narrative Art (which is said to be lacking) as compared to a full page dedicated to Judges as Historiography, another full page about the Archaeology and Social World, and a full half page addressing the Levitical Sponsorship. Boling, "Judges, Book of" 1113–6.

[6] P. Trible ignited the trend of examining particular stories with "An Unnamed Woman: The Extravagance of Violence," and, "The Daughter of Jephthah: An Inhuman Sacrifice," both in *Texts of Terror: Literary-Feminist Readings of Biblical Narratives.* Philadelphia: Fortress Press, 1984. M. Bal's approach was to examine the entire book of Judges, but using a particular methodology and examining specific issues. M. Bal, *Death and Dissymmetry: The Politics of Coherence in the Book of Judges.* Chicago Studies in the History of Judaism (Chicago: The University of Chicago Press, 1988). It is striking that despite the importance of these and following works written from a feminist perspective, most general references, such as Boling's bibliography in *ABD*, do not refer to this important body of scholarly literature.

[7] M. Brettler, "Literature as Politics," *JBL* 108 (1989) 412; M. Sweeney, "David Polemics in the Book of Judges," *VT* 47 (1997) 517–29.

The book of Judges is concerned with seeking an answer to a straight-forward question, "Who is going to lead Israel?" The book begins with this question (Judg 1:1) and a variation is repeated towards the end (Judg 20:18). Throughout the text different titles and characterizations for leaders, both within and outside Israel, are introduced, almost as if a test is being made of different forms of control. The stories in the book are less about battles and the reasons for them than they are about such issues as how the various judges attained their office, what individuals did in order to express their leadership, what judges' relationships were with the deity, their reasons for fighting, how much power they wielded before and after their major battle/s, and what other actions they carried out which impacted their relationship with the Israelite deity and set the stage for the next generation. The book begins with Othniel, the model judge, and ends with Samson, who is so negatively evaluated that he not only dies in battle with foreigners, but his death leads to anarchy in Israel. These poles, Othniel and Samson, highlight the steadily decreasing worth of the judges over time, and at the same time, the downward spiral of all of Israel. An implicit evaluation of the later kings Saul and David is also included in Judges through the many qualities, often negative, of the various leaders.

Chapter 2 describes the very limited role foreseen for whatever non-Israelite people are left in the land. This role implies a number of guiding principles which ought to underpin Israelite behavior. The Is-raelites are told to destroy them, and are certainly neither to intermarry with them nor take on their religious practices. Yet all of the judges, with the possible exception of Othniel, adopt at least some of these practices. The nature of the judges' offenses worsen over time so that Samson, the worst of the judges, is remembered to have sought out only Philistines throughout his lifetime. By the end of the book, then, even the leader designated by the deity does not follow the practices incumbent upon all Israel. This leads to a situation in which there are no leaders in Israel and, as a result of which, Israel turns on itself in war.

One of the major components affecting the evaluation of the judges is the role of women in their lives. With the exception of Ehud, Tola, Jair, Elon, and Abdon, the stories of the individual judges contain some reference to a woman, either by name or description of relationship to them, who heavily affect the judge's character and actions. The book begins with Othniel who married into the only pre-existing family of Israelite rulers. The last individual judge's life ended because of his habit of chasing women. Finally, in the last story of the book, the Israel-ites destroy whole villages and institute rape/marriages for women, actually preventing their fathers and brothers from protecting them, in order to sustain the tribe of Benjamin.

Saving the tribe of Benjamin through the rape/marriage of women highlights the constant north/south, David/Saul tension which flows through the book. This tension appears already in the book's second line where the tribe of Judah is the answer to the question of "who will begin to lead Israel" (Judg 1:2). The final story implies that all Benjaminites, including the future King Saul, are descendants of a male warrior and a raped/married woman from Jabesh-Gilead or Shiloh. This is just one example of how hints to the north/south, David/Saul conflict permeate the book.

The final story is another example of the tension between the northern tribe of Benjamin, and the rest of Israel, which is also related to the David/Saul conflict. Saul is from the tribe of Benjamin. Gibeah, a Benjaminite town, is depicted in Judges 19–20 as sexually depraved and saved only through Israel's decision not to destroy a tribe in Israel (Judg 21:2). The Israelites offer the Benjaminites the opportunity to rape/marry women from Jabesh-Gilead and Shiloh to continue the tribe (Judg 21:9-12, 19-23). The implication of the final story is that all succeeding generations of Benjamin, including the future King Saul, are descendants of a male warrior and a raped woman from Jabesh-Gilead or Shiloh. Northern Benjamin is contrasted with Judah, the tribe of the future King David and therefore authoritative enough to rule all of Israel. Already in the second line Judah is the answer to the question, "who will begin to lead Israel" (Judg 1:2), and reappears at the end of the book in response to the question who will lead Israel against the tribe of Benjamin (Judg 20:18).

All of these themes reaffirm the central insight that the book of Judges is most fundamentally concerned with the relationship of Israel to its deity. Tenets of the relationship are broken in the first chapter necessitating a reminder to the people of what the deity had already done for the Israelites in the past and what were, as a result, their responsibilities. The following scenarios reflect instances where the deity repeatedly comes to Israel's aid despite their continuing to go astray. The relationship worsens so that whereas the earliest judges had fought their battles on behalf of the Israelite deity and the people of Israel, Samson would fight merely for personal revenge, and ultimately, in the civil war with which the book concludes, the Israelites no longer know the reason for their actions but simply react.

The worsening situation in Israel concerning the relationship between the people and her deity is also reflected in Israel's evaluation of her situation and how it might be remedied. At the beginning of the book, the Israelites cry out to the deity and attempt to mend their ways. Again, by the time of Samson's story they no longer cry out but, much to the contrary, are angered by someone who fights the enemy. At the end of the book there is no longer any external enemy because Israel has turned on itself as its own enemy.

The text relies heavily on specific words and phrases to highlight the worsening situation of Israel reflected in the search for leadership, role of women, north/south, David/Saul polemic, and relationship to the deity. A number of specific words and phrases are used early in the book, with apparently positive connotations and results, which by the end of the book are seen as negative and which lead to destruction. For example, many of the specific terms used with Achsah in the first chapter of the book such as, "donkey," "heart," and, "father," and which lead in that case to a positive outcome are also used later with the raped *pîlegeš*. In that latter case, they lead to her death and dismemberment, which then becomes the catalyst for a civil war. Many of these terms are used throughout the book in modified versions, so uniting the narrative while at the same time highlighting the gradual decline of Israel's state regarding how her deity demands she act.

The text also employs irony frequently to reveal the worsening situation of Israel. Again the case of Achsah is apt. At the beginning of the book Achsah carries out actions which contain within them hints of irony. Yet it is only when these actions reappear in the final story of rape and civil war is the extent of the ultimate irony apparent.

Themes which recur throughout the book, use of terminology as leitmotifs, and irony reveal that one encounters in Judges an integrated text which constantly reinforces the theological argument of the book, that Israel's leaders do not follow the commandments of the deity, do not destroy the surrounding nations, and, as a result, adopt their customs. Israel's deteriorating leadership leads the people to a worsening situation so that towards the end of the book the Israelites do things for the deity which are expressly forbidden. Israel's moral compass is lost through lack of leadership, establishing the need for a monarchy in Israel. Despite much commentary to the contrary, the terminology and themes expressed in the opening chapters do not disappear only to reappear again in the final three chapters, nor are they only tacked onto the beginning or end of the individual stories, but are integrated throughout the book. Judges does not have theology merely tacked onto it at the end but thoroughly incorporates the theme that Israel's straying from her deity is the cause of her distress.

Overview

The book of Judges begins with the question about leadership which is asked following the death of Joshua, the last deity-appointed ruler. The first chapter examines the status of each of the tribes, highlighting not only where their successes had been, but, more prominently, how they failed to recover the land, thereby transgressing the deity's commandments. In chapter two the text back-tracks to the time surrounding Joshua's death, providing details of the Israelites' responsibilities and highlighting how they have already transgressed. Also included is a summary of the general cycle that follows in the rest of the book. Chapter three begins with a list of the nations that the deity left in the land in order to test Israel.

The third chapter also begins the accounts of the individual judges with Othniel who becomes the model. Othniel is the model because the text describes his actions and the way in which he accomplished the deity's expectations. Elements of his story that are not relevant or may detract from that image but were already narrated in Judg 1:12-15 are not included.

Chapters four through sixteen contain stories of the individual judges. Traditionally scholarship has classified them as falling into two groups: charismatic and minor. Charismatic judges are those for whom a story, and about whom some detailed information, is supplied. The minor judges are those about whom the text states the fact that they judged, supplies their name, place of origin, and some limited information about them, but does not define a battle or episode which legitimates their role as judges.

It is difficult to define the characteristics definitive of the heros granted the action of judging in the book. The responsibilities change throughout the narrative time, highlighting Israel's worsening state. The earliest judges Othniel, Ehud, and Shamgar fight battles and are clearly military heroes. There is no indication that they had any other functions. Beginning with Deborah and Baraq there is a change. Deborah is the only judge who functions in a judicial context, and this occurs prior to the battle. In fact, Baraq is the intended military leader but fails to live up to that role, so Deborah is forced to take on a military role in addition to her judiciary responsibilities. The judges continue to assume more power with Gideon, who is offered kingship and claims not to accept it. But his children (not only Abimelech but his other children as well) behave in such a way as to reveal elements of leadership which are rooted in their father's military victory, although they are not military leaders themselves.

The situation worsens with the minor judges who follow, who rule despite there having been no apparent battle or enemy to necessitate their leadership or validate it. Jephthah demands powers beyond those of the military even before accepting the military role. Samson completely reverses the trend, though not for the better, by taking neither a military nor any other form of leadership role, but instead by acting merely for self-gratification and revenge.

Each judge is rooted in a specific region; in this the book reflects Israel's fragmented state. Only at the beginning and end are the Israelites clearly gathered as one group. Throughout the stories only a few tribes appear at any one time to fight in any particular battle. Even in this regard a worsening situation appears. In chapter one Judah receives the leadership status from the deity and immediately fights on its own behalf (Judg 1:3-4). The situation of single tribes fighting on their own is not considered to be an issue until chapter five when Deborah castigates a number of tribes for not having appeared to fight with the others (Judg 5:14-18). The situation worsens with Gideon/Jerubbaal when Ephraim claims they had not even been invited. However, in that instance the angry Ephraimites were placated by compliments (Judg 8:1-3). In Jephthah's story, Ephraim complains once again about the lack of invitation, but this time they cannot be placated and the slight leads to a small scale civil war (Judg 12:1-6). In the final story, apparently all of Israel manages to gather to fight Benjamin, but even in this instance one tribe does not appear. In this final case, the failure to appear is consistent with the anarchy which prevails at the end of Judges, and leads to a clan's destruction (Judges 19–21).

This last example shows how, despite the absence of individual judges in the last five chapters, the final stories are thoroughly integrated into the book in terms of the themes and terminology which are used there. The situations reflected in the final stories can take place only because of the increasingly poor leadership Israel had received throughout the book.

The final judge is from the tribe of Dan and chapter seventeen begins with the movement of this tribe. In fact the tribe may have moved at this time as a result of the Samson episode and its aftermath. In the resulting anarchy, Israel no longer cries out to its deity and everyone in the story takes matters into his own hands. The tribe of Dan decides on its own where it will live; Michah tries to please the deity by making a graven image from stolen money and promotes a priest who nonetheless leaves for a better job.

The following story (Judges 19) concerns another Levite who is also of questionable character. This man takes his *pîlegeš* from the security of her father's house into a situation where an entire town requests illegitimate sexual liaisons with the Levite, who, instead of complying, throws his *pîlegeš* out of the house to be gang-raped all night. After mustering all of Israel by retelling his story, while pointedly deleting his role in it, all of Israel goes to war against Benjamin (Judg 20:1-7). Lack of leadership is most evident in the final war where the Israelites presumably fight because a woman was raped, but in so doing impose the same fate on more women in an effort to restrain the tribe of Benjamin (Judges 20–21).

A final note concerning kingship follows the civil war, the almost complete destruction of the tribe of Benjamin, and the enforced rape/marriage of the women of Jabesh-Gilead and Shiloh to save the Benjaminites. The final note that there was no king in Israel and so every man did what was right in his own eyes summarizes what had happened during the narrative time of Judges and hints at what is needed in the future (Judg 21:25).

Dating of the Book

Most commentaries on Judges discuss the redaction of the book, the period to which the stories purport to relate, and when the book was finally redacted to its present form. How and when the stories originally were written, and when and how they came to be in the present order are issues which, while worthy of consideration, are beyond the scope of this study. The approach of this series is to treat each book of the Hebrew Bible as a literary whole, and the redaction history of the book is not relevant to its present literary character. The Masoretic Text (hereafter MT), referring to the standard text of the Hebrew Bible derived from the tradition of the Masoretes of Tiberias, is the form of Judges under discussion in this volume.[8]

References in the Book

This series is intended to be used by scholars and lay people alike. This author has attempted to limit the use of footnotes, but not at the expense of deleting the sources to which one can turn for further examination of an issue. I have used the *Anchor Bible Dictionary*, *Hebrew and English Lexicon of the Old Testament (BDB)*, and *The New Encyclopedia of Archaeological Excavations of the Holy Land*, as the primary references since they are all easily accessible, are somewhat up-to-date, and provide bibliography for the reader. A more extensive bibliography for studies concerning the book of Judges is included at the end of the book.

---

[8] For more on the Masoretes see E. J. Revell: "Masoretes," *ABD* 4:593–4; "Masoretic Studies," *ABD* 4:596–7; "Masoretic Text," *ABD* 4:597–9.

Many commentaries and studies have been written about the book of Judges. It is not possible to refer to all of them and keep the number of footnotes within limit. A number of commentaries were published in the early 1980s, and a few more have been published since that time. Those published in the early eighties incorporated much of the scholarly discussion prior to their publication, so the older phase of commentaries will not be referred to extensively here. Instead, those which were published in the early 1980's and form the foundation for much of the scholarship of today will be addressed since they are the primary texts addressing the book of Judges as a unified text. The commentaries used extensively here are R. Boling, *Judges: Introduction, Translation and Commentary,* J. Gray, *The New Century Bible Commentary: Joshua, Judges, Ruth,* and J. A. Soggin, *Judges, A Commentary.*[9] It is necessary to rely on these commentaries because they express the scholarship and understanding of the book up to this time. Again, although there has been much work done on Judges in the last twenty years, much of that work concerns specific stories within the book or trace a particular theme. As a result they do not treat the book as a narrative whole, the focus here.

Throughout this book there are references to biblical passages. If not marked otherwise the translation is the author's. There are quite a few of these but because most translations obscure many of the recurring words which are critical for following the themes in the book, this is the best way to convey this information to the reader. Other translations are also important because they are the basis upon which most English speakers gain access to the text and are the texts from which most people form their understanding of Judges.

As a compromise I use three standard texts. I use the King James Version because it is an older translation, considered authoritative by many, and formed the basis for much of the English discussion of the book for more than 450 years. The Revised Standard Version became standard for many and reflects translation practices and interpretations from the middle years of this century and was important especially for the previous round of Judges commentaries. Finally the new Jewish

---

[9]David N. Freedman, ed. *The Anchor Bible Dictionary,* 6 vols. (New York: Doubleday, 1992); Ephraim Stern, ed. *The New Encyclopedia of Archaeological Excavations in the Holy Land,* 4 vols. (New York: Simon & Schuster, 1993); Francis Brown, S. R. Driver and C. A. Briggs, *Hebrew and English Lexicon of the Old Testament,* (Oxford: Clarendon Press, 1951); R. G. Boling, *Judges: Introduction, Translation and Commentary,* The Anchor Bible (Garden City: Doubleday and Company, 1981); J. Gray, *Joshua, Judges, Ruth,* The New Century Bible Commentary (Grand Rapids, MI: Wm. B. Eerdmans, 1986); J. A. Soggin, *Judges: A Commentary,* Old Testament Library (Philadelphia: The Westminster Press, 1981.)

Publication Society version will be employed. This is a translation from a Jewish perspective, it was published more recently, and reflects some of the most recent translation practices.[10] These are used, primarily, to show the variety of interpretations which are possible in understanding the text and how certain themes in the book have been masked through translation practices.

---

[10] The NRSV is not used here because the RSV and KJV represent Christian traditions and JPS reflects not only a Jewish perspective but also the more recent trends.

Chapter 1
SETTING THE STAGE
Judges 1:1-36

The opening chapters of Judges introduce the themes of the book and are the starting point for the major trends, sub-themes, and language plays used throughout the text. The first two chapters are traditionally treated as a conquest narrative added to the text at some later time by the Deuteronomist.[1]

Such a treatment overlooks: how the opening functions within the book, how closely it is tied to following units, how it relates intimately to the rest of the book, how words, themes, and issues raised in this unit are used throughout the book, and how much in this initial unit is later resignified in the final chapters in an ironic debacle.[2] Understanding the subtle references in the first chapter is essential to understanding the book as a whole, though at this stage many of the references are only hints of what is to come in the final chapters.

The first chapter of Judges contains introductory material. The text contextualizes the period in Israel's history. The central questions concerning leadership, which are faced by the characters in the rest of the text, are first raised here. The main characters, namely the Israelites, their deity, their enemies, and their relationships to each other are introduced. The chapter lays the groundwork for all the situations that follow.

---

[1] R. Boling, "Judges, Book of," *ABD*, vol. 3, ed. D. N. Freedman (New York: Doubleday, 1992) 1107–17; W. Richter, *Traditionsgeschichtliche Untersuchungen zum Richterbuch*, Bonner Biblische Beiträge no. 18 (Bonn: P. Hanstein, 1963); and *Die Bearbeitung des 'Retterbuches' in der deuteronomistischen Epoche*, BBB no. 21 (Bonn: P. Hanstein, 1964); J. A. Soggin, *Judges: A Commentary*, Old Testament Library vol. 4, (Philadelphia: The Westminster Press, 1981).

[2] M. Sweeney ties the unit to the rest of the book through syntax ("David Polemics in the Book of Judges," *VT* 47 [1997] 517–29).

Setting in Time: Judges 1:1-3

The book of Judges begins with the same phrase as the book of Joshua, "It happened after the death of PN" (Josh 1:1; Judg 1:1).[3] Following this mention of the previous leader's death the two books diverge, yet the similarity of this first phrase sets up the contrast between them. The book of Judges purports to follow the period of Joshua's conquests, not only in content of the discussion, but even in the phraseology of the initial sentence.[4] In the book of Joshua, following the announcement that the leader (Moses) had died, the deity is quoted as speaking to the new leader of Israel, Joshua, a leader who had been appointed by the deity during the lifetime of the previous deity-appointed leader, Moses (Josh 1:1). In the case of Judges, no leader was appointed in the reign of Joshua to take over upon his death. The people do not know what to do and therefore inquire of the deity.

The first sentence of Judges reflects a paradigm shift which takes place in the governing of the Israelites in the transition from the wilderness and conquest experiences. Beginning with the first sentence of Judges the deity no longer informs the people and guides them directly; the people now lead themselves. The sense of fear and panic on the part of the Israelites is apparent from the continuation of the sentence, "Who will go up for us in the beginning to the Canaanite to fight against him?" (Judg 1:1). The Israelites, who have depended on the deity or the leader appointed by the deity, have no idea how to proceed. Though most translations use the term "Canaanites," in the plural, the Hebrew is actually singular, "Canaanite." The Canaanites are treated as a singular force whom the Israelites fear. The singular usage creates a more personal situation. It is not a nameless horde but a personal enemy.

The first sentence ties the book of Judges to the book of Joshua in phraseology and themes. According to the conventions of Hebrew narrative, the first word, *wayĕhî*, signals the resumption or continuation of an ongoing narrative. Its use here intimately ties it in to the preceding narrative, indicating that the beginning of Judges is actually the continuation of a much larger story. A hint of condemnation exists because Joshua's task is not finished and no preparations had been made for continuing leadership. Had Joshua succeeded in his task the present community would not be facing the hazards before it.

---

[3] PN is a standard convention which means Personal Name. All biblical translations are the author's unless otherwise noted.

[4] There is much discussion in commentaries on Judges addressing its placement in time. According to information in the book and its placement in the canon, Judges reflects the period between the conquest of the land by Joshua and the period of the early monarchy described in Samuel.

The condemnation is not necessarily condoned by the narrator. This is indicated by the question being placed in the mouth of the Israelites. The unacceptable nature of the Israelites' request is implied in the formulation of the question. Only two other places in the Hebrew Bible employ the terminology, "who will take us up." One reference is in Judg 20:18, which will be discussed later in this volume. *mî* in the MT is in Deut 30:12, again in the context of the death of an Israelite leader. The Deuteronomy citation appears before the death of Moses when the people are frightened about their future. The phrase is in the mouth of Moses who states, "It is not in the Heavens, that you should say 'Who among us can go up to the heavens and get it for us and impart it to us that we may observe it?'" (Deut 30:12, JPS). The Deuteronomy passage is rhetorical; no one can do what is asked, which implies that the question is not a legitimate one to ask. If this is the case, is there a similar connotation that the request for a leader is not legitimate? Deuteronomy 30:13 further rejects the legitimacy of the question by noting that the people have been given the answers in Moses' teaching from the deity. The Deuteronomic refrain which says that following the law brings prosperity and rejection of the law brings disaster appears in the first sentence of Judges both in the request for a leader other than the deity, and the phraseology used to make the request.

A time restraint is included in the initial request for a leader by stating "who will go up for us in the beginning" (Judg 1:1). Phrasing the question in this way raises the issue of a possible dynastic line or a monarchy in the first sentence. The children of Israel are not asking for a line of rulers but only for someone to initiate the process of settlement. No title for this potential leader is mentioned and the question is phrased so that the action of leading is the verb; in other words, the people do not ask for a specific office to be filled but rather for a task to be done on their behalf.

Questions concerning who should lead Israel and how they should rule plague the Israelites throughout the book and is one of its main themes. Judges begins with the question of leadership and the episodes in the following chapters focus on various means of finding a leader, what qualities that leader should have, as well as problems associated with rulers. The text is filled with various titles for rulers. It is not clear whether this reflects an historical situation where all the nations had different titles for their leaders, or, more likely, whether it is a literary device used to indicate Israel's background research into leadership options. The lack of a title for the role of leading in the first sentence allows for a range of activities and qualities for leaders to be revealed in the following chapters.

The answer to the people's question subtly turns to the issue of a long-lived monarchy by the deity's response, "Judah will go up. Here I give the land to his hand" (Judg 1:2). The response is a double-entendre. On the one hand, it fits the immediate context and means that the deity will give the land, presumably presently under Canaanite control, to Judah, and so provides a direct answer to the previous question. Yet the response would have a prophetic ring to a community living under the Judite monarchy, or even to those living after its destruction, since the reader knows that the response addresses both the short term situation of Judges as well as the reality of the children of Israel long after the period of the Judges. The double meaning of the deity's statement is further enhanced because the deity does not answer the people's question but "says" *wayyōʾmer* the statement. In this way, the text indicates that the deity does not really answer the people directly, rather the deity makes statements which are interpreted by the people to be the answer to their query.

The text does not address where and through which medium the inquiry was made. Many commentators answer the question despite the lack of textual support. Boling notes that "asking the question" really means that they sought oracular guidance at an amphictyonic sanctuary.[5] Soggin agrees that the root *š-ᶜ-l* in "contexts like this" always carries with it the sense of "inquire by means of the oracle" but qualifies the situation by noting that there is no mention of a central sanctuary nor any implication that there was one.[6] Gray ties this to the similar question asked in Judg 20:18, locating the site at Gilgal or Shiloh as the Joshua passages would seem to indicate.[7]

From a literary standpoint, not noting where the people are or who is asking emphasizes Israel's confused state. Israel had nowhere to go and no one specific to ask the question concerning leadership. Israel did not yet have a centralized location nor was there a leader to designate such a place. Since no priest is mentioned as asking the question, the implication is that there was no functioning priesthood prepared for such an action. This is highlighted at the end of the book where similar questions are asked and although Israel is further along in the process, they are not in a better situation (Judg 20:18).

In the following verse, Judah takes the leadership role and does not attempt to help all the tribes but displays partisanship by turning to its brother tribe Simeon (Judg 1:3). Again the situation could be read on two levels. On one level, Judah helped Simeon first with its immediate concern which was the conquest of the land from the Canaanites. On

---

[5] R. G. Boling, *Judges: Introduction, Translation and Commentary*, The Anchor Bible (Garden City: Doubleday and Company, 1981) 53.

[6] J. A. Soggin, *Judges*, 20.

[7] J. Gray, *Joshua, Judges, Ruth*, The New Century Bible Commentary (Grand Rapids, MI: Eerdmans 1986) 235.

another level, a later audience would interpret the situation as Judah looking out for Judah, which by that time included Simeon.[8] It is difficult to determine if this is a judgmental critique of Judah, or simply a depiction of the perceived historical situation. At this point in the story the role of Judah as leader is clear, but to what extent Judah is to lead is not yet as obvious as it will be in the final story.

The Bezek Incident: Judges 1:4-7

The role of Judah, especially concerning Benjamin and Saul, is raised obliquely in Judg 1:3-7, although these verses are not traditionally treated in this way.[9] Ironically, these lines seldom warrant discussion in terms of the development of the book despite the fact that they describe the first battle in the book. The verses focus on the battle against the Canaanites and Perizzites at Bezek. In this battle the Israelites smote their enemy, captured the enemy ruler, and cut off his fingers and toes. Following his dismemberment the ruler of Bezek commented on the act and compared it to actions he had taken himself.

The reference to Bezek does not appear particularly relevant to the general story at first glance. Locating Bezek is problematic because the text does not note its location with any specificity.[10] Yet the question concerning its location is pressing because the reader wonders why the Judites began there. The dismemberment of Adoni Bezek's fingers and toes is unusual. Most scholars treat the dismemberment as a military action to prevent Adoni Bezek, either actually or symbolically, from taking up arms against Israel.[11] Yet there are no other examples of finger

[8] Judah and Simeon are full brothers, both children of Leah and Jacob (Gen 29:33, 35). Specific tribal boundaries are never listed for Simeon. The only cities listed for Simeon are found in Josh 19:1-9 and are located in the most southern area of Judah's territory. Thus Simeon was dependent upon Judah and functioned as part of Judah.

[9] Most discussions of the Bezeq incident concern the actual name of the ruler of Bezek (Boling, *Judges*, 55; Soggin, *Judges*, 27), where Bezeq should be located, this person's relationship with Adoni-Zedeq (G. E. Wright, "The Literary and Historical Problem of Joshua 10 and Judges 1," *JNES* 5 [1946] 105–14), and how this relates to Jerusalem (E. J. Hamlin, *Judges: At Risk in the Promised Land*, International Theological Commentary [Grand Rapids: Eerdmans, 1990] 26).

[10] The site is associated with Khirbet Ibziq because of the geographical characteristics given in the biblical sources (A. Zertal, "Bezek" *ABD* 1: 718).

[11] Hamlin sees the cleansing role of thumbs and toes in the passages cited below as marking the end of the Canaanite order of sacred kings. He adds that "A corrupted Canaanite social order with false claims to divine sanction came to an end

and toe dismemberment in battle or against enemies in the biblical text.[12] When fingers and toes are mentioned in the Hebrew Bible they appear in the context of cleansing someone to make them holy, such as the ordination of Aaron and his sons (Lev 8:23, 24), or the cleansing of a leper upon their recovery (Lev 14:14, 17, 25, 28).

The importance of Bezek, more likely, relates to what happened there in 1 Sam 11:7-11. In those passages in Samuel, Saul takes a census of the people during his Jabesh-Gilead campaign. The Israelites' call to arms for this particular battle was a dismembered yoke of oxen which had been sent to all the tribes. The reference to Bezek, where people would have been mustered because of a dismemberment, when combined with this partial dismembering of the ruler of Bezek, are forms of foreshadowing. The reference is the first hint foretelling the devastation that will take place, at the end of the book, when the dismembered body of a raped woman is used to muster the Israelites to fight a civil war between the tribes of Israel and the tribe of Benjamin, Saul's tribe (Judges 19–21). Bezek is the first site captured by the Israelites. The presentation of the story raises issues surrounding Saul/Benjamin and David/Judah that become crucial to the Israelites at the end of the book and in later Israelite history.

The person who suffered the finger and toe dismemberment is referred to as Adoni Bezek. Adon could be translated as "Lord/ruler" of Bezek; so, Adoni-bezek could be the man's name, the whole thing could be a title, or it could be a satirical name.[13] The problem is that, because each is possible, determining which is most probable is difficult. It is evident that in every episode in Judges the Israelites seek a leader and encounter foreign leaders of different kinds. Numerous titles are used for the leadership roles both of Israelites and her contemporaries. In a book where the search for a leader is so fundamental, the appearance of so many different titles for leaders can hardly be accidental. Any one of the aforementioned interpretations of the leader's name fills the role of this as the first reference to a ruler from another community and a possible model for the Israelites to evaluate.

---

with the dethroning of this last Canaanite king in the south" (*Judges*, 27). Boling claims the dismemberment was to keep him from taking up arms and took place in anticipation of his dispatch to Jerusalem in order to instill fear there. He refers to similar practices involving decapitated bodies mentioned in Mari (*Judges*, 55).

[12] Gray notes this sort of mutilation is known from records of the Athenians and Hannibal of Carthage who cut off the great toes of his captives, though no citation is provided (*Joshua, Judges*, 237).

[13] Adoni-Bezek as: "ruler" (D. G. Schley, "Adoni-Bezek," *ABD* 1: 74), as a title (Boling, *Judges*, 55), or a satirical name (Hamlin *Judges*, 26).

After his dismemberment, the ruler of Bezek makes a statement which, although difficult to translate precisely, means something like, "Seventy kings, with thumbs and big toes cut off, used to pick up scraps under my table: as I have done so God has requited me" (Judg 1:7, JPS). This comment reads as the arrogant boasting of a captured, defeated, and dismembered ruler. It also serves as a prophetic commentary; in the words of a foreign ruler the Israelites are already acting like the Canaanites.

Jerusalem enters the opening scenes of the book as part of the Bezek incident, though for no clearly stated reason. While most translations do not punctuate the text in this way, the death of Adoni Bezek in Jerusalem is included in the same sentence as his boast. Some unidentified "they" brought Adoni Bezek to Jerusalem where he died (Judg 1:7). The reader wonders who "they" might be. The active characters in the narrative, to that point, had been the Judites, who originally captured Adoni Bezek (Judg 1:4). In the course of Adoni Bezek's boast, he talks about the seventy kings, who theoretically could be considered another "they." The text offers no explanation for Jerusalem's involvement in the incident nor does it say what, if any, relation Adoni Bezek had with the city. In the rape narrative at the end of the book, dismemberment plays a key role in the narrative, and Jerusalem is again an important factor. Thus there is a literary need to have Jerusalem introduced into the narrative in the beginning of the text, especially in relation to the Bezek incident.

Jerusalem's Status: Judges 1:8

According to the masoretic notation, the following verse begins a new section. It continues to discuss the status of Jerusalem and the Judites' role in it. In this way, the city of Jerusalem ties the previous narrative to the following unit, in which the role of Judah becomes more prominent as the leaders of the Judges generation. Judah's status is highlighted, not only in regard to their actions in battle, but through legitimating relationships to the previous generation, specifically through Caleb. The reappearance of the topic of Jerusalem allows a smooth transition between the Bezek incident and Judah's new role.

The status of Jerusalem is confused by the following verse where the Judites attacked, captured, put to the sword, and burned Jerusalem (Judg 1:8). There is no explanation in the text for why this was done. What the Judites did to the city is clear; they destroyed it. They did not inhabit it along with the inhabitants resident at that time, they avoided, thereby, the problem of cohabiting with the residents and adopting their ways. The Judites' actions contrast sharply with Jerusalem's status and Judah's actions towards that city which had been described in the book of Joshua. In Joshua 10, five kings joined to fight Joshua. In the Joshua episode, the Israelite deity caused the sun to stand still (Josh 10:13-14) and hurled stones from the sky to aid the Israelites (Josh 10:11). Following the details of the capture of the enemy kings and their fates, the text recounts the attack and destruction of each of their five cities with one exception, Jerusalem. There is no attack or destruction account for Jerusalem. In Josh 15:63 the Judites are also associated with Jerusalem but, at that time, the Judites could not dispossess the Jebusites, the inhabitants of Jerusalem. Instead they dwelt with them, according to the text of Joshua, "until this day."

The Joshua references highlight a contrast made in the opening verses in Judges. In the book of Joshua, neither the Israelites nor the Judites could capture or dispossess the Jebusites from Jerusalem. In the book of Judges, in the first chapter, the Judites set fire to Jerusalem rather than dwell with the inhabitants. In contrast, the tribe of Benjamin, towards the end of this chapter (Judg 1:21), did not dispossess the inhabitants of Jerusalem but, on the contrary, dwelt with them, which is one cause of the tragic civil war at the end of the book (Judg 20–21). In this case, the tribe of Judah accomplished something it had not been able to do in the book of Joshua, while the tribe of Benjamin is saddled with, what had been, in the book of Joshua, Judah's weakness. This is another example of Judah becoming stronger in Judges as the other tribes, especially the tribe of Benjamin, are weakened. The contrast between Judah and Benjamin, with regard to Jerusalem, is an expression of the David/Saul, north/south polemic in Judges.

Generational Transition: Judges 1:9-11

After burning Jerusalem, the Judites continued attacking the hill country, the Negev, and the Shephelah, finally turning against the Canaanites in Hebron (Judg 1:8-10). Hebron was attacked and then Debir (Judg 1:11). The narrator notes that the Judites defeated various peoples from the region of Hebron (Judg 1:10), a situation similar to one recounted in the book of Joshua yet with key factors differing between the two accounts. In Joshua, the incident is preceded by the notation, "In accordance with the Israelite deity's command to Joshua, Caleb son of Jephunneh was given a portion among the Judites, namely Kiriath-arba, that is Hebron" (Josh 15:13). In the book of Joshua the deity gave a direct command concerning leadership. In the similar, possibly identical, incident in Judges, the deity was not directly involved in the conflict and Judah replaces Caleb, the previous deity-appointed leader.

This shift in focus from Caleb to Judah is reinforced by a shift from plural to singular in the Judges text. When referring to the encounters in Bezek and Jerusalem the term for the leader of Israel is, "the children of Judah" (Judg 1:4, 8). Suddenly in verse 10, when the focus of the action is against Hebron, the text employs the term Judah in the singular. The shift from plural to singular forms a closer parallel with the incident in the book of Joshua, further highlighting Judah's prominence in the period of Judges. By deleting Caleb as the leader of these battles, the text focuses on the new situation in Judges where the focus and answer to the call for leadership is Judah.

The shift from Caleb leading the battle in Joshua to Judah leading it in Judges raises the question of Caleb's continuing authority or right to land. Caleb is a prominent character in other biblical books, but this is one of the few references to him in Judges.[14] In Joshua, Caleb's announcement that he will give his daughter to the man who captures the city is not out of context, since the text is examining the future of areas under his control. Caleb's rights to land are noted in a number of places. He is the only person other than Joshua from the desert generation who is allowed to enter the land (Num 14:6).[15] More importantly, the deity grants land to Caleb by stating, ". . . him will I bring into the land that he entered and his offspring shall hold it as a possession" (Num 14:24, JPS). In Judges, Caleb is still imbued with the deity's blessing from the Numbers passage, yet he has no active part in the present situation since the battles in Judges are carried out by Judah.

Caleb is finally introduced by name and with the statement that he will give his daughter, Achsah, as a woman/wife to the man who attacks and captures Kiriath-Sepher/Debir (Judg 1:12).[16] While Caleb is

---

[14] References in other biblical books to Caleb include: Num 13:6, 30, 14: 6, 24, 26:65, 32:12, Deut 1:36, Josh 14:6-15, 15:13, 1 Chr 2:18-24, 42-55, 4:13-15

[15] Caleb was allowed into the land because he did not fear the Canaanites who were in the land when it was originally investigated. He was also given Hebron as a gift in Josh 14:14, and 15:13.

[16] In Hebrew the word for woman and wife is the same. Most translations decide for the reader which meaning is intended. There are many cases in the MT where the intended meaning is ambiguous. What processes must be completed for a woman to be considered a wife are never explicated by the text, nor are the responsibilities or benefits in status. As a result, this author will translate, "wife/woman," and let the reader determine which is the better translation.

still an important figure, his only function in Judges is as a conduit from his generation, the generation led by a deity-appointed ruler, to this newer generation led by Judah. What had been Caleb's accomplishments earlier are now Judah's achievements and the only action available to him is to give his daughter to the next generation. Ironically, Caleb's announcement, as is the case in Joshua as well, indicates that he will grant his daughter to a military man who has proven himself in battle. His younger brother, Othniel the Kenizzite, captured Debir, and Caleb gave him his daughter Achsah as woman/wife (Judg 1:13).

Caleb, Achsah, and Othniel: The First Relationships: Judges 1:12-16

In Judges 1:12 Caleb clearly identifies who is to be given as woman/wife by referring to her as "my daughter" and also by her first name, Achsah.[17] While referring to both of these two aspects may not seem unusual, it is unique when one considers that most of the women who appear in the book of Judges lack names and their status is seldom clearly defined.[18] The nature of the relationships between Achsah, Caleb, and Othniel is established prior to their consummation. Othniel won Achsah in battle. As a result Achsah became a woman/wife, apparently the highest rank a woman could attain in her relationship with a man in Judges. She was given this rank by her father, one of two from the desert generation allowed into Canaan (Num 14:6).[19]

The relationship between Achsah's man/husband and her father is identified and solidified by the reference to Othniel as Caleb's younger brother.[20] Regardless of their precise relationship, this reference ties the two men together in brotherhood with Caleb as the older and possibly

---

[17] Achsah is identified as the daughter of Caleb in 1 Chr 2:49, though this passage raises questions concerning the identity of her mother. Boling (*Judges*, 56) presents an uncertain etymology for her name, tying it to seductive anklets that attracted attention, as in Isa 3:16-18, and relates this feature to some of her later actions.

[18] Important women with no names include: Abimelech's mother, Jephthah's daughter, Samson's mother, Samson's first betrothed, the prostitute Samson visits in Gaza, Micah's mother, and the raped *pîlegeš*.

[19] The other is Joshua who, according to Judges, was dead when this story begins (Judg 1:1), though in the book of Joshua he was alive when Achsah's marriage took place (Josh 15:13-19).

[20] A problem in terminology exists with reference to terms of relationship of men, such as husband, especially in the story of the *pîlegeš* where their relationship to each other is ambiguous. Othniel's specific relationship with Caleb is not entirely certain either. In 1 Chr 4:13 he is identified as the son of Caleb's brother, and in 1 Chr

more authoritative. Both were war heroes where Othniel proved himself according to terms set by Caleb. Thus the marriage was organized and consummated with and by the correct parties following a predetermined sequence of events.

Caleb's offer of his daughter in marriage is the first time that a promise or oath is made before a battle in Judges. In this scenario the reference is tame, almost a standard practice. A military man offered his daughter to another man with, presumably, similar characteristics as the father which are identified through some act by which the suitor proves his worthiness. In fact Hamlin interprets the situation as proof that Caleb was a good father who arranged for his daughter's marriage to a man of Judah.[21] As with many other incidents in Judges, when an event or idea first occurs it is in a legitimate context but by the end of the book the same concept causes terrible results. This case of a military leader making an oath or promise before a battle reappears later both in Jephthah's promise, leading to the subsequent sacrifice of his daughter (Judg 11:30-31 and 11:39), and in the final story, where the Israelites swore they would not give their daughters to Benjamin, which led to the rape/marriage of women from Jabesh-Gilead and Shiloh (Judges 20–21).

The character of Achsah in the book of Judges has been ignored, or otherwise treated as: merely an element of the Othniel story, or as depicting the model woman in a model male-female relationship, or as a metaphor for Israel.[22] She is a vehicle to connect Othniel, through Caleb, to the chain of command which linked the Sinai generation to the period of the Judges.[23] The verses concerning her are translated and interpreted in such a way as to depict her as, "an image of ideal Yahwist

---

27:15 Othniel appears as a clan or a tribal name. Here he is named the younger "brother." The term "brother" can be used in many senses such as "brotherhood," especially in Judges, and it is not clear that in this instance the inference is specifically to the son of either of his parents.

[21] Hamlin, *Judges*, 31.

[22] Achsah has been ignored in such major commentaries as Soggin (*Judges*) and Gray (*Joshua, Judges*). As an element in the Othniel story see, Mark J. Fretz, "Achsah," *ABD* 1:56-7. For the model relationship see, L. R. Klein "The Book of Judges: Paradigm and Deviation in Images of Women," *A Feminist Companion to Judges*, The Feminist Companion to the Bible vol. 4, ed. A. Brenner (Sheffield: Sheffield Academic Press, 1993) 55. As a metaphor for Israel see, L. R. Klein, *The Triumph of Irony in the Book of Judges*, JSOTS/Bible and Literature Series vol. 14, (Sheffield: The Almond Press, 1989) 26.

[23] It is interesting in light of the role of the *pîlegeš* at the end of the book, that according to 1 Chr 1:46-50, Caleb has two women who bear him children and both are referred to as *pîlegeš*. The text does not indicate whether Achsah was the descendent of one of these women, a woman/wife, or another woman.

womanhood."[24] Yet a careful reading of the text indicates that Achsah may not be the docile ideal of womanhood. Achsah is the first woman introduced into the Judges narrative and serves as a starting point for how women are treated at the beginning of the period. She does function indeed as a comparison by which one might document the status of women, but exactly what her role and status are demand a careful reading of the relevant passages.

The text takes no note of Achsah's attitude toward the marriage or the legitimacy of such a contest to win a bride. It begins to describe her role in the narrative by stating that, when she came, she (Achsah) induced him (presumably Othniel) to ask her father for land (Judg 1:14). Most translations and discussions of the text focus on the second verb, "induced," with almost no discussion of the first. While the subject and meaning of the second verb are crucial for understanding this passage, it is also necessary to understand the subject and meaning of the first, which in turn facilitates understanding the second. One possibility seldom examined is that the first and second verbs have different subjects. The first verb is usually translated, "when she came to him" (Judg 1:14). The *h* at the end of the verb is the directional *h* which conveys the meaning, "when he came toward her."[25] *BDB* includes one meaning of the verb "to come" as, "of bride coming into her husband's house," under which our text is listed, but notes that the subject of the verb is rarely a woman.[26] In this context the connotation would be sexual, referring to the sexual consummation of the marriage. This meaning would not be out of place here since in most cases when a marriage takes place there is reference to the sexual consummation of that union. One would expect, however, some sign of consummation, particularly in this context, since Caleb gave his daughter as a woman/wife in verse 13, making verse 14 the first time that Othniel and Achsah were together as husband and wife. As a result, a better meaning for the first verb in the sentence would be, "he came (sexually) to her."

The subject and meaning of the second verb are difficult because traditional commentaries fear tarnishing Othniel's image by having the request come from Achsah and prefer the LXX which states that, "*he* nagged *her*."[27] Soggin feels that it is "manifestly absurd" to follow the

[24] Klein, *Triumph*, 26. Even Bal views Achsah as the "model daughter" (*Death and Dissymmetry: The Politics of Coherence in the Book of Judges*, Chicago Studies in the History of Judaism (Chicago: The University of Chicago Press, 1988) 155.

[25] I would like to thank Kevin Mellish for noting this option in class. See also Klein, *Triumph*, 56.

[26] *BDB*, 98.

[27] Boling goes so far as to claim that, "Caleb's daughter Achsah ignores the request of her husband, who will be Judge in 3:7, and substitutes her own desire

MT since it must be Othniel who did the "prompting" because, "the reading is obviously wrong since the 'father' is her father."[28] His assumption is that since it is her father controlling lands it would make more sense for her to ask him. This interpretation ignores the present situation where the father controlling the land just gave his daughter away as a prize to a man who won a military battle, providing no indication that her wishes were considered relevant by her military commander father. The Hebrew text clearly has a feminine subject for the second verb; therefore, according to the MT, Achsah was the character carrying out the action of the second verb. Achsah's precise action is controversial. The verb *s-w-t* means, "to allure, incite, instigate."[29] Soggin adds a more sexual connotation translating, "seduce, tempt."[30] Other translators prefer "nag" for reasons not elaborated.[31] It is difficult to know what Achsah's precise action was, but it was an attempt to persuade Othniel, through whatever means, to ask Achsah's father for property.[32] Some view Achsah as the more likely candidate to make such a request since it is her father who was asked. But Achsah was a woman with limited inheritance rights, who had just been given away as a battle prize, and it is not that difficult to understand why she may have considered her recently victorious warrior husband the more appropriate one to make the request.

In light of the sexual connotations of the first verb of verse 14, discussed above, the second verb, "seduced," may be delicately timed. If the first verb refers not to Achsah's arrival but to a sexual encounter, possibly their first, then her requesting something from Othniel immediately following that union may be the reason why Achsah's actions

---

(surely the editor implies a contrast with the Shiloh maidens in Judg 21 and the quick thinking elders who there attend to the future of all Israel)" (*Judges,* 64).

[28] Soggin, *Judges,* 22.

[29] *BDB,* 694.

[30] Soggin, *Judges,* 22. Note Bal's discussion on the ideologically based problems behind many of the interpretations of this verb, both in terms of who carries out the action and what the action is (*Death and Dissymmetry,* 152–3).

[31] "Nag" means, "to engage in persistent petty fault-finding, scolding, or urging," (*Webster's Third New International Dictionary of the English Language Unabridged,* ed. P. B. Gove [Springfield, MA: G. & C. Merriam, 1968] 1499). Boling translates "nag," but feels that Othniel is the subject, though he admits that having Achsah as the subject does, "less damage to the image of the first 'savior judge' [3:7-10] and may be taken as a tendentious development" (Boling, *Judges,* 56–7).

[32] P. G. Mosca sees Caleb as the direct object of Achsah's actions. The problem with his thesis is that it provides no explanation for why she must travel to her father asking him again for the same thing ("Who Seduced Whom? A Note on Joshua 15:18//Judges 1:14," *CBQ* 46 (1984) 18–22).

immediately follow Othniel's. This would again be in keeping with the tone of Judges where sex and its impact on men is used by women for various reasons.[33] There are a number of concepts introduced in the opening chapter of Judges which either lead ultimately to the Israelites' civil war, or are used against Israel later in the text, such as the role of Jerusalem and the dismemberment of Adoni Bezek. The translations of the verbs discussed here follow that pattern and will be used against Israel later in the narrative of Judges.

Regardless of Achsah's precise action to convey her wish that her husband make the request of her father, it was not effective because the continuation of the verse has her carrying out still more actions to achieve her goal.[34] In verse 14, Achsah dismounts from her donkey at her father's house. While the verb used for Achsah's action concerning the donkey has received much attention, her arrival on a donkey has received little. The donkey *ḥămôr* as a mode of transportation appears infrequently in Judges and it is no accident that it appears in the stories of both Achsah and the raped *pîlegeš*.[35] The text says nothing about Achsah's ascent to the donkey, only her descent from it. The Levite's raped *pîlegeš* rides a donkey, but only after she has been gang raped. In that case she does not descend but only ascends.

Some scholars see Achsah's action of dismounting as problematic. According to the MT, "she dismounted from her donkey and Caleb asked her, 'What is the matter'" (Judg 1:14, JPS). The LXX has a different interpretation, translating, "she murmured and cried out." Another translation is, "she clapped her hands."[36] The assumption is that because of the question asked by Caleb, Achsah must have done something beyond descending from her donkey to gain her father's attention.[37] Driver goes so far as to suggest a connection with the Akkadian

[33] Most obvious are Delilah's actions in order to gain the secret to Samson's strength (Judges 16), and possibly Jael's actions (Judges 4–5).

[34] Note that though the terminology is different, Deborah must verbally coerce Baraq into fighting and, when that was not enough, she too undertook another action in order to fulfill the necessary events (Judges 4).

[35] Other references to a "donkey" in the book of Judges are: Judg 6:4, and 15:15-16.

[36] Soggin, *Judges*, 22.

[37] Soggin, *Judges*, 22. M. Bal believes that she clapped her hands because it explains and enhances the narrative structure of the story, adds an interesting case for the study of the anthropology of gesture in the ancient Near East, explains why other cases where a person dismounts to extend a greeting use a different verb, provides insight into the particular kind of body language used by the daughter in addressing the powerful father whose object or gift she is, and enhances the performative aspect of a symbolic gesture whose phatic function relates physical to verbal

verb *sanāḫu* translating, "she broke wind."[38] Klein sees the act of descending from the donkey as unimportant, what matters is that Achsah bowed low and prostrated herself before her father.[39] In her interpretation, Achsah's father was puzzled by her prostrating herself which in turn prompted his question.[40]

The issue concerns not only the precise meaning of the verb *ṣ-n-ḥ* but the interpretation and significance given to that action.[41] Many arguments against it meaning simple descent assume that the action must be special in order to gain Caleb's attention. The previous verse explained Achsah's marriage to Othniel and the beginning of this verse either refers to her arrival at her new home or to her sexual union with her husband, presumably in his home. Achsah's action of leaving her new home and returning to her father is significant in itself. Her use of a donkey as a mode of transportation indicates that her new abode was not near her father's but some distance away. The only other Israelite woman in Judges to leave her father after consummating a relationship with a man is the Levite's *pîlegeš* at the end of the book, further cementing the beginning and end of the book together. What is significant here is that Achsah left her husband. Her descent from the donkey is not as important as her traveling alone and leaving her husband. Her descent in front of her father signifies her arrival at Caleb's place where he was not expecting her.

Achsah's actions were enough to gain her father's attention because he responded by asking, "What is with you?" (Judg 1:14). A new verse begins with Achsah's response, "Give me a blessing. You have given me away as Negev land, give me springs of water" (Judg 1:15). Achsah used the imperative with her father.[42] It is unusual for women to speak in Judges, so the use of the imperative, especially with her father, is shocking. She asked for a blessing but defined the content, a specific parcel of land, leading some to translate the word in question as "present" instead of blessing (JPS, RSV).[43] Achsah even provided a reason why Caleb should do this when she says, "You gave me away." Her comment reads like a reprimand. She was angry either because he gave

---

language, and hence exemplifies the materiality of speech-acts (*Death and Dissymmetry*, 155).

[38] G. R. Driver, "Problems in Judges Newly Discussed," *ALUOS* 4 (1964) 6–25.

[39] Klein, *Triumph*, 26.

[40] Ibid., 26

[41] The root is used in the story of Jael's murder of Sisera in Judg 4:21.

[42] Note that the Josh 15:19 passage uses *n-t-n* rather than *y-h-b*, though the meaning is the same, and both are in the imperative.

[43] Soggin translates "favor" (*Judges*, 22), KJV translates "blessing."

her away as a prize or because the area in which she was forced to live was problematic.[44]

Another interpretation of this scene sees Achsah representing Israel. Klein suggests that this is the first appearance of the biblical metaphor of Israel as bride.[45] According to Klein, "The bride is a reward to the hero who proves his worth, she leads to honorable occupation of the land, and she asks for life-giving water."[46] She relates this request to reproduction, not of the moment but of time.[47] Achsah emerges, in her view, as the image of ideal Yahwist womanhood.[48] Other scenes involving women in Judges are often interpreted as related to women and children, despite the presence of only two women who are described with their children in Judges.[49] There is no evidence from the book of Judges to support the claim that Achsah asked for children, wanted children, or ever had children.[50] Achsah asked her father for better land because her husband would not ask for her.

Achsah's request of her father was granted. The Hebrew is not grammatically correct, but this is done to create the word play with her father's name, *kālēb*.[51] The translation is, "and he gave her according to heart" (Judg 1:15). While one would expect "according to her heart," the addition of the possessive *h* at the end of the verb would destroy

---

[44] Note that the Rabbis were also upset with the method by which Caleb found a husband for Achsah. According to the Mishnah, four men made improper vows; Caleb is one of three who abused their authority over their daughters. Here their concern is that the nature of his vow was foolishly formulated, and Caleb could have a slave or a Canaanite as a son-in-law (Leila L. Bronner "Valorized or Vilified?" *A Feminist Companion to Judges,* The Feminist Companion to the Bible vol. 4, ed. A. Brenner (Sheffield: Sheffield Academic Press, 1993) 75–6.

[45] Klein, *Triumph,* 26.

[46] Ibid.

[47] Ibid.

[48] Ibid.

[49] Samson's nameless mother is the only woman seen from pregnancy through part of her child's life (Judg 13:2-14:16), and Michah's nameless mother appears only briefly, but in some relationship to her child (Judg 17:2-3). Other mothers such as the mother of Abimelech (Judg 8:31, 9:1 and 9:18) and Jephthah (Judg 11:1-2) are referred to, but are never named or seen, and the legitimacy of the circumstances in which they were conceived are questioned by the text. Sisera's mother speaks but, ironically, it is only after her son's death, though that information is known only to the reader (Judg 4:28-30).

[50] In the genealogy list in 1 Chr 4:13, Othniel is listed as a son of Kenaz and has two sons. Achsah's name is not included.

[51] Another interpretation is to follow the LXX and say that "according to her heart" has dropped out by haplography (Boling, *Judges,* 57).

the word play using the name Caleb. The word play is essential from the literary standpoint because a variation of this phrase is used in the story of the Levite's *pîlegeš* (Judg 19:3).

Achsah is clearly an important character. Her story describes a woman using all the skills available to her to achieve her goal. She acted on her own because the men in her life, who had authority and control over her, were not carrying out her wishes, for reasons that are never elaborated. As with other themes in the book, the image of a woman carrying out actions to accomplish her needed result begins on a positive note, with Achsah receiving the desired lands, but degenerates through the period so that the *pîlegeš*, who carried out many of the same actions, was raped and murdered (Judges 19).

Achsah, as the first woman, functions as a model to which other women's situations in Judges are evaluated. She was the daughter of a war hero. She was married to another war hero through means defined by the text. She is named by the text. She left her father's house safely and returned to Caleb safely. Her father granted her wishes. While these ideas may not appear unusual, in Judges they are. The following sections of the book depict women unprotected, even in their homes (Jael, Judg 4:17-21), sacrificed by their fathers (Jephthah's daughter, Judg 11:34-40), and institutionally raped (Judges 21) as evidence of Israel's degeneration without a strong central leader.

The Rest of the Players: Judges 1:16-36

The transition from Caleb to Othniel through Achsah precedes the discussion of the peoples still in the land whom the Israelites could not displace. Othniel and Achsah serve as a bridge from one generation to the next but also function as a bridge to the discussion of the status and whereabouts of the other tribes. The verses following the Achsah narrative place the Israelite tribes geographically in relation to the other tribes and record how well each is following the laws which are supposed to be governing their behavior. The behavior of the various tribes is key to understanding the alignments throughout the book, especially in the final scenes.

This unit, concerning the status of the other tribes of Israel, is introductory. The first chapter of Judges is drafted like a modern movie script; it begins with action scenes laying out the major issue (the cry for leadership, the Bezek and Achsah incidents) and then backtracks to provide the background from which the narrative progresses. As a result, the material in this unit is introductory but it is conveyed through statements, rather than descriptions, as was the case with the stories seen thus far.

The first group discussed in this unit is the Kenites (Judg 1:16). The text retreats to history by noting that the children of Ken, the father-in-law of Moses, joined with the children of Judah and settled with them. The text begins with the discussion of the Kenites joining Judah because the previous passages concern Caleb and his daughter's marriage. Since the text focuses on Caleb, using him as the transition from the previous generation, it is necessary to relate Caleb and the Kenites as closely as possible with Judah. This verse provides a smooth transition from the discussion of Caleb and Achsah and brings the focus back to Israel, and more specifically, to Judah. It legitimates Judah's position as leader since the only person from the desert generation who remains is Caleb, who was given land directly by the deity. Moses' name further justifies Judah's role as leader because of its association with, and incorporation of, the Kenites through Caleb. Caleb becomes the conduit from the previous generation and Judah's inclusion of that group in its self-definition provides more legitimation for Judah's leading role.

The text immediately turns to the status and activity of Judah, again noting that Judah is closely tied to its brother-tribe Simeon (Judg 1:17). They began their incursion with Zephath, destroyed it, and changed its name to Hormah, a reflection of what they had done to it (Judg 1:17). The new name of the city, Hormah, is another prophetic play on words.[52] The name of the city comes from the Hebrew root *ḥ-r-m* which means, "a devoted thing," usually referring, in the strictest application, to a thing which is to be either destroyed or set apart.[53] In this case it refers to something that had been destroyed and is related to cleansing. The term is used one other time in Judges, in reference to the destruction of the population of Jabesh-Gilead (Judg 21:11) as part of the final horror of the civil war against Benjamin.[54]

Judah then moved on to Gaza, Ashqelon, and Ekron (Judg 1:18).[55] The LXX includes, "Ashdod with her territory." Boling follows the LXX with the explanation that these words fell out through haplography.[56] As Hamlin points out, from a literary point of view the text need not be modified because as it now stands it mentions only those cities which are relevant for the later Samson stories.[57] The text notes that the deity

---

[52] The town was allotted to Judah in Joshua 15:30 but was part of Simeon's allotment in Josh 19:4.

[53] *BDB*, 356–7.

[54] Hamlin, *Judges*, 33.

[55] The LXX reads that Judah did not capture these cities.

[56] Boling, *Judges*, 58.

[57] The cities visited by Samson are: Ekron (Judg 14:1), Ashqelon (Judg 14:19) and Gaza (Judg 16:1) (Hamlin, *Judges*, 35). Samson does not actually visit Ekron but nearby Timnah.

was with Judah in this endeavor, and that Judah took the hills but could not take the valleys because "they" had metal chariots. The text specifically states that the deity was with Judah, something that is not included following the description of the status of the other tribes. The reference to the metal chariots provides a legitimate reason for the inability of Judah to take the valleys. This too can be seen with a slightly ironic sense since in a few chapters the metal chariots will be the source of a Canaanite loss (Judges 4-5).

The text returns to Caleb by stating that a non-specified "they" gave Hebron to Caleb, as Moses had promised (Judg 1:20). Since the last plural subject was the Judites, it is a likely subject for this verb as well. The verse continues with a singular non-determined "he" who is said to have driven the three Anakites out of there (Hebron). The corresponding passages in Joshua are useful in understanding this passage. Joshua 15:13-18 contains very similar statements to these, including the Achsah narrative, but in a very different order and arrangement. In Joshua, the section begins, "In accordance with the deity's command to Joshua, Caleb son of Jephunneh was given a portion among the Judites, namely Kiriath-arba, that is Hebron" (Josh 15:13). In Joshua, Hebron was given to Caleb according to the deity's instructions, whereas Judges gives the impression that the Judites alone carried out the actions that Moses promised. In Judges the Judites are depicted either as the ones carrying out Moses's instructions or as usurping authority in the new era with little direct contact with the deity.[58]

The different arrangement of the Caleb passages in Judges influences the second part of the Judges verse. In Joshua, following the handing over of Hebron to Caleb, Caleb dislodged the three Anakites: Sheshai, Ahiman, and Talmai, descendants of Anak. In Judg 1:10 the Judites defeated Sheshai, Ahiman, and Talmai. Earlier in the Judges passage the enemies are not defined as Anakim but simply as peoples dwelling in that region. It is only in verse 20 that they are referred to as Anakim and said to have been driven out by Caleb. In Judges, Judah battled the three enemies, and the few tasks left to Caleb are described only after the Kenites were brought under Judite control.

The Achsah narrative is also affected by the different configuration of the passages from Joshua to Judges. In Joshua, Caleb was given Hebron because the deity promised to do this, Caleb defeated the peoples of Anak, who are listed by name, and only then, after Caleb had proven

---

[58] J. C. Exum examines the role of the deity in Judges, pointing out the complexity of the deity in the book. While not addressed in her piece, the idea of Judah usurping some of the deity's powers follows her model ("The Centre Cannot Hold: Thematic and Textual Instabilities in Judges," *CBQ* 52 (1990) 410–31).

himself and taken land did he offer his daughter as a prize. This is not the case in Judges. Here Judah took Hebron and defeated the three groups living there. Only then did Caleb, appearing from nowhere, make the offer of his daughter. Only after the text incorporated the Kenites into Judah is Caleb granted a victory. The text uses the flow of the narrative to displace the other tribes and heroes and place Judah in their stead.

The text moves immediately from describing the situation of Judah to describing the situation of the Benjaminites. This contrast highlights the David/Judah versus Saul/Benjamin polemic prevalent in the book, and so prepares the reader for the final chapters. The text states that the Benjaminites did not dispossess the inhabitants of Jerusalem (Judg 1:21). This contradicts the previous verses where Judah destroyed Jerusalem (Judg 1:8). The previous reference to Jerusalem contrasts Judah's actions with Benjamin's. The contrast raises the issue of the city's status to parallel the final chapters. Judah's actions to non-Israelite Jerusalem are compared favorably to Benjamin's; Judah destroyed them and did not live there.[59] The Benjaminites' actions do not receive a favorable evaluation; they did not rid Jerusalem of its inhabitants and continued to dwell with them. The problem of living with local non-Israelite neighbors becomes apparent in chapter 2. According to later chapters, Benjamin's decision to dwell with the inhabitants of Jerusalem leads to their misbehavior, resulting in the Israelite civil war, which reinforces why there is no reference to the deity's presence with Benjamin at this time.

The next group discussed is the house of Joseph. The Josephites are placed in the region of Bethel (Judg 1:22). The text notes that the deity was with them. In the context of this account is a reference to the capture of a town, the inhabitants of which were put to the sword (Judg 1:25). The person who helped them to take the city was spared, he founded a new city in the Hittite country, and the town was renamed Luz (Judg 1:26).

The role of Luz and its relationship to Bethel is complicated. There are a number of references to Bethel in the biblical text and it is not clear that they are all referring to the same geographic location, or whether to a house *bêt* of a deity *ʾēl*.[60] It is more complex when seen in

---

[59] For example Judg 1:19, since the Judites could not dispossess them they did not live there.

[60] It is mentioned by the patriarchs (Gen 28:10-22, 35:7, 35:15), the burial site of Deborah, Rebekah's nurse (Gen 35:8), a place of inquiry (Judg 20:26-28), a place where Samuel periodically judged the people (1 Sam 7:16), a cult center for Jeroboam (1 Kgs 12:29-33), which aroused opposition from Hosea (10:15) and Amos (3:14), and was finally defiled by Josiah (2 Kgs 23:15).

light of Joshua 16:2, where the two names refer to separate places. In the context of the book of Judges, the city went through a change. The name change in this story indicates that even if it had earlier been changed (Gen 28:10-22, 35:7) it is now once again considered to be Canaanite and must be made Israelite anew. Despite the later importance of the city, no particular significance is given to it in the context of this narrative. There are no hints triggering the reader's memory to earlier events. However, many scholars follow the LXX which states that Bethel, which becomes a major sanctuary, is actually where the Israelites meet a few verses later, rather than Bochim.[61]

The reference here is to the site of Bethel, while in a few verses there follows another to a site named Bochim, and each place and name must be addressed in its respective context. At the end of the book Bethel is the site where the Israelites gather after the civil war against Benjamin to determine their fate (Judg 21:2). Thus, for the narrative of Judges it is necessary that the town and how it became Israelite are addressed early in the narrative.

The episode recalls Rahab and the spies (Joshua 2) and involves making a deal with inhabitants in the land. The text of Judges strictly forbids such actions in Judg 2:2, and this would be the northern tribes' first transgression. The deity is said to be present at the beginning of the episode (Judg 1:22), but following this scene the deity is never described as being with the other tribes. The text continues by addressing the tribes of Manasseh and Ephraim. First Manasseh did not dispossess Beth-shean, Tanaach, Dor, Ibleam, or Megiddo (Judg 1:27). Again a contrast is made with the previous tribe since, while saving one person, the Josephites had otherwise rid the town of its previous inhabitants. In this case the Manassehites could not dispossess them. When they did gain an upper hand, rather than ridding the land of its residents, they subjected them to forced labor (Judg 1:28). According to Gray, this type of forced labor is a characteristic Canaanite institution, illustrated in administrative texts from the palace at Ugarit.[62] If so, this is another example of the Israelites already dwelling with and incorporating the traditions of the Canaanites. The practice will be exercised again in Israelite kingship with Solomon (1 Kgs 5:27-30). There is no reference to the deity's presence with Manasseh.

Significantly less text is dedicated to the plight of the other tribes: Ephraim (Judg 1:29), Zebulun (Judg 1:30), Asher (Judg 1:31-32), and Naphtali (Judg 1:33). A similar pattern is recounted for each. It begins with the name of the tribe, which is followed by the inhabitants and the

---

[61] Boling, *Judges*, 67; Soggin, *Judges*, 30; and Gray, *Joshua, Judges*, 242.
[62] Gray, *Judges*, 241.

name of the town or towns in which they continued to dwell. The final
aspect is an account of what happened to the inhabitants. Here too a
pattern can be seen, with Ephraim and Asher living in the midst of the
previous inhabitants and Zebulun and Naphatali subjecting the inhabitants to forced labor. Neither practice is legitimate according to Judg 2:2
and the deity is not said to be present with any of these tribes.

The final tribe listed is that of Dan which follows a different pattern.
The pattern for the previous four tribes began with the name of the
tribe, described the areas they could not rid of inhabitants, and noted
how the situation was resolved. Verse 34 lists the Amorites first, making them the subject and the Danites the object. The text notes that the
Amorites kept the Danites from entering the plain and that they were
also active in Har-heres, Aijalon, and Shaalbim (Judg 1:35). The continuation of the verse refers to the house of Joseph, not the tribe of Dan.
The text continues by saying that somehow, despite the strength of the
Amorites, the House of Joseph enforced labor. In this review of the status of the tribes' conquest of the land, only the tribes of Judah and the
House of Joseph enjoyed the presence of the deity. The chapter ends
with a summary of the Amorite's territory (Judg 1:36), not that of a
tribe or house of Israel. Though the book is about the Israelites and
their territory, the analysis ends by focusing on the area controlled by
the Amorites, thereby highlighting the problem; the Amorites are in the
land and control areas promised the Israelites.

While most scholars do not end the unit at this point, from a narrative perspective this is the end. The next chapter begins with the discussion of leadership and ends with a summary of the status of the
different tribes, to a certain extent explaining why the tribes other than
Judah were unacceptable candidates for the job of leading. The following unit, while still somewhat introductory, examines the theme of the
Israelites' misbehavior. It covers many of the issues already addressed
in chapter 1, but rather than describe the situation through the actions
of the tribes, it generalizes them. Thus the first chapter begins with a
question of leadership and ends with the result of the lack of leadership
by describing the territory of the Amorites.[63]

Summary

The opening chapter of Judges functions as an introduction by presenting the major themes, sub-themes, words, and actions that are im-

---

[63] For a similar construction of units, based on structural reasons see M. Sweeney,
"Davidic Polemics in the Book of Judges," *VT* 46 (1997) 1–13.

portant for understanding the rest of the book. The opening chapter raises the major theme of the book, namely, who will lead Israel in the land, and to a certain extent, in what manner anyone other than the deity is designated to lead Israel. The problem is exacerbated by Israel's inability to conquer the land and refusal to destroy the previous inhabitants when it gained the upper hand. The major players are the various tribes of Israel, especially Judah, who enjoyed the most approval by the deity, and the various inhabitants who still occupied territory which Israel considered to be land which had been promised to them by their deity.

Many sub-themes are presented in the first chapter. Achsah's story introduces the role of women, who will serve as a barometer of how the Israelites fare in the land by noting women's status. Different aspects of leadership, such as titles of rulers, longevity of rulers and the ruler's house, what other rulers do and do not do, are presented in this first chapter and regularly throughout the text, almost as a study for the Israelites. The role of the tribe of Judah is key in the leadership question but is also connected to the David/Saul polemic. Israel's relationship with the previous generation and the local inhabitants are presented here but become the basis for many of her problems throughout the book.

Many important words and actions which are presented in an initially positive manner but which slowly erode and lead to the final civil war are in place by the end of the chapter. Places such as Jabesh-Gilead and Bethel are introduced. Benjamin and Judah are already contrasted through their differing treatments of Jerusalem. The Achsah story lays the foundation for many of the terms and actions later twisted in the story of the raped and murdered *pîlegeš* (Judges 19). Othniel is introduced, though not as Judge yet, as someone who serves as the transition from the desert generation to the period of Judges. The incorporation of local inhabitants, particularly by the northern tribes, is introduced. The final note, focusing on the amount of territory still in the hands of the Amorites, lays the groundwork for the following battles. Thus all the major pieces are introduced. In the following chapter the text proceeds to less literary and oblique language and categorically states its Deuteronomistic theology.

Chapter 2

A LOOK BACK AND A LOOK AHEAD

Judges 2:1-23

Judges 2 begins with communication between the Israelites and their deity, looks back to the time of Joshua where precedents had been set, provides an overview of what is to come, and ends with what happens when the Israelites do exactly what they are prohibited from doing. There are many problematic features in this unit such as: the duplication of Joshua's death, the role and meaning of the meeting at Bochim, and the relationship of 3:1-7 to the preceding and following texts. The Deuteronomistic terminology compliments the idea of most scholars that this unit is a secondary Deuteronomistic interpolation.[1] Regardless of the history of composition, the narrative is not as choppy as these scholars claim. Concerning the storyline, the previous unit set the stage by describing what happened in the period of Judges and this unit serves as background history.

Judges 2 provides the background material against which the previous chapter functions, and elaborates the patterns followed in the rest of the book, especially when the previous chapter is treated as the introduction to the major themes and issues governing the book. From a narrative perspective, this unit could not appear earlier in the book because the problems were not yet established. If the people had not transgressed, an admonition would be inappropriate. The new relationship with the deity, which does not include direct communication with the deity or a deity appointed ruler, had not yet happened nor had

[1] R. G. Boling, *Judges: Introduction, Translation and Commentary,* The Anchor Bible (Garden City: Doubleday, 1981) 64; J. Gray, *Joshua, Judges, Ruth,* The New Century Bible Commentary (Grand Rapids, MI: Eerdmans, 1986) 242; J. A. Soggin, *Judges: A Commentary,* Old Testament Library (Philadelphia: The Westminster Press, 1981) 31.

the ramifications of that scenario been felt by the Israelites. The relationship of this segment with the similar unit in the book of Joshua (Joshua 24) is important. Rather than assuming the unit in Judges as secondary, the differences between the two must be examined and analyzed for what they indicate about the book of Judges.

Most commentaries on Judges do not regard the Israelites' actions in Judges 1 as particularly negative and thus view the reprimand in this chapter as a reference to earlier books. As seen in the previous chapter, the episode with Adoni Bezek revealed Israel already to be assimilating Canaanite practices. Judah was designated to begin leading, but usurped excessive authority. Caleb and Othniel treated Achsah as a prize to be handed out to any winner. When the rest of Israel was fighting for land, Achsah simply asked her father for land and received it. The actions of the other Israelite tribes, at the end of the chapter, were in direct violation of the commandment, at least in Joshua (Josh 23:6-7), not to dwell with the local inhabitants. By Judges 2, Israel had already committed serious offenses against the Israelite deity, and the placement of Judges 2 is the logical result.

The Meeting at Bochim: Judges 2:1-5

Judges 2 begins a new unit because the previous chapter had focused on the status of the Israelite tribes and set the stage for the major issues of the book, while Judges 2 provides background material. Verses 1–5 serve as a transition from the previous chapter. They set the stage, and introduce the characters, the new situation in which they find themselves, and the new problems they face. The following unit hearkens back to the days of Joshua's death to provide background to what the Judges period follows and to which it is being compared.

The chapter begins with a messenger going up from Gilgal to Bochim reminding the Israelites that:

> I brought you from Egypt to the land which I had promised on oath to your fathers. And I said, "I will never break my covenant with you. And you, for your part, must make no covenant with the inhabitants of this land; you must tear down their altars. But you have not obeyed me—Look what you have done! Therefore, I have resolved not to drive them out before you; they shall become your oppressors, and their gods shall be a snare to you" (Judg 2:1-3).

The people realized that their actions were addressed directly and they broke into weeping, thus naming the site Bochim (weepers), and offered sacrifices to their deity (Judg 2:4).

Many scholars at this point discuss the relationship of Bochim with Bethel because of the LXX reading of Bethel here and the absence of other references to Bochim in the biblical text.[2] The ramifications of Bochim being Bethel are interpreted as indicating that this is a use of the later sanctuary at Bethel, in the northern kingdom of Israel, with the deity's decision to punish Israel causing the nations to remain in the land as a snare.[3] Most interpretations follow the LXX reading of Bethel here over the MT. Bethel was the home of one of the golden calves placed by Jeroboam I for the northern Kingdom of Israel in place of the Jerusalem Temple following the division of the United Monarchy (1 Kgs 12:29-33), and became a "cause of guilt" (1 Kgs 12:29, JPS). The deity's decision to punish Israel in Judges by causing the nations to remain in the land as a snare is considered in keeping with the site's later role in Israel. The reality is that the MT states that the event happened at a place named Bochim and includes an explanation for the name.

Concerning the flow of the narrative in the book of Judges, the occurrence of this event at a previously unknown site is fitting and sets the tone for the following narratives. The event follows immediately upon the discussion concerning the initial election of a leader and the Israelites' first attempts at expressing leadership, followed by the tribes not destroying the previous inhabitants of the captured lands. The result is that the people were gathered and admonished by their deity. The rebuke did not come directly from the deity, because there was no longer a clear communication link with the deity, but through an unnamed messenger. The people's reaction of crying indicates that they understood the nature of their offense and were aware that they were at fault. The event occurring at a new site ties into Israel's present crisis. Israel was facing new situations, in a new land, and their first action of repentance is represented by tears at a new location.

The use of Bochim prophecies a contrast with the final chapter, the only other time in the book when the people gathered to weep. In Judg 21:2 the people gathered at Bethel (in both LXX and the MT) and the people again wept bitterly. In the Judges 2 context the people misbehaved, the deity reprimanded them, they recognized their faults, and sacrificed to the deity. At the end of the book, the people erred in a much more drastic and destructive way, and yet did not understand why calamity struck despite their sacrifices and tears. Yet at the end of the book, after all the experiences described in Judges, the people gathered to weep at Bethel, a traditional site with a history and future. Again, elements are included in the beginning of the text and reappear

---

[2] Boling, *Judges*, 62; Gray, *Judges*, 242; Soggin, *Judges*, 30.
[3] M. Sweeney, "Davidic Polemics in the Book of Judges," *VT* 46 (1997) 5–6.

at the end revealing Israel's journey through the narrative period represented by Judges.

Another Look at Joshua: Judges 2:6-10

Joshua re-enters the picture in verse 6. The text notes that when Joshua dismissed the people the Israelites went to their allotted territories and took possession of the land (Judg 2:6). The previous generation is praised by stating that the people served the deity during the lifetime of Joshua and the older people who lived on after Joshua who had witnessed the deity's deeds (Judg 2:7). The text notes Joshua's death at the age of one hundred and ten years. Joshua is described as a servant of the deity. His burial took place on his own property, at Timnath-heres in the hill country of Ephraim (Judg 2:9). The section concludes with reference to the demise of that entire generation (Judg 2:10).

This unit raises a number of questions. Does this historical note cover the same period of time which had just been described, or is the text confused and chronologically out of order since the first sentence of the book purports to address the period following Joshua's death?[4] Since a similar story occurs in Joshua, how the two compare and contrast is relevant. The dismissal of the people and announcement of Joshua's death in Joshua 24 differ considerably from the situation in Judges and those differences are, to a large extent, related to their differing contexts.

In Joshua the dismissal of the people happens at Shechem, where the people made a covenant with their deity, recorded it, and witnessed it (Josh 24:25) only after the history of the people's relationship with their deity was recounted (Josh 24:2-18). The text states that the people were dismissed and went to their allotted portions (Josh 24:28). This statement follows Joshua 23 which states that the people and land were at rest and the necessary territory captured. Immediately following this report Joshua died and was buried. The passage following Joshua's death in the book of Joshua does not concern the people of Israel but Joseph by noting that the bones of Joseph, which had been brought up from Egypt, were buried at Shechem, in the ground which Jacob had purchased from the children of Hamor (Josh 24:32).

It is no accident that the house of Joseph is the last Israelite group not following the deity's directions at the end of the previous chapter

---

[4] According to Klein, Judges 2 covers the same time period as Judges 1 but this time from the deity's point of view (*The Triumph of Irony in the Book of Judges*, JSOTS/ Bible and Literature Series 14 (Sheffield: The Almond Press, 1989) 32.

(Judg 1:35). In Judges 1 the status of the tribes, the land they controlled, and the status of the inhabitants of those areas are described. The list begins with the Kenites, followed by Judah, and then the House of Joseph. The House of Joseph appears again, following the discussion of Dan and prior to the summary of the territory controlled by the Amorites. This is another example of irony in Judges; the hero honored by burial following Joshua's death in the book of Joshua is the ancestor of the house that is discredited directly before the admonition by the deity and the summary of past events in Judges.

The rest of the statements surrounding Joshua's death read differently when they follow the events of Judges 1, especially since these are not the same events recounted in Joshua. In Judges, the Joshua dismissal follows a reprimand of the people. Joshua has not been dead long and already the people have strayed. In Judges 2 the reference is background to what happened, highlighting the new situation. The text states that the people served their deity during the lifetime of Joshua, but because of the opening sentence the reader knows that Joshua was no longer alive. The rest of Judges 1 informs the reader that the people have already strayed. Both texts include reference to, "those who had witnessed all the marvelous deeds that the deity had wrought for Israel," but, according to the MT, the only person from the desert generation who entered the land was Caleb, and in Judges many of his deeds already were carried out in the name of Judah.

The book of Joshua ends with the death of Joshua, the reburial of the bones of Joseph, and the death of Eleazar, son of Aaron. The previous leaders were gone. As discussed in the previous chapter, Judges begins with a search for new leadership upon the death of the previous generation, therefore the description of Joshua's death serves a completely different function in Judges. In Judges the second reference to Joshua's death reminds the reader of the previous generation as a comparison. Since those deaths, one of which is mentioned in the first line of Judges, the people have already strayed. Judges 2:1-10 provides a bridge to the following segment which summarizes what is to come.[5]

---

[5] Sweeney has shown that the texts bridge together in a slightly different way. He focuses on the last time that the messenger of the deity met with Joshua at Gilgal. He stresses that the switch from Gilgal to Bochim takes the reader to the literary setting of Josh 5:13-15. He sees this as another example of recalling Israel's covenants with the Canaanites made in violation of their covenant with their deity. He also notes that the perspective is initially on the past period of Joshua but shifts to the future period by pointing to the following generations that did not know Joshua or the works of the deity ("Davidic Polemics in the Book of Judges," *VT* 46 [1997] 6).

The same sentence recording the death of the previous generation also informs the reader that a new generation arose which did not know the deity or the deity's actions on behalf of Israel (Judg 2:10). The formulation of this sentence fragment is the same as that of Exod 1:8, "A new king arose over Egypt who did not know Joseph." In Exodus the sentence indicates that a new period was initiated, one in which the Israelites suffered because the present generation of Egyptians forgot the acts of the previous generation, namely the actions of Joseph, leading to slavery for the Israelites. The message is the same in Judges.

The oblique reference to Egypt and the memory of Joseph's actions in Egypt reinforces the contrast with the Israelites' situation in Joshua. In the book of Joshua, Joshua's death was followed by the burial of Joseph's bones (Josh 24:32). In Judges, the reference to Joseph does not appear. What follows, Joshua's burial, is not a direct reference to Joseph. Instead, a sentence is used which was used upon the death of Joseph. The irony is that in the Exodus context Egypt forgot; here the Israelites forgot Egypt. The sentence recalls the ramifications of forgetting, especially the deeds of Joseph. In Egypt forgetting led to the enslavement of the Israelites, in this context it led to a similar type of enslavement. The idea of "enslavement" is reinforced later in a number of stories that note that Israelites "served" ʿ-*b-d*, using the same root meaning "serve," the other nations because they forgot their deity (Judg 3:8, 14; 10:6).

The New Generation: Judges 2:11-19

The previous sentence highlights the contrast between the previous generation of Joshua and the new generation, which forgot the actions of their deity. The direct result of not serving their deity is expressed in the next verse by stating that the Israelites "did the bad thing in the eyes of the Israelite deity and served Baalim" (Judg 2:11).[6] The appear-

---

[6] The author will repeatedly translate this as, "the bad thing." The Hebrew construction is the definite article followed by the nominal form of "bad," hence, "the bad thing." The specific object which is "bad" never is defined. While the translation, "the bad thing," appears to be a poor form of English slang, this translation best reflects the Hebrew. Translations such as, "evil," impose modern interpretations onto the text which this author is attempting to avoid. The term will be translated consistently in this way so that the reader can see the repetition of the phrase in its many contexts and can evaluate the author's interpretation of the term and its context.

ance of this verse, directly after noting that a new generation arose that did not know the deity, implies a connection between the two actions. Thus, as a result of the Israelites not knowing the deity, and because of the reference to forgetting, they carried out actions unacceptable to their deity.

Many texts translate, "the Israelites did what was offensive to the LORD" (JPS), "in the sight of the Lord" (KJV and RSV), as opposed to, "in the eyes of the deity" (AT). The problem with these translations is that they obscure the ironic force of how the actions of the Israelites differ from, and are the same as, comments in following chapters that, "every man did what was right in his own eyes," which appear twice later in the book (Judg 17:6; 21:25). This phrase becomes a signal that the Israelites were judging good and bad in their own eyes rather than by standards set by their deity. The origins of the cycle of the Israelites not doing what was right in the eyes of their deity appears already in Judges 2. The issue of seeing good and bad is established at the beginning of the book and the deity is the judge of that evaluation. The implication is that the deity has made what is good and bad known to the Israelites. The later statements of, "doing what was right in his own eyes," are in direct contrast to this statement. Not only were the Israelites doing what was wrong, but they came to the point where they felt that they, not their deity, judged good from bad.[7]

"The bad thing" that the Israelites commit concerns serving other gods. They come into contact with those gods and their rites through intermarriage because they did not destroy the previous inhabitants (Judg 2:11). The above pattern appears already in Judg 1:28-35. It is clarified in Judg 2:11-19 which notes the pattern the Israelites will follow in the rest of the book of abandoning the deity who delivered them from Egypt, following and serving the gods of the surrounding people, thereby angering their deity, who, as a result, gives them to plunderers who plunder them. The deity then raises someone to deliver the Israelites who saves them during that person's lifetime because of the pity the deity felt for the people. Upon the deliverer's death the pattern is repeated and the Israelites revert to practices unacceptable to their deity.

---

[7] Note that there are other cases where the Bible makes similar comments and seldom are the outcomes positive. For example, Abram told Sarai to do to Hagar what is "good in her eyes," and Sarai plagued her until Hagar ran away (Gen 16:6). Similarly Lot offered his two virgin daughters to the mob of Sodom and told them not to take the messengers but his daughters and do to them what is "good in their eyes" (Gen 19:8).

Judges 2:6-10 focuses on actions at the time of Joshua and the works of the deity, leading the reader into Judg 2:11-23, which states the basic pattern of apostasy, punishment, repentance, and deliverance that appears in the individual narratives of the Judges.[8] Judges 2:11-23 indicates that the pattern is cyclical and simply repeats itself, especially the reference that during the lifetime of the leader the people would act appropriately but upon the deliverer's death would return to their previous practices (Judg 2:18). What is not recognized is that the cycle does not repeat itself at the same level but repeats in descending order, with each cycle and generation beginning from a lower level of obedience to the deity than the previous period. This will become more apparent as the text progresses.

The term used for Israel going after other deities is translated, "prostituted after" (Judg 2:17). The root *z-n-h* means "commit fornication, be a harlot," but it can also be used metaphorically in reference to "improper intercourse with foreign nations," and our case is considered to refer to *"intercourse with other deities*, considered as harlotry, sts. involving actual prostitution."[9] This terminology is powerful in a text where some of the major characters have close relations with prostitutes (Judg 11:1; 16:1 and 19:2 where the final conflict is initiated by a woman carrying out this action). Regardless of the precise meaning of the verb, according to Israel's deity, this was an action the Israelites should not be doing.

The Other Nations: Judges 2:20–3:4

Judges 2:20 provides closure to this unit by noting the deity's anger against Israel's actions, "Since that nation has transgressed the covenant that I enjoined upon their fathers and has not obeyed Me, I for my part will no longer drive out before them any of the nations that Joshua left when he died" (JPS). In this way the deity explained why all the nations were not destroyed. It exonerates the previous generation of any wrongdoing by stating that Joshua and his generation intentionally left nations in the land to test Israel.

The final line of this unit and Judges 2 ties the unit to Judges 1 and provides closure by ending the references to Joshua. The text quotes the deity stating that the deity will no longer drive out any of the nations that Joshua left when he died (Judg 2:21). The next verse provides the

---

[8] So too in Sweeney, "Davidic Polemics," 5.
[9] *BDB*, 275.

reason; they will be a test to see whether the Israelites will walk in the ways of the deity as their fathers had done (Judg 2:22). The final statement in the chapter says in other words what the Israelite deity just proclaimed; that the deity left nations in the land rather than driving them out at once, explaining why they were not delivered into Joshua's hands (Judg 2:23).

These last few verses summarize the chapter, explain the deity's position, and exonerate Joshua and his generation, one of the main focuses of the chapter. As a result they explain the present situation, the preceding and following verses and their placement. Judges 1 focuses on Israel's reality in the time of Judges; there was no leadership, the land had not been conquered, and there were still enemies in the land. To a certain extent, Joshua could easily be blamed for the situation. Thus Judges 1 includes hints that the Israelites already were not following their deity's instructions.

Judges 2, especially the last few verses, exonerates Joshua and places the blame on the present generation. The chapter begins with a messenger of the deity explaining the terms of the covenant with the deity to them again. Because Judges 1 already describes situations where the Israelites transgressed, it is an easy step to point out their faults to them and remind the Israelites of their history. This chapter provides, for Judges, the parameters within which the Israelites should act. The role of Joshua is crucial because his job was completed. But the book of Judges, with its repetition of Joshua's death and a different presentation of the order of events, places the blame on the present generation. These last three lines blatantly state what the text was hinting at by recounting Joshua's death. It is not Joshua's generation that is at fault but the present one. Joshua left people in the land to be a snare to the present generation as a test, which, because of Judges 1, the reader already knows they failed.

Summary

Judges 1 introduces the Israelites, their new reality, and their reactions to it. There were hints in that chapter to contrasts with previous generations, especially that of Joshua. Judges 2 addresses the issue of Joshua specifically. It must follow Judges 1 so that the new pattern set by the following generation is already established. The chapter ends by exonerating Joshua so that the book can focus specifically on the period of Judges.

Chapter 3

FINAL BRIDGE TO THE NEW GENERATION

Judges 3:1-14

This chapter includes the final introductory material, which focuses on the first and prototypical judge Othniel. According to the Masoretic notes, a new unit begins with 3:1. New themes are introduced at this point, though the unit is well integrated into the previous chapter. Judges 3:8-11 is the last of the bridges from the introductory material to the individual accounts of actual judges. This unit begins with a list of the peoples remaining in the land as a test to the Israelites, followed by the actions committed by the Israelites which had angered their deity, and caused the deity to sell them to the hands of their enemies. The Israelites cried out and the deity responded by presenting them with a savior, Othniel. Despite the paucity of text dedicated to him, the components of Othniel's service function as the model by which later judges are evaluated.

Most scholars consider Othniel to be the ideal judge (i.e., an embodiment of perfection) rather than the model Judge (i.e., a standard of excellence). In this sense, Othniel, although not perfect, becomes the standard by which later judges will be evaluated. If one views the book of Judges not as merely cyclical, but as also representing a descending spiral of social and moral behavior in the eyes of the Israelites' deity, one would expect the behavior of the first to be exemplary. The problem with Othniel is that he was already introduced with a reading that casts a slight blemish upon him.

Israel's Test: Judges 3:1-7

The first seven verses of Judges 3 function as transitional material. The difficulty scholars have in separating these verses from the preceding and the following testifies to the art with which the editor wove the text of Judges together. In most discussions, Judg 3:1-6 is considered to be part of the Deuteronomistic introduction, beginning in Judg 2:6, because it lists the nations that the deity left as a snare to the Israelites, thereby highlighting the theme of the continued presence of the Canaanites as a test.[1] The first lines of Judges 3 list the groups that Judg 2:23 notes remained in the land.

Contrary to this popular notion, Sweeney argues that, while the passage relates thematically to the preceding material, it is distinguished formally by the introductory phrase, "and these are the nations that YHWH left, by which to test Israel, i.e. all who did not know all the wars of Canaan."[2] He points out that the *waw* consecutive (this refers to a construction of Hebrew wherein the word *"waw"* introduces relative time to the verb in such a way that the *waw* does not transform the following form into a past tense verb but links the verb to which it is attached to a past situation) formulation of Judg 3:7, "and the children of Israel did what was bad in the eyes of the deity," establishes a syntactical relationship between Judg 3:1-6 and 3:7–16:31. His thesis continues that the premise of the deity leaving people in the land and the Israelites intermarrying with them and serving their gods introduces the individual judge's narratives, which address precisely this issue. Judges 3:1-6 serves as a literary and thematic bridge between the previous introductory material in Judg 1:1–2:23, but also begins a new topic, that of the individual judge stories.

This textual bridge emphasizes the shift in generations by noting that the test group of Israelites were those who had not known any of the wars of Canaan, so that the succeeding generations might be made to experience war. The text separates the generations and prepares the reader for the next units which focus on specific judges and their actions. As noted previously, Judges 2 ends by focusing on Joshua and finishes the discussion of the previous generation, exonerating them, specifically Joshua, and clearing the way for the new topic and focus of the book, the period of judges.

The text lists explicitly the nations that the deity left behind: the five rulers of the Philistines, all the Canaanites, Sidonians, and the Hivites (Judg 3:3). Ironically these are not the only groups with whom the Israelites must battle in Judges. This unit is tied to the previous one by stat-

---

[1] R. G. Boling, *Judges: Introduction, Translation and Commentary,* The Anchor Bible (Garden City: Doubleday, 1981) 78–9, J. Gray, *Joshua, Judges, Ruth,* The New Century Bible Commentary (Grand Rapids, MI: Eerdmans, 1986) 247–8, J. A. Soggin, *Judges: A Commentary,* Old Testament Library (Philadelphia: Westminster, 1981) 40–4.

[2] M. Sweeney, "Davidic Polemics in the Book of Judges," *VT* 46 (1997) 6.

ing that these nations served as a means of testing Israel, more specifically, to learn whether they would obey the commandments which their deity had enjoined upon their fathers through Moses (Judg 3:4). This sentence does not differ significantly from Judg 2:22-23, which also notes that the nations were left behind as a snare. The difference is that the earlier passage was in a chapter focused on the concerns of the generation directly preceding Judges, i.e., Joshua and his generation, and as a result refers to them specifically. This reference places the Israelites in the larger context of Israel's history, hearkening back to the time of Moses. The focus is not only on the actions of the previous ancestors of Israel but reminds the Israelites of the deity's specific commandments and covenantal relationship.

The text continues, stating that the Israelites settled among the Canaanites, Hittites, Amorites, Perizzites, Hivites, and Jebusites (Judg 3:5), a slightly different list from that which appeared just two lines earlier. This statement follows the reference to the law and ties directly to the following line which notes that the Israelites took "their" (referring to the people who remained in the land) daughters to wife, gave their daughters to their sons, and worshiped (served) their gods. These actions led the Israelites to worship the Baalim and Asheroth (Judg 3:8).

The first few sentences in Judges 3 directly connect the story that is to follow to Judges 2 and take it in a new direction. The beginning sentences tie in with the same issues found at the end of Judges 2; enemies remained in the land to test the Israelites. The next sentences turn the focus toward the main transgression of the Israelites; intermarriage leading to the worship of other deities. According to the story, this is the reason for Israel's inability to capture the land.

Into the Hand of the Enemy: Judges 3:8-9

The previous section ended with a summary of Israel's actions which had caused the problems first encountered in this unit. The Israelites' transgressions are that they settled among the previous inhabitants of the area, and intermarried with them, which led them to worship foreign gods and ignore their deity. Judges 3:8 is considered a new section here because, although it is intimately related to the previous section in theme, it includes the deity's response. The deity's direct response to the Israelites' previous actions was anger resulting in selling them into the hand of a king, Cushan-rishathaim of Aram-naharaim, to whom the Israelites were subject for eight years (Judg 3:8).

There are many difficult questions, with no clear answers, concerning this king: who was he, where was he located, how and why could he have ruled areas relevant to the Israelites, and to what historical period does he relate? Aram-naharaim is often considered to be Mesopotamia, but more accurately refers to the area of upper Mesopotamia around the great bend of the Euphrates in northern Syria.[3] The other four examples of the term in the biblical text identify it as the home of Abraham's family (Gen 24:10), of Balaam, the son of Beor (Deut 23:5), and a source of troops David fought (1 Chr 19:6). The situation is made even more confused by the later sentence which describes the place ruled by Cushan-rishathaim as Aram, rather than Aram-naharaim (Judg 3:10).

Since it is doubtful that Othniel, who is associated with Judah, would be fighting so far from home, other explanations have been sought. The name of the ruler has been explained in Talmudic tradition as meaning, "of double wickedness," "chief of Athaim," and "chief of the Temanites."[4]

Possibly more relevant than the location of this ruler's kingdom is understanding his placement in the text. According to the terminology used to refer to this ruler and his kingdom, neither he nor the area he controlled were on the list presented a few sentences earlier of the peoples left to act as a snare to the Israelites (Judg 3:3), or with whom the Israelites cohabited (Judg 3:5). The first example in the text indicates that while the peoples of the land were left as a snare to test the Israelites, the actual enemies who would function as the punishment could come from beyond that group.

The text presents the situation involving Cushan-rishathaim as one of cause and effect. The Israelites intermarried and the deity took direct action. It was only when the people cried to the deity that the deity responded. In this case the Israelites cry out directly to the deity. The hand of Deuteronomy is strong here. What is described here is precisely what the deity had declared would happen if the Israelites did not follow instructions (Deut 7:4) and is, to a large extent, the reason they were tested (Judg 3:1-4).

Othniel's Story: Judges 3:9-11

Othniel, the first judge, is considered by most scholars to be an ideal. According to Boling, the story offers the relationship between Othniel and Israel as exemplary.[5] It is told at the beginning of Judges in such a

[3] W. Pitard, "Aram-Naharaim," *ABD* 1:341.
[4] J. R. Bartlett, "Cushan-rishathaim" *ABD* 1:1220.
[5] Boling, *Judges*, 81.

way as to introduce the problems with which Israel and the deity would be confronted in Israel's memory throughout the rest of the era.[6] While in many ways this is true, this unit cannot be considered the beginning since it is the third chapter of the book, Othniel was already introduced earlier, the Israelites have already transgressed, and the cycle that the deity will impose on the people has been described. As a result, Othniel can be considered the first leader for a problem that was introduced in the first chapters. He serves as a model for the office of judge, so aspects of his heritage, marriage, and experiences are not included here so that the structure of a model judge may be revealed.

Some have noted that the story of Othniel is added to provide a judge from the tribe of Judah.[7] Othniel's inclusion serves as a literary link to the original question asked in the book, "who will lead in the beginning" (Judg 1:1). Both beginning points provide the same answer, Judah. The first beginning set the stage and provides background to the situation. At this point in the narrative, the text is about to enter its second stage, the account of the individual judges and again Judah, or a Judite ruler, led first.

Othniel is the perfect candidate for the first judge because he was introduced earlier and is a known character, has an established military record (Judg 1:13), is related to Caleb, one of the two people from the desert generation who were allowed to enter the land, is married to an Israelite and is a member of the tribe of Judah, which has been designated as leader. Just as Caleb was the bridge from the previous generation of desert and conquest to the Judges generation, so, too, Othniel serves as a final link with the desert generation. He was not elected by the deity to judge in the first narrative concerning him; only later, after the previous generation has passed on and the pattern to be followed is set does he bear an official role.

Othniel is introduced as a judge after the Israelites transgressed. The transgression which is specified is that they had intermarried with those surrounding them. The reader already knows that Othniel had married the daughter of a war hero and that she is not only an Israelite but a Judite. The previous story of Othniel enhances his role in this case. The reader knows he was not guilty of the crimes that caused the situation in the first place, intermarriage with the local inhabitants. Othniel was the only one who could bear this role since he was the only one whose background and marital relations are legitimate.

---

[6] R. Boling, "Othniel," *ABD* 5.51.

[7] W. Richter, *Die Bearbeitung des 'Retterbuches' in der deuteronomistischen Epoche,* Bonner Biblische Beiträge, no. 21 (Bonn: P. Hanstein, 1964) 53–6, and G. Wallis "Die Geschichte der Jakobtradition," *WZH* 13 (1964) 436–8.

Othniel's married status is important in light of the status of the various judge's wives and relationships they have with women, some of which become major components in the way they are criticized. Othniel is shown to have already cleared this hurdle by the previous narrative. The cycle of stories about individual judges begins with the pattern whereby the judge's relations with women are the cornerstone of the critique of the leader's strength or legitimate behavior, in this case on a positive note since the woman was an Israelite. When Othniel is introduced in this cycle, he is not the son-in-law of Caleb, nor is his wife even mentioned, but he is the younger brother of Caleb.

Since Othniel's role as first judge serves as a model for what is to come, including too much information on him in the section concerning his judgeship could threaten the function of his role in that office. The description of his tenure in office reveals the bare essentials of the office. This is the perfect situation for a model. Too many particulars would confuse the essential elements. The downward spiral of Israel is reflected in her later judges who erred in the elaboration and details of the model set by Othniel. To a certain extent, too many details concerning Othniel, especially if one wants to question the legitimacy of Caleb's vow and Othniel's winning Achsah, could tarnish his image. It is important for Othniel to be married to Achsah in terms of continuity, legitimacy, and the role of Judah, but it is just as important that the details of that situation be separated from the text of his tenure in office.

The reason for separating the previous information concerning Othniel reinforces the ideas presented thus far concerning the organization of the material. The narrative begins with information setting up the dire circumstances of the present, bridging it closely with the previous period (the period of Joshua). The text then backtracks to provide relevant information in order to contextualize what will happen. The narrator conveniently includes the information that is relevant to the future, though not necessarily all the details of the past. When the text returns to the present situation (Othniel), it returns to a character already familiar to the reader and one who bridges all the generations presented, making him the only person to begin and continue the task. Structurally the story is at a new point in the narrative. The text is now focused on individual judges and the pattern which is followed for the next thirteen chapters begins.

Although Othniel had already won his wife through his skills as a warrior, that is not mentioned here. After noting that he was raised by the deity to save Israel, the text explains that the spirit of the Israelite deity descended upon him (Judg 3:10). The absence of a resume of his previous military career here emphasizes the role of the "spirit of the deity," not Othniel's previous military prowess. The "spirit of the Israelite deity" is a phrase that is used a number of times throughout the book (Judg 6:34; 11:29; 13:25; 14:6, 19; 15:14). According to Boling, "references to the spirit of Yahweh occur sporadically throughout Judges differently manifested in various individuals."[8]

According to Boling, in the Othniel case, "the spirit of the deity," stands for, "an impersonal power or force which can be absorbed or can so envelop a person that he or she becomes capable of extraordinary deeds."[9] This conclusion is based on little evidence in Othniel's case since the data concerning the ramifications of the presence of "spirit of the Israelite deity" are meager. After Othniel received this spirit he judged Israel, went out to war, and the Israelite deity delivered King Cushan-rishathaim of Aram into his hands (Judg 3:10). The result was quiet in the land for forty years (Judg 3:11). In this case the final results of the spirit are clear but the specific actions taken by Othniel as a receptor of the spirit are not.

While "the spirit of the Israelite deity" helped the Israelites in this situation, later in the narrative it precedes actions that lead to the ruin of judges' reputations as legitimate leaders, leading Boling to separate the results of the spirit in Othniel from the other Judges. The "spirit of the Israelite deity" next enveloped Gideon who, as a result, rallied the troops (Judg 6:34). This happened after he tore down the statue of Baal in his village, but the following incident indicates that though the deity showed proof once, Gideon needed more evidence of the deity's power. When Jephthah was on his way past Mizpah of Gilead the spirit of the Israelite deity descended upon him and he made his vow which caused him to sacrifice his daughter (Judg 11:29).

The remaining instances concern Samson. The spirit of the Israelite deity descended upon him and he went to Timnah to find a Philistine wife (Judg 13:25). The second time Samson was gripped he was again on his way to Timnah, this time to arrange his marriage with the Timnite woman, and he destroyed a lion with his bare hands (Judg 14:6). The third time follows Samson's hearing that the Philistines solved his riddle, and his response was to go to Ashqelon and kill Philistines for their clothing (Judg 14:19). The last time the spirit of the Israelite deity gripped Samson he gained strength to shed his Philistine bonds at Lehi (Judg 15:14). From the examples in Judges it seems that "the spirit of the Israelite deity" gives characters physical strength to carry out the physical and military actions necessary, but possibly blinds them from making intelligent choices.

---

[8] Boling "Othniel," *ABD* 5:51.
[9] Ibid.

This use of "the spirit of the Israelite deity" is another example which reflects the downward cycle of Judges. In the first example it led to a military victory (Judg 3:10). In the second case it led to a military victory but reflected a lack of trust in the deity, the source of the strength. In Jephthah's case the spirit descended upon him but he was either unaware of it or it led him to make an illegitimate vow resulting in the sacrifice of his daughter. In Samson's cases it led to personal acts of revenge. His actions resulting from "the spirit of the Israelite deity" did not help Israel as a whole but only Samson personally, often in pursuits in which he should not have been engaged. Othniel is the example of how the "spirit of the Israelite deity" should affect one, confirming his role as the model judge. That he was already an accomplished military man is separated from the narrative concerning his role as judge. To include his military prowess would have confused what was necessary for a model judge and what was personal to Othniel.

Othniel's relationship to the enemy ruler again sets him up as the model. The text obliquely raises the issue of capturing the enemy ruler, but is not straightforward about the matter. While the text does not elaborate on the issue, many later judges are concerned with what happens to the foreign ruler and much text is dedicated to that task; Ehud (Judg 3:18-21), Baraq (Judg 4:17-22; 5:24-27), Gideon (Judg 7:25–8:21), Abimelech (Judg 9:53), and even to a certain extent Samson (Judg 16:27-30), and often the actual killer of the enemy leader brings out character flaws in the Israelite judge. The reasoning behind the need to capture the foreign ruler is never stated but it ties into the theme of the book concerning what happens when non-Israelites remain. This may also tie into the David/Saul polemic since Saul's ultimate rejection as king was because he did not destroy King Agag of the Amalekites (1 Samual 15). It appears that the risk of being influenced by a foreign ruler presents an even greater risk of negative influence, or possibly reconquest. The concept of capturing the ruler also relates to the theme of what characteristics an Israelite leader should have. Othniel again functions as the model judge because in 3:10 the text states that the deity delivered the King of Aram to his hand.

A final note concerns the voice of the narrator. In 3:10 the text states that after Othniel went out to war the Israelite deity delivered the king of Aram. Since Othniel's voice is not heard in this unit, the reader does not know who Othniel considered responsible for the victory. The narrator attributes the victory to the Israelite deity, and does not allow the judge to claim it. This, too, is an element of the judge model since many of the later leaders erred by claiming the victory for themselves rather than attributing it to their deity. In Othniel's case the issue is raised and then circumvented by the narrator.

The same verse that notes that the land had quiet for forty years also records Othniel's death (Judg 3:11). The place of burial is not recorded. There is also no report of any children in Judges, though a Judite Othniel with a brother named Caleb, son of Jephuneh, is recorded as having had children in 1 Chr 4:14. Othniel did the job demanded of him at that time and left behind no problems as would be encountered by later judges. This too can be considered part of the model built around Othniel. The military leader was concerned with their generation and the immediate crisis. The text hints that some of the later judges either built or tried to build their own dynasties, or had problems with their burial place and what that represented. The biblical text in a later book attributes children to Othniel, but just as it distances Othniel's military prowess and marital connections from his role as judge, so too this information is separated from him. The concept of Othniel as a model controls the placement of the material. In order to form the model so that others can detract or elaborate on it, the text is careful to distance extraneous information from Othniel, at least in the portion of text where the model for a judge is created.

Summary

This unit relates what has happened in the previous chapters to the following narratives concerning individual judges. After an introduction tied thematically but separated syntactically, the text turns to Othniel. The character of Othniel serves as both bridge and model for the future because the text had already introduced him and established his relationship to the previous generation and his wife.

The text uses Othniel to describe the key elements of a judge, which are areas in which later judges erred. Othniel was deity-chosen. He received the "spirit of the Israelite deity" and used that to fulfill his primary goal of saving Israel from its immediate oppressor. He captured the enemy ruler and destroyed him. The responsibility for the victory was given to the deity. The result of the action was quiet in the land for a generation. Othniel died and was buried in an unknown place with no children to cause dynastic problems. All of these elements will be abused or misused by the later judges, eventually leading to civil war.

Chapter 4

EHUD

Judges 3:12-30

Ehud is the first leader for whom the narrator provides a story and detailed information about the situation encountered. A careful analysis of the story reveals the David/Saul polemic, tension with Ephraim, and foreshadowing of tales to come as the judges deteriorate from some of the attributes found in the Othniel model.[1]

The Israelites Offense: Judges 3:12-15

The episode begins in Judg 3:12 with the information that the Israelites continue to do "the bad thing" in the eyes of its deity. This is a pattern set in Judges 2 when the narrator first explains the events which are unfolding. Many translate the phrase "the Israelites again did what was offensive" (JPS, KJV, RSV). As Boling indicates, when the text intends "again," the word *ʿôd* is used.[2] In Judg 11:14 Jephthah uses "again" when he is referring to a second round in negotiations. In Judg 3:12 (and Judg 4:1; 10:6 and 13:1) "again" is not used and thus the Israelites continue doing "the bad thing" in the eyes of their deity. The implication of continuation, rather than repetition, is that when the previous leader judged, the Israelites did not cease committing the

---

[1] The absence of women in this story is striking since the previous Judge gained stature through his marriage (though it is not noted in the preceding text but only in the opening chapter) and the following charismatic judge is a woman.

[2] R. G. Boling, *Judges: Introduction, Translation and Commentary*, The Anchor Bible (Garden City: Doubleday, 1981) 85.

45

offensive acts. When the next hero took control, the people have not returned to a former practice but were continuing it. The implication is that Othniel may have protected Israel on the military level but did not enhance their situation concerning compliance with the deity's commandments. This information is not stated when setting out the model but only after the model was established.

The translation of r^c includes the definite article "the," making the term definite, hence the translation "the bad thing." The inference is that the Israelite actions, to which the text refers, were not general misconduct but some specific action. The previous story concerned Othniel who was married to an Israelite.[3] The story directly preceding his actions concerns the general statement by the narrator summarizing the status of the remaining peoples in the land and the Israelites' settlement among them. The negative aspect of that situation concerns the intermarriages that occurred, which resulted in the Israelites worshiping other gods. Thus the text is not focusing on evil in general but a specific negative action which led to a series of actions; settling among the peoples of the land led to intermarriage which led to worship of other gods.

The result of continuing to defy the Israelite deity is that the Moabites, under King Eglon, prevailed over Israel (Judg 3:12). King Eglon brought the Ammonites and the Amalekites together under his command, defeated Israel, and occupied the City of Palms (Judg 3:13). This is the second time the enemy to which Israel is subservient is not one listed in Judges 2 but is from outside the boundaries of Israel. It is possible that the reason for this was already mentioned by the text, that the Israelites did not consider the people of the land enemies any more because they were doing "the bad thing," namely settling with the peoples on the list, intermarrying with them, and worshiping their gods. In this scenario, selling the Israelites into their hand would have had no effect since they were already ensnared by them.

Many scholars consider the reference to the "City of Palms" to be an epithet of Jericho, based on a reference in Deuteronomy. In Deuteronomy, when Moses was shown the land before his death, the text states, "from the valley of Jericho, the city of palm trees, as far as Zoar" (Deut 34:3).[4] The problems with this meaning in Judges are many. The city was already mentioned in Judges 1 referring back to the Kenites joining the Judites (Judg 1:16). In that context Caleb had just given his daughter to a Kenite and the text established Judah's status inherited from

---

[3] See the discussion above in both chapters 1 and 3 of the present study and the corresponding biblical text in Judg 1:13.

[4] Y. Kobayashi, "City of Palm Trees," *ABD* 1:1052–3.

Caleb. The specific reference has the Kenites going up from the City of Palms and settling among the people in the Negev land, leading to intermarriage and worship of other deities.

In the present context the most famous Judite in Judges, Othniel, has just died. The people continued to offend their deity, apparently by cohabiting with the local inhabitants. The next scene is at the City of Palms where the last judge's clan was last mentioned carrying out the action the text just reminded the reader was unacceptable. The result was that the enemy took the city. The text reminds the reader of the connection between Othniel, the City of Palms, and the continuation of bad actions in the eyes of the Israelite deity.

The Israelites' situation deteriorated and they served Eglon, King of Moab, for eighteen years (Judg 3:14). The Hebrew states that the Israelites "served" ʿ-b-d the king, using the same verb used earlier in the chapter in reference to the Israelites serving foreign deities. The subject of the verb is Israel, meaning that the king was not prevailing over them but that the Israelites served the king. The use of "serve" in the Hebrew leaves open the possibility that the Israelites were not only subject to the king but may have adopted various modes of worship.

The Judge Ehud: Judges 3:15

The Israelites cried out to their deity and this time the Benjaminite Ehud, son of Gera, a left-handed man, was raised as a savior (Judg 3:15). This first description of Ehud is powerfully loaded since each element, that he is a Benjaminite, a son of Gera, and a left-handed man, relates to the David/Saul polemic.

Ehud's Benjaminite lineage is almost expected. Since the previous Judge was a Judite it is not surprising that the next leader would be a Benjaminite, establishing a comparison and contrast between the two tribes. Because the first answer to the question of who would lead was Judah, a Judite judge had led first. The inclusion of a Benjaminite leader following the Judite judge is another example of the David/Saul rhetoric. The book presents a decent judge from the tribe of Benjamin early in the narrative to highlight the extent of the downward spiral, especially by the tribe of Benjamin, exhibited in the book's final stories.

Ehud's designation as "son of Gera" is normally considered to be a clan name and is only a minor point in most discussions.[5] In light of the strong Judah/Benjamin, David/Saul themes in the book, the reference

---

[5] Boling *Judges*, 86; B. Halpern, "Ehud," *ABD* 2:414; J. A. Soggin, *Judges: A Commentary*, Old Testament Library (Philadelphia: Westminster, 1981) 50.

to another member of the Gera clan in 2 Sam 16:5-13 and 19:16-19 must be considered. 2 Samuel 16:5 recounts an incident during the Abshalom rebellion when David was leaving Jerusalem and a man named Shimei, son of Gera, a member of Saul's clan, hurled insults at David, and threw stones at him and his courtiers while all the troops and warriors were at his right and left. The second reference takes place after the death of Abshalom (2 Sam 19:16-19). King David was about to cross the Jordan on his return to Jerusalem and the Judites went to Gilgal to meet him. Again, Shimei, son of Gera, the Benjaminite hurried to meet them, accompanied by a thousand Benjaminites and Ziba, the servant of the house of Saul, to escort the king's family. At this point Shimei confessed his guilt for his actions at the previous encounter:

> Shimei son of Gera flung himself before the king as he was about to cross the Jordan. He said to the king, "Let not my lord hold me guilty and do not remember the wrong your servant committed on the day my lord the king left Jerusalem; let your Majesty give it no thought. For your servant knows that he has sinned, so here I have come down today, the first of all the House of Joseph to meet my lord the king." Thereupon Abishai son of Zeruiah spoke up, "Shouldn't Shimei be put to death for that—insulting the LORD's anointed?" But David said, "What has this to do with you, you sons of Zeruiah, that you should cross me today? Should a single Israelite be put to death today? Don't I know that today I am again king over Israel?" Then the king said to Shimei, "You shall not die"; and the king gave him his oath (2 Sam 19:19-24, JPS).

Another hint demanding a reading of the two stories in light of each other is that both David's second crossing and the Ehud incident occurred at Gilgal. The incidents in Samuel highlight animosity between the Benjaminites/Saulides and David. Enough similarities in the Ehud and 2 Samuel episode exist to read the David/Saul issue in the background of the Judges incident.

Ehud's description introduces him not only as a Benjaminite but, more specifically, one from the Gera clan which will insult David when his kingship is in trouble. Whereas Othniel's designation "younger brother of Caleb" ties him to the previous generations, highlighting his legitimacy, Ehud's designation relates him to Saul through the remnant of Saul's kingship which will gloat at King David's misfortune. Again the contrast favors Judah the victor over what will be the destroyed and humiliated remnants of Saul. Even before Ehud carries out any actions he is already not the model depicted by Othniel. This is another example of the polemic about David and Saul which appears as foreshadowing of events and names in Judges.

Ehud's final designation is that he is "son of the right, restricted in the right hand." The first reference is a play on words since "son of the right" is almost the same as "the Benjaminite" with the exception of the spacing and the inclusion of the *hey* indicating "the" *ben-hayĕmînî*. Continuing with the word play is the second element, often translated, "left-handed." The Hebrew actually reads, "restricted in his right hand," which does result in left-handedness, but the situation is characterized as a restriction. This word play functions on a number of levels. In this story Ehud turned his restriction into a strength against a man who was restricted in movement (the text does not state it as such but implies it when referring to his size). Ehud's left-handedness is also relevant in light of the civil war at the end of the book where the Benjaminite warriors were all left-handed and particularly accurate fighters (Judg 20:15).[6]

Ehud was raised by the deity to be a savior, not a judge. The title of judge is never ascribed to him, nor is he the subject of the verb "to judge." Ehud was raised by the deity as a direct response to the cries of the Israelites.

The Story of King Eglon: Judges 3:15-29

Conveniently enough, the Israelite tribute was delivered to King Eglon of Moab by Ehud (Judg 3:15). At some undetermined point, Ehud fashioned a special two-edged dagger which he girded on his right side under his cloak, and then presented the tribute to King Eglon (Judg 3:16). The timing of Ehud becoming a hero in relationship to his career delivering tribute is not explicit in the text. The implication, as the story progresses, is that this was Ehud's job and therefore the Moabite king knew him and possibly trusted him to a certain extent. There is no designation in the text of a specific point when the deity chose Ehud, Ehud did not have a revelatory experience where he realized he was chosen by the deity, nor did the spirit of the Israelite deity descend upon him.

The text states explicitly that Eglon was very fat (Judg 3:17), though the LXX has "handsome" for the term. The Hebrew Bible, like short stories, seldom adds details about people's appearances unless they are relevant to the story or plot line. The mention of such a detail is striking and raises the question concerning how this will impact the story.

---

[6] B. Halpern understands the use of "restricted" as an indication that Ehud was schooled in the use of the left hand for war. *The First Historians: The Hebrew Bible and History* (San Francisco: Harper & Row, 1988) 40–3.

After mentioning Eglon's weight, the text continues to say that when Ehud finished presenting the tribute he dismissed the people who had brought it (Judg 3:18). These people are called, "the carriers of the tribute," which might be a word play. The term used is the participial form of *n-ś-ʾ*, "to carry."[7] The term does not differ much from *n-š-ʾ* meaning "to beguile."[8] Bringing the tribute was a trick to gain Ehud an entrée to the king. Since the difference in the writing is a matter of pointing (the system, not original to the Hebrew text, but invented and introduced into the text by the Masoretes, of representing vowels by the inclusion of small points under the consonants), the shift is subtle and could easily be read both ways. The carriers of the tribute were also the beguilers, setting the king up without his knowledge.

After returning from Pesilim near Giglal, Ehud spoke again with the king, telling him that he had a secret for him (Judg 3:19). The king commanded those in attendance on him to leave his presence (Judg 3:19). The word which describes the room where the meeting took place is difficult to decipher. Most view it as a cool upper chamber, where the king would be comfortable and which could be cleared of attendants.[9] According to Halpern, the room was a bathroom, which justifies the later actions of Eglon's attendants.[10] This part of the story reads almost like stage directions. The author is setting all the people in place, Ehud hiding a dagger, and the fat king sitting alone in a bathroom with no attendants. The sense of excitement builds since the audience senses what must come and it is all the more thrilling because the reader knows what the king does not.

Ehud continued to lure the king to an inappropriate level of comfort by telling him that he had a message from Elohim (Judg 3:20). Rather than give him a verbal message Ehud reached his left hand into his garment, drew the dagger from his right side and drove it into his (presumably Eglon's) belly (Judg 3:21). In a rather grotesque continuation the reader learns that the fat closed over the blade and the hilt which went in after the blade, and he (Ehud) left it in his (Eglon's) belly (Judg

---

[7] *BDB*, 669–73.

[8] Note the difference is in the way the shin/sin is pointed. This difference plays an important role in the Shiboleth/Siboleth incident, where it was used to detect Ephraimites (Judg 12:5-6). This is possibly another example, this time of a word play which is playful in its first manifestation in Judges but later carries with it disastrous ramifications. The connection is strong because both stories involve Ephraim and fording the Jordan. *BDB*, 674.

[9] Boling states that the place must have been near Jericho because of the Gilgal reference and that the only cool place would have been on the roof (*Judges*, 86).

[10] Halpern, *First Historians*, 43–58.

3:22). The scene finishes with some kind of filth coming out of the king's body (Judg 3:22). According to Halpern, since Eglon was in the bathroom, a specific filth exited, one whose smell would not arouse suspicion from his attendants.[11] In this encounter Israel's military leader killed the enemy ruler even before the battle occurred.

The king's lack of protection is further highlighted, as the story continues, by Ehud exiting, shutting the doors and locking them. After he left, Eglon's servants saw the closed doors and thought, "He must be relieving himself in the cool chamber" and waited until they found their king dead (Judg 3:25). Their wait gave Ehud time to return safely, gather his troops, and carry the day. The term used to refer to those working for Eglon is "servant" *ebed*, the same root as the verb used to describe the relationship between Israel and Eglon at the beginning of the chapter (Judg 3:14).

Eglon, the king of Moab, is only the second foreign ruler for whom there is a description thus far in Judges, since the previous king had been mentioned only by name. Eglon is depicted as fat, slow-moving, and naive. The fact that "filth came out of him" and that his servants took this smell as a sign that he needed to be left alone, depicts the king as rather crude, or at least interested in the simple systems of the body. It also exposes rather personal elements of hygiene generally not discussed in the Hebrew Bible or about a ruler of a nation. Israel's second encounter with a king does not place kingship in a flattering light.

Eglon's courtiers provided Ehud enough time to escape and call up his troops before the Moabites responded (Judg 3:25-27). Ehud sounded the ram's horn throughout the hill country of Ephraim and all the Israelites descended with him from the hill country, with Ehud taking the lead (Judg 3:27). The narrator states that all of Israel was involved in this battle. The issue of who joined the military expeditions is another point which later shows the unraveling of Israel since, in the following story, only certain tribes participate in the battle (Judg 5:14-18).

Ehud stirred the troops by stating, "Follow me closely for the deity has delivered your enemy Moab into your hand" (Judg 3:28). In this case the main character noted that it was the deity who was responsible for the victory. In the previous case Othniel did not make such a statement, but the narrator informed the reader of the deity's role. This element is another aspect that deteriorates with later saviors, first sharing the victory with the deity (Judg 7:20), and later claiming the entire victory for themselves (Judg 9:17).

The troops followed Ehud, seized the fords of the Jordan, let no one cross, and slew ten thousand Moabites (Judg 3:28-29). The easy destruc-

---

[11] Ibid., 59–60.

tion of the Moabites once their leader was dead speaks to the larger question of leadership; without a king troops are easily destroyed. The reference to seizing the crossing of the Jordan functions as another case of foreshadowing since a similar event occurs later in Judges. In the later case it is Israelites against Israelites (more specifically Gileadites against Ephraimites) and as a result forty-two thousand Ephraimites died (Judg 12:5-6).

The author continues to deride the Moabites by referring to them as "fat and brave." While many translations use "robust" to describe the Moabite warriors, the Hebrew uses the word, "fat or oil" *šāmēn*. The question is whether the text is depicting them as a difficult group to defeat and so chooses a word which strengthens their character, or is describing them negatively. Since the text already jokes about the bulk of the Moabite, ruler it would not be out of line to depict his countrymen in the same light.

The story ends with Moab submitting to Israel, adding that the land was tranquil for eighty years. In the MT, Ehud is not called a judge, though in the LXX he is. The text also does not state that the land was tranquil because of him but only that Moab submitted to Israel and as a result of that the land was tranquil. The tribe Benjamin did produce an important deity-sanctioned military leader, but he is pointedly not called a judge.

Summary

Ehud was a Benjaminite who used left-handedness in a beguiling fashion. Ehud is not called a judge but rather a "savior" *môšîʿa*.[12] The text does not mention how this happened or if he was aware of it. Ehud did not need an introduction to the situation (as we will see with later judges) but led his people when they needed him. The text is careful to state that he did so for the Israelite deity, not for his own glory or credit.

As a result of Ehud's actions the land had peace, but he is not held directly responsible for that, nor does the text add that he ever judged Israel for any length of time.

---

[12] *BDB*, 446.

Chapter 5

DEBORAH

Judges 3:31–4:24

The story of Deborah shows how the spiral continues downward. This is done through the figure of Baraq, who should have been the judge and primary hero. His shortcoming, according to the world-view espoused in the biblical text, is that he allowed many of his responsibilities to be coopted by a woman. Women are prominent in this story—Deborah, Jael, and in the poetic version, Sisera's mother. The book continues to examine various forms of leadership. Criteria for evaluating judges, already seen in the earlier stories, continue, such as whether they capture the foreign ruler, what their reason for fighting is, what the role of the deity in battle is, and new categories are introduced.

This chapter will examine the transitional reference to Shamgar ben Anath, and then the contents of Judges 4. The same episode is covered in both Judges 4 and 5 but each conveys different information and the two diverge in some areas. The poem of Deborah is one of the oldest pieces of literature in the Bible and, because it was written first, its material has often been treated as primary despite where it appears in the present version of the MT. Judges 4 preceding Judges 5 means that information included in Judges 4 colors how the reader views the following poem. What details are included in Judges 4 and how the various incidents are presented is crucial for understanding both chapters. As a result, the Song of Deborah (Judges 5) and how the two relate to each other will be considered in the following chapter, only after the background material provided in Judges 4 is evaluated.

Placement of Shamgar Ben Anath: Judges 3:31

The function and placement of this sentence are complicated. The difficulty appears as early as some manuscripts of the LXX which place this unit after the Samson cycle in Judg 16:31 because of the reference to Shamgar's interactions with the Philistines.[1] The story of Ehud ends in Judg 3:30 but in Judg 4:1, the line following the Shamgar reference, Ehud is mentioned again. There is no reference to apostasy on the part of Israel preceding Shamgar's arrival on the scene. Shamgar is not named a Judge or even a savior. The deity is not involved in the story, which is common among the minor judges, but the other minor judges are grouped together. In this study the verse will be treated as part of the Deborah narrative because of references in those chapters to Shamgar.

There is a fair amount of information in favor of associating Shamgar with the end of the Ehud episode. Judges 3:31 begins by stating, "After him . . ." The "him" is presumably Ehud since he had been the protagonist in the previous chapter. Boling follows the LXX and assumes that the line indicating Ehud was a judge has fallen out of the MT because of a haplography due to homoioarcton.[2] In the present state of the MT Ehud is not referred to as a judge and therefore ties in nicely with Shamgar, who does not bear that title either.

The problem in associating Shamgar with the previous chapter is that he is referred to again in the Song of Deborah (Judg 5:6). In the Judg 5:6 context the reference occurs early in the poem and sets the stage for the events involving Deborah and about which she sings. If it is used to set the stage for Judges 5 and appears in the line before Judges 4, it is not hard to imagine it serves a similar function for the narrative aspect of the Deborah cycle. The verse must be interpreted as setting the background for understanding what is about to happen during the events soon to be related. Since there is little information in Judg 5:6 about who Shamgar was, its inclusion here provides information that will be relevant later in the account (in this instance in the poem), a device used extensively in this chapter.

---

[1] R. G. Boling, *Judges: Introduction, Translation and Commentary*, The Anchor Bible (Garden City: Doubleday, 1981) 89.

[2] Ibid., 87. Haplography and homoioarcton are names scholars have given to two of the ways in which textual variants are understood to have developed in a tradition. For a better understanding of textual transmission and variants see E. Tov, *Textual Criticism of the Hebrew Bible* (Minneapolis: Fortress Press, 1992). Tov defines haplography as, "the erroneous omission of one of two adjacent letters or words which are identical or similar" (237), and homoioarcton as the phenomena of the erroneous omission of a section influenced by the repetition of one or more words in the same context in an identical or similar way found at the beginning of a verse or unit. Presumably the eye of the copyist or translator jumped from the first appearance of a word to its second appearance, so that in the copied or translated text the intervening section was omitted together with one of the repeated elements (238).

Neither Ehud nor Shamgar is referred to as a judge. The verse recounting Shamgar's actions forms a bridge between Ehud, a major
non-judge, and Deborah, the only woman who judges. The reference in
Judg 3:31 to Shamgar parallels the reference in Judg 5:6, whose literary
function sets the stage for the events in the time of Deborah.

Who Was Shamgar ben Anath?

If the role of Judg 3:31 is to provide background for the upcoming
events, then the name or incidents relayed must be meaningful to the
readers. While little information is included in the Shamgar narrative
there are hints at its meaning since the name is not Israelite. Anath is
the name of a Canaanite goddess. This is the first battle with the Philistines in the book of Judges, and the first reference to an enemy the Israelites face who was on the original list of peoples left in the land to
entice the Israelites.

Since most scholars treat the book of Judges as an historical rather
than literary document, many have sought the historical referent for
the Shamgar episode. Thus the name Shamgar ben Anath receives
much scholarly attention. The name Shamgar is non-Semitic and probably of Hurrian origin.[3] While this is usually considered significant, the
significance is not so much that the name is Hurrian, but what the
name says about the one bearing it. Hurrian names appear referring to
people from Canaan in both the Middle Bronze and Late Bronze Ages.
The relevance here is that the name might indicate that its bearer was
part of the pre-Israelite population of Canaan.[4] Shamgar is said to be
"son of Anath," a phrase which has a number of possible interpretations, all with different ramifications for how the reference impacts the
understanding of Shamgar and his position in the narrative. One interpretation is that "ben Anath" means that he came from the town of
Beth-anath in Galilee.[5] Another possibility is that the label was a military designation involving the name of the goddess Anath, who was
consort of Baal.[6] Proponents of this interpretation find analogical evidence connecting Anath with the semi-nomads, known as Haneans, in
the Mari texts who provided sizable military contingents to the king of

[3] R. G. Boling, "Shamgar," *ABD* 5:1156.
[4] Soggin raises the possibility that Israel is saved by a non-Israelite [*Judges: A
Commentary*, Old Testament Library (Philadelphia: Westminster, 1981) 59]; M. Morrison "Hurrians," *ABD* 3:335–8.
[5] W. A. Maier III, "Anath," *ABD* 1:226.
[6] Boling, *Judges*, 89.

Mari on several occasions.[7] After comparing inscriptions on two arrow-heads dating to the late twelfth and eleventh centuries Cross believes that "ben anath" simply refers to Shamgar's father; i.e., that Shamgar is literally the son of a man named Anath.[8]

A final option for the meaning of "ben Anath" relates to the actual goddess Anath in the ancient Near East. There are few references to this goddess in the biblical text, but the appearance of her name before the story of Deborah, where a woman is the leader and judges, makes some relationship with this goddess at least worth investigating. Anath is an ancient goddess who was worshiped from Mesopotamia through Egypt.[9] There is too much literature relating to her to represent all of it here but some salient points will be mentioned.[10] According to Walls, Anath embodies the tensions and paradoxes of feminine power in an androcentric world.[11] She disdains feminine social roles and domestic responsibility, and engages in the masculine activities of hunting, warfare, and politics.[12] She is a female independent of male authority when according to ancient social ideology she should have been a submissive wife and mother active within the domestic sphere.[13] Walls' description of Anath is not a bad depiction of Deborah, and possibly Jael. The inclusion of Shamgar, whose name embodies a reference to Anath, is a foreshadowing which prepares the reader for other women who engaged in warfare and politics and were not controlled by clear male authority.

While Shamgar's name foreshadows the following roles of the women in the story, it contains no Israelite aspects, though this is not stated explicitly. Either Shamgar and his actions are condoned by their inclusion in the text, indicating that it was legitimate for Israelites to accept help from non-Israelites, or it depicts the decline of the leaders that Israel relied upon for help.

Shamgar's Actions and Enemies

Shamgar's actions and enemies are important to the narrative because of the role the Philistines play later. The narrator states that

---

[7] Ibid., 87.

[8] F. M. Cross, "Newly Found Inscriptions in Old Canaanite and Early Phoenician Scripts," *BASOR* 238 (1980) 1–20.

[9] Maier, "Anath," 225–6.

[10] For more information on Anath and her literature and bibliography see N. Walls, *The Goddess Anat in Ugaritic Myth*, SBL Dissertation Series 135 (Atlanta: Scholars Press, 1992).

[11] Ibid., 217.

[12] Ibid.

[13] Ibid., 218.

Shamgar slew six hundred Philistines with an oxgoad. This is the only place in the Hebrew Bible where the term "oxgoad" appears. The term is the causative of *l-m-d*, though it is unclear how this could refer to a weapon. Boling relates the term, with a bit of sarcasm, to the wooden paddle once used in schools.[14] It may simply mean that Shamgar "taught them a lesson." It is noteworthy that such a simple weapon is used preceding the Deborah story where the Israelites' enemy is better equipped with technologically advanced weaponry.

The mention of the Philistines in this verse was once viewed as a reference to the arrival of pre-Philistine invaders.[15] In recent years much archaeological work has been conducted on the coastal plain of Israel in an effort to understand the Philistine arrival and method of settlement.[16] Because the biblical text provides little information concerning the location of Shamgar's battle, correlating these two bodies of data is difficult at best. Understanding Shamgar's name as placing him near Beth-anath in Galilee does not help, since there is little archaeological evidence for Philistines in that region.

Instead of seeking a historical referent for Shamgar it is more worthwhile to understand the reference as part of the construction of the book of Judges. The story directly preceding the outbreak of civil war at the end of the book concerns Samson and the tribe of Dan, which was forced to move as a result of the Philistine control of their region. Mentioning them here, at the beginning of the book, means that their later appearance need not be explained.

If Shamgar's name and actions are used as a literary device to introduce the Philistines, the question still remains why this occurs here as opposed to earlier or later in the book. As already mentioned, Shamgar ties in nicely with Ehud since neither is referred to by the MT as a judge and Shamgar is referred to in the Song of Deborah. The Anath element of his name may be an oblique reference to Anath or the attributes associated with her. This would connect the Shamgar passage with the story of Deborah more firmly since Deborah, Jael, and Anath share character traits unusual for women. The reference to a goddess warrior,

---

[14] Boling, *Judges*, 90.

[15] Ibid.

[16] See, M. Dothan, "Ashdod," *NEAEHL* 1.93–100; L. Stager, "Ashkelon," *NEAEHL* 1.103–7; T. Dothan and S. Gitin, "Miqne, Tel (Ekron)," NEAEHL 1.1051–9; A. Ovadiah, "Gaza," NEAEHL 2.464–7 (though at the time the article was written no Philistine levels had been unearthed) and E. Stern, "Zafi, Tel," *NEAEHL* 4.1522-4. Concerning whether or not Tel Safi is ancient Gath see A. Rainey, "The Identification of Philistine Gath: A Problem in Source Analysis for Historical Geography," *EI* 12 (1975) 63*–76*; and W. Schniedewind, "The Geo-Political History of Philistine Gath," *BASOR* 309 (1998) 69–78.

even if, or maybe especially, one from a foreign people, sets the tone for the following narrative. The prominence of Anath among the Canaanites, the people whose customs Israelites are prohibited from acquiring, serves as a notice about the assimilation of Canaanite customs into Israel.

The final note states that Shamgar saved Israel. Again he is listed with no tribe, no place, appears to be a foreigner, and carries out the same function as Ehud, who has all the correct attributes concerning Israel. This indicates that the Israelites are already not maintaining their traditions and have assimilated to such an extent that they allowed a non-Israelite to save them. The appearance of this brief line preceding the story where an Israelite woman and a non-Israelite woman saved Israel serves as another indictment of the men of Israel who were no longer saving their people but instead relied on foreigners and women to carry out that task for them.

The Story of Deborah: Judges 4

Judges 4 begins, as did the previous episode concerning Ehud, with the children of Israel continuing to do "the bad thing" in the eyes of their deity, but with two significant differences. In the previous chapter the reference to the Israelites continuing their bad actions followed the notation that the Judge Othniel died. While the Israelites' actions are still a continuation of previous acts, the text leaves open the possibility that there was some period when the Israelites did not misbehave. The other difference is that the transition from Othniel to Ehud is a transition from a judge to a leader who is not termed a judge in the MT. This case presents the transition from a non-judge (Ehud), to a foreign savior (Shamgar), to a female judge. The model judge embodied in Othniel has diminished considerably.

The impact of Ehud's death is not clear. An episode exists between the peace following Ehud's defeat of the Moabites and the reference to the Israelites' continuation of negative actions. Scholars attempt to solve this problem in a number of ways. One possibility, as expressed in the LXX, is to end Judg 3:30 with a reference to Ehud's death and to his having judged them until he died. In the LXX, the reference to Ehud's death does not appear, having been added earlier. An explanation for this is haplography due to homoioarcton.[17] In this case Boling does not accept this explanation and notes that there is no way to explain this as an addition in 4:1. Instead it contributes to the initial building up of suspense by the narrator concerning the Israelite deity's

---

[17] Boling, *Judges*, 94.

administrative strategy.[18] So, the reason Shamgar is missing is that his story did not speak directly to the need for wide-ranging organizational ability as did the story of Ehud.[19] In his interpretation, the reference to Ehud in 4:1 means that the Shamgar episode should be deleted.

As previously indicated, the Shamgar sentence was not deleted in the MT but this reference is included directly preceding the Deborah episode and is incorporated into the poem of Chapter 5. The MT does not call Ehud a judge, and the notice of a foreigner, Shamgar, saving Israel reveals a further degeneration on the part of the Israelite leaders. The reference in Judg 4:1 to Ehud reinforces the idea that although Shamgar saved Israel, he was not an Israelite, the land did not have rest following his actions, and it is Ehud who must be considered the primary protagonist in the text. In other words, the reference to Shamgar is to a key episode, but one in which Shamgar should not be considered a major player, and the place from which the story continues is Ehud's reign.

The result of Israel's negative actions was that their deity sold them into the hand of another oppressor, this time the Canaanites, another one of the people left in the land by the deity for this purpose. More specifically, the Israelites were sold to Jabin, king of Canaan, who reigned in Hazor. His army commander, Sisera, is also mentioned by name. He too plays a major role and functions as a leader of the Canaanites in this episode (Judg 4:2). Since a Jabin, King of Hazor, designated the head of the Canaanites, is active and then killed in the book of Joshua (Josh 11:1-13), more investigation into these two characters is warranted.

In Josh 11:1-5, King Jabin of Hazor sent messages to gather the kings in Canaan to fight Joshua and the Israelites at the waters of Merom. After defeating the coalition, Joshua captured Hazor and put her king to the sword (Josh 11:10). At this point the text notes that Hazor was the head of all those kingdoms. Joshua proscribed Hazor; put everyone to the sword, burned down Hazor, captured all the other royal cities and their kings, and also put them to the sword (Josh 11:11-12). The text continues by noting that Hazor alone was burned and that the Israelites killed all the inhabitants of the other cities (Josh 11:14). If this is the same Jabin, King of Hazor, then Judges directly contradicts the book of Joshua.

There are a number of attempts at resolving this contradiction. One theory sees Jabin as a dynastic name for the kings of Hazor.[20] Support

---

[18] Ibid.
[19] Ibid.
[20] P. Benjamin "Jabin," *ABD* 3.595.

for this interpretation is found in the Mari texts, the Amarna letters, and other Egyptian documents, since all refer to the city of Hazor, as well as modern archaeological excavation which has uncovered an impressive Late Bronze Age city.[21] There are problems with this theory. Hazor was destroyed earlier than the other Canaanite cities, meaning there was a time gap between the destruction of Hazor and the other cities.[22] The theory does not explain how, if Jabin was a dynastic name at Hazor and the Joshua story is correct and Hazor was destroyed by the Israelites, where and how the family dynastic line continued in Judges.

A second theory sees both the Joshua and Judges accounts as two varying traditions of the same event. Not far removed from this point of view is the theory that in Judges 4 Sisera is central to the story while the poetic account in Judges 5 does not mention Jabin at all. Proponents of this theory posit that the account in Judges is about Sisera, who governed in Harosheth Hagoyim. This theory posits that it is possible that the battle of Merom took place subsequently to the battle of Deborah. In this scenario, the Deuteronomistic Historian used the two episodes to contrast the strength of the enemies and the victory that is possible when the leaders are obedient to the deity.[23]

The purpose here is to understand how the phrase functions within the book of Judges. As noted in discussing the opening chapters, there are many references to the period and events of Joshua's time and these are used to highlight how much has changed between the initial conquest and the circumstances faced in Judges. It is possible that Judg 4:2 follows this pattern. In Joshua's time kings fought battles. In the period of Judges, the king, if he existed at all, was overshadowed by both his general and even the general's mother. The king did not take counsel with other kings as he did in the time of Joshua but the general's mother took counsel with her counselors (Judg 5:29). The contrast is particularly marked in this chapter where both Israel's commander and the person who kills the foreign leader were women.

The use of Jabin, King of Hazor, and Sisera his commander ties into the use of different titles and their related functions in Judges. In Joshua's period kings were active. While Israel did not have a king in the period of Joshua, there was a leader designated by the deity, namely Joshua. One of the basic questions repeatedly raised in Judges, and in particular in this chapter, concerns the role of leadership; who should have it and what are the responsibilities of leading? It is only fitting that the various roles played by the surrounding peoples would be

---

[21] Ben-Tor, "Hazor," *NEAEHL* 2.594.
[22] Ibid.
[23] Benjamin, "Jabin," 596.

questioned. This may be an indictment or a mockery of the role of the king, who is completely absent in this episode. This is not out of context following the Eglon episode where the enemy king is depicted as fat, naive, and disgusting. In this episode even the generals, both Israelite and Canaanite, are of questionable leadership ability.

Sisera is the second character introduced in Judg 4:2. Sisera's name is problematic because it is neither Hebrew nor Canaanite.[24] The text states that he lived at Haroshet Hagoyim, which has not been located with certainty. The location is further complicated by the LXX translating the phrase to mean "forests of the nations" rather than as a place name for a town or city. Recent archaeological excavations in the Jezreel region reveal that while urban activity in the region declined, the Egyptian presence remained strong in the north, particularly in the region of Beth-shean.[25] The home of Sisera could as easily refer to an encampment in the forest or a town.

One of the problems in understanding Sisera is his relationship to Jabin. Judges 4 contains the only reference to Jabin in Judges. Sisera in Judges 4 is subject to Jabin but in Judges 5 is the only ruler and therefore the main protagonist. This is reinforced by Sisera's activities, the Israelites' interest in his capture, and the prominence of his mother. It may be more profitable to understand Sisera not from his hometown but from the way his title, actions, and role function in the text.

In 4:2 Sisera is called the "the sar of his army" *śar-ṣĕbāʾô* ("his" refers to Jabin). This term is traditionally translated as "army commander" (JPS, RSV). The term *śar* is fairly common and carries the meanings, "chieftain, chief, ruler, official, captain, prince."[26] The specific English term used to translate it is determined by the noun with which the word is in construct or the context in which the term appears. In Judg 4:2 the term is in construct with "army," hence the translation "commander" rather than "prince," or "chief." All the various translations of this word imply that the person bearing the title is in charge of some area, but is not the final authority. In every appearance of this term there is someone with higher authority over this person. Such is the case in Judg 4:2 with reference to Jabin. Without Jabin's presence a different term could be applied to Sisera indicating that he was "king" or "ruler."

The second tier aspect of Sisera's title is relevant in light of the following events and creates parallels with the different players in the ensuing

[24] Boling, *Judges*, 94.
[25] M. Hunt, "Harosheth-Hagoiim," *ABD* 3.63, A. Mazar, "Beth-Shean," *NEAEHL* 1.217-22, and P. McGovern, "Beth Shean," *ABD* 1.694.
[26] *BDB*, 978.

story. Sisera is not the sole leader and must answer to someone. Whether Jabin was a living person or a dynastic name, the text describes Sisera as second to him. Sisera's secondary status is particularly important when analyzing the power structures of the different parties involved.

Baraq is ostensibly the leader of the army, yet he too takes orders from and therefore acts as second in command to, Deborah. Her gender makes this more striking. Though the text only refers to Sisera's mother at the end of the poetic account in 5:29, she too has "commanders" *śārôt* of her own. Because the noun "commanders" appears in the feminine plural and is not modified by a noun in construct such as "army," as in Sisera's case, the term is usually translated as something less strong in terms of power and position such as "her ladies" (JPS, RSV). Regardless of the noun to which it is or is not in construct, the term carries the connotation of someone in a high office with a fair amount of power, exactly like Sisera. At the same time, the term denotes one who is in secondary status to someone else. Ironically enough, Sisera is a *śar* to someone while his mother has her own *śārôt*.

Since Baraq is second in command to Deborah, an ironic parallel is created between Sisera and his mother. This parallel would have been irrelevant and unbelievable in the story had the text originally listed Sisera's mother as a ruler. The inclusion of Jabin sets Sisera's status as secondary from the beginning of the story. It is only at the end of the entire episode that the reader learns to whom he is actually second. Sisera's status in life parallels the irony of Sisera's death, to be discussed in more detail below.

Israel's Response: Judges 4:2-3

The Israelites respond to their new status by crying out to their deity (Judg 4:2). The text notes that the deity sold the Israelites to Jabin and Sisera, and when the Israelites cried out to their deity the reason stated is that "he" (this is singular, and therefore could refer to either Jabin or Sisera) had nine hundred chariots of iron (Judg 4:3). Like Judg 1:19, which notes that the Israelites could not dispossess the people of the plain because they had iron chariots, this verse has been used to relate the book of Judges to history through the appearance of iron in the region. Boling claims, "The iron age in Canaan began with the arrival of the Philistines, who controlled their secrets of ironworking under monopolistic conditions that were not finally broken by Israel until after the time of Saul."[27]

[27] Boling, *Judges*, 94.

While the transition from bronze to iron is an important topic, the reference here is fraught with so many difficulties that using this as evidence for the arrival of iron to the region is meaningless. The text states clearly that Jabin is a Canaanite, and while it does not provide a designation for Sisera, since he is listed as an officer of a Canaanite, one cannot assume he was a Philistine ruler. If the Philistine/iron argument were relevant to the Deborah story, and determined that the arrival of iron in the region should be attributed to the Philistines, one would have to develop a theory explaining why the Philistines shared their secret with the Canaanites and not the Israelites.

Focusing on the appearance of technology neglects the statement the text makes about the source of Israel's plight and how they viewed it. The Israelites cried out "because" *kî* the opposition was better equipped technologically than the Israelites; this was their interpretation of the source of their oppression. They did not consider their own actions or an absence of leadership as the cause of their distress but technology, a new event in the book. The Israelites' lack of faith in their deity is highlighted by the previous savior's victory with a low technology weapon.

The Israelites' cry for help here is very different from the previous cases where they did "the bad thing," were punished, served other rulers or peoples, cried out to the deity, and the deity raised a leader for them. In this case the response to the Israelites' misbehavior was Ehud's death. Only after that proclamation were they punished. When they cried out their appeal was not for a leader but technology. In this case the deity did not respond by raising up a savior. Instead, following the Israelites' cry to their deity, the text notes that "he" oppressed Israel for twenty years.

Deborah the Prophet: Judges 4:4-5

Deborah is introduced only when the backdrop is in place. The Israelites' cries thus far in the book had been answered by the deity appointing a leader. In this case there is a shift; a *waw* consecutive does not precede Deborah's introduction, rather a connecting *waw* is used. Some translations attempt to convey this shift by translating "Now Deborah . . ." (RSV) or "And Deborah . . ." (KJV). The result in the Hebrew, as well as these translations, is an abrupt shift to a focus on Deborah, highlighting the way in which this case does not follow previously established patterns.

If one includes the name Deborah, which is a feminine noun, her introduction begins with a string of seven feminine nouns, including one defining her husband (Judg 4:4). While this may not be surprising, considering that a woman is being described, the list is striking since there are so few women named or described in the biblical text. Translating this introductory line is difficult, evidenced by the many differing translations:

> "Deborah was a prophetess, the wife of Lappidoth. She was judging Israel at that time" (Boling).

> "Deborah, wife of Lappidoth, was a prophetess; she led Israel at that time"(JPS).

> "And Deborah, a prophetess, the wife of Lappidoth, she judged Israel at that time" (KJV).

> "Now Deborah, a prophetess, the wife of Lappidoth, was judging Israel at that time"(RSV).

At first glance the differences seem minor, but they include such important issues as: how the topic is introduced, the use of the verb "to be," placement of various components, translation and tense of the verbs, and which elements are thought to belong to the same sentence. The problem is rooted in the list of seven feminine nouns, one of which is a personal pronoun.

As already noted, use of the connecting *waw*, rather than a *waw* consecutive, creates an abrupt transition. The first element introduced is the name Deborah. While not all female names end with the feminine *h*, this ending on her name enhances the feminine nature of this row of feminine nouns. The name itself means "bee."[28] Another relationship between this story and that of Samson later in the book may be represented by the bee element.[29]

The second noun is the word meaning woman, wife, or female *ʾiššâ*.[30] The term is problematic because the decision as to which meaning to translate, is, as always, a function of the translator's interpretation of the text. Since little work has been done on how the noun *ʾiššâ* functions and is used in word plays, it is not always clear how to translate the noun in each context.[31] In the above translations the translators

---

[28] *BDB*, 184. According to Klein, bees are depicted in the biblical text as vanquishers and attackers of men [*The Triumph of Irony in the Book of Judges*, JSOTS/Bible and Literature Series 14 (Sheffield: Almond, 1989) 41–2].

[29] Boling, *Judges*, 94.

[30] *BDB*, 61.

[31] For example, the case of Gen 12:13 when Sarah was in Egypt. The term is traditionally translated "woman" when the reader knows she is Abram's "wife" but seen as "woman" by the Egyptians.

view this noun as modifying the following noun "prophetess" *naḇîʾah* by making it feminine. While this may be its function, the noun used for prophet is already in the feminine form. The noun must function, at the least, as emphasizing the femaleness of Deborah or her status as prophet, a title rare for women in the Bible. A translation acknowledging the noun would read, "Deborah was a female prophetess," or possibly more emphatic, "Deborah was a woman, a prophet."

The use of *ʾiššâ* here may simply emphasize the femaleness of Deborah, but it forms an ironic parallel with the leaders Ehud and Othniel. Both Ehud and Othniel appeared as a response to the Israelites' cry. Following the introduction of their name, each was identified by two relationships, thus far interpreted as, first, identifying their primary ties, then, a slightly larger affiliation, followed by some type of epithet or anecdote about them. Othniel is son of Kenaz, brother of Caleb, the younger (Judg 3:9), and Ehud, son of Gera, son of the right, a man restricted in his right hand (Judg 3:15). Deborah has a relationship listed but it is not the first piece of information presented. Following the previous pattern, Deborah's primary affiliation is not to a family or a spouse, as would be expected for a married woman, but to her profession, prophecy. The first *ʾiššâ* here replaces the "son of" in the previous cases. The relationship of *ʾiššâ* to *něḇîʾâ* "female prophet" is reinforced by the Masoretic notes which unite the two words as a unit.

The third feminine noun is *něḇîʾâ*, the feminine form of the noun prophet. Judges 4:3 is the only place where the term appears in Judges, even though most scholars do not consider the beginning of prophecy to take place until the book of Samuel. There are a few individuals in the Torah who are called "prophets," but most consider these to be anachronistic uses of the term.[32] Miriam, the sister of Moses, bears this title but most are quick to point out that she performs actions that exhibit a character that is more cultic than prophetic (Exod 15:20).

Modern scholars define prophecy based on how it appears in the biblical text and state that the main use of prophecy is later, despite the application of the term to both Miriam and Deborah. To say that Miriam and Deborah do not carry out the action of prophecy ignores the data. The aspects of Deborah's character, actions, or responsibilities emphasized in the reference to her as a prophet remain undefined. Her status as prophet is her primary affiliation, and is apparently separate from her role as judge which appears later in the sentence.

The noun *ʾišāh* is applied a second time to Deborah. In this case the noun is in construct with the following feminine noun and usually translated as "wife of Lappidoth" (JPS, KJV, RSV). The term *ʾišāh* in this

---

[32] J. Schmitt, "Prophecy (Pre-exilic Hebrew)," *ABD* 5.482.

position is consistently translated "wife" because it is followed by what is understood to be a male proper name. Yet the husband's name is somewhat suspect because it is the only appearance of the name in the MT and the form is unusual. It is interpreted as a feminine abstract form of the Hebrew word *lappîd (lappîdôt)*. *lappîd* means "torch" in biblical Hebrew and is somewhat common in Judges (Judg 15:4 (2x); 15:5; 17:6 (3x); 7:20).[33] Nowhere else does it have the feminine abstract ending. The standard interpretation is that Deborah is the wife of a man named Lappidoth and it was coincidental for the construction of this sentence that his name has a feminine ending which perpetuates the feminine flow of this sentence.

Some scholars have trouble with the strange name Lappidoth. Boling notes that it is probably her husband's nickname meaning "flasher."[34] He assumes that this is a nickname for the other male player in the story, Baraq, who must be Lappidoth and therefore Deborah's husband.[35] The evidence is that *bârâq* means "lightning," which is not far removed from "flasher." Others note that since the text identifies Baraq as originating in the northern part of Israel, this identification is unlikely.[36] The text never states that Baraq is Lappidoth. What must be addressed is why the text would mention Deborah's marital status, at this point in the sentence and narrative, and how that affects Deborah's role.

The second *'iššâ* must be examined in light of the previous saviors before assuming it addresses Deborah's marital status. After introducing each savior, his primary relationships are defined. In Othniel's case, after his first two relationships are noted, the text states that he was the younger one (Judg 3:9). With Ehud the text states that he was the son of Gera, a son of the right, a man *'îš* restricted in his right hand. In Deborah's introduction, the reference to her being a woman/wife of Lappidot *'ēšet*, parallels the third aspect of the characters' introduction describing a more personal characteristic. Thus one possible interpretation could be that she was, "Deborah, a woman, a prophet, a fiery one."[37]

---

[33] *BDB*, 542.

[34] Boling, *Judges*, 95.

[35] Ibid.

[36] K. Lowery, "Lappidoth," *ABD* 4. 233; Soggin, *Judges*, 64.

[37] Other, primarily feminist, scholars, have looked at other meanings for the term. C. Exum translates it, "spirited woman" ("Deborah," *HBD*, 214); and M. Bal translates "a woman of torches" [*Death and Dissymmetry: The Politics of Coherence in the Book of Judges*, Chicago Studies in the History of Judaism (Chicago: University of Chicago Press, 1988) 208].

The translation, "wife of Lapiddoth," implies that she was married. Since women in the ancient world were known either by their father, brother, or husband, it is fitting that the text would present the name of Deborah's father, or, if she were married, her husband. But the primary and even secondary relationships for both Othniel and Ehud are listed as the first and second epithets. In Deborah's case, following the pattern established by Othniel and Ehud, "wife of Lappidoth" should be her primary designation if it refers to her husband. Instead, her primary designation is as a woman and a prophet. The third element, according to the pattern described above, notes a quality about the character, so far whether they were either younger or left-handed. The concept of a fiery personality is more in keeping with that position in her introduction than is her marital status. In fact, this third component of her characterization is close to Anath who is described, at least by modern scholars, as having a fierce and violent temperament, dare one say "fiery."[38]

If Deborah was married other questions need to be asked concerning her role in Israel. Would her actions outside the home be acceptable for an ideal Israelite wife?[39] Thus far the only explicitly stated roles for women in Judges is that they be and marry Israelites. Even this aspect is not stated about Deborah. Serious doubt is cast on Deborah's married status because: her primary description is female and prophet, not wife, her later fiery actions, the restrictions that would have been imposed on her if she were married, and the unusual feminine ending on her supposed husband's name.

Even if the designation "woman of Lappidoth" reflects Deborah's married status, the statement's placement does not follow the previous cases. The information in the primary position in the MT is that Deborah is a woman and a prophet. Only secondarily is the information that she is a wife or fiery noted. Whether she is considered married, or married to her work, her primary signifier is the occupation of prophet.

The two feminine nouns following *lappîdôt* are separated by the Masoretic notations indicating that, at least in the eyes of the Masoretes, these two should be related to each other forming their own phrase or, possibly, a new sentence. The first is the third person feminine

---

[38] Walls, *Goddess*, 1.

[39] This was the approach that the rabbis took, who viewed Deborah negatively because she did not follow the correct rules of a dutiful wife and thus the rabbis were more interested in her husband. L. Bronner, "Valorized or Vilified? The Women of Judges in Midrashic Sources," *A Feminist Companion to Judges*, A. Brenner, ed., The Feminist Companion to the Bible 4 (Sheffield: Sheffield Academic Press, 1993) 79.

personal pronoun "she" followed by the verb, "she judged" *šôpṭāh*. While the presence of the personal pronoun is not necessary, its use is not unwarranted if the author wanted to clarify the gender of the subject of the verb. Since this would be the only case where a female was the subject of this verb in Judges, the use of the pronoun would be a way to ensure that the feminine form was not considered a mistake. Its function continues to highlight the female subject of the verb.

The action is the verbal form of the term which gives its name to the book, judge *š-p-ṭ*. While the simple translation of "judge" is clear, JPS translates "led" as a way of explaining the actions associated with the verb in this context. The problem is that, while later Deborah functions on as many levels as the male judges in the book, in terms of leading military campaigns, at this point in the narrative she has not performed any of those actions. At this point in the narrative the term could refer to something rather different, as will be discussed below. The text's claim that she judged all of Israel reinforces the notion that her role was different than Othniel's, at least at this point, since the previous judge was involved in regional military actions prior to and during his tenure as judge.

The following verse elaborates on Deborah's job by stating that she sat under the Palm Tree of Deborah and that the Israelites would come to her for judgment (Judg 4:5). Unfortunately the placement of the event and her precise actions are fraught with problems. Some see the term for "sit" *yôšebet*, as carrying a connotation of "presiding" as in Isa 28:5-6.[40] Whether the verb denotes "to preside" or "to sit," the Israelites came to her for judgement *mišpāṭ*. The term is a nominal form derived from the same root which both supplies the name of the book and the title she received in the previous verse. Since Deborah was just labeled a judge, it is not surprising that people would come to her seeking judgments. What is unique is the reference appearing in a book where the others who held that office attained their position only after leading a military event. In this case Deborah held an office prior to her involvement in military affairs. This may be another ironic situation since the only person qualified for the office prior to military battle was a woman.

Deborah's job is unique in that she was one of only two people to whom people went for judgment, the other was Moses when the Israelites were in the desert (Exod 18:13). While at this point in the story that resemblance is not a major issue, the role of Moses and his line becomes more important later in this story (Judg 4:11), and at the end of the book (Judg 18:30), making this another example of foreshadowing for both those later episodes.

[40] Boling, *Judges*, 95.

Deborah sat underneath the tree of Deborah between Ramah and Bethel in Ephraim, a noteworthy site. The area of Bethel is not a surprising place for a character to choose to serve as judge since the site was frequented by many biblical characters in connection with the deity and judgment. Abram erected an altar between Bethel and Ai (Gen 12:8) and visited it again on his return from Egypt (Gen 13:3, 4). Jacob, too, erected a pillar marking the place where he saw the messengers and the ladder (Gen 28:10-22), and on his return from Haran set up another pillar there (Gen 35:7). Samuel would visit this city periodically to judge the people (1 Sam 7:16). Later still this would be one of the sites where Jeroboam would place the golden calves (1 Kgs 12:29). The site was a mid-point between the northern and southern parts of Israel. The site relates to the larger Judges story appearing at the end of the book where judgments of dubious merits were made concerning the men of the tribe of Benjamin and a source of wives for them.

The site was not only a place of judgment, but relates Deborah to another woman for whom a tree was planted. Rebekah's nurse, who traveled with her to Canaan, was also named Deborah. After she died she was buried under the oak near Bethel which was henceforth known as *ʾallôn-bākût* (Gen 35:8). It is striking that the only women for whom trees were named bore the same name. Since there is so little information about that first Deborah, what the connection may be between the two, or what such a reference could mean in this context is vague, if any exists at all.

Baraq: Judges 4:6-10

Baraq is introduced into the story only after Deborah and her position are presented (Judg 4:6). That she holds a position superior to his is emphasized by his coming when Deborah sent someone to summon him. In the first reference to him Deborah is the subject, and Baraq is ordered to appear before her. From the outset he is second in command. He is introduced as Baraq, son of Abinoam, from Kedesh Naphtali. Like Ehud and Othniel before him, he is introduced first by his name, followed by his family name, followed by his clan name, none of which are included for Deborah.

Deborah began her instructions by emphasizing that the deity, the deity of Israel, commanded her actions (Judg 4:6). In previous cases the text notes that the spirit of the deity descended upon or raised up the saviors Othniel and Ehud, but there are no references to whether that was acknowledged by the savior. In this case there is no evidence that the deity was working through Deborah but the text is explicit that she viewed herself as acting on behalf of the deity. The narrator implies that Deborah was the deity's representative through her victory and the actualization of her predictions.

Deborah commanded Baraq to take ten thousand men of Naphtali and Zebulun, and committed herself to drawing Sisera, again referred to as Jabin's commander, with his chariots and troops toward Baraq to deliver him (Judg 4:6-7). Baraq insisted that he would only go if she went with him (Judg 4:8). Deborah agreed but added a prophetic quali-fication that there would be no glory for him because the deity would deliver Sisera into the hands of a woman (Judg 4:9). Deborah accompa-nied Baraq, who gathered his ten thousand men (Judg 4:10).

The reference to Sisera's death at the hand of a woman states a number of principles in no uncertain terms. By stating that no glory will come to Baraq because he would die at the hand of a woman, the text highlights what women should not be doing in the story where they did it. Women should not be capturing the opponent's military commander. When women fight in battles men lose glory. The implica-tion is that men, or maybe especially Israelite men, fought for glory or renown, not, as Deborah stated, because the deity commanded it. This may be another element of foreshadowing, since the reason for fighting becomes a critique of the later judges Gideon/Jerubbaal (Judg 8:18), Jephthah (Judg 11:6-11), and Samson (Judg 15:7; 16:28).

Baraq's punishment, that he would not capture the enemy ruler, emphasizes how important the capture of the enemy commander is in Judges. This image appears in the first story with the capture of Adoni Bezek (Judg 1:6), is key in Ehud's story (Judg 3:20-30), and continues here. The focus on Sisera as the person to capture points to him as the primary leader in the story. Designating him as the person to capture, despite his introduction as second-in-command, does not necessarily indicate the disparity between Jabin and Sisera, but that between Debo-rah and Baraq since both Baraq and Sisera fought the battles, yet both must report to, take commands from, and are secondary to someone else. Baraq's reprimand, which came true, implies that his comment that he would fight only if Deborah joined him was not a legitimate request.

A number of scholars are uncomfortable with Deborah's reprimand and role in this incident. Boling describes these sentences as dealing with the theme of camaraderie in the administration and notes the irony in Baraq's casuistic acceptance of the apodictic command.[41] His suggestion for the continuation of the verse found in LXX, "for I never

---

[41] Ibid., 96.

know what day the Yahweh envoy will give me success," is that Baraq
had been going out and coming in from battle without benefit of ade-
quate or proper inquiry.[42] Soggin goes so far as to state that the difference in styles between Deborah and Baraq is that Baraq, because he
was more interested in the welfare of his troops, was waiting for strate-
gic reasons whereas Deborah was fired by excitement for the deity but
was without military insight.[43] It is clear that most scholars have trouble
with Deborah's command to Baraq to lead the battle and his refusal to
do it without her presence, despite the roles of such ancient Near Eastern goddesses as Anath and Ishtar in military battles.[44] Regardless of
how difficult it is for someone to believe, according to the MT, Deborah
commanded Baraq to lead the battle.

Kenite Interlude: Judges 4:11

The narrative shifts abruptly to relay information concerning Heber
the Kenite (Judg 4:11). The information is conveyed here so that when
suspense surrounding Sisera's death builds later in the story, all the
characters are in place, allowing the story to continue without interrup-
tion. What is important to note is on how many levels this brief comment relates to later events, not only in this chapter but also to events at
the end of the book.

The text suddenly introduces "Heber the Kenite" who, according to
the text, was separated from Cain (Judg 4:11). The Kenites are defined
as the, "sons of Hobab, the father-in-law of Moses." The narrator notes

---

[42] Ibid.

[43] See especially his comments below concerning field strategy for Judg 4:13. It is
ironic how blatantly Soggin's description of the roles of Deborah and Baraq in this
instance is governed by sexist notions of men being in the "real world." The following quote indicates the extreme stance that he takes, with no evidence from the
biblical text, in order to protect the image of the male warrior, the notion this text
questions. "Thus the text here contrasts two opposed attitudes: that of the faith
which accepts on trust, sometimes in a way which humanly speaking can seem almost irresponsible, the call of the word of God, and which in the face of that authority is either ignorant of the risks or ignores them; and that of a man of the world,
responsible for himself and others, accustomed to weighing the actions and only
incurring risks on the basis of certain guarantees" (*Judges*, 73). The biblical text provides no evidence of Baraq's worries for his troops or his rootedness in the "real
world."

[44] For Anath see N. Walls, *The Goddess Anat*. For Ishtar/Inanna as a warrior god
see T. Frymer-Kensky, *In the Wake of the Goddesses: Women, Culture, and the Biblical
Transformation of Pagan Myth* (New York: The Free Press, 1992) 63–7.

that "he" (presumably Heber) pitched his tent at Elonbezaanannim, which is near Kedesh. The information is sudden and brief but necessary in order to place characters in their proper places for later events. On the most basic level this verse introduces the Kenites so that when Sisera flees the battle and finds Jael, the reader knows who she was and why she was there, allowing the rest of the story to flow smoothly. The story is placed so that the reader has relevant information that the characters do not necessarily have.

When the story reaches Sisera's situation, the Kenites' relationship to the Canaanites is stressed. At this point in the story the Kenites' relationship to the Israelites, through Moses, is the focus. The Moses reference raises questions concerning the identity of the Kenites, the consistency of the biblical references, and how they relate to Moses and the Israelites.

The Kenites first appear as the descendants of Cain in Genesis. Tubal Cain, their ancestor, is introduced as the founder of metallurgy (Gen 4:22). There is agreement among scholars that the etymology of the word involves metal working, meaning, "to forge."[45] The early Kenite traditions in Gen 4:17-24 depict Cain as a prime culture-hero.[46] The relationship of the Kenites to metal-working is another use of irony in Judges since Deborah's story begins with the Israelites lamenting their lack of technology, to a large extent in the area of metallurgy, and their ironic savior, Jael, was from a tribe specializing in that industry to which the Israelites are related through the marriage of Moses.

The history of the Kenites, provided in Judg 4:11, introduces Moses to the scenario. As mentioned above, an oblique reference to his role in Israel is implied in Deborah's job description, serving as a judge to whom the Israelites brought their disputes. The statement that Moses was related to the Kenites through his father-in-law is problematic because whether the name of his father-in-law is Jethro (Ex 3:1; 18:1) or Reuel (Ex 2:18; Num 10:29 [actually in this reference Hobab is the son of Reuel]), he is always referred to as a Midianite. One solution is to follow the LXX and translate "son-in-law" instead of "father-in-law." This solves the relationship problem but not the Midianite/Kenite issue. Another way of addressing the problem is by placing the Kenites in a Midianite league.[47] Other discussions use archaeological material to show that there were pastoralist Kenites in the region and the authors

---

[45] *BDB*, 883. In the biblical text it appears only as a gentilic, but cognate languages include meanings like Aramaic, "fit together, fabricate," Syriac and Palmyrene, "metal worker."

[46] B. Halpern, "Kenites," *ABD* 4.18.

[47] Ibid.

must have been using the information of their day to reconstruct the Judges material.[48]

How the Kenites function in the book of Judges and how that impacts the material provided sheds light in this case. As mentioned in Chapter 1 of the present study, the reference to Moses and his father-in-law depicts Caleb as a bridge from the previous generation of Moses to the period of Judges (Judg 1:20). Caleb's Kenite background enhances Judah's reputation since the tribe of Caleb, which was related to the Kenites, was incorporated by Judah. Judges 4:11 ties Judah to Jael, one of the heroes of the story. The reader is informed about the relationship of the Kenites to the Israelites, but the information provided at the time of the events does not include those details, nor does the character most impacted by them, namely Sisera, necessarily know them.

The objective historical reality of the relationship between Moses and the Kenites is almost inconsequential. Instead, the text states that there was a relationship, or that the Kenites, or maybe only Jael, considered the relationship of the Kenites to the Israelites as primary in this instance. The author plays with irony by hinting to the reader which side Jael will take by providing the reader with information the character Sisera either does not have or is not considering.

A final question concerns whether Heber is a single person, taking his personal family to this area that happens to be near an impending major battle, or whether this is a larger tribal group, where everyone is related to Heber or descendants of Heber.[49] The size question is not of major relevance at this point in the story, but has serious ramifications later in the text when Jael is introduced. Related to this is Heber's introduction, though he plays no role in the story. Jael, who is the major player in the story, is not introduced or even mentioned here. This technique builds suspense. The information is presented in such a way as to appear almost irrelevant to the story at this point, yet has great impact on what the reader knows, as opposed to what the characters know, later in the story.

This one line insertion ties the Kenites to the Israelites and places them precisely where a major battle is about to occur. The name of the site where the Kenites pitched their tents is Elon-bezaanannim. The word elon *ʾēlôn*, a terebinth of some sort, is another literary touch since both of the key women in this story are associated with and situated near trees.[50]

[48] Ibid.

[49] J. Gray, *Joshua, Judges, Ruth,* The New Century Bible Commentary (Grand Rapids, MI: Eerdmans, 1986) 258.

[50] *BDB,* 18.

The Battle: Judges 4:12-17

The description of the battle is short, especially considering the many verses introducing the characters and placing them in their context. This is not surprising since in most stories in Judges the battles are recounted briefly, indicating that the battles were unimportant, compared to who fought them, why, and for whom. The case of Deborah is a slight anomaly since the poetic account uses more verses to describe the battle, but the nature of the description continues the pattern seen thus far; the battles are not the focus of the narrative.

The text continues to relate that an unnamed "they" informed Sisera that Baraq had gone up to Mt. Tabor (Judg 4:12). Sisera ordered all his chariots, specified as nine hundred iron chariots in case the reader had forgotten their technological military advantage, and all his troops and moved them into place (Judg 4:13). Deborah responded by issuing Baraq a command, "Get up!," informing him that this was the day that the deity would deliver the troops (Judg 4:14).

Deborah commanded Baraq with the imperative, "Get up!" (Judg 4:14), as one would expect with a command, though many scholars have trouble with the form. Soggin goes so far as to translate Deborah's command as, "Have courage," deleting the commanding aspect of Deborah's appeal.[51] Soggin is so uncomfortable with Deborah making the decision determining the time of attack that he claims, "Barak, who is a leader and a man of the world, and therefore accustomed to weigh up the odds, cannot share the charismatic enthusiasm of Deborah."[52] While the tactics employed by the army of Israel and her leaders throughout the book may be questionable in terms of military strategy, Deborah's actions were no less responsible than those of Ehud or Gideon. All used rather unusual strategies which reflected creative approaches and resulted in military victories.[53]

Deborah's command ties the narrative into the theme of imperatives used by and toward women in the book. Early in Judges Achsah used the imperative with her father in order to gain land, which she received (Judg 1:15). Later in this chapter another imperative is used when Sisera demands something of Jael (Judg 4:20). Ironically, in that case, the wrong gender was used, the action was not carried out, and

---

[51] Soggin, *Judges*, 61.

[52] Ibid., 73.

[53] As will be noted in the discussion of the poetic account in Chapter 5, Deborah responded to the weather (Judg 5:20-21), Ehud rallied the troops only after he killed the enemy leader King Eglon of Moab (Judg 3:27), and Gideon sent the foreign troops into disarray by using a surprise attack at night (Judg 7:19-22).

he lost his life as a result. In the story of the *pîlegeš*'s rape the same imperative was directed at the raped woman draped on the doorstep of what should have been her refuge. In that case the Levite, who should have been her protector, demanded the same of her, "Get up!" (Judg 19:28). Again a woman did not respond to the man's demand, though in this case it was because she could not. Thus Deborah's command to Baraq is a powerful statement in the context of this chapter, the battle, and other themes in the book.

Baraq obeyed Deborah's command and marched down Mt. Tabor followed by his men (Judg 4:14). Sisera, his chariots, and army were thrown into a panic (Judg 4:15). Sisera leapt from his chariot and fled on foot, while Baraq pursued the chariots and the soldiers (Judg 4:16). The text states that all of Sisera's soldiers fell by the sword. The narrative omits a number of items that will be explained in the poetic account (Judges 5). Judges 4 does not describe why or how Deborah knew that the day the deity had commanded had arrived, why all of Sisera's chariots and soldiers were in a panic, nor how Sisera could have escaped. All are answered in the poetic account, our first indication of how the two complement each other.

The text highlights Deborah's role. Sisera saw Baraq and his troops, but she determined the time of the battle. The text indicates that Deborah issued the command to Baraq, telling him to get up and fight. She was explicit that the real general was the deity. However, only because Deborah was with him did Baraq follow orders.

While Baraq followed Deborah's instructions and destroyed the enemy he did not capture the prize. Once the enemy army was in a panic Baraq went after the chariots, not the leader. The Israelites at the beginning of this chapter cried out for help from their deity not because of oppression but because of the military and technological advantage that the Canaanites enjoyed because of their chariots. Here Baraq again focused on the technology, not on the leader of their oppressor. As a result he did not notice the prize slipping from his grasp into the hands of a woman, just as Deborah had prophesied that it would.

Sisera and Jael: Judges 4:17-22

At this point in the battle Sisera fled the scene and encountered Jael. This episode, and its counterpart in the poetic version, highlight a number of points. They focus on the power of women in this story, reinforce the prophetic aspect of Deborah's earlier statements, take the capture of the foreign ruler away from Baraq, and maintain the sense of irony. The language used and the way the scene is composed continues to stress important words, sexual innuendo, the role of women, and irony.

While Jael is the hero of Judges 4 and proclaimed as such by the poetic version in Judges 5, both rabbinical commentaries and modern scholarship have not treated her as such. Some state that she committed murder and violated a treaty, or at least the rules of hospitality.[54] Thus it is important to understand who Jael was, what she was exposed to, how she acted and reacted, and how she was judged by the biblical text since later scholarship has treated her differently.[55]

Sisera's first action was to flee on foot, indicating how different the situation had become since the beginning of the story. The chapter begins by noting how much superior the Canaanites were militarily because of their technologically advanced chariots (Judg 4:3). In the previous sentences the reader is told that those chariots had become useless, and the poetic section will explain why. Here the general was reduced to running away from the scene, alone and on foot. The mighty had already fallen, to a certain extent, yet the reader was forewarned that his death would be even more humiliating.

The first line of this subsection functions in a similar way to Judg 4:11 by laying the groundwork of the scene. The difference is that in this sentence the information relayed is what Sisera knew about the situation, or the information he was considering, which governed his actions. The line notes that Sisera fled to the tent of Jael, woman/wife of Heber the Kenite, because there was "peace" šālôm between the king of Hazor and the family of Heber the Kenite (Judg 4:17). The narrator had earlier provided information about these people, but now different aspects and relationships are presented. The contrast builds the suspense and irony of the scene. King Jabin, who has not done anything in the story, is listed as the representative of the relationship between the two peoples. This causes the reader to wonder what impact he could have. The person representing King Jabin in this scene was his general Sisera, who was depicted in this sentence as defeated, alone, and without technological support.

Other contrasting information governs with whom Jael will side. Earlier the relationship between the Kenites and the Israelites was said to have been rooted in marriage bonds (Judg 4:11). Now the relationship is through treaty, though the members who were related to the šālôm, King Jabin of Hazor and Heber the Kenite, were not present or

---

[54] L. Klein, *Triumph of Irony*, 42–3, and K. Lowery, "Jael," *ABD* 3.610-11.

[55] Jael is viewed positively by the sages, evidenced by the midrash which lists her among the Judges of Israel. Bronner, "Valorized or Vilified," 87.

active (Judg 4:17). The LXX heightens the suspense over which side Jael will take by adding after the Kenite, "his friend."

Sisera fled to the tent of Jael, the woman/wife of Heber the Kenite, who is presented almost as though the reader should already know her. Her only introduction is that she was the woman/wife of Heber. Her relationship to Heber may not be as straightforward as being his wife. When Heber was mentioned earlier in the text, he was related to the Israelites through Moses, but no woman was mentioned. Here Heber is in a *šālôm* relationship with Israel's enemy and the obvious question is how that affects Jael. She is listed by name in the reference that relates Heber's peaceful relationship with King Jabin. The twist is that the reader received different information previously, and it is not King Jabin of Hazor who arrived at Jael's tent.

Most scholars do not question the translation "wife" for Jael's relationship to Heber, though another possible translation is, "woman of," meaning any woman of his family or clan. Heber's group is first introduced without any information regarding the size of his group, how many generations and people fall under the title, or even how many wives he had. There are hints in the story, and by the way it appears in Judges, that a husband/wife relationship should be questioned. Jael and Heber are never depicted together; in fact, Heber never appears.

Jael functions independently. She is not always referred to by the title "woman/wife of" Heber (Judg 4:18, 22). Jael appears in a story with many other women acting independently, with little or no male supervision. This story has already introduced Deborah, whose marriage to an actual person named Lappidoth is suspect. The roles of the women in this story are another signal of the downward spiral since women and their actions were no longer defined by their husbands, and men no longer cared for their women. The present situation reveals women not defined by marriage taking matters into their own hands.

Jael's tent is a source of much discussion. The final descendant of Cain before the flood is Lamech, whose wife Adah bore Jabal, the ancestor of those who dwell in tents (Gen 4:19-20). The reference to Jael dwelling in a tent ties her neatly to the Kenites. What interests many scholars is the question of who had access to the tent, who controlled the tent, and who should and should not have been allowed inside the tent. This is especially complicated in terms of what Jael did both inside and outside the tent and the legality of her actions, especially concerning the codes of Middle Eastern hospitality that are often invoked in this conversation. Bal neatly points out the hypocrisy of many of these arguments in her critique of Gray. Gray notes that Heber is more likely a clan name when referring to Judg 4:11, but, when he discusses Jael and her tent, Heber is said definitively to be her husband and Jael must take extreme actions to defend her honor, even though, in Gray's opinion, she may even be an "older, discarded wife of Heber."[56]

Bal's critique of Gray confronts the discussion of the nature of Jael's tent since Gray presumes that there are two possibilities: either the tent was that of her husband or the screened harem section of the long Bedouin tent.[57] Gray, among other scholars, is quick to draw parallels with modern Bedouins despite the lack of evidence that modern Bedouin practices parallel the biblical tradition. Using modern examples ignores indications within the biblical text that women had their own tents. Genesis 18:6 depicts Abraham hastening to the tent where Sarah was, though there is no indication that it was her own tent as opposed to their tent. When Isaac met Rebekah he took her to "the tent of Sarah his mother," though Sarah was dead at this point (Gen. 24:67). Genesis 31:33 says quite explicitly that Jacob, Rachel, Leah and the maidservants each had their own tents.

What is never stated or addressed is how much autonomy a woman had in her own tent, who had access to it, and under what conditions. In Rachel's case (Gen 31:33-34), Jacob gave Laban the right to search her tent, and after the search claimed that Laban had rummaged through all his (i.e., Jacob's) things. Laban's search is an unusual case because he was searching for his family idols and Jacob authorized the search to clear his name (Gen 31:31-36). The Rachel situation shows that each of the wives and maidservants had their own tent, but it is not clear if the tents were considered Jacob's possession and that he determined who had access to them.

Returning to Judges, in the next verse Jael went out of her tent, greeted Sisera, called him "my lord" and invited him in, reassuring him that he should not be afraid (Judg 4:18). He entered her tent, and she covered him with something.[58] Issues here concern why Jael left her tent, whether Sisera was correct to enter her tent, and whether she offered hospitality she should not have offered, or conversely, whether he should not have entered her tent and so therefore deserved what happened to him.

The first issue concerns Jael's actions. She went out to greet Sisera (Judg 4:18), raising the question why, if she was married, she greeted a foreign man outside her tent and then invited him into her tent. In light of her actions, both here and later in the story, it is clear that she knows who Sisera was, though how is not stated. It is not clear that being out-

---

[56] Bal, *Death and Dissymmetry*, 211–2; citing Gray, *Judges*, 259.

[57] Ibid.

[58] What she covers him with is often referred to as a blanket though this is the only reference in the biblical text of the word *šĕmîkâ*.

side her tent was a proper place for a woman to be, especially with a major battle not far away.[59]

There are indications inside the book of Judges that women waited (Judg 5:28), and went outside to greet their menfolk when they returned from battle (Judg 11:34). In Judges 5, while Sisera's mother waits, the reader knows the irony that he will not be returning home. When Jephthah's daughter went outside it signaled her death by the hand of her father. While it was not to wait, the *pîlegeš* at the end of the story was thrust outside to meet her death. When the women of Shiloh went out for a festival they were kidnapped and forced into rape/marriages with the Benjaminites (Judg 21:21-23). Thus in Judges, the act of a woman going outside carries great import.

The terminology used to invite Sisera inside is laden with comfort overtones. The term "turn aside" *s-w-r* means to turn aside from attacking, turn aside to shelter, revealing how Jael's invitation was phrased to lull Sisera into a sense of false security.[60] She left the security of her tent to greet him. She treated him with reverence by calling him "my lord." She assured him that he should not be afraid. Once he entered the tent she covered him. All her actions led him into a sense of comfort, an ironic sense.

At this point Sisera asked for water, even saying please, because he was thirsty. Jael opened a skin of milk, gave him some to drink, and covered him again (Judg 4:19). Her actions are open to a number of interpretations, most indicating some sort of scheme concerning why she gave Sisera milk instead of water. She may have been a pastoralist and that was all she had. Another view sees her trying to show him hospitality, since he asked for water and she showed herself to be a good hostess by offering him something better, further lulling him into a sense of comfort and safety. More forethought is attributed to Jael when consideration is given to Sisera's mood, after a long day of losing a battle and running to safety. Jael knew that milk or any sort of dairy product would have a soporific effect on him and so the milk was served to drug him.[61] Sexual allusions can also be read into the text, interpreting Jael as giving Sisera her breast leading to other acts which exhausted him.[62] Regardless of the motive behind her actions the result was the same; Sisera was lulled into a sense of security, exhausted enough to fall asleep.

[59] Regardless of where the battle occurred, according to the text, it was close enough for Sisera to flee to where Jael was, on foot, in the same day.

[60] *BDB*, 693.

[61] Boling, *Judges*, 98.

[62] This was the interpretation of some of the midrashic rabbis. Bronner, "Valorized or Vilified," 89.

Sisera's raised comfort level is clear when he commanded Jael to stand at the entrance of the tent. He told her to say no to anyone who asked if there were a man there (Judg 4:20). His command is prophetic and ironic since the next person who happened by was the man Sisera feared. When Baraq arrived, Sisera's words would be true.

Sisera used the male imperative when he told Jael to "stand" *ʿămōd*. Boling notices this incongruity and states that it is best resolved by re-pointing the MT to read an infinitive absolute with a strong imperative force, as in the Decalogue (Exod 20:8 and Deut 5:12).[63] While it was definitely a mistake to use the masculine command with Jael, who was clearly a woman, it is not as obvious that the mistake was on the part of the writer or copyist; instead, the masculine form may have been intentional.

Sisera's grammatical mistake heightens the image of a tired general who was falling asleep and not concentrating. In this first speech act he asked for water politely, even saying "please" (Judg 4:19). He then laid down, possibly with a warm blanket after drinking some thick dairy product (or having a sexual encounter), believing that he was in a friendly camp, in the company of a mere woman who treated him with nothing but honor and respect. Sisera felt comfortable enough to command her. Since he was an army leader he was presumably used to issuing commands, particularly in the masculine imperative. Its use here magnifies how comfortable and unsuspecting he was.

Sisera's relaxed state allowed Jael to act. She is referred to again as the "woman/wife of Heber," possibly to highlight the irony by reminding the reader of the shalom between Heber and the Canaanites (Judg 4:21). The reference also emphasizes Jael's occupation, legitimating the presence of the tools available to her. Jael took a tent pin and grasped a mallet (Judg 4:22). The text continues to build the suspense by noting that this happened when he (Sisera) was fast asleep from exhaustion. Only then did she approach him and drive the pin through his temple until it went down into the ground.

A certain amount of force is implied by reference to the pin going all the way into the ground. The verb used to describe the pin's descent is the same used to describe Achsah's descent *ṣ-n-ḥ* from her donkey (Judg 1: 14). The verb has a feminine subject which could refer to the mallet, Sisera's temple, or possibly Jael's dropping down. Regardless of the subject, the verb's action does not bode well for men in Judges since this time the verb determines the army commander's death at the hand of a woman. The entire battle between the Canaanites and the forces led by Deborah and Baraq use fewer verses than the account of Sisera's death.

[63] Boling, *Judges*, 98.

Only now did Baraq appear on the scene in pursuit of Sisera (Judg 4:22). Jael again went out of her tent to greet the military man. The phraseology is identical except that in verse 18 Jael went out to meet Sisera and here the text states that she went out to meet "him" (presumably Baraq). Jael again invited the man inside her tent but this time to show Baraq the man he sought. Baraq entered and found Sisera dead, actualizing Deborah's prophecy.

Summary of Events: Judges 4:23-24

The summary of the episode states that on that day Elohim (this is the first time this term is used for the Israelite deity by the narrator) subdued King Jabin of Hazor before the children of Israel (Judg 4:23). Throughout this story both the narrator and Deborah are explicit that the Israelite deity was responsible for the victory, not Baraq or Deborah. The result of the victory is described in the following verse that the hand of the children of Israel bore harder on King Jabin of Canaan until they destroyed him (Judg 4:24).

The role of King Jabin of Canaan is one that is often discussed in connection with Deborah. Soggin notes the absurdity of the title "king of Canaan" since we know that there was no such thing.[64] Yet Judges declares in the first sentence its interest in leadership. Many different forms of leadership are examined throughout the following stories. In light of that, a general carrying out all actions without being a king makes a powerful image. The untimely death of the military commander, which led to the destruction of the people, is a powerful statement. In Judges, most of the leaders were military figures who were later given a title that carried more weight than military leadership. A statement like this, revealing a king's status when the military is gone, is quite a lesson.

The dichotomy between King Jabin and Sisera's roles and duties is especially strong in the context of Judges, particularly at this point in the story. One previous leader carried the title of judge, but the duties of a judge are not explained and the characters never are depicted carrying out functions beyond those of a military leader. This chapter begins with an unusual leader, a woman, who was functioning as judge and prophet. As a result of the unwillingness of the military leader to actually lead the military campaign the judge took on a pseudo-military role. The problem is that the leader was a woman and the text is explicit

[64] Soggin, *Judges*, 70.

about the degradation accompanying a military leader who either dies at the hand of a woman, or loses his prey to a woman, and both happen here.

The military versus political aspects of leadership are highlighted since the Canaanite political leader in this story is not the military leader, but the destruction of the military leader led to the end of the political. The following stories reveal the impact of this on Israel, whose situation changes. The next few military leaders are depicted either debating the extent of their duties as political leader (Gideon/ Jerubbaal), trying to usurp those powers (Abimelech), or being unwilling to take on the role of military leader without an agreement beforehand to also obtain the political powers (Jephthah). The relationship between Jabin and Sisera, whether they were historical figures, literary characters, or historical figures that were turned into literary characters, plays an important role in the book as pivotal in the dichotomy of functions of the leaders depicted in Judges.

Summary

The narrative portion of Deborah's story is tied to the preceding stories and the entire book through its language and themes. The story focuses on Israel's plight and her need to rely on foreigners and women as a result of the decline in Israel's leadership. The decline is not because of Deborah's actions, which are praised in Judges, but because she had to carry them out at all, since the men would not. Following this episode the dichotomy between military and political leadership changed in Israel.

Topics such as how Deborah knew it was time to attack, how the Israelites won, and what happened to all those chariots are not explained by the prose but are described in the poetic account. The prose account stresses issues that are important to the book of Judges such as: leadership, responsibilities of a leader, the role of women, and the role of the deity in the Israelites' battles. The poetic account fills in many of the details of the episode, though it introduces minor contradictions.

Judges 4 introduces the following poetic account in a number of ways. The Poem of Deborah is believed by many to contain some of the oldest literary material in the Bible.[65] While this study is not concerned with whether the poem was modified or not when incorporated into Judges, the poem was certainly modified by its placement following

[65] Gray, *Joshua, Judges*, 261–2; Soggin, *Judges*, 60.

the prose. The prose account introduces most of the major players and events which are retold in the poem. The characters portrayed in the poem are viewed through the lens of the information already recounted in the prose section. This means that aspects of the poem, which may have had certain meanings if the poem stood alone, are now modified by the information already provided the reader in the prose account.

The two units, prose and poetic, complement each other. The prose presents material that is related to the main issues and themes of Judges using terminology and phraseology in keeping with the literature of the book. The poem may have been written earlier and could be a unit within itself. Placing the poem after the prose ties it to the prose through the modification of its characters by presenting them, after they were already introduced in the prose narrative, in a way that ties them to the rest of the book. The prose does not address issues better or already more elegantly described by the poem, demanding the inclusion of the poem, and therefore both chapters, into the text.

Chapter 6
THE POEM OF DEBORAH
Judges 5:1-31

The poem of Deborah is a complicated text because it may contain some of the oldest literature in the MT.[1] Many of the words which appear in it are otherwise unknown or difficult to translate because the forms are so archaic. It is poetry, rather than prose, and it is difficult to translate poetic license. A glance at the various translations will provide an overview of how complex the poem is for modern translators.

In this section, rather than attempting an explanation of every line, those lines that are relevant to themes noted thus far and which tie into the previous chapter will be examined. Since the poetic account traditionally is considered to be the older version, it is often treated first despite its appearance following the prose in the present form of the book. While it is doubtful that the poem was modified internally it must be considered to have been modified by its inclusion following the prose account, and phrases that may have had one function on their own, when following the prose, carry a slightly different nuance. For example, by the time the reader reads the poem they know that Deborah, not Baraq, led the battle, Baraq did not capture the enemy leader, and Sisera was killed by Jael.

Because of the complexity of the poem a few specific aspects will be examined. A first concern will be how the poetic account portrays the events and its characters. Another focus will consider how information about the various characters and incidents differs from that recounted

[1] J. Gray, *Joshua, Judges, Ruth,* The New Century Bible Commentary (Grand Rapids, MI: Eerdmans, 1986) 261–62; J. A. Soggin, *Judges: A Commentary,* Old Testament Library (Philadelphia: Westminster, 1981) 80.

in the prose narrative. What is relevant, and will be elaborated upon, is how the prose account took themes, possibly originally used for some other reason in the poetic account, and modified their meaning by placing them after the prose account, further tying them into the style, form, and themes of Judges. Comparing how the prose and poetic versions complement each other is crucial when viewing the book as a literary whole. Finally, we will examine how this account connects with the rest of the book of Judges.

The Bridge: Judges 5:1

The first verse links Judges 4 to 5. Some would claim that prior to the insertion of the poem, this line was followed directly by the exclamation of Judg 3:31.[2] The problem with interpreting Judges 4 as a later text with the poem inserted following its composition, is that such things as what happened during the battle and how the Israelites won despite the chariotry of the Canaanites, are not included in the prose narrative. The discussion of the role of the deity in the eyes of the Israelites only appears in the poetic version. If the prose is considered later, which is a possibility, then it had to have been written to accommodate and accentuate the poetic account.

Introducing the Poem: Judges 5:1

The relationship of the two accounts begins with the first verse, which states that Deborah and Baraq sang (Judg 5:1). The characters introduced here as subjects would not be known without the previous prose narrative, which introduces Deborah in great detail. The difficulty in the poetic text is that while there is a dual subject, Deborah and Baraq, the verb is singular and feminine. This stresses the role that Deborah played as key, with Baraq as secondary. If the poem is earlier then the role of Deborah is original and pivotal for both stories. The role of Baraq is elaborated more fully in the prose account. His role in the poem is elucidated only through the prose which ties the poem more closely into the themes and plots running through the rest of the book.

The first line of Judges 5 reinforces the identity of Deborah as a non-married woman. As noted previously, the reference to Deborah as

---

[2] R. G. Boling, *Judges: Introduction, Translation and Commentary*, The Anchor Bible (Garden City: Doubleday, 1981) 105.

"woman/wife of Lappidoth" parallels the references to the previous judges which note their primary affiliation and then some noteworthy characteristic. In this reference Deborah has no affiliation, only Baraq does. Following the prose account Baraq still needs his full designation. In Deborah's case her epithet in the prose narrative as the "woman/ wife of Lappidoth" places her in parallel with, while at the same time contrasted to, the previous military leaders of Israel. In the poem the introductory verb agrees with her and she needs no modifier.

Background: Judges 5:3-13

Verse 2 is a good example of how complicated translating this poem is. It has been translated as variously as, "When they cast off restraint in Israel, When the troops present themselves . . ." and, "When locks go untrimmed in Israel, When people dedicate themselves . . ."(JPS).[3] These translations reflect more the intent of the translators or their interpretation than the meaning of the text. In general Boling views most references in Judges to something military, thus his translation here, while JPS serves a Jewish community and is less concerned with finding military references everywhere.

What is noteworthy for the present interpretation are word plays. The term for "to cast off" *p-r-ʿ* and the term for "hair" is spelled the same way. The problem is that the meaning behind each is obscure. Could it be that the Israelites "let their hair down?" The following line contains a word play telling the "potentates" to "give ear." The Hebrew for "ear" *ʾ-z-n* and "potentate" *r-z-n* are similar. The sound of the two words is not exactly the same, the role of the *r* and how it may have interacted with a soft laryngeal could have been another play with the sounds. The poem plays with words and their sounds and is elegantly written, though its meaning is now obscure.

The next few lines are poetic references to the history of Israel while also referring to the situation at hand. They mention that the deity came forth from Seir, advanced from Edom, the earth trembled, heavens dripped, and the mountains quaked (Judg 5:4-5). The deity and extreme weather are compared often in war ballads and psalms.[4] The references set the stage by praising the deity for past actions and marshaling the elements, including the heavens and earth, to battle.

---

[3] Boling, *Judges*, 101.

[4] For comparisons as war ballads, see J. Blenkinsopp, "Ballad Style and Psalm Style in the Song of Deborah," *Biblica* 42 (1961) 61–76, and as psalms, Boling *Judges*, 108–9.

The poem continues to place the event by mentioning the days of Shamgar ben Anath, Jael, and the cessation of caravans (Judg 5:6). As with the introduction of Deborah and Baraq, the reference would be meaningless without the antecedents provided by the prose account. Soggin would like to delete the reference to, "in the time of Jael," stating that the woman plays a role only at the end of the song and so it does not perform a function here.[5] If one treats the poem as completely separate from the prose account then he has a point. But the present version of the book includes the prose version before the poetic. The reference to the days of Jael is meaningful; it conjures up for the reader the political situation between the Kenites and Canaan and between Israel and the Kenites. It is possible that in the poem's original state this was not the function, but it carries that impact now. In either case the reference highlights the importance of Jael; time could be reckoned based on her existence.

The Shamgar reference now functions in the same way. It too may have functioned originally in the poem in a different manner, it now follows important information pertaining to Shamgar and his role in Israelite history. He was a non-Israelite. He saved Israel. He used technologically simple equipment. His reference appears in the same sentence which provides background about another non-Israelite who saved Israel. These meanings would not be relevant if the poem stood alone but they are fully integrated into the reader's understanding of who these characters are since they are grouped together and follow the detailed accounts of the two in the previous unit.

The poem treats Jael as primary, and Heber is not even mentioned. Shamgar and Jael are treated together. In the prose account Jael is identified as related to Heber in some way and his relationship to both Israel and Canaan are specified. What is clear from the prose is that Heber is non-Israelite and has relationships with both Israel and Canaan but on different levels. Since Israel's relationships to Shamgar and Jael are not clarified in the poem, the references to them in the previous chapter clarify their appearance in the poetic account. In the prose account they are completely integrated into the themes and focus of the book. Their subsequent appearance in the poem ties the poetic account more closely into the Deborah episode and, through that, the rest of Judges.

Shamgar and Jael are further grouped together by their association with caravans in the poem. The prose notes Jael's relationship to tents, which could be considered an aspect of the caravan trade, though that aspect of her life or livelihood is not noted. The tent residence in the

[5] Soggin, *Judges*, 85.

prose explains her appearance so close to the scene of the battle and why she had certain tools at her disposal. Little detail concerning Shamgar is provided in the prose account and none of the information included suggests any relationship with caravan trade. In light of the new information provided about Shamgar in the poem, his previous struggle makes more sense in the context of caravan trade, and how and why he may have helped Israel, and is another example of how the poetic account focuses on different aspects of the incident. Again the prose modifies the poem by providing background information to aspects presented in the poetic account.

The Problem: Judges 5:7-8

The next few lines address the problem that deliverance ceased and the people went after new gods until Deborah arose (Judg 5:7-8). Ehud is not mentioned. The problem addressed is that appearing throughout Judges in general; the Israelites followed other deities. The problem is portrayed as impacting other issues such as trade and travel. While the terminology "the bad thing" is not used, the problem of going after other deities is specified. Deborah is described as the person who saved Israel both militarily and spiritually.

Deborah is called, "a mother in Israel" (Judg 5:7). It is an odd reference for Deborah since she is not referred to in the poetic version as anyone's wife. The text contains no reference to children related to Deborah and there is no evidence of her as a biological mother. The reference stands out since, although in the previous account there is an overwhelming number of epithets and designations for Deborah, nothing like judge or prophet is used in the poetic account. With no evidence of children, the use of the term must refer to a meaning beyond that of childbearing.

As noted above, both Baraq and Sisera are in secondary roles even though they are the primary male characters, particularly regarding military actions. It was also noted that Sisera is compared to Jabin King of Hazor despite Jabin's absence in the text. In the poetic account Jabin is not mentioned at all but Sisera retains a secondary position to his mother. The reference to Deborah as "a" mother in Israel may serve the literary function of paralleling Deborah with Sisera's mother.

The following verses refer to the types of problems that occurred prior to the battle (Judg 5:9-11) exhorting Deborah to awaken (Judg 5:12). Boling notes that the reference is not so much to awakening but to getting on with the singing. In his interpretation the reference is not to the poem itself but to the role of the "womenfolk" when the warriors return.[6] This would be another allusion to women going out to meet the men upon their return from battle. Following this trajectory women were expected to go out and meet the men after battle. If so, the reference heavily impacts the interpretation of Jael's going out to meet Sisera in the prose, and Jephthah's later vow (Judg 11:30).

Baraq is exhorted to "Get up!" (Judg 5:12), as he was in the prose version. In the poem no specific character commands him, whereas in the prose Deborah commands Baraq. In both cases Baraq did not command but was commanded. The difference is that in the poetic account both Baraq and Deborah were commanded, apparently by the deity. Deborah's position of importance is highlighted since the command in the poem uses the identical verb and tense as Deborah used in the prose. These words were already spoken by Deborah, emphasizing her working relationship with the deity when Baraq was commanded. Baraq's refusal to follow his orders unless Deborah joined him combined with the reader's knowledge that Baraq did not accomplish his second command, places the poetic verses concerning Baraq in a different light.

The continuation of the verse notes that Baraq should take his captives, using the plural. This verse contains a sense of irony that is set up by the prose version. The captive Baraq most wanted, according to the previous chapter and following the pattern of military leaders described thus far, was Sisera, singular. Yet the reader already knows Baraq chased after the chariots and as a result did not capture Sisera. The text uses the plural "captives," which ties the prose to the poetry so that the poetic reference functions as an indictment of Baraq. The implication is that Baraq was too concerned with many captives, similar to the Canaanites later in the poetic account who were interested in women, slaves, and loot, and lost Sisera. It is unlikely that this was the original intent of the poem, but its present placement in the narrative connects it intricately with the prose on this issue.

Who Fights: Judges 5:14-18

The poem continues with a catalogue of the Israelite tribes who joined the battle (Judg 5:14-15) and those who did not (Judg 5:15-18). Not all the tribes appear in these lists. Many scholars have tried to find historical elements in some of the more unusual references, such as the reference to Dan lingering by ships (Judg 5:17).[7] Regardless of the pos-

---

[6] Boling *Judges*, 111.

[7] A. Malamat, "The Danite Migration and the Pan-Israelite Exodus-Conquest: A Biblical Narrative Pattern," *Biblica* 51 (1970) 1–16; F. Spina "The Dan Story Histori-

sible historical referents, this is the first time that someone in the book condemns Israelite tribes for not appearing. The description of the first battle in the book states that only two tribes fought (Judg 1:3), yet Deborah's poem is the first reprimand for such behavior.

Earlier in the book there was a sense that each tribe was expected to fight for its own territory. Deborah's comments indicate that in this battle help from some tribes would have been appreciated but it was not offered. As the book progresses so does this theme, which eventually culminates in the destruction of an entire clan because they did not take a vow with the rest of the community (Judg 21:8-12).

The Battle: Judges 5:19-23

The poem discusses the battle only once the background is established. Judges 5:19 places the final players *in situ* by referring to the Kings of Canaan coming to fight. The poem continues by providing the reason for Israel's victory; the stars fought from heaven, which caused a huge torrent in the Kishon. The Kishon is a *wadi*, a river bed which, since Israel is a desert, often flash floods in the winter months and dries out during the summer. In other words, a massive rain storm suddenly sent water rushing through the valley rendering the feared chariots useless.

The poetic account provides a reason for victory and explains how Deborah knew the correct time for battle. Her timing reflects savvy strategy (contra Soggin above). The reference is couched in poetic terminology and consists of two verses. Judges 5:20 refers to the stars fighting from heaven, which as a reference alone would not be particularly useful. Only in Judg 5:21 is the effect of the stars' participation in the battle made clear. The massive rain storm and flooding rivers explain the Israelite victory but the text still does not use much space in recounting the battle. As was the case with the prose narrative, the text stresses the role of Deborah, particularly over Baraq, and the Israelite deity in the events, not the military prowess of Baraq.

Jael: Judges 5:24-28

After the battle Jael is introduced again (Judg 5:24). The author of the poem, who, according to the text, is Deborah, is straight-forward

---

cally Reconsidered," *JSOT* 4 (1977) 60–71; and Y. Yadin, "And Dan, Why Did He Remain With the Ships?" *AJBA* 1 (1968) 8–23.

about Jael's elevated status. She is referred to as, "most blessed of women." The poem devotes a fair amount of text to describing her and her actions (in fact only slightly less than is given to the battle itself). She is: "most blessed of women," "woman/wife of Heber the Kenite," and, "most blessed of women in tents." Because the references are in a poetic account it is difficult to determine whether the three epithets for her, two of which are rather similar, are for metrical and aesthetic reasons or if they are intended to provide relevant information about the ensuing scene.

Jael's blessed status is important because it indicates that the actions Jael is about to take (and has already performed in Judges 4) are condoned. Despite some modern scholars' trouble with Jael's actions (they express their displeasure by not commenting on them), the biblical text is clear about them; Jael is blessed. All the reader knows about her from the poem is her blessed status and some of her actions. The prose account originally introduces Jael in a way that is neither positive nor negative, nor is there an evaluation of her actions. It is only in the complementing poetic account where her actions, which involve killing the enemy general, are evaluated and determined to be positive. Again the poem complements and adds necessary information to the prose narrative.

After stressing Jael's blessed state the poem recounts her actions. These follow the general story line presented in the previous chapter with slight modifications. The poem notes that "he," without stating an antecedent for the personal pronoun, asked for water and she offered milk and brought it to him in a special bowl (Judg 5:25). Paralleling the prose account, the substitution of milk or cream instead of water is a significant element in the story. As in the prose, it is difficult to ascertain if the function of the dairy product was to serve as a sedative, or whether she was creating a sense of comfort because she served him more than he requested.

In the poetic account Jael's use of a special bowl further lured him into a relaxed state by accentuating her hospitality. It may replace Jael's protective stance at the door, a detail found in the prose account but not in the poem. The dialogue between Jael and Sisera, which appears in the prose but not in the poem, emphasizes the ironic and Deborah's prophetic statement. In the poetic account Jael carried out her next actions immediately. This difference highlights the varying foci of the two accounts. The poetic version is not so much focused on the Deborah versus Baraq elements of the story as it is on the victory over the Canaanites, regardless of who was involved. In the poetic version Jael reached for the tent peg (Judg 5:26), struck Sisera, and crushed his head. He sunk at her feet, destroyed (Judg 5:27).

The two accounts differ in the placement of Sisera during his final moments. In the previous chapter Jael was at the door, in Sisera's mind protecting him so that he could sleep, and he had laid down and was asleep when Jael struck. In the poetic account, Sisera fell at her feet, which implies that he was standing when the attack occurred. The poem deletes some of the suspense and irony provided by the narrative account where he commanded her, she apparently complied, and then attacked him while he was sleeping. In the poem the action happened almost immediately, is more graphic, and focuses less on Baraq and Sisera and more on Jael and Sisera.

In the poetic account both characters' actions contain possible sexual allusions, as did the prose narrative. When Sisera fell, it was between her feet, a reference that could be sexual. The reference to offering him milk instead of water could be interpreted as sexual, offering her breast rather than water, although this is less likely since the poem refers to the vessel in which the beverage was served.

Sexual allusions are in keeping with the women who have appeared thus far in Judges and will appear later. Achsah made a request of her husband after their first sexual union (Judg 1:14), Jephthah's mother would be of questionable sexual legitimacy which will be the basis for his status in his tribe (Judg 11:1), his daughter's virginity will be a major issue (Judg 11:37-40), the women in Samson's life all play significant sexual roles (Judg 14:15-19; 16:1, 4-20), and a civil war ignites over the rape of a *pîlegeš* (Judg 19:25). Clearly the sexuality of the majority of women in Judges is significant to plots concerning them and would not be out of place in this context.

Regardless of the exact chain of events, the specific actions, and Sisera's location at the time of death, both the narrative and poetic accounts view Jael's actions as pivotal to the story, positive, and worthy of as many lines, if not more, than are allotted to the entire battle. In the poem Baraq does not appear after the battle. Instead the focus of the battle in the poetic account is on the role of the weather/deity and Jael. Baraq did almost nothing and Jael receives praise.

Sisera's Mother: Judges 5:29-31

The poetic account contains a segment regarding Sisera's mother which is missing from the prose narrative version. This episode is crucial for tying the poetic account into the prose narrative, setting up parallels with Deborah which frame the entire episode, and highlighting the irony in the episode. It examines for the first time in Judges a mother/son relationship. In fact, this is the only mother/son relationship included before the Samson story. Like Samson's mother, Sisera's mother is not named.

The text notes that Sisera's mother peered through the window and asked a question which, according to the text, was something of a lament or wail, wondering why her son tarried (Judg 5:28). Her precise action is difficult to determine because the term *y-b-b* appears only here in the MT. The verb is translated variously as: "cry shrilly," "wailed," and even "whine" (JPS).[8] The differences in the translations appear minor but they carry with them some cultural ramifications that lead to differing interpretations of the verse. If Sisera's mother was, "crying shrilly," or, "whining," the modern reader envisions a whiny non-active figure with all the negative connotations of an overbearing mother. If one translates "wail" or "lament," then her actions were more dramatic and serious. A wail is an action which in some cultures and contexts is ritualized behavior. Thus translating "wail/lament" indicates ironic prophetic insight on the part of Sisera's mother; without knowing it she acted appropriately for the situation since she had just lost her son.

Viewing Sisera's mother as insightful and possibly in mourning provides the reader with sympathy for her initially. Establishing some positive feelings for her is important if one wants to read an ironic sense into her later statements and to her reactions to what she was hoping the end result of the battle would be. Irony is introduced since Sisera's mother is asking why he was late when the reader had just read of his death.

Sisera's mother continued by asking where the clatter of his wheels was. The chariot was key to the Canaanites' superiority over the Israelites and the main source of the Israelites' distress according to the prose version. The reader knows that the technological advance that was such a threat was in reality no match for the weather harnessed by the Israelite deity who rendered those vehicles useless. This reference, while not necessarily originally intended to do so, ties the end of the poem to the beginning of the prose unit through the theme of the technological superiority of the Canaanites (Judg 4:3).

The response to Sisera's mother's question comes from one of a group of women waiting with her. The woman is referred to as the wisest of her *śārôt*, the feminine plural form of the term *śar*. When the term appears in its masculine form, either in singular or plural, it is translated as "advisor," "minister," or, periodically, "courtier" (Gen 12:15).

---

[8] *BDB* translates "cry shrilly," (*BDB*, 384), Boling translates "wailed" (*Judges*, 104).

Judges 5:29 is the only place where the term appears in the feminine plural. In this context it is translated as "her ladies" (JPS, KJV, RSV). When the term appears in the masculine, both in singular and plural, the implication of the terms used to translate it indicates that the holder/s of this title is in some official governmental capacity, usually as advisors to political officers. The one time the term appears in the feminine plural it suddenly refers to a group of women sitting around whining.

The use of the term in this context, if interpreted as a feminine plural form which has the same meaning of the term in the masculine, places these people in some official capacity *vis à vis* Sisera's mother. This would in turn place Sisera's mother in a role other than simply the one who had given birth to a general, but possibly someone of importance in an administrative or ceremonial capacity. Though few, there were queen mothers both in Israel and the surrounding lands who were important in their husband's or son's political administrations.[9] Other women may not have had political powers but carried out important ceremonial functions, necessitating an official entourage.[10] The important role Sisera's mother's entourage serves in the story is obscured when translating the term simply as, "ladies."

As noted earlier, Sisera is repeatedly placed in a secondary position to Jabin in the narrative section of the text despite Jabin's absence from the story. One suggested reason for this was that in the prose section Baraq functioned in a secondary role to Deborah, paralleling Sisera. In the poetic account Deborah is called a "mother in Israel," Baraq plays almost no role, Jabin does not appear, and Sisera is only mentioned at his death. Suddenly the scene shifts to Sisera's mother who has a host of advisors. His mother's advisors carry the same title as Sisera, *śar*. The only difference in their titles is that Sisera's is modified by the term 'army' and the women's title is in the feminine plural. This again places Sisera in a secondary position but the person in the more primary position was a woman, the exact parallel to Baraq's status in the text second to Deborah, a mother in Israel.

---

[9] Note some of the more famous women, such as: Hatshepsut who ruled as Pharoah, Adad-nirari's mother Sammuramat (legendary Semiramis), Naqi'a-Zakutu, Nabonidus's mother, Athaliah, and Jezebel.

[10] For example, in the el-Amarna letters, Tushratta of Mitanni gave his daughter, Tadu-Hepa to Amenophis III in marriage and thus she appears in much of their correspondence discussing matters of state as well as her marriage gifts and entourage. EA tablets 22, 23, 24, 26, 27, 28, and 29 (W. Moran, *The Amarna Letters* [Baltimore: The Johns Hopkins University Press, 1992]). Another example, from the biblical text, is Solomon's marriage to an Egyptian princess (1 Kgs 3:1; 7:8; 9:16, 24).

The following statements reinforce the idea that while Sisera's mother may have been genuinely interested in his well-being, she had political issues on her mind also. Her female minister spoke aloud Sisera's mother's thoughts concerning what Sisera was doing. She claimed that they (presumably the men) must be dividing spoil/booty (Judg 5:30). The list of booty includes cloth of all sorts for Sisera and others, but these are not the first items mentioned.

The first item listed is captured women, one or two for each man. The term used is rather graphic. Though usually translated "damsel" the term is from the root *r-ḥ-m* whose primary meaning is, "to be soft, wide," leading to, "female cavities," often translated as, "womb."[11] The reference to women not as women but as wombs indicates that the immediate priority was to use these women for rape and potential bearers of future slaves.

The booty Sisera sought, and his mother's legitimation of it serve an important function in the story. The irony of the whole scenario is established since the unit begins with his mother lamenting his absence. Originally Sisera's mother appeared to be a concerned mother worrying over her delayed son. Suddenly the mother is not just a mother but someone with advisors and concerned with the booty she hoped her son was collecting. The irony is apparent. She was visualizing her son having a good time raping captive women and bringing in booty while the reader knows that a woman, possibly a potential rape victim, just killed him.

The rape reference in the poem further legitimates Jael's actions. The prose notes that there was a treaty between the Canaanites and the clan of Heber but does not explain how that would have affected Jael. In light of Sisera's mother's wish for her son, Jael may function in the story as the only named potential rape victim and thus her actions could be seen as a preemptive strike. The reference to Sisera's mother legitimating actions she hoped her son was carrying out serves as a notice of a Canaanite practice. The reference, and implication that someone else in the group was also thinking it, reveals that raping captive women would not be a unique experience but standard practice. This reference foreshadows the end of Judges where the children of Israel do precisely the same when they attack in order to capture women to function as wombs (Judg 21:8-12), though different terminology is used. While the reason stated for the Israelites' later actions is not identical, the procedures and outcomes were, the Israelites legitimated it, and modern translators refer to the event as "marriage."

---

[11] *BDB*, 933.

This unit never depicts Sisera's mother receiving word of Sisera's death but the final line alludes to it. The last line asks that all "your" (presumably Israel's or the Israelite deity's) enemies may perish the same way and that friends be as the sun rising in might (Judg 5:31). This summarizes the situation asking that enemies be like Sisera and friends like Jael. Again the reference praises Jael, a non-Israelite woman, and hopes that Sisera, as enemy, will suffer.

The unit concludes by noting that the land was tranquil for forty years. Baraq is not listed as a judge nor is he or Deborah listed as the reason or cause of the ensuing peace.

Summary

The poetic account focuses on issues slightly different from those in the prose version. Because the poem is interested in the battle it does not necessarily contain many of the themes evidenced in the book, which are major elements of the prose narrative. Themes stressed in the prose narrative concern the role of leadership, seen in the contrast between Deborah and Baraq, how one leads (like the active Sisera or the absent Jabin), who leads (king or general, prophet or general, man or woman), and foreigners helping Israelites (Shamgar and Jael).

The poem is concerned with the battle and praising the deity. While it is doubtful that the poem was modified internally, it was modified by its inclusion after the prose account. Aspects that may have functioned in a particular way if the poem functioned as a document on its own mean something different when encountered following the prose. This is evident in the role of Shamgar and Jael, the references to Baraq, the deity's commands, Sisera's death, and the inclusion of Sisera's mother at the end, which completes the circle with the beginning of the prose where Deborah is the woman/wife of Lappidoth.

While elements in the poem were modified by its placement, the prose account functions with an eye towards the poem, which clarifies and magnifies many elements so that the two units need each other. The battle itself, the role of the deity, and the final segment with Sisera's mother create a bond between the two units so that neither can stand alone and both are tied into the themes and style of the rest of book.

Chapter 7
GIDEON/JERUBBAAL
Judges 6:1–8:35

In the chapters which focus on Gideon/Jerubbaal, Israel's relationship with the deity continues to decline. The issue of leadership is again prevalent here, with a focus on such aspects as: how a leader is chosen, reasons for fighting, rewards, and succession. The character of the individual heroes has reached such a low level that Gideon, the leader contacted directly by the deity, demanded proof repeatedly from the deity, had personal reasons for the campaign, and flirted with the notion of taxation, kingship, and dynasty.

This chapter flows neatly from the previous ones through the themes of the Midianites/Amalekites and trade. An ironic twist appears in the juxtaposition of the previous unit with Gideon's story. The Gideon cycle follows an episode where women are the dominant characters, both in the military and political sense, yet no women with names are mentioned in relation to Gideon, and the focus is primarily on men and male war culture, almost a reaction to the previous story. Despite the absence of specific women in this episode, the question of women's status is raised indirectly by statements made that are part of the evaluation of the judge and lead to and impact the following episode involving Abimelech.

The narrator emphasizes more strongly than in previous chapters the theological theme that the Israelites' victories derive directly from the deity. Thus far the heroes were cognizant of the deity's role but the narrative does not stress the point. In this chapter the hero no longer accepts the role of the deity as a fundamental belief. The deity must now both save Israel from her enemies and battle to reestablish the deity's role within the community of Israel.

Many modern scholars treat the theological aspects sarcastically since it is considered to be a later theme that has corrupted the original story. The general consensus is that Gideon and the battle are primary and the theological components of the story in some way mask its essence.[1] Although the theological aspects may indeed be a later addition, in the present form these elements are fundamental to understanding the placement of the episode, its structure, and main themes. It is important not to minimize those aspects but to examine them for what they do to the story and how they carry the plot of the episodes concerning Gideon and the book of Judges. The focus on the battle and strategy may be important for modern scholars trying to understand the history of the period, but it is not a focus or essential characteristic of the narrative flow of the text.

The attitude of modern scholars concerning the theological components of this chapter almost falls into the category of irony. Many scholars seem almost annoyed at what the author or redactor of Judges has done by taking authority and power away from Gideon. These scholars miss the focus of the text which is structured to highlight just that point. According to the text the people strayed to such an extent that they no longer readily listened when the deity contacted someone directly. This theological message is then elaborated throughout the rest of the story and, to some extent, the rest of the book.

Background: Judges 6:1-10

This unit begins with the Israelites again doing "the bad thing" in the eyes of their deity and being given to the Midianites for seven years (Judg 6:1). The "bad thing" is not specified. Since the same terminology for the Israelites' action is used as in previous episodes and the "bad thing" uses the definite article it may be that intermarriage leading to the worship of other deities is again the issue. This contention is supported by the previous story where Israelites were led and saved by non-Israelites, indicating a high degree of interaction with non-Israelites. There are hints later in this story that intermarriage continued to be a problem, possibly within the family of Gideon/Jerubbaal.

[1] R. G. Boling, *Judges: Introduction, Translation and Commentary*, The Anchor Bible (Garden City: Doubleday, 1981) 135; J. Gray, *Joshua, Judges, Ruth*, The New Century Bible Commentary (Grand Rapids, MI: Eerdmans, 1986) 205–11; J. A. Soggin, *Judges: A Commentary*, Old Testament Library (Philadelphia: Westminster, 1981) 110–34.

The previous story is obliquely recalled by references to the Kenites who were earlier listed as descendants of Moses' father-in-law. The father-in-law mentioned in Judges does not have the same name as that listed in the other biblical books (Jethro [Ex 3:1; 18:1] and Reuel [Ex 2:18; Num 10:29]), but in all contexts he is referred to as a Midianite. Since in the previous story the Kenites are related to Moses' father-in-law (Judg 4:11), and the Kenites/Midianites saved Israel through Jael, some special relationship is established. Though the previous story notes the relationship between the Kenites and Moses' father-in-law, his Midianite origins are not stated there. In the story following the Jael episode Israel returned to mixed marriages with the result that they were given to the Midianites, the people who had previously saved them. The juxtaposition of stories implies that the results of the previous story contribute to the present situation.

The juxtaposition introduces an ironic situation. In the previous episode the Midianites, sometimes an ally and sometimes a foe, saved Israel through a woman. In this episode the saving group becomes Israel's oppressor and overlord. If the "bad thing" perpetrated by the Israelites was intermarriage leading to the worship of other deities, possibly in this case with the Midianites, the Israelites brought the calamity on themselves.

The following lines provide the background against which the next story must be viewed (Judg 6:2-6). The result of Israel's transgression was that the Midianites prevailed over Israel and Israel had to take refuge in caves and strongholds in the mountains (Judg 6:2). When Israel finished sowing, Midian, Amalek, and the children of Kedem would come up and raid them, destroying the produce of the land all the way to Gaza and denying Israel any means of sustenance (Judg 6:4). The Midianites had livestock and cattle, which were as thick as locusts and innumerable camels, and they would invade the land and ravage it (Judg 6:5). Israel was reduced to utter misery by the Midianites, and the children of Israel cried out to their deity (Judg 6:6).

The Midianite situation in Judg 6:2-6 is ironic on another level. One of the problems mentioned in Deborah's poem was the cessation of the caravan trade (Judg 5:6-7). Possibly as a result of Sisera's demise, the caravan trade, now in the hands of the Midianites, appears to be thriving (Judg 6:2-7), but at Israel's expense. The nomadic lifestyle was the reason why Jael was in a place that she could kill Sisera in the last episode. One chapter later what had been Israel's salvation became the source of disaster.

As a result of the crisis facing Israel they cried out to their deity (Judg 6:7). This time the deity reacted by sending a prophet to speak to Israel (Judg 6:8). The prophet was not impressed with Israel's distress and reminded them that the deity of Israel brought them out of Egypt, freed them from the house of bondage, rescued them from the Egyptians and oppressors, drove them out before them, and gave them their land (Judg 6:9). The prophet reminded the Israelites that the deity had told them that they were not allowed to worship the gods of the Amorites, in whose land they dwelt, but that the Israelites did not obey (Judg 6:10).

This section is often described as a straightforward insertion by the Deuteronomistic Historian of the standard party line that if the Israelites followed their instructions and were loyal to their deity they would prosper, and if they strayed from the path they would suffer, as they were at this point in the story.[2] That is one function of the passage but the reference is relevant from the literary standpoint. In a few verses, when Gideon is introduced, he questions the deity and the deity's role in Israel's present predicament (Judge 6:13). The placement of this passage contextualizes and to some extent counteracts Gideon's upcoming statements.

Boling notes that "Amorites" here refers to westerners in contrast to the previous notes about the easterners (Judg 6:3).[3] It is the Amorites, and various forms of them such as Canaanites, Hittites, Perizzites, Hivites and Jebusites, that the deity left in the land to be a snare for Israel (Judg 3:5). Ironically, in the previous chapter where the foe was the Canaanites, the hero who helped them defeat their enemy was a descendant of their present foe. The concept of intermarriage with non-Israelites leading the Israelites to other gods is highlighted again.

The reference to a prophet ties this unit to the previous episode through his introduction and use of the term "man" ʾîš reading, "a man, a prophet" (Judg 6:8) just as Deborah was ʾiššâ, "a woman, a prophet" (Judg 4:4). In contrast, however, the prophet here is unnamed, has no business address, no regularly stated position, nor tribal affiliation. The absence of name, place, and tribal affiliation may lend this prophet a pan-Israelite perspective which emphasizes Deborah's earlier complaints that all the tribes did not participate (Judg 5:16-18).

The text uses the direct speech of the prophet to state the reason for Israel's distress, reinforcing the Deuteronomistic gloss and substantiating the cause of the present situation. The prophet asserted categorically that at this point the Israelites were, in the eyes of the deity, worshiping other gods. This emphasizes the present author's contention that the "bad thing" mentioned in Judg 6:1 is intermarriage leading to apostasy.

[2] Boling, *Judges*, 125–7; Gray, *Joshua, Judges*, 283–4; Soggin, *Judges*, 112–3.
[3] Boling, *Judges*, 126.

Gideon/Jerubbaal's Introduction: Judges 6:11-32

Gideon is introduced through the direct intervention of a messenger of the deity. The meeting took place immediately following the prophet's message to the Israelites in response to their crying out to the deity. The prophet's message from the deity ended by stating that, "you (Israel) did not obey me" (Judg 6:10). The word translated as "messenger" here is often translated as "angel" (JPS, KJV, RSV). This being usually presents itself to biblical characters in human form. This messenger's appearance follows the message from the prophet of the deity which had served to reprimand the people. Is the messenger sent because the people were now prepared because of the prophet's work, or, did the prophet's message not work, making more radical measures necessary? In either case it is clear that without direct contact with the deity the Israelites would not obey. At this point in Israel's history the Israelites no longer sought to discover the deity's wishes, as they had at the beginning of the book, but the deity had to be proactive, sending messages to them.

Gideon's introduction begins by noting that a messenger of the deity went to sit under the terebinth at Ophrah, which belonged to Joash the Abiezrite, who was the father of Gideon (Judg 6:11).[4] Hamilton notes that this terebinth may be something like Deborah's palm seen in the previous story.[5] The irony is that in Deborah's case the palm was used for prophecy for the Israelite deity while here it serves a similar function, but in the service of Baal rather than the Israelite deity. The reference to a tree place ties Gideon's story to the previous episode while emphasizing Israel's descent.

The character of Joash is ironic. Joash is a Yahwist name yet a few verses later he has an altar to Baal (Judg 6:25). At this point in the narrative he is associated with the terebinth at Ophrah (Judg 6:11) which appears as a cultic object or place and is later associated with an altar to Baal and an Asherah (Judg 6:25). He is called an "Abiezrite," a family in the clan of Manasseh (Josh 17:2) named for the male progenitor (1 Chr 7:18). The name means, "my father is help," or, "father is help," a name fitting for the story, since this is precisely what Joash did for Gideon.[6]

---

[4] The precise location is uncertain, but most scholars (J. M. Hamilton "Ophrah [Place]," *ABD* 5:27-8) agree with the identification of Affuleh, originally proposed by Y. Aharoni, in the center of the Jezreel Valley in the territory of Manasseh (*The Land of the Bible: A Historical Geography: Revised and Enlarged Edition* trans. A. Rainey. [Philadelphia: Westminister, 1969] 263).

[5] Hamilton, "Ophrah (Place)," 27–8.

[6] D. G. Schley, "Abiezer," *ABD*, 1:15.

Though the story focuses on Gideon, his father is introduced first. It is his father who was related to a clan, and a few sentences later it is his father who owned land and apparently had wealth and prestige in the community (Judg 6:25-32). While including a father's name is a standard form of reference in the biblical text, and previous judges have been introduced by their fathers already in the book (Ehud, Judg 3:15; possibly Shamgar, Judg 3:31; Baraq, Judg 4:6), this is the first time that the father of a hero plays any role in the text. Since later the role of Gideon's children becomes an issue (Judg 8:20-24), especially in the following story of Abimelech (Judges 9), this introduction of the father before the hero is another example of foreshadowing.

The text continues by noting that Joash the Abiezrite's son Gideon was beating out wheat inside a wine press to keep it safe from the Midianites. The implication is that because of the Midianites the Israelites had to carry out their agricultural roles in hiding. The name Gideon comes from the root *g-d-ʿ* meaning, "to hew, hew down, or off," so that the name means something like "hacker," exactly what he was doing when first introduced (Judg 6:11).[7]

The messenger of the deity appeared to Gideon calling him a "mighty man of valor" (KJV and RSV; "valiant warrior" JPS). The messenger spoke directly to Gideon stating, "the deity is with you," employing the second person singular (Judg 6:12). Gideon's response indicates that he either had not heard the earlier prophet's words or did not believe them because he asked the messenger why, if the deity were with Israel (the text says literally "with us") difficult things had happened to them. He was so arrogant as to ask where all those wondrous deeds talked about by their fathers were (Judg 6:13).

On a basic level Gideon's response can be interpreted to mean, "What have you done for us lately?" His statement highlights the different realities faced by the desert generation and those presently in the land since, for Gideon's generation, the stories of the Exodus were already just that, stories. Gideon revealed no recognition of any fault on Israel's part, an issue raised by the prophet only a few lines earlier (Judg 6:7-10). Gideon's answer, using the first person plural, implies that he was speaking on behalf of all Israel. This use of a first person plural indicates that Gideon ignored the messenger's direct speech in which the singular was used to address him specifically.

At this point the deity, presumably still speaking through the messenger, told Gideon to go in this strength of his and deliver Israel from the Midianites, even offering to make him his messenger (Judg 6:14). Exactly what strength was being referred to was as unclear to Gideon

---

[7] *BDB*, 154.

as it is to the modern reader, and Gideon responded by asking how he could deliver Israel when his clan was the humblest in Manasseh and he was the youngest in his father's household (Judg 6:15). The deity, through the messenger, did not discuss the issue but reiterated what he had said to Gideon, speaking directly to him in the second person singular, saying "you will defeat Midian" (Judg 6:16).

Gideon's questioning himself as a leader because he was the youngest person in a household that was the humblest in the clan is reminiscent of Moses with another ironic twist. The deity's response here is almost a direct quotation of Exod 3:11. The differences between the scenes parallel and highlight the irony of the comparison. In Exod 3:11 when Moses spoke to the deity at the burning bush, saying, "Who am I that I should go to Pharaoh and free the Israelites from Egypt" (JPS), he was tending the flock of his father-in-law, a priest of Midian and was being harbored by Gideon's present enemy. In Exodus, Moses was contacted by the deity to lead the children of Israel out of Egypt, an event Gideon considered so old as to allow him to demand new proof of the power and role of the deity for his generation.

Gideon's response raises the issue of position in the family as a method for determining status and power. Gideon claimed to be the youngest in an inconsequential family as a means of avoiding this service which the messenger of the deity requested directly of him. This story, and its continuation with Abimelech, raises many issues concerning inherited rule and one's position within the family. The irony is that Gideon's oldest and youngest sons later play roles in this story regarding similar issues (Judg 8:20-21; 9:5-21). King David was also the youngest in his family (1 Sam 17:12-14; 1 Chr 2:13-14), so this is another example of the David polemic imbedded within the text.

Gideon did not believe either the identity of the messenger or the power of the deity and as a result asked the messenger for proof by a sign (Judg 6:17), Gideon's first test of the deity. Gideon told the messenger not to leave where he was until he returned with an offering. It is unclear at this point in the text if Gideon realized who was visiting him and whether, when he told the messenger to wait, he intended on making a meal or an offering. The difference in intentions relates to Gideon's order because while not a direct command, to some extent, Gideon issued the messenger of the deity orders.

Gideon prepared an offering of a kid and unleavened bread and brought them to the terebinth (Judg 6:19). The text is fairly detailed about the order in which the items were prepared, how they were prepared, even how much flour was used. There are a number of places in the biblical text where meals were prepared for foreign travelers (later in this book the Levite of the *pîlegeš* was twice a traveler; Judg 19:4-8,

21), some of whom were also messengers of the deity (also by a tere-binth, Gen 18:1-8, and with the same travelers in Genesis 19). In the book of Judges alone there are two cases of visitors who were messengers of the deity (this case and Samson's birth in Judg 13:2-20) and two others where the visiting travelers were not divine (Judg 18; 19:4-8). The issue of hospitality is often raised, comparing the various stories to determine what legitimate behavior would be in each case.

The problem with comparing the different episodes is that because each is situated in a story with a particular theme, plot, and, presumably, point to make, many of the specifics of the preparation may be particular or relevant to that story alone. It is difficult to ascertain whether Gideon prepared more than Lot did for his guests.[8] Determining precisely what Gideon was trying to do and which element of the offering indicates that point is not clear. If he used excessive amounts, is it because he was trying to impress the visitor, which would ruin the idea that he was from a small or weak family? It may indicate that Gideon did not know what he was supposed to do, typically for his times, at least according to the comments of the prophet made just prior to the incident.

After receiving the offering, the messenger instructed Gideon to place the meat and bread on the rock and spill out the broth (Judg 6:20). Gideon followed his instructions (Judg 6:20). The messenger touched the meat and unleavened bread and fire sprang from the rock consuming the offering and the messenger disappeared. It is only at this point that Gideon realized with shock, and apparently horror, who the messenger was and that he had seen the deity face-to-face (Judg 6:22).

The passage suggests more parallels with Moses since he was the only other person thus far to have seen the deity face to face (Deut 34:10). As in the earlier case, the parallel is not exact. Moses really did see the deity face to face, while Gideon encountered a messenger. As in the earlier parallels to Moses and characters from the previous desert generation, the scenario serves to compare the situations of the characters and their actions while highlighting the differences. The contrast with Moses is extreme since for Moses the drama of leaving Egypt was unfolding whereas Gideon and his generation had already strayed from the deity to such an extent that they had to be reminded by a prophet of how the Israelite deity led the Israelites out of slavery in

---

[8] G. Moore suggests that the quantity (more than a bushel) is disproportionate, and he compares it with 1 Sam 1:24 where an *ephah* of flour was enough unleavened bread to go with a three year old bullock (*Judges*, The International Critical Commentary [New York: Harper, 1969] 187). Boling notes that Gideon never did anything in proportion (*Judges*, 133).

Egypt. Israel's problem was that even after Egypt and Sinai the deity still had to show proof of power and the people still did not obey.

The deity, who was apparently still present though no longer in the form of a messenger, reassured Gideon that he should not fear and that he would not die as a result of the encounter (Judg 6:23). This is the first time in Judges that an Israelite did not recognize who he was meeting, though this theme will appear later with Samson's parents (Judg 13:22-23). In both cases the Israelite man had to be reassured that nothing would happen to him. In this case the deity was present and it was the deity who reassured Gideon.

As a result of the incident Gideon built an altar to the deity and named it "Adonaishalom" which, according to the text, still stands in Ophrah of the Abiezrites (Judg 6:24). The timing of this notice is relevant. After meeting the deity Gideon built an altar, but the next few sentences inform the reader that while he was brave enough for that, he was still wary of tearing another one down. This is another sign of the trouble inherent in Israel, the Israelites did not see how the worship of the gods surrounding them angered the Israelite deity they were supposed to be worshiping, which caused their present predicament.

That night Gideon received his first instructions. The deity told him to take a young bull belonging to his father, to tear down the altar of Baal which belonged to his father, and to cut down the Asherah beside it (Judg 6:25). The implications of this verse confirm much of what the prophet noted earlier; that the Israelites were worshiping other deities (Judg 6:10). Gideon's father, who bears a Yahwistic name, had his own altar to Baal and an Asherah beside it. This raises the status of Gideon's father since it seems unlikely that a person of the lowly status claimed earlier by Gideon, would possess such things. The deity was clearly planning on giving Gideon the reigns of leadership. In light of the cultic situation Gideon was ordered to address, leadership in this case was not purely military but contained a religious component. This is the opposite of the previous story where Deborah had religious and judicial powers and only secondly, under duress, took military control.

The deity's instructions continue, commanding Gideon to build an altar to the Israelite deity on level ground on top of the stronghold (Judg 6:26). Gideon was to take the bull and offer it as a burnt offering, using the wood of the Asherah that he had cut down (Judg 6:26). Gideon's response was mixed; he carried out the action with the help of ten of his servants but was afraid to do it by day, "because of his father's household," and the people of the town (Judg 6:27).

This verse reemphasizes many aspects of Gideon and his family that were noted previously. Gideon had ten servants available. The term used to refer to Gideon's helpers is "servant" ʿ-b-d.[9] It is the same term used of the Israelites when they were slaves in Egypt. The term can also be applied to worshipers of the deity, especially in the sense of levitical singers, and sometimes in polite address of a person's equals or superiors.[10] The term is used in the verbal form in Judges to refer to what Israel did to some of the foreign countries which it "served" (Judg 3:8, 14). It is difficult to deny the implication that Gideon employed either servants or had slaves, nullifying the idea that his family was overly weak. It may also be another play on the Moses motif since Moses freed the Israelites from slavery in Egypt so they could serve (same root) their deity. This is contrasted with Gideon, who had servants of his own, whom he is only now using in the service of the deity.

Gideon's fear of the reaction of his father's household highlights his family's role in the episode since they are, with their Baal altar in their home as well as an Asherah, apparently doing exactly what Israel was forbidden to do. On the larger level the townspeople were exerting an influence on Gideon's actions. The ethnic and religious origin of the townspeople is never identified so the reader does not know if they were all Israelites who were not worshiping only their deity or whether they were Amorites with whom the Israelites were dwelling. Neither is a legitimate stance for the Israelites (Judg 3:5-7). Gideon's father has a Yahwistic name but he also made use of the religious artifacts of the Amorites. Gideon's fear of reprisals from both groups indicates their positive feelings toward these symbols of the Canaanites.

Gideon's response of fear to both the village and his family is a comment on his leadership. He was carrying out these actions because the deity had recently commanded him to do so. Like Baraq in the previous story, he carried out the actions only under duress. The saviors of Israel no longer acted out of any sense of commitment to Israel or their deity but had to be recruited. Baraq was recruited by a contemporary woman. The situation in this chapter has deteriorated to the point that now the deity had to oversee recruitment.

The following verse shows that Gideon's fears were legitimate since in the morning the townspeople's response to finding the altar and the Asherah torn down and a new altar erected with an offering upon it (Judg 6:28) was to seek the perpetrator of the act. They were led to Gideon, the son of Joash (Judg 6:29). They reacted by commanding Joash to bring out his son and kill him for his actions (Judg 6:30). The text is still not specific about the ethnic and religious identity of the townspeople nor whether Israelites were involved in the decision to kill

---

[9] *BDB*, 713.
[10] Ibid., 714.

Gideon. It would be helpful here because it would indicate if the text is describing more practices of the Amorites or if it reveals how far removed from the worship of the Israelite deity the Israelites had moved.

At this point in Judges fathers do not kill their children (Judg 11:39), or at least their sons, and Joash refused (Judg 6:31). Instead Joash asked, somewhat rhetorically, if it would be better to contend for Baal, asking the townspeople if the people must vindicate him, presumably referring to Baal. He stated that whoever fought his (Baal's) battles would be dead by morning (Judg 6:31). He finished by noting that if Baal was a god he could fight his own battles. Joash not only defended and saved his son but made a theological statement concerning the power of the Israelite deity. Joash did not go so far as to state that Baal was a non-god but questioned his power. He distanced himself from Baal's altar noting that it was Baal's altar (Judg 6:31) although when the deity gave Gideon his instructions it was said to be "his father's altar" (Judg 6:25). Gideon never made an impassioned plea for the Israelite deity to the townspeople, but his father Joash questioned Baal's power in front of his neighbors.

Following the destruction of Baal's altar Gideon's name was changed. According to the text they named him Jerubbaal, explaining the meaning of the name as, "Let Baal contend with him since he tore down his altar" (Judg 6:32, JPS). Most discussions of the text center around redactional problems without addressing the final form of the text, thereby missing the irony that Gideon did not really contend with Baal but his father did.

Mustering the Troops: Judges 6:33-40

The story returns to Israel's crisis with Midian, Amalek, and the sons of Kedem who joined forces and were encamped in the Jezreel valley (Judg 6:33). The spirit of the deity descended upon Gideon and the following statement claims that the Abiezrites rallied behind him (Judg 6:34). Gideon/Jerubbaal sent messengers throughout Manasseh, which also rallied behind him (Judg 6:35). He sent messengers throughout Asher, Zebulun, and Naphtali and they too came up to meet him. Here again not all of Israel was summoned, but only specific tribes. As noted earlier, this had been the case since the first battle in Judges (Judg 1:3) but only in the Song of Deborah was it considered a problem (Judg 5:15-18). In this case the men of Ephraim will take umbrage at not receiving an invitation (Judg 8:1).

Gideon's conviction waned after he rallied the troops and he tested the deity again. Gideon needed proof that the deity intended to deliver

Israel through him (Judg 6:36), and he even chose the experiment. He informed the deity that he was placing a fleece on the threshing floor and that if dew fell only on the fleece while the ground remained dry he would be convinced (Judg 6:37). Note that when Gideon was first introduced he was threshing in a wine press, now he was fleecing on the threshing floor. Gideon did nothing in the appropriate place.

The next day Gideon checked and the experiment was a success (Judg 6:38) but for some reason it was not enough. He asked the deity not to be angry but said that he wanted one more test (Judg 6:39). Gideon admitted that he was testing the deity, even using the same term used by the deity when explaining why Canaanites remained in the land after Joshua (Judg 3:1). The second test was the opposite of the first; the fleece would be dry while dew remained on the ground. On some levels the second test parallels the deity's test of the Israelites by leaving Canaanites around them and demanding that Israel remain free of their ways. The deity passed the second test to Gideon's satisfaction (Judg 6:40).

Preparing for Battle: Judges 7:1-14

One of the more famous scenes in the Gideon/Jerubbaal cycle concerns the preparation for battle with the Midianites. The text notes that Jerubbaal, that is Gideon, and all the troops arose early the next day (Judg 7:1). The Israelites were positioned at Ein Harod with the camp of the Midianites below in the plain when the deity informed Gideon that he had too many troops (Judg 7:2). The text is explicit about the deity's reasoning; with so many troops the Israelites could easily say that the reason for the victory was because of their numbers and not because of the deity. Clearly the deity did not trust the people to acknowledge the deity for the victory.

The reference to the large number is often viewed by scholars as a later addition inserted by the redactor. But the structure of the book, particularly the episodes involving Gideon/Jerubbaal, makes this theme primary and provides the framework for the episode. The story begins with the prophet telling Israel that they had not carried out their part of the covenant with their deity. The deity went through a series of tests establishing the deity's designated leader. This passage emphasizes the continuing mistrust between Israel and their deity. This is the only indication that the deity was not pleased with Gideon's tests.

The deity instructed Gideon/Jerubbaal to announce to the men that anyone who was fearful or timid could return, and twenty-two thousand turned back, leaving ten thousand behind (Judg 7:3). The number was still too great, so the deity suggested an experiment to decide who would join and who would not (Judg 7:4). The deity stated, "I will smelt them for you" (Judg 7:4). In the previous story the deity commanded through Deborah who in turn commanded Baraq. Here the deity was directly involved in the battle, actually choosing the soldiers. The level of leadership in Israel had declined to such an extent that the deity no longer trusts even the deity-designated leaders with military strategy.

The remaining troops were brought to the water and those who "lapped like dogs" were separated from "those who get down on their knees to drink" (Judg 7:5). Those who lapped were in the minority, a mere three hundred (Judg 7:6). The deity chose the three hundred, dismissing the rest (Judg 7:7). The three hundred lappers took the provisions and the shofars, trumpets made from ram's horns, from the others who were sent back (Judg 7:8).

There are many interpretations of the deity's method for choosing those who were to remain to fight. Mendenhall notes that, according to the census lists of Numbers 1 and 26, Manasseh's quota was precisely thirty-two clan units, totaling approximately three hundred men which would represent roughly a thirty percent levy of the able-bodied men.[11] Boling uses the Moab inscription, the mid ninth century inscription of Mesha, king of Moab, to show how three hundred would be a great fighting force since Mesha bragged about bringing an army of two hundred men.[12] He concludes that the test was one of alertness. In his view the men who lapped the water scooped up with their hands, instead of lying down.[13] As proof he cites Gaster who noted that the scoopers "show themselves more watchful and ready to meet any sudden emergency, such as an attack from the rear."[14] According to this theory the deity chose the smaller and more suitable group.

In light of the deity's previous statement about wanting to be responsible for the victory, it is no surprise that the smaller group was picked. It may be that the lappers were the less militarily able group, but the text does not state that explicitly. The text is clear that the deity will take responsibility for the victory that will occur. If the troops were separated based on military expertise then it would have taken away from the deity's role in the victory. The exercise was intended to be

[11] G. Mendenhall, "The Census Lists of Numbers 1 and 26," *JBL* 77 (1958) 61–4.

[12] Boling, *Judges*, 144.

[13] Ibid., 145–6.

[14] H. Gaster, *Myth, Legend, and Custom in the Old Testament* (New York: Harper, 1969) 420–2, 531.

non-militarily focused, something seemingly meaningless in order to serve its point of bestowing the entire victory on the deity.

There is little discussion concerning what happened to those who did not take part in the battle. To a large extent this is the result of translations of later passages, to be discussed below. But, in order to understand the later events, the movement of those who did not take part in the original battle is crucial. According to the text, the first group, consisting of twenty-two thousand, left because they were afraid. The text notes that they "turned back" *y-š-b* (Judg 7:3). Once they left ten thousand remained who were subjected to the lapping test. The deity informed Gideon that the three hundred lappers would fight and "all the nation they will go, each man to his place" (Judg 7:7). At that point they (presumably the three hundred lappers) took the provisions and the shofars of the others and "each man of Israel was sent to his tent" while the lappers stayed (Judg 7:8).

Most translations note that the first group was sent home as was the second, implying that neither played any other role in the battle and that there was no intention of using them in the battle. Yet the text defines two different destinations for each group and neither group is sent "home" *bayit*. The first group was sent each to "his place" (Judg 7:7). It is not clear precisely what the implication of the phrase is. This first group was composed of those who were too afraid to take part in the battle and were already defined as less brave than those that remained. Not sending them home, but to their place, allows the understanding that each individual was allowed to decide where he belonged, something that becomes problematic later in the story.

The second group was sent each to "their tent" *ʾōhālāyw* (Judg 7:8), not "home," despite some translations that convey this idea (JPS, RSV). The translation of this term as "home" implies that the Israelites were living in tents, a concept not borne out by the stories recounted thus far. By sending the rest of the group to their tents and not home leaves open the possibility that they were still under some type of military command but not taking part in the battle itself.[15] The use of tent is ironic since thus far it has only been used of the Kenites, and more particularly Jael (Judg 4:11, 18; 5:24). The only thing that had happened so far in a tent in Judges was the death of the previous enemy military leader. The implication is that the present Midianite enemy also lived in tents, but that point is never stated explicitly.

---

[15] Soggin notes that later, in the context of Gideon summoning the troops for the chase, logistically speaking, it seems "absurd" that he would send them home only to recall them. Reading "to his tent" as referring to their military tent, not home, avoids this problem later (*Judges*, 147-8).

According to the text, that same night the deity said to "him" (apparently Gideon) that it was time to attack the camp (presumably the Midianite camp) because he would deliver it (Judg 7:9). The deity told him that if he were afraid, to first go down to the camp with his attendant Purah (Judg 7:10). This was a preemptive test on the deity's part since Gideon tested the deity repeatedly. It also functions as a comment on Gideon. The deity used Gideon but was testing his courage. The troops may have respected Gideon but the reader knows that his courage was not what Deborah's was, and that he did not readily trust the deity. Gideon was even less enthusiastic about leading his troops to battle than Baraq had been.

Gideon was told to go down with his "attendant" *na῾ar* Purah. This is the first appearance of term "attendant," which appears a number of times later in the book. The term is difficult to translate precisely but is usually applied to a young man, often some kind of attendant.[16] In this case the major military commander took a person who was not even a soldier, possibly because he did not want his soldiers to see his fear evidenced in the next sentence, to follow the deity's command and investigate the enemy.

The deity instructed Gideon and his attendant to listen to what the Midianites were saying because that would give him the courage to attack the camp (Judg 7:11). The narrator portrays the camp in a way similar to the earlier descriptions; Midian, Amalek and Kedem were spread over the plain as thick as locusts and their camels were as numerous as the sands of the sea (Judg 7:12). This poetic description of a battle it is in keeping with the theological bent of this episode and Judges in general. In the previous story the enemy was superior militarily because of technology, which was not, however, superior to the Israelite deity. In this case, the enemy was more numerous than the Israelites, so the deity took steps to make the Israelite army even smaller in number to magnify the victory.

At this point Gideon overheard one enemy soldier narrating a dream to another (Judg 7:13). The dream entailed a commotion caused by a loaf of barley bread whirling around the Midianite camp. According to the dreamer, the loaf struck a tent, it (the tent) fell, turned upside down, and collapsed. The other man interpreted the dream as representing the sword of the Israelite Gideon, son of Joash (Judg 7:14). He continued that it was because *hā᾽ĕlōhîm* (not the deity's personal name) would deliver Midian and the camp into his hands. The meaning of the dream and the reference to the bread relate to Gideon's name and previous occupation. Gideon the hacker originally threshed

---

[16] *BDB*, 654–55.

wheat, hence the bread in the dream, and now the farmer was destroying their camp.

The use of a dream is powerful in this context. Israel's hero and leader doubted his deity's role in history since he had not seen it in his time (Judg 6:13). He demanded proof of the deity's power numerous times. The deity, knowing Gideon was still afraid, set up another incident to provide him with proof. Hearing from the enemy that they feared both Gideon and his deity and that the deity would be delivering them into his hand was a powerful statement of the power of Gideon's deity. The impact of overhearing the retelling of the dream is evident in Gideon's response. When he heard the dream, and more importantly its interpretation, he bowed, returned to the camp, and awakened the camp claiming the deity had delivered the Midianites (Judg 7:15).

The Battle: Judges 7:15-8:3

The text states that Gideon sprang into action when he heard the interpretation of the dream and "its breaking" *šibrô*, usually translated as "its interpretation" (JPS, KJV, RSV). The root means "to break" and this is the only context in the Hebrew Bible where the verb is used for the interpretation of dreams.[17] The use of this root forms another wordplay since, as a result of hearing the dream and "its breaking," Gideon made a commotion by breaking jars. The companion of the soldier broke the dream, possibly providing Gideon with the idea of how to attack.

Gideon's first command to the troops is the imperative of *q-w-m*, "Get up!" (Judg 7:15). This case illustrates how differently the term is translated depending on the gender and situation in which it appears. When Deborah informed Baraq to, "Get up!" Soggin translates, "Have courage," because she was over-zealous and not concerned enough with her troops.[18] Yet Soggin has no trouble translating the term as simply "Up!" in the context of Gideon rousing the troops because he overheard an enemy's dream. Despite differing translations, the imperative of this verb is legitimate since in both cases the deity guided the troops through an appointed ruler.

Boling has less trouble using the imperative with Deborah, translating "up" and noting that she used the phrase "this is the day . . ." to prod Baraq at last to victory.[19] His translation in the Gideon scenario is

---

[17] BDB, 991.
[18] Soggin, *Judges*, 73.
[19] Boling, *Judges*, 97.

consistent with that of Deborah's, "Up!" He also notes that, just as in the Deborah context, the imperative in the Gideon story is a signal preparing the audience for a description of intense fighting.[20] He offers no explanation why Gideon's plan is more inspired than Deborah's.[21]

This author understands this as another case of irony not within the text, but the text recounting the battles in the stories of both Deborah and Gideon stresses that the victories belong to the deity, yet modern scholars refuse to accept the text's interpretation of the incidents. In both contexts the narrator stresses that the deity accomplished these acts. Attacking an army with chariotry in the rain when that chariotry would be useless, even a liability, was no less an inspired plan than Gideon's rushing into the enemy army while making noise. Where the stories diverge is important. Deborah attributed the success to the deity whereas in the Gideon/Jerubbaal episode the deity had to orchestrate a scenario so that it would be difficult for Gideon to claim the victory for himself. This difference between the story of Deborah and Gideon emphasizes how the Israelites continued to slip downward in their relationship to their deity.

Gideon divided the men into three columns and equipped each with a ram's horn and an empty jar, with a torch in each jar (Judg 7:16). He commanded the troops to watch him and do what he did, instructing them to blow the horns and shout "For the deity and Gideon" (Judg 7:17). Gideon's plan was to cause the commotion revealed in the dream. Already the deity's fears were actualized; Gideon took partial responsibility for the victory even before it was accomplished.

The troops followed Gideon's orders, sounding the horns and smashing the jars they had with them while shouting for both the deity and Gideon (Judg 7:20). The troops arrived with Gideon at the outposts at the beginning of the middle march. Just after the sentries were posted they made the commotion (Judg 7:19). The event was timed so that one set of guards would have just gone off duty and would be tired while the second group would not yet have had time to accustom themselves to the darkness and noises. Gideon's troops struck at the time of transition when things were confused.

The noise and confusion achieved the desired outcome and the Israelites stood their ground while those in the enemy camp ran about yelling and took to flight (Judg 7:22). Even here the deity took extra precautions, turning every man's sword against his fellow throughout the camp (Judg 7:22). The result was that the entire host fled as far as Beth Shittah and on to Zerah, as far as the outskirts of Abel-meholah,

[20] Ibid.
[21] Ibid., 147.

near Tabatah.[22] As with many of the site names in Judges, very little is known about these locations.

The text notes that each man turned on his fellow (Judg 7:22). The term used for fellow is that used in a number of key places in Judges. In the dream just recounted, the first soldier related his dream to his companion (Judg 7:13). The picture drawn in that scenario was of two army buddies talking at night, one fellow helping another. Suddenly, only a few lines later, the same people, companions or fellows, turned their swords on each other. The use of the term in the earlier passage was clearly a means to introduce this term originally in a friendly form of camaraderie to highlight them turning on each other a few lines later. The term will be used later in the Samson story with similar results (Judg 14:20).

The next few lines concern the inevitable chase. At this point other tribes joined in the pursuit. The text states that "the men of Israel from Naphtali and from Asher and from all of Manasseh" were summoned (Judg 7:23). The Ephraimites were ordered to go down ahead of the Midianites and seize the crossings of the Jordan at Beth Barah, which they did (Judg 7:24), cutting off the Midianite retreat. "They," presumably the mustered troops, pursued the Midianties and captured their two army leaders, Oreb and Zeeb. Both were killed; Oreb at the rock of Oreb and Zeeb at the winepress of Zeeb. Proof was brought back to Gideon from the other side of the Jordan in the form of the heads of both (Judg 7:25).

The tribes did not rest, and the men of Ephraim immediately question, apparently Gideon/Jerubbaal, why they had not been invited to fight the Midianites, rebuking him severely (Judg 8:1). Gideon/Jerubbaal answered by appealing to the importance of each tribe's produce, "Why, Ephraim's gleanings are better than Abiezer's vintage" (Judg 8:2, JPS). Gideon/Jerubbaal reminded Ephraim that the deity delivered the Midianite generals Oreb and Zeeb into their hands, which he implied was more important than what he accomplished. Again the stress is on capturing enemy leaders. Gideon/Jerubbaal's speech caused their anger to abate (Judg 8:3).

Ephraim's questions raise issues concerning: the invitations offered to join the battle, in what capacity, the ramifications of the players involved, the actions surrounding them, carried out against them, and irony. The first issue concerns the immediate reaction after the rout of the camp when the troops were rallied (Judg 7:23). Boling follows the LXX in translating the verb "rallied" $ṣ$-$ʿ$-q (Judg 7:23).[23] In his under-

---

[22] None of these sites have been identified.

[23] Boling, *Judges*, 150.

standing of the verse, "the Masoretes were no longer alert to the contextual implications of ṣ-ʿ-q (to appeal in person, not merely 'to call') and treated the verb as passive."[24] Boling's understanding assumes that the troops referred to were the ones that had already taken part in the original battle. Another way to understand the verse is to follow the MT which translates the verb as a passive form of "summon."[25] According to this interpretation the summons would only be relevant for the troops that had already been sent "to their place" and needed to be recalled.

Understanding the verb as "summon" has much in its favor. It allows the MT to stand as it is. There is also support for it in the preceding episode with Deborah, earlier references in this episode, and a number of following episodes. The text does not state that those who responded to the initial call to arms were sent home but that they were sent to their tents. If one considers that to be a reference to their going home, little is left to relate the previous reference to this. Yet if the earlier reference to sending the troops to their tents (Judg 7:8) were understood to mean that the troops were retained but not employed in the present battle the summons makes sense. They were standing by awaiting this summons to move them into active duty.

The translation "summons" as opposed to "rally" fits well in the immediate context of this story but also ties into the larger themes of the book. The episodes surrounding this incident stress the role of summons as a means of describing the unity or lack thereof in Israel. The poetic version of Deborah lists those tribes which responded to the call to arms and those which did not (Judg 5:14-18). Many of the tribes that did not join Deborah were summoned and appeared for Gideon/ Jerubbaal's battle (Asher, Zebulun and Naphtali; Judg 5:17-18). As noted above, the Deborah passage was the first reprimand for some tribes not helping all other tribes, though the practice began in the book's first battle (Judg 1:3). It is in keeping with the irony of the book that these tribes would readily arrive to help when the incident impacted them but not the rest of the tribes.

Considering later events in the Gideon story, and later in Judges, the role of the different tribes in capturing foreign leaders, and possibly the glory and booty which would come with them, becomes important (Judg 12:1-7). Ephraim would be upset that it was not invited to the battle (Judg 8:1). In later stories the invitation to the battle was almost as important as whether the battle ended in victory. By the end of the book the response to a summons to fight is the difference between life

[24] Ibid., 151.
[25] *BDB*, 858.

and death of a clan (Judg 21:5-14). In this case there would be no need
to rally the troops since, in all stories up to this point, it has been standard operating procedure to chase the enemy rulers after the battle
until they were captured. The idea of "summons" here refers to the lack
of unity in Israel, which emphasizes the ongoing downward spiral.

The sentences surrounding the end of the battle and the chase of
Oreb and Zeeb play with a number of ideas. They underline the importance in Judges of capturing the enemy leader. In this case Gideon, in
trying to pacify the Ephraimites, depicts the capture of the enemy
leader as more important than routing the camp. Gideon's political tac-
tic would not work if there were not some preexisting notion that capturing the enemy leaders was significant. The episode emphasizes not
only the breakdown of unity but the awareness of it.

Gideon's pacification of the Ephraimites reestablishes problems in
Gideon's character and the upside-down nature of situations in this
story. When Gideon was first introduced he was threshing wheat in a
wine press, according to the text, because of the Midianite threat (Judg
6:11). This is often interpreted to mean that he is unable to thresh the
wheat out in the open where it should be done. In his speech with
Ephraim he notes how their wheat is better than Abiezerite wine. Yet
the text makes no reference to the Abiezrites' wine and the winepress is
only mentioned in terms of threshing wheat. If this reference means
that the Abiezrites were known for wine, then the wine press reference
means that they were reduced to raising wheat. In either case, both references reinforce the unusual nature of the period.

The names and deaths of the rulers also play into the idea that
things in this story are out of place. Each was killed on an element
named after them. It is not clear from the text if their deaths at these
spots were what created the name or if it is an ironic twist that they
were killed there. It should be noted that Zeeb was killed on a wine
press. Again, throughout the Gideon story actions not related to the
making of wine were carried out at a wine press.

Both Oreb and Zeeb are referred to as Midian's *śārîm*, often translated in this context as: "commanders," "generals" (JPS), or "princes"
(KJV and RSV).[26] All of the translation texts have trouble with this
noun. Not only do the translations disagree with each other but they
are not internally consistent. For example, KJV translates "prince" in
this context, but when referring to Sisera (Judg 4:2), who bore the same
title, they translate "captain." So too the JPS translates "general" in this
context whereas Sisera's status was that of an "army commander." In
Sisera's context the noun is in construct with the following noun "army"

---

[26] For the translation "commanders," Boling, *Judges*, 150.

and thus an attempt is made to translate the term into something understandable in English. The problem is that in the present case the term stands alone, the individuals concerned were captured by soldiers in a battle, and they are in the parallel position to Sisera, therefore also in a parallel position in the hierarchy of the military in the story. The translation "prince" implies a relationship with the individuals captured later in the chapter who are called "kings," something the text does not emphasize.

What is important about the translation of *śar* is not simply the issue of consistency but addresses meaning. The book of Judges examines different forms of leadership. This is stated outright in the first sentence and every episode considered thus far examines various aspects of leadership both inside and outside Israel. If the narrator uses the same term in different places it is important to understand how that term functions. Using different English options in translation of the same word masks the repeated appearance of this particular type of leader in the text, which bars the reader from evaluating their roles.

In this context the importance of seeing these *śārîm* in a position parallel to Sisera's relates to the actions carried out against them and the effect that had on Israel. According to the prose version of the Deborah narrative, the day Sisera was killed was the day that the deity subdued King Jabin of Hazor (Judg 4:23). The text stresses that while killing Sisera was important, especially because of his military role, it was not the ultimate goal. King Jabin, despite his absence in the story, was the goal. It is only in the following sentence, as a result of the death of Sisera, that Israel bore down harder on King Jabin until they destroyed him (Judg 4:24). The same is true in this case. While the capture of Oreb and Zeeb was important in terms of winning the battle, it did not declare its end. Instead, much text is dedicated to capturing the real power, Zebah and Zalmuna.

The Leaders of Amalek: Judges 8:4-21

Gideon was not satisfied with the capture of only Oreb and Zeeb so he crossed the Jordan in pursuit with his three hundred troops (Judg 8:4). By the repetition of the number three hundred the text implies, without explicitly stating it, that the troops traveling with Gideon at this point were the same three hundred lappers mentioned above, which, assuming they had stayed with him the whole time, also explains their hungry and thirsty state. As a result of their hunger Gideon told the people of Succoth to give him some loaves of bread for the men who were following (Judg 8:5). He also informed the people of Succoth that they were pursuing Zebah and Zalmuna, the kings of Midian. The officials of Succoth questioned his ability to capture the Midianite kings, almost sarcastically, by asking, "Are Zebah and Zalmunna already in your hands that we should give bread to your troops?" (Judg 8:6, JPS) Gideon's response was to swear that when his deity delivered the leaders into his hands he would thresh their bodies upon desert thorns and briers (Judg 8:7). Gideon proceeded to the next town, Penuel, made the same request, and received a similar answer (Judg 8:8). Gideon threatened that he would tear down their tower (Judg 8:9).

Gideon did not bring provisions with him nor did he rest the troops before the pursuit. According to the text he had time to call up the other troops, even tribes not originally summoned, send them out on a mission, congratulate them on accomplishing their mission, all before pursuing the Midianite kings. The honor Gideon bestowed upon the Ephraimites, and that was heaped upon those who captured and killed the enemy ruler, combined with portrayals of Gideon thus far provide the reason. Gideon wanted to capture the leader with his troops. He had already claimed partial glory for the victory which his deity had arranged for him and others had already captured part of his goal. It was not winning the battle to save his people that interested Gideon but the glory of capturing the foreign leaders that drew him, possibly even at the expense of his troops. As will become more apparent, Gideon/Jerubbaal had something personal at stake and it was not just any enemy leader that interested him but these two in particular.

The names of the enemies are relevant. Zebah means, "sacrifice."[27] According to popular etymology, Zalmunna means, "shadow is withheld" in Hebrew.[28] According to Boling, the name means, "protection refused," but he says both Zalmunna and Zebah are distorted names.[29] He claims these names are narrative distortions which reflect early Yahwist sympathy for Zebah and Zalmunna.[30] In his view these are not the original names nor can the originals be recovered. Mendenhall uses other recensions which provide different readings to understand the names. He claims that the LXX and Vulgate have preserved the correct vocalization which is a composite with the divine name *Sade alm* and the verb *m-n-ʿ*, "Salm protects." He associates the name with a god at Taima, attested as early as the sixth century B.C.E. which survives well into the Roman period as far north as Palmyra and Transjordan.[31]

[27] *BDB*, 257–58.
[28] G. Mendenhall, "Zebah," *ABD*, 6.1055.
[29] Boling, *Judges*, 155.
[30] Ibid.
[31] Mendenhall, "Zebah," 1055.

The names are important if one desires to find out who these people were, in a historical reconstruction of the text, but as a literary device the names function well as they are. At this point their names indicate the tribulations Gideon faced. Gideon needed food, a form of protection. He pursued these kings so he could kill them, making them sacrifices. "Search for protection" is what Gideon sought, both immediately for his troops, protection from hunger, and protection from the threat that these two enemies were for Israel. Thus their names neatly fit the irony of the story.

Gideon's demand for food from Succoth and Penuel, the cities' responses, and his final threats reveal a great deal about Gideon and his role in leadership, more so than anything particular about the cities. Both cities are mentioned as important points in Jacob's return from Paddan Aram; wrestling with the angel messenger at Penuel (Gen 32:25-32), and building booths (hence the name "Succoth," which means "booths") at Succoth (Gen 33:17). According to the book of Joshua, Succoth was allotted to the tribe of Gad (Josh 13:27). Judges places both cities on the "other side of the Jordan," that is the eastern side, and provides no comment about their population's ethnic affiliations. Succoth is usually identified with Tell Deir 'Alla in the Jordan valley and Penuel with Tell edh-Dhahab esh-Sherqiyeh on the brook of Jabok.[32]

Neither Gideon nor the narrator provide any reason why the cities of Succoth and Penuel should provide food for Gideon. Gideon did say "please" in his initial request for food, but there was a threat in his explanation. By referring to Gideon's search for Zebah and Zalmunna in the body of the request, he implied an assumption, that he would capture the enemy leaders. Gideon also assumed that it was in the best interest of these cities to help him. Their responses indicate that the cities thought they were better served by waiting for the outcome of Gideon's pursuit before choosing sides between those who were apparently ruling the area (the Midianites) and this new upstart.

Gideon's reaction appears severe. He asked cities for food without having provided them with a reason other than that the Israelites would soon take control. When they refused he threatened them. These, then, were Gideon's first actions as a ruler, threatening cities. Boling notes that at this point the story shifts to Gideon in action without any participation by the deity, nor reference to the deity, except in Gideon's own words.[33] Boling implies that textually this is for the better.

---

[32] For Succoth, J. H. Seely, "Succoth," *ABD* 6.218, and Penuel, J. C. Slayton, "Penuel," *ABD* 5.223.

[33] Boling, *Judges*, 158.

The present interpretation views the lack of references to the deity and Gideon's acting on his own as a deliberate action on the part of the narrator to highlight the problems that arose when Israelite military leaders were given a free hand; they became like the other rulers, abandoned the deity's reason for enabling them, and forgot their deity. The text nowhere either condones or condemns Gideon's actions, though the following story of Gideon's son Abimelech may be his indictment.

The verses concerning Gideon's threatened punishment of Succoth and Penuel further tie this episode with later problems surrounding Abimelech. According to Soggin, the root *d-w-š* denotes the threshing of grain and explains Gideon's name in context. Gideon was planning to thresh the cities with something, the word which is used to describe it is used only here in the Bible. But it is reminiscent of the thorn references later used by Jotam to explain what would happen with Abimelech's rule (Judg 9:20). This is heightened by the reference to Penuel's punishment, and the destruction of a tower, the future source of Abimelech's death (Judg 9:52-53).

The story reverts back to the enemy leaders noting that Zebah and Zalmunna were at Karkor with their army of fifteen thousand, all that remained of the Kedemites who had once been one hundred twenty thousand (Judg 8:10). Gideon marched up the road of the tent dwellers and routed the camp that was off-guard (Judg 8:11). At that point Zebah and Zalmunna took flight, Gideon followed, captured the two kings, and threw the whole army into panic (Judg 8:12).

These sentences reinforce a number of previous issues. While some scholars see the number of Israelites who were said to have been picked as reflecting real historical numbers, such as those found in the Moab inscription, or similar to a fighting unit in a nearby community, according to the narrator the force Israel was fighting was one hundred twenty thousand. Regardless of whether this number is based on some historical reality or reflects an inflation of the historical number, the point of the text is that the enemy had a large fighting force and the Israelite troops were significantly smaller to emphasize that the victory belonged to the Israelite deity.

This unit implies either that the Kedemites and the Midianites were interchangeable or that the Midianites were in charge. Zebah and Zalmunna are repeatedly referred to as Midianites and here the text refers only to the Kedemites but includes Zebah and Zalmunna in that term. The text reminds the reader of the previous story by referring to tent dwellers. As mentioned earlier, the only tent dweller encountered prior to this episode was Jael. It is in keeping with this story that the tent was thrown into a panic since confusion and things being in the wrong place are repeated themes in this episode.

Gideon did not immediately destroy his enemies, instead the text relates that on his return from the battle at the Ascent of Heres (Judg 8:13) he captured a young man from the people of Succoth and interrogated him. Gideon had him draw up a list of the "commanders" *śārîm* and elders of Succoth numbering seventy-seven (Judg 8:14). With the list in his possession, Gideon came to the people of Succoth and showed off the captured Zebah and Zalmunna about whom the people had mocked him previously (Judg 8:15). Gideon took the elders and punished them with the briars as he had earlier threatened them (Judg 8:16). He went to Penuel, destroyed its tower, and killed its townspeople (Judg 8:17).

After the capture of Zebah and Zalmunna, while Gideon was on his way to take his revenge on the cities of Succoth and Penuel, he is introduced again as Gideon, son of Joash (Judg 8:14). This may be because he was beginning to take revenge on a series of issues rooted in his lineage. Tying him to his family, especially his father who had been so important earlier in the story, recalls these issues to the reader's attention just as Gideon's family is about to resurface as an issue in the narrative.

The titles in this unit are significant. The young man whom Gideon captured is called a *na'ar*, the same term that was used of Purah who accompanied Gideon to listen to the dreams of the Midianites (Judg 7:10) and will be seen later in the rape story as an important person. The town of Succoth had both *śārîm* and "elders." The appropriate translation for the word *śārîm* and an understanding of their role has been problematic in a number of places in the book. The term is sometimes translated as "officials" (JPS, RSV) and sometimes as "princes" (KJV). In this case, the idea that these people were second-in-command in status is buttressed by the presence of the elders as a significant component necessary for Gideon's revenge. When Gideon destroyed the cities it was the elders who were killed.

These verses reveal a side of Gideon not yet emphasized; that of a thin-skinned ruler seeking revenge. The towns of Succoth and Penuel did not give him food, so he destroyed them. One may argue that the action was carried out because they placed Gideon and his troops at risk, or that the deity commanded him to take such an action, or that it was somehow related to the task at hand. Gideon said that his main reason was that they mocked him (Judg 8:15). Gideon used the power granted him by the deity to unburden his people and to take revenge for a personal affront. This unit is the precursor to what Gideon is about to admit, namely that he had used the Israelite army to achieve personal revenge.

After destroying the cities that mocked him, Gideon attended to the kings of Midian, Zebah and Zalmunna by questioning them. He asked them what the men that they killed at Tabor were like (Judg 8:18). They replied, "They looked just like you. Like sons of a king." Gideon declared that those men were his brothers, sons of his mother (Judg 8:19). He swore by his deity that if they had spared his brothers he would not kill them now.

This is Gideon's explanation for fighting these people, personal revenge to avenge his brothers. A question that must be asked of the text concerns whether the reader believes that the deity chose Gideon because of this or despite it? Gideon was the first judge motivated by personal reasons. Prior to Gideon the leaders of Israel responded to the Israelites' circumstances. None of the previous judges received personal gain, either money or revenge. Gideon represents a paradigm shift where personal revenge becomes the prime motivation for the subsequent leaders. The text does not explicitly condemn or condone this reasoning, but it indicates a lack of motivation on the part of Israel's rulers for the glory of their deity and the relief of the Israelites' misery.

These verses explicitly introduce the concept of kingship within Israel. Gideon asked the Midianite kings about those they killed. The captured kings respond that they looked like Gideon, sons of a king. Their statements are ironic on a number of levels and the motivation behind their speech and its meaning could be interpreted a number of different ways. The kings could have said anything since they knew their death was imminent and so they were mocking Gideon. Or, stating that he was like a king could have been an effort to sweet talk Gideon into sparing their lives.

Another option is that the kings were speaking the truth, at least in terms of the story line of the text. In their minds those that they killed looked like Gideon and looked like "sons of kings." The implication of this could be that they were dressed like kings, or carried themselves regally, or had the accouterments of kings, indicating that there was already some hierarchical ordering in Israel. This would also assume that Gideon was somehow dressed or looked different from his troops.

Another option is that the brothers were literally the sons of kings killed at Tabor, but that they were Canaanites. Gideon called them the sons of his mother, not his father. Since prior to this episode the Israelites were accused of doing "the bad thing," which was intermarriage leading to worshiping other gods, the text could be hinting that Joash had married a Canaanite princess. Gideon's mother being a Canaanite would explain the presence of the statue of Baal and the Asherah. Gideon might have looked, not like the son of a king, but the son of a queen.

Further evidence for the Canaanite ancestry of Gideon's mother may be seen in the relationship of Gideon to his brothers and the place of their death. He referred to them as his brothers, sons of his mother, who died at Tabor. The previous battle took place at Tabor where the enemy was the Canaanite, the Midianites were their saviors, and Gideon's tribe was not listed as having participated (Judg 5:14-18). In order for his brothers to have been active in that battle they would either have been part of another tribe, or been on the other side. The side that lost, and was more likely to have been killed, were the Canaanites.

His mother's origins have ramifications beyond this particular interpretation. Gideon claimed that they were the sons of his mother, not his father. This is a powerful statement from someone who was recently referred to as the son of Joash and whose father earlier saved his life (Judg 8:13). In the next story, the role of a different mother was the motivating factor behind Abimelech's actions of claiming kingship. The role of the mother as separating brothers is raised already with Gideon's parentage. The idea of parentage and the question of to whom one belongs continues to be a major theme from this episode through the end of the book.

The story continues on the family theme with Gideon commanding his oldest son Jether to "Go kill them" (Judg 8:20). The boy, who is called a *na'ar*, did not draw his sword because he was timid, still being a *na'ar* usually translated here as "boy" (Judg 8:20, JPS, "youth," RSV). Zebah and Zalmunna taunted Gideon, saying that he should slay them, for strength comes with manhood (Judg 8:21). Gideon killed Zebah and Zalmunna and also took the crescents that were on the necks of the camels.

The role of Gideon's son is crucial for this story, the theme of kingship, especially inherited kingship, and the following story of Abimelech. Jether, Gideon's oldest son, was with him in battle. This is not unusual since this would be where soldiers were trained, and his father was the military leader. Jether and Purah (Judg 7:10) are both referred to as *na'ar*. If the term simply refers to their age, namely that they were young, why did Gideon take another *na'ar* to listen to the Midianites' dream when his son was with him? It is not clear why he would take a young boy with him to listen to the dreams of the Midianites rather than one who could actually help him in some capacity. The reason could only be that, as mentioned earlier, Gideon was afraid and did not want his troops, or especially his son, to see his fear. It is fitting that here his son was too timid to kill the enemy leaders.

The role of the oldest son is important concerning kingship and inheritance. In Israel there are a number of cases where the eldest son does not inherit the kingship. David took the kingship though not the oldest even in his own family. Gideon claimed earlier in the text to be the youngest from an insignificant family, which raised the question of family placement and leadership early in the story (Judg 6:15). What was not included at that time was that Gideon's brothers had been killed, though whether all of his older brothers were dead is not stated. What this text states clearly is that Gideon's eldest son was timid and too afraid to kill the enemy rulers, the act considered the most important in winning a battle. The boy's rejection of the opportunity to kill already captured enemy rulers makes a statement about his capacity for military leadership, an issue that will be raised in the Abimelech story.

Zebah and Zalmunna either legitimate the son's refusal to kill them or taunt Gideon through his son by stating that "strength comes with manhood" (Judg 8:21). Since the text referred to him as a *na‘ar*, it is not necessarily true that this was an act that a *na‘ar* should have accomplished. Yet a jab at Gideon is embedded in their statement since Gideon's eldest son was not man enough to carry out their execution and, as a result, Gideon had to kill them.

After killing the enemy leaders Gideon took the crescents that were on the necks of their camels. In other words he took booty. This action has parallels with Achan's actions in Joshua 7–8. There Achan, son of Carmi, took proscribed objects (Josh 7:1). In the following verses Joshua sent a small number of men to take the city of Ai, since it was a small town (Josh 7:2-4). The Israelites were defeated (Josh 7:5), as they learned a few verses later, because Achan's action so angered the deity (Josh 7:10-26). In Joshua, Achan, a Judite, committed the offense. In Gideon/Jerubbaal's case a leader of Israel committed the crime.

Gideon/Jerubbaal's actions follow the account in Deborah where Sisera's Canaanite mother thought Sisera was collecting booty while she awaited his return (Judg 6:30). The parallel is even stronger since one of the items mentioned in Sisera's mother's list was embroidered cloth round every neck as spoil (Judg 6:30). While she was referring to what they would have around their necks, booty from the necks of captured items appears prominently in both stories. Gideon, whether actually the son of a Canaanite, possibly royal woman, or not, was acting precisely as Sisera's mother wanted Sisera to act, as a Canaanite warrior, and how the Israelite deity did not want him to behave.

Gideon's Dynasty: Judges 8:22-27

The men of Israel reacted to the victory by asking Gideon, his son, and his grandson to rule over them (Judg 8:22). Their reason was Gideon's saving Israel from the Midianites. This is the first outright request in Judges for a judge to become a dynastic ruler. The Israelites were forthright about their request and its continuation. They felt that their request was legitimate because Gideon had saved them from the Midianites, a situation the deity took careful precautions to prevent from happening. Gideon provided the correct answer by stating that the deity alone should rule over them (Judg 8:23).

Gideon provided the correct answer but then requested from them the earrings they received as booty (Judg 8:24). The text explains, almost as an aside, that they (presumably the Midianites) had golden earrings because they were Ishmaelites (Judg 8:24).[34] The people agreed and spread a cloth onto which everyone could throw the earring they had received as booty (Judg 8:25). The text details the weight of the golden earrings noting that, in addition, there were pendants, purple robes worn by the kings of Midian, and collars from the necks of the Midianites' camels (Judg 8:26). Gideon made an *ʾēpôd* of this gold and set it up in his own town of Ophrah and his household. Israel prostituted after the *ʾēpôd* and it became a snare to Gideon and his household (Judg 8:27). This case shows that though Gideon refused dynastic kingship he was not opposed to receiving extra payment or the trappings of kingship. The final result of the booty was so unacceptable that even the text condemns it by stating that it became a snare to Gideon and his household (Judg 8:27).

This episode is the first time a hero was asked to take on a role beyond that of military leader. In the previous chapter Deborah, a prophet who served as judge prior to battle, was forced to take on a military role and in the next situation the people asked to combine the political and military. While Gideon rejected the title of king, he accepted the payment that would be due the Canaanite military leader evidenced by Sisera's mother. The narrator manifests his condemnation by not naming Gideon/Jerubbaal a judge. The hero acquired titles and position not granted by the deity while the people requested he take even more power.

Summation of Gideon/Jerubbaal: Judges 8:28-35

The episode finishes with a conclusion of the end of Gideon's rule. It notes that Midian submitted to the children of Israel and did not raise its head again (Judg 8:28). The text includes the standard notation in Judges that the land was quiet for forty years in Gideon's time (Judg

[34] Midian appears as a half-brother of Ishmael (both children of Abraham by different mothers) in Gen 25:1-6.

8:28). Only after the land reference does the text add that Jerubbaal returned to his house (Judg 8:29). This is usually interpreted as relating to
what follows with Abimelech, who returned to the house of his
mother.[35] But the verse does not say that Jerubbaal returned to his father's house but to his house *bêtô*. The contrast is ironic since in this
verse the hero is again referred to as both Jerubbaal and the son of
Joash.

The following lines summarize Gideon's later activities and tie the
Gideon story neatly to the next episode by stating that he had seventy
sons of his own issue (literally who came out of his body), because he
had many women/wives (Judg 8:30). This verse has ramifications for
the following story. The number seventy was the number of people
who had gone down to Egypt with Joseph (Gen 46:27), and it is enough
to begin a nation. Boling sees a political aspect to the number since it
was also the number of kings who had once shared Adoni Bezeq's table
and were mutilated by him (Judg 1:7). Ahab was also credited with
having seventy sons (2 Kgs 10:1-7).[36] Thus Gideon generated a significant number of descendants.

The stated reason for having so many children is that he had many
wives. The precise status of these females is complicated because of the
woman/wife translation problem. Its precise meaning would be helpful because in the next line the text notes that Gideon also had a son by
a *pîlegeš* in Shechem, whom he named Abimelech (Judg 8:30). In this
instance there is a differentiation between a *pîlegeš* and an *ʾiššâ*.

The term *pîlegeš* is usually translated as "concubine" (JPS, KJV,
RSV). That translation has caused many scholars trouble. According to
Soggin it does not really refer to a concubine but rather to a secondary
wife.[37] Bal suggests the term refers to a wife from a patrilocal (therefore
matrilineal descent) as opposed to the traditional biblical state which is
virilocal (patrilineal descent).[38]

The English translation is troublesome because it has as loose a definition as our understanding of the Hebrew term. According to *The
American Heritage Dictionary of the English Language*, a concubine is, "A
woman who cohabits with a man without being married to him. In cer-

---

[35] Boling, *Judges*, 160.

[36] A. Malamat ("Origins of Statecraft in the Israelite Monarchy," *BA* 28 (1965) 34–
50) and Boling (*Judges*, 162) make the parallel with the seventy sons of Ahab that
they were all killed in a bloody coup carried out by Jehu. It is an even stronger parallel if Jehu was a disgruntled son of Omri. See Schneider, "Rethinking Jehu," *Biblica*
77 (1996) 100–7.

[37] Soggin, *Judges*, 159.

[38] Bal, *Death and Dissymmetry*, 176–7.

tain polygamous societies, a secondary wife, usually of inferior legal and social staus."[39] Since it is not clear what benefits the biblical status of woman/wife accorded in such areas as inheritance, legitimation of offspring, and inheritance of offspring, it is even more difficult to determine what they would be for others.

There are few references to this status in the biblical text and only two in Judges, though all share some common characteristics. A *pîlegeš* is associated with a man who has sexual relations with the woman. Often she is provided for in some way by the man, though there are cases where that is not clear (here for example). In all of the cases except for the raped *pîlegeš* in Judges 19, the men with whom they are associated are married to other women who are named woman/wife. Kings have many of them (2 Sam 5:13; 16:21, 22; 19:6, 1 Kgs 11:3; Esth 2:14).

There are two major issues concerning *pîlegeš* regularly highlighted in the biblical stories: the status of their children *vis à vis* the children of the "wives," and what a *pîlegeš* of a ruler means politically (and often the two are related, especially when determining who inherits power).[40] In Genesis the text states explicitly that the children of Abraham's *pîlegeš* received gifts but were sent away (Gen 25:6). Sons sleeping with their father's *pîlegeš* became an issue when Reuben slept with Bilhah (Gen 35:22), when Abner slept with Saul's his *pîlegeš* (2 Sam 3:7), and when Absalom slept with David's *pîlgašîm* (2 Sam 16:21-22; 20:3).[41] Other references show them to be counted when numbering how large a king's harem was but shows that they were not of the same status as women/wives since they are listed after women/wives (2 Sam 19:6, 1 Kgs 11:3). Beyond that there is little data. None of the characteristics common to other biblical references to a concubine fit the definition of concubine in this text, raising the question of what the term really means. Since the translation "concubine" does not fit this context a transliteration of the term, rather than an inaccurate translation, will be used.

The question concerning Jerubbaal's *pîlegeš* in Shechem is this: If he already had a number of wives, and plenty of children as a result, what was the need or objective of having a *pîlegeš* in another town? Gideon/Jerubbaal's son by the Shechemite woman is named Abimelech mean-

---

[39] *The American Heritage Dictionary of the English Language* (New York: Houghton Mifflin, 1969) s.v. "concubine."

[40] Note the contrast between Gen 25:6, where the children of the *pîlegeš* of Abraham received gifts but were sent away and Gen 36:12 where the children of Essau's *pîlegeš* were not less important.

[41] The Reuben situation is noted in the text where no action is taken (Gen 35:22) but it is expressed negatively in the final blessing from Jacob (Gen 49:3).

ing, "my father is king" (Judg 8:31). According to Boling, "It is virtually impossible to exaggerate the narrative's sustained contempt for Abimelech."[42] The narrative does not show contempt for Abimelech here since the story is not about Abimelech yet, but is concluding its discussion of Gideon/Jerubbaal. The name may connote a sense of arrogance, though it is not clear who was arrogant. The text states that, "he placed his name" *wayyāśem ʾet šĕmô* which is not the usual formula for naming a child but is used in renaming circumstances (2 Kgs 17:34; Neh 9:7; Dan 1:7). Since the subject of the verb "placed" is not specified, the namer could have been Gideon, or Abimelech may originally have received another name and then chosen this name himself. The sentence is placed in a section dealing with Gideon/Jerubbaal, his women and children, his actions, and the transition to the following episode. The contempt or arrogance espoused by the name is intended for the one who named the child but it is not clear who that was. If Gideon/Jerubbaal named the child he would be the only man in Judges who names his child.

When Gideon died, at an old age, he is referred to as the son of Joash and was buried in the tomb of his father Joash (Judg 8:32). This time following the death of the leader the children of Israel did not do "the bad thing" but prostituted themselves after Baals and adopted Baal-berith as a god (Judg 8:33). This information is key to the following story because the god of Shechem was Baal-berith, highlighting the importance and prominence of that city.

Gideon's story does not end on a pleasant note. The children of Israel gave no thought to their deity who saved them from their enemies (Judg 8:34). According to the next line they did not even show loyalty to the house of Gideon/Jerubbaal in return for the good that he had done for Israel (Judg 8:35). There may be ironic justice in these concluding lines. Gideon went into the battle not believing in the deity, and later it was revealed that he fought for personal reasons. It appears that he reaped what he sowed; he showed no thanks to the deity and so too he did not receive thanks or respect from the people he helped. The text never calls Gideon/Jerubbaal a judge.

Previous chapters ended on less than happy notes, however this is the lowest thus far. The Israelites even strayed in the lifetime of the leader. The leader even helped lead the people astray. The leader laid the seeds in his lifetime for even more corruption to follow upon his death. The spiral has begun to plummet.

---

[42] Boling, *Judges*, 170.

Summary

Gideon/Jerubbaal's story reveals that the judges have strayed considerably from the model established by Othniel. The people of Israel also have strayed and their leader did not take the necessary steps to keep them on the path designated by the text. The story began with the people no longer crying out to their deity for help. The deity had to send a prophet and even that did not help reestablish the relationship between the Israelites and their deity. The deity handpicked a man who was so unbelieving that he tested the deity repeatedly. The deity took extra precautions to ensure that the leader did not claim the victory and yet that still happened. As the story progresses the reader learns that the leader went to battle for personal revenge.

The character of the leader has decreased considerably. The hero showed few signs of bravery. The hero fought for personal revenge. The leader's son was not brave enough to carry out the ultimate victorious gesture against the enemy leaders even when they were already captured. There are even hints questioning his Israelite background.

The episode ends with the leader leading the people astray. Gideon/Jerubbaal rejected the kingship they offered but it is not clear how vigorously the offer was rejected, especially in light of the following story. He did accept extra gifts for his victory, which, as was repeatedly stressed, was accomplished because of the Israelite deity. He went so far as to lead the people astray religiously by setting up an ʾēpôd which the text condemns so thoroughly that Gideon/Jerubbaal did not even receive the title judge. The object was considered so odious that in the hero's lifetime it became a snare to them. The final horror is that he left behind a situation which led Israel to the destructive episode of his son Abimelech.

Chapter 8

ABIMELECH

Judges 9:1-57

Abimelech continues Israel's degeneration. Abimelech took power, possibly from Gideon/Jerubbaal's sons, in what was a blatant attempt at kingship. Neither the deity nor any actions on behalf of the deity or the people of Israel are referred to in the context of this effort to gain control. There is little to recommend any of the players in this passage and Israel is described both as leaderless and as having no expertise at making correct choices about what a leader and leadership should be.

In the previous stories the deity was involved in the choice of the leader, though comments about how the leaders conducted themselves before, during, and after the battles are included. Here the aspects of leadership under discussion center on the issue of family ties, particularly which ties should contribute to choosing a leader. Following the previous leader, many of these issues are bound up in family relations in which the role of a woman, though again unnamed, is central to the matter.

Rise to Power: Judges 9:1-3

Abimelech is introduced in the previous chapter in the context of Gideon/Jerubbaal's final acts (Judg 8:31). He is introduced before his father's death thereby cementing the two stories together. When he is first mentioned key factors about his birth and status within Gideon's family are accentuated, namely that he was not one of the seventy sons of Gideon's women/wives (Judg 8:30), but the son of his *pîlegeš* from Shechem (Judg 8:31). The narrator comments that someone (either

Gideon/Jerubbaal or Abimelech himself) named him Abimelech, meaning, "my father is king." When Abimelech is introduced again in Judges 9, his relationship to Gideon and how he was different from the other sons already has been clarified (Judg 8:31).

The difference between Abimelech and his seventy half-brothers is crucial in Abimelech's first action as a main character. The text states that Abimelech, son of Jerubbaal, went to his mother's brothers in Shechem and spoke to them and the whole family of the house of "my father his mother" (Judg 9:1). In this verse Abimelech's relationship with Gideon/Jerubbaal is reinforced. At the same time, the role of his mother and her family is emphasized. The Hebrew is obscure, as indicated in the literal translation offered here, but the thrust seems to be that Abimelech is appealing to his mother's family, rather than his father's. As mentioned earlier, there may have been a similar situation with Gideon/Jerubbaal where he claimed to be brothers with people through his mother, not his father. Abimelech was not dealing with his own brothers but the brothers of his mother because his own brothers rejected him. In fact, he is about to kill all of them.

According to Judg 9:1, Abimelech went to them in Shechem. The implication of the use of this verb of motion is that he had been somewhere other than Shechem beforehand. This occurs repeatedly throughout the story. Abimelech never appears to live in Shechem but was connected to the city through lineage and used it as a power base.

The use of Shechem is relevant in light of events which occurred there in Genesis and would occur there in the future according to 1 Kings. Dinah, the daughter of Jacob, was raped by Shechem, son of Hamor, the Hivite (Gen 34:2). Shechem decided to marry Dinah, and Shechem's father asked for her as a wife for his son stating, "Intermarry with us: give your daughters to us and take our daughters for yourselves" (Gen 34:9, JPS). Jacob agreed but later, after all the men of Shechem were circumcised and in pain, Dinah's full brothers Simeon and Levi slew all the males and the rest of the sons plundered the town, saying that it was because their sister had been defiled (Gen 34:25-29). Jacob's response to Simeon and Levi was, "You have brought trouble on me making me odious among the inhabitants of the land"(Gen 34:30, JPS). In Judges the city of Shechem was involved again in a situation where the brothers of a woman who had sexual relations with a man (it is not clear whether the relationship was consensual or not) was involved with the man's family. This situation contains an ironic twist; the woman possibly defiled (Abimelech's mother) was not necessarily an Israelite and the probable defiler was an Israelite, even an Israelite leader. In the time of Judges, Hamor's request would have been considered an action leading to apostasy (Judg 3:5-6).

The ethnicity of the Shechemites is not discussed in the text. As noted above, there were Canaanites living there who wanted to intermarry with Jacob's children as early as Genesis. According to Joshua 24, just prior to his death, Joshua conducted a covenant ceremony at Shechem. During that ceremony the people forswore other gods. Since the status of towns in Judges is different from the situation in the book of Joshua, it is not clear who the people of Shechem were presumed to be in this account, and what their relationship was to Israel.

If the residents were Israelites then this is an internal battle of Israel, almost a precursor to the civil war which breaks out later. According to Boling, proof of this is that following Gideon/Jerubbaal's death the text does not state that the Israelites again did "the bad thing" in the eyes of the deity.[1] If they are not considered Israelites then Gideon/Jerubbaal may not have considered her a wife because she was not an Israelite. It would also mean that he was cohabiting and producing non-Israelite, possibly Canaanite, children. The status of Shechem is necessary to understanding the context, though the text does not provide this information.

Shechem played an important role for Israel in the period of Joshua. At the end of the book of Joshua, Joshua assembled all the tribes of Israel at Shechem (Josh 24:1). At that time he recounted the history of Israel and the role the deity had played in it, and made a covenant for the people which was recorded, and a great stone was set up at the foot of a sacred tree (Josh 24:2-28). Boling sees the connection between the Joshua passages and Abimelech as so strong as to claim, "The objective of Gideon and Abimelech had been to weld together a nation-state centered in Shechem, which was decisively situated in the north central hill country."[2] His statement implies that Abimelech and Gideon worked together and that Abimelech's actions were condoned by Gideon, an idea that is neither substantiated nor contradicted by the text.

Shechem continued to play an important role in Israel's later dynastic history as the place where Rehoboam went for all Israel to declare him king (1 Kgs 12:1). Jeroboam learned of the event (1 Kgs 12:2), returned from Egypt (1 Kgs 12:3), and demanded Rehoboam lighten the labor load which King Solomon had imposed upon Israel (1 Kgs 12:4). Rehoboam's elders recommended that Rehoboam comply with the people's request, noting that to grant their request would ensure their loyalty (1 Kgs 12:7). Rehoboam ignored their advice and responded in

---

[1] R. G. Boling, *Judges: Introduction, Translation and Commentary*, The Anchor Bible (Garden City: Doubleday, 1981) 170.

[2] Ibid., 184

the negative (1 Kgs 12:6-14), which caused the split between northern Israel and Judah. Shechem was the first place where Israel was united in the land (Joshua 24), the place where an Israelite first sought kingship, and the place where the United Monarchy collapsed. This is another reference in Judges with barely veiled allusions to the north/ south conflict. The story in 1 Kings is a fitting referent for Judges since it concerns an Israelite ruler who exerted power based on the actions of his father, ignored the needs of his people and advice of his counselors, and made decisions which led to the destruction of the United Monarchy. In 1 Kings, as here, the text stresses the negative evaluation of an Israelite ruler (1 Kgs 12:15).

The story continues with Abimelech saying that they should place a question in all the ears of the lords of Shechem asking which would be better, to be ruled by seventy men, all the sons of Jerubbaal, or be ruled by one man (Judg 9:2). He added that they should remember that he was their own flesh and blood. This verse both contains elements already raised in the transition to Abimelech and hints at elements from Gideon/Jerubbaal's reign that appeared differently earlier. The nature of the question implies that Shechem was already under some kind of control by the seventy sons of Jerubbaal. Abimelech used the same verb *m-š-l* that the Israelites used when asking Gideon to rule over them (Judg 8:22). While Gideon claimed that neither he nor his children wanted to rule, he did nonetheless take booty (Judg 8:23). The verse concerning Abimelech assumes that Gideon/Jerubbaal's sons were ruling. If they were not, then Abimelech would not have needed to make the comparison but would simply have offered to rule them. This is another indication that Gideon/Jerubbaal, or his other children, began a dynasty and Abimelech was attempting to take that rule from them.

It is not clear how much prestige Abimelech had in Shechem. He did not go to the council himself to present his case but went to his family in Shechem and asked them to make the proposition to the council. He had to go to Shechem in the first place. It is possible that because of his mixed origin he did not have authority in either community, a situation not far removed from that of Jephthah which follows.

At this point Abimelech's mother's brothers carried his message to the lords of Shechem who were won over to Abimelech (Judg 9:3). Their reasoning was that they thought that, "he is our kinsman." This is the first example in Judges where lineage and clan loyalties influenced the community to such an extent that they chose their own leader. Thus far there were only hints at tribal loyalties breaking down in Deborah (Judg 5:16-18), and in the previous episode (Judg 8:1). The role of clan and tribal loyalties will grow to such an extent that it becomes a contributing factor to the civil war at the end of the book, and again in resolving what was almost the destruction of the tribe of Benjamin in the final episode (Judges 20-21).

Taking Power: Judges 9:4-7

Abimelech's family convinced the city elders to accept him as ruler since some unspecified "they" gave him seventy shekels from the Temple of Baal Berith, and Abimelech used these funds to hire "worthless and reckless fellows," who followed him (Judg 9:4). Abimelech went to his father's house in Ophrah and killed his seventy brothers, who are referred to as the "sons of Jerubbaal" (Judg 9:5). This is more evidence indicating that Gideon's children established a dynastic house. It is also a way to condemn what would eventually be the Northern Kingdom since seventy children were enough to begin a dynastic house in Israel, and were destroyed by Jehu (2 Kgs 10:1-17). The text describes the death as "seventy men on one stone." Jotham, the youngest son of Jerubbaal, survived because he went into hiding. Gideon/Jerubbaal's sons are called "men" *ʾîš*. While that could be a term used simply to identify them, it is not necessary in the text but highlights rather their age and, possibly, status. The last time a legitimate son of Gideon/Jerubbaal's appeared in the text it was his oldest, who was only a *naʿar*, young, timid, and too afraid to kill the captured enemy leaders (Judg 8:20).

Note that it is the youngest, not the oldest, who survived. In the previous story the oldest was depicted as timid (Judg 8:21), and now only the youngest remained. The first time the text introduced Gideon/Jerubbaal he too was hiding, working to protect the produce (Judg 6:11). Gideon/Jerubbaal also claimed to be the youngest in his father's household (Judg 6:15), and so the story has come full circle.

Only after the sons of Gideon/Jerubbaal had been killed does the text note that all the lords of Shechem and all Beth Millo convened and proclaimed Abimelech king at the terebinth of the pillar at Shechem (Judg 9:6). This supports the position that the sons of Gideon/Jerubbaal had had some political authority over Shechem. If not, they would not have waited until their deaths to make their proclamation.

Jotham, Gideon/Jerubbaal's youngest son, reappeared. The text states that when he was informed, presumably that Abimelech had become king over Shechem, he went to stand on top of Mt. Gerizim and called out to an undefined "them," "Lords of Shechem, listen to me, that Elohim may listen to you" (Judg 9:7). He did not use the Israelite deity's proper name but a generic one that could be used of the Israelite deity and also by other cultures (as did Ehud when speaking to Eglon [Judg 3:20] and as the dreamer's interpreter did [Judg 7:14]). He could be referring either to the Israelite deity, using a title for gods, or referring to Canaanite gods. This is not surprising since Gideon/Jerubbaal's later actions did not recognize the Israelite deity, indicating that, at least after the battle, he was not motivated by the Israelite deity. This has often been interpreted as the true historical story coming through the later theological framework imposed on the text, but the absence of theology at this point is part of the story and emphasizes that this is the theological low point in Israel's relationship to the deity. The Israelites no longer recognized their deity's preeminence.

Jotham proceeded to recount a fable about kingship, using different trees as examples (Judg 9:8-15). Lindars claims that the whole curse of Jotham welds together the story, which was made up of a variety of originally independent traditions that were added together, and creates a promise that is fulfilled at the end of the book.[3] The interest in this treatment is on how the final form works together, and this story does not tie it all together but follows the format that has been noted thus far. The book is in search of leadership, how leaders were chosen, who chose them, what happened to that role, what characteristics a leader should have, and where the areas for abuse of power were. Jotham's fable addresses the issue of how leaders are chosen and the abuses that can result from those choices.

Jotham's Fable: Judges 9:8-22

The fable recounts the search of the trees who want to find a king to anoint over them. Their first choice was the olive tree (Judg 9:8). The olive tree declined noting, "Have I, through whom God and men are honored, stopped yielding my rich oil, that I should go and wave above the trees" (Judg 9:9, JPS). The word translated as "God" in the preceding quotation is the same ambiguous term (Elohim) noted earlier. Next they turned to the fig tree who was not prepared to give up making sweet fruit, but made no reference to Elohim (Judg 9:10-11). Next they asked the grapevine to rule over them. The vine rejected them because it was not prepared to give up making wine which gladdens Elohim and men (Judg 9:12-13). Finally they asked the thorn bush (Judg 9:14). The thorn bush provided a mixed message, "If you are acting honorably in anointing me king over you, come and take shelter in my shade;

[3] B. Lindars, "Yotham's Fable—A New Form-Critical Analysis," *JTS* 24 (1973) 355–66.

but if not, may fire issue from the thorn bush and consume the cedars of Lebanon" (Judg 9:15, JPS).

At this point Jotham made the connection with his family. He noted that if "you" (presumably still speaking to the lords of Shechem) have acted honorably and loyally in making Abimelech king and done right by Jerubbaal and his house (Judg 9:16). This is a rhetorical statement and his position on the situation is made explicit with his following comments which reminded them that his father fought for them and saved them from the Midianites at the risk of his life (Judg 9:17). He stated that they had turned on his father's household, killed his sons, seventy men on one stone, and set up Abimelech, the son of his "hand-maid" *ʾāmâ*, as king over the citizens of Shechem just because he was related to them (Judg 9:18). He became rhetorical again by telling them that if they had acted honorably then they ought to have joy in Abimelech and he in them (Judg 9:19). He also reminded them that if they have not acted loyally that fire may issue from Abimelech and consume the citizens of Shechem and Beth Millo and fire may issue from the citizens of Shechem and Beth Millo and consume Abimelech (Judg 9:20). With that Jotham is said to have fled to Beer and stayed there because of his brother Abimelech (Judg 9:21).

The premise from which Jotham and most modern scholars work is that because Gideon/Jerubbaal was hand-picked by the deity, and Jotham's prophecy came true, Jotham and his family are the heroes of the story. But the previous story noted that Gideon did not immediately believe in the deity, claimed half of the victory before it occurred despite the deity's efforts to keep that from happening, was motivated by revenge for his brothers, accepted booty, and despite stating that he would not rule or create a dynasty may have done so, or his children did. All indications in this chapter are that the brothers exercised authority over Shechem although the text never states this categorically. Although Jotham's statements may be correct, there is an ironic sense that he was making them at all.

At the root of his fable is the issue of leadership and it is not clear what the view of kingship is. The fable uses kingship as the paradigm for rule. It is likely that kingship had already been established when the book was finally redacted, but, according to the information provided in the book, this form of leadership had not yet taken hold in Israel. The paradigm of kingship as an implementation of rule that would be picked is a commentary on kingship but whether Jotham used this paradigm because the sons of Gideon/Jerubbaal were practicing it, or because Abimelech was, is not clear.

The depiction of kingship is not favorable. The trees chose their rulers without discussion as to the characteristics of any particular tree.

All the trees who declined kingship depict ruling as "waving above the trees" (Judg 9:9, 11, 13). All the trees that rejected kingship did so because they felt that they were already doing something more important. Both the fig and the olive noted that their produce benefitted "God (Elohim in Hebrew) and men" (Judg 9:9, 13). It was only the thorn bush, that does not produce anything, that accepted kingship and even then only under certain conditions.

The conditions under which the thorn bush accepted are prophetic for this story since they foretell how Abimelech would die and have ramifications for leadership in Israel in general. The bramble claimed that a king can provide shade/protection if the subjects are honorable and loyal, but if not, will consume the people with fire. The implication is that the people who designate the ruler have as much responsibility as the ruler. Without the loyalty of the people, destruction by the leader is legitimate. Since the book of Judges is concerned with the search for leadership, one of the major issues about which Israel and its deity contend is whether the deity should be the supreme ruler. Already in the last story even the deity-designated ruler forgot that point. Jotham claimed that in his eyes his family was wronged, whereas according to the rules established by the deity, the deity was wronged by the hero, his family, and the Israelites.

Jotham stated in the transition from the fable to his description of his family's situation that when they (the people of Shechem) were deciding upon Abimelech, they should take into consideration whether they had dealt well with Jerubbaal and his household (Judg 9:16). Jotham used his father's military efforts on their behalf as the major issue to consider. This statement reinforces the notion that Gideon/ Jerubbaal, or at least his children, forgot or neglected the role the deity played in the battle. In the previous episode the deity chose the lappers specifically so that the Israelites would not be able to claim the victory over the Midianites themselves (Judg 7:2), yet this is precisely what the descendants of the deity designated leader did. Again the theology of the book is fundamental to the construction of the story and emphasizes the downward spiral of both the Israelites and the children of the rulers.

Ironically, Jotham ignored his own neglect of the deity and depicted the lords of Shechem as having turned on his father's household, killed his sons, and set up Abimelech. On some levels the lords of Shechem have not done that since they chose a son of Gideon/Jerubbaal. As a result Jotham had to separate his brothers and himself from Abimelech. He did this by referring to Abimelech as the son of "his handmaid" (Judg 9:18). Using *ʾāmâ* here was intended to denigrate Abimelech by degrading his mother and her status. By using this term he took away the legitimacy of Abimelech as a true son and heir to Gideon/Jerubbaal.

The term used here is as difficult to understand as other terms referring to the status of women because it is never defined. This case is more difficult because in the narrative Abimelech's mother is referred to as a *pîlegeš* (Judg 8:31), not an *ʾāmâ* (Judg 9:18). Jotham used the reference as a taunt to diminish Abimelech's legitimacy, so the term *ʾāmâ* must have been an insult, referring to some position with lower status than a *pîlegeš*.

Understanding the term *ʾamah* is problematic because the term is often translated into English using the rather ambiguous term "handmaid" (JPS). According to BDB the term means, "maid, handmaid," and is more servile than a *šipḥâ*.[4] It can also be used in address, referring to the speaker in a tone of humility.[5] In English "handmaid" means, "personal maid or female servant or attendant."[6] Dandamayev treats the term as interchangeable with "slave" and includes the term *naʿar* and its feminine form as younger versions in the classification "slave."[7] Bal translates Abimelech's mother's status as concubine, though also part of the matrilocal as opposed to the virilocal system.[8] The root of the problem is that while women of this status were slaves, they sometimes had a procreative function not found in male slaves (Exod 21:4). For example, Jacob's handmaid bore children when his wives could not (Gen 30:3).[9] Complicating this is that Jacob's sons from those unions were considered full brothers in terms of inheritance and the definition of Israel. This is in direct contrast to this case where Abimelech was separated and not allowed to inherit because of the status of his mother, which was claimed by his brother Jotham, who never recognized him as his equal.

Jotham disassociated himself from Abimelech because of the status of their different mothers. Since the text notes that Gideon/Jerubbaal had many wives, apparently explaining how he had so many children, the situation with Abimelech's mother must have been different. Despite Abimelech's treatment as illegitimate because of his mother, his mother's denigration by Gideon/Jerubbaal's son, and Jotham's granting extreme

---

[4] *BDB,* 51.

[5] Ibid.

[6] *Webster's Third New International Dictionary of the English Language, Unabridged* (Springfield, MA: G & C Meriam Co, 1968) s.v. "handmaid."

[7] M. Dandamayev, "Slavery (OT)," *ABD* 6. 63.

[8] M. Bal, *Death and Dissymmetry: The Politics of Coherence in the Book of Judges.* Chicago Studies in the History of Judaism (Chicago: University of Chicago Press, 1988) 133.

[9] Note that Bilhah and Zilpah both are named *ʾamah* (Gen 30:3; 31:33), and *šipḥāh* (Gen 30:4, 9, 10).

rights and privileges to his brothers because of something his father had been enabled to do through the help of the deity, Jotham is viewed with great sympathy by modern scholars. Most scholars claim that the narrative presents him as the only likely candidate for Judge in his day.[10] Even the fact that he escapes without changing the situation, thereby allowing Abimelech to rule over Israel for three years (Judg 9:22), gains him the sympathy of modern scholars.[11]

While it is clear Abimelech is not regarded sympathetically either by the text or its readers in any age, it is not clear that Jotham is viewed with sympathy in the text. Thus far no leader's children had inherited any type of leadership role from them. Gideon/Jerubbaal said that he did not want to rule, nor did he want his children to rule (Judg 8:23). Jotham should not be considered the correct person to bear any leadership role. Jotham carried out no positive action for the deity or leadership. The only reason he was alive at this point was that he hid while his brothers were killed (Judg 9:5). He did not stay to fight for leadership but ran and hid, just as his father, who was first introduced while hiding, had done (Judg 6:11). Only later the text revealed that his brothers were killed (Judg 8:19). Jotham never mentioned the Israelite deity's name and instead used the generic term Elohim. The text emphasizes the degenerated state of Israel, or at least its leadership, rather than anything positive about Jotham.

Abimelech ruled over Israel for three years after Jotham's departure (Judg 9:22). The term used, *wayyāśar*, from the root *ś-r-r* is not the form of leadership that Israel requested when asking Gideon/Jerubbaal to lead them, nor had it been used in any other situation in the text thus far. The word is the verbal form of a noun which appears repeatedly and which means "second in command" *śar*. The word is used infrequently in its verbal form in the Bible. When used it often appears in a context where someone acted like a prince, without necessarily being one, hence the translation "to be, or act as, prince."[12] According to Boling, the verb must mean something other than "to rule" because Abimelech had already been made king, so therefore it must mean that he saw active service on behalf of what Boling called the Yahweh confederation as a "field commander."[13] Regardless of its precise meaning, the

---

[10] Boling *Judges*, 172; J. K. Kuntz, "Jotham," *ABD* 3.1022.

[11] Boling, *Judges*, 172.

[12] *BDB*, 979. Other contexts where it is used: Isa 32:1; Prov 8:16; Num 16:13, and Hos 8:4, though not all are in the same verb group.

[13] Boling goes so far as to say that, "God had to put up with it for three years" (*Judges*, 175).

text questions the legitimacy of Abimelech's reign by the verbs chosen to describe it.

Abimelech's Fall: Judges 9:23-57

Abimelech's fall was divinely imposed. The text states that Elohim (the only name used for the deity in this story) sent a spirit of discord between Abimelech and the lords of Shechem who thereupon broke faith with Abimelech (Judg 9:23). The text explains that this was to end the crime committed against the seventy sons of Jerubbaal, to avenge them and to have their blood recoil upon their brother who had slain them, and the lords of Shechem who had allowed it to happen (Judg 9:24). Revenge has become a legitimate motivating factor and continues as a major cause for Israel's leaders throughout the rest of the book. The goal has changed, and is no longer obedience to the deity but revenge. In this case even the deity was involved.

The lords of Shechem planted ambushes on the hilltops, robbed whoever passed by them on the road, and Abimelech heard about it (Judg 9:25). Since Abimelech had to hear about it, the text implies that Abimelech was not in Shechem, although he was the ruler. Abimelech's absence from Shechem is reinforced and the problems with it are highlighted as the story continues to say that Gaal ben Eved and his brothers came passing through Shechem and the lords of Shechem gave him their confidence (Judg 9:26).

Gaal's name plays a role in the story since *g-ᶜ-l* means to abhor or loathe and his full name means, "loathsome son of a slave." It is an ironic twist since Abimelech, whose name means, "my father is king," was, according to his brother, the son of a slave. What Gaal ben Eved was doing in Shechem is not clear. According to Boling he was on the prowl, like the wild animal in 2 Kgs 14:9 (a story which he sees as coming from the same repository as did Jotham's), and Saul and his servants looking for the lost asses of Kish.[14] Soggin sees him as a Shechemite, which is supported a few lines later when Gaal ben Eved claims to be a Shechemite (Judg 9:28).[15] But in either case it is not clear why he decided to appear in Shechem at this time.

The scene changes suddenly and an unidentified "they" is said to go to the fields, gather and tread out the vintage of their vineyards,

---

[14] Ibid., 176–77.

[15] J. A. Soggin, *Judges: A Commentary,* Old Testament Library (Philadelphia: Westminster, 1981) 185.

make a festival, enter the temple of their god, eat, drink, and revile Abimelech (Judg 9:27). The name of the festival and who took part in it are not explained. It is a festival in which someone went to the field, festivities followed, and the local god was involved. There have been numerous references to grapes and wine, yet in each there is a twist. Gideon was first introduced beating wheat in a wine press (Judg 6:11). Zeeb, the Midianite general, was killed at the winepress of Zeeb (Judg 7:25). Gideon/Jerubbaal calmed Ephraim from their anger at not having been invited to the battle by reference to wine (Judg 8:2). Now a wine festival marked the beginning of the end for Abimelech. As with so many other references and themes in Judges, this appears at the end of the book as well, for the final rape and kidnap of the women of Shiloh would occur when they went out to the vineyards for what would appear to be a similar festival (Judg 21:20-22). As with other themes, the wine reference begins innocuously enough yet will turn into another crime committed by the Israelites on behalf of Benjamin.

Gaal ben Eved was involved with some aspect of the festivities because in the next line he questioned who Abimelech was and whether "we" Shechemites should serve him (Judg 9:28). He continued noting that "this son" of Jerubbaal and his lieutenant Zebul once served the men of Hamor, the father of Shechem, so why should we serve him. In this line Gaal ben Eved planted the seed of contention between Abimelech and Shechem. In the next line Gaal ben Eved continued, rather dramatically, "Oh, if only this people were under my command, I would get rid of Abimelech" (Judg 9:29, JPS). His not subtle comment challenged the fundamental issues concerning who should rule, under what conditions, and who is to make that decision.

Why Gaal ben Eved raised the question of leadership although his relationship to the city is never stated is not evident. He repeatedly uses the first person plural "we" including himself with the Shechemites. In terms of placing his opponent, he reemphasized Abimelech's relationship to Gideon/Jerubbaal to the exclusion of Abimelech's name. His reference to, "this son of Jerubbaal," is a means of denigrating Abimelech by not using his name but associating him with the name of the family which rejected him. Gaal ben Eved cannot insult Abimelech the way that Jotham did because it would also insult the Shechemites. He honored Jerubbaal by implying that he was a legitimate force but, "this son" was no match. Gaal ben Eved created more trouble for Abimelech by reminiscing about how Abimelech and his lieutenant *pĕqîdô* once served the men of Hamor. By naming Hamor and Shechem specifically as people, the text reminds the reader again of the story of Dinah's rape since both are named specifically in both stories.

Gaal ben Eved created the sought-after trouble because when Zebul, the second in command *śar* of the city, heard his words he was furious (Judg 9:30). In this context Zebul is referred to as the second in command of the city, whereas earlier he was called a lieutenant *pāqîd*. The two terms are not contradictory and the use of these two different terms must be intentional. Gaal ben Eved tried to insult both Abimelech and Zebul in his speech, hence the use of the term *pāqîd* rather than a more flattering term. While it is clear what Gaal ben Eved's intentions were concerning Abimelech, the reader does not know who Zebul was. To read later, in the words of the narrator, that Zebul's real title and position were governor of the city *śar-hā'îr* signals the reader what Gaal ben Eved attempted to do regarding Zebul.

Zebul took action by sending messages to Abimelech at Tormah informing him that Gaal Ben Eved and his brothers had come to Shechem and were inciting the city against Abimelech (Judg 9:31). He instructed Abimelech to set out at night with the forces with him and conceal himself in the field (Judg 9:32). The plan was that early the next morning Abimelech and his troops would descend on the city and they would, "do to him as your hand finds" (Judg 9:33). While the parallel is not precise, it is similar to the significant phrase which appears toward the end of the book that, "each man did what was right in his own eyes" (Judg 21:25). The concept is that determining what is the correct action to take is determined by each man as what is "right in their own eyes" as opposed to following the deity's instructions. Throughout all these events, Abimelech was not in the city.

Abimelech followed the plan laid by Zebul and all the men who were with him set out at night and disposed themselves against Shechem in four hiding places (Judg 9:34). Gaal ben Eved came out and stood at the entrance to the city gate, apparently when Abimelech and the army were emerging from concealment (Judg 9:35). Gaal ben Eved saw the army and said to Zebul that he saw an army marching down from the hilltops, but Zebul reassured him that he was just seeing shadows that looked like men (Judg 9:36). Gaal ben Eved spoke again, noting an army marching down from two different directions (Judg 9:37). Finally Zebul admitted it was an army but taunted Gaal by stating, "Where is your boast, 'Who is Abimelech that we should serve him?' There is the army you sneered at; now go out and fight it" (Judg 9:37, JPS).

From these few verses it appears that Gaal ben Eved acted on his boast, or was thinking of doing so and was interested in the city gate and on the lookout for attack. Similar to the situation in the previous story, the concept of boasting and then throwing it back into the taunter's face was important to the leaders, especially the military leaders Gideon/Jerubbaal, Zebul, and Gaal ben Eved. It reveals that

Abimelech gathered an army, though from where and peopled by whom is not clear.

Gaal ben Eved, at the head of the lords of Shechem, fought Abimelech (Judg 9:39). Zebul is not mentioned and apparently the lords of Shechem sided with Gaal ben Eved. The text states that an unidentified "he," presumably Gaal, fled and Abimelech pursued him, slaying many all the way to the entrance of the gate (Judg 9:40). Again, the capture of the leader of the enemy was essential. Apparently Abimelech did not succeed because the next line states that Abimelech stayed in Arumah while Zebul expelled Gaal ben Eved and his brothers and kept them out of Shechem (Judg 9:41). Again, Zebul was in Shechem and Abimelech was not, which in this case sets the stage for the next day.

The next day the people (*ʿam*) of Shechem were attacked. The text notes that Abimelech was informed when people went out to the fields (Judg 9:42). He took the army, divided it into three columns, laid an ambush when he saw the people coming out of the city, pounced on them, and struck them down (Judg 9:43). Abimelech took a position at the entrance of the city and the other columns took those that were in the open, striking them down (Judg 9:44). Abimelech fought against the city all day, captured it, massacred the people in it, razed the town, and sowed it with salt (Judg 9:45).

Abimelech's limited relationship with the town is apparent throughout the story, most obviously in his absence from the city. According to the text his main connection with the city, and how he gained control in the first place, was through family connection with it. The use of *ʿam* and the text reiterating that they destroyed the entire city and the inhabitants implies that he destroyed his family. This would not be the first time that Abimelech destroyed his family, yet it does reveal a pattern. It may be another commentary on the concept of leadership revealing the extent to which a leader will go to make his point, especially if he was ruling a city in which he did not live.

The lords of Shechem were not part of the general massacre because the next verse notes that when the lords of the tower of Shechem learned what happened they went into the tunnel of the Temple of Berith (Judg 9:46). This is the first time that the group is referred to as the lords of the tower of Shechem rather than the lords of Shechem. Since they learned of this because they had not experienced the massacre themselves, where they had been and what their role in the city was is unclear. There are a number of different types of leaders in this story but none of them protected the people of the city since they were all concerned with their own well-being. Their own personal well-being was what led them to make choices that led to the destruction of the city.

News travels quickly in the book of Judges and Abimelech was informed that all the lords of the tower of Shechem had gathered (Judg 9:47). Abimelech and all his troops with him went to Mt. Zalmon (Judg 9:48). Abimelech lopped off a tree limb, lifted it onto his shoulder, and had his troops do the same (Judg 9:49). His troops followed his lead, marched behind him, laid the branches against the tunnel, and set fire to the tunnel over their heads, thus all the people of the tower of Shechem perished, about a thousand men and women (Judg 9:49). So too came true the first half of Jotham's fable.

The distinction between those called the lords of Shechem and the lords of the tower of Shechem is problematic and continues to be so with their death. Up to this point they appeared as a ruling body that was involved in the decision to make Abimelech their king (Judg 9:6). After the people (ʿam) were killed, the phrase was applied to the lords of the tower of Shechem, apparently separating it from Shechem itself. The tower of Shechem may be another name for the Beth Millo mentioned earlier in the episode (Judg 9:6).[16] One might consider them the upper echelon of the city, "citizens" according to JPS. The text does not define them, but they are implicated initially by Jotham for condoning and trying to benefit from Abimelech's massacre of his brothers, and thus their death was foretold. They are another example of poor judgment in choosing leaders, being responsible for appointing Abimelech in the first place.

The troubling aspect of the text is that not only did the lords of the tower of Shechem perish but, "all the people of the tower, about a thousand men and women" (Judg 9:49). Prior to this verse the text referred to the lords of Shechem, a ruling body mentioned above. In this verse the text states that they were the "people" ʾanšê of the tower of Shechem. The text is more explicit in its separation of these people from the lords by stating that there were both men and women among those who died. In this case not only the leaders and soldiers suffered but unprotected people were massacred because of poor leadership. The inclusion of women as the difference indicates that a barometer for how poorly society was functioning was the status of women. Here the text says explicitly that they too were destroyed.

Once Shechem was destroyed Abimelech proceeded to Thebez where he encamped and which he occupied (Judg 9:50). There is no explanation concerning why or how this city was involved. The only parallel appears in the following verse which explains that there, too, was a fortified tower and all the men, women, and the lords of the city shut themselves in and went to the roof of the tower (Judg 9:51). In this

---

[16] Boling's suggestion (*Judges*, 180).

case the text lists all three categories, men, women, and lords, each connected with a *waw*. The text is explicit about the different categories of people present in the tower, indicating that each component is important in the story.

Abimelech pressed forward to the tower, attacked it, and approached the door of the tower to set it on fire (Judg 9:52). A woman dropped a millstone on Abimelech's head and cracked his skull (Judg 9:53). His first reaction is in keeping with the Jael story. He cried out to his young boy *na'ar*, his arms-bearer to draw out his dagger and finish him off so that they would not say a woman killed him. His *na'ar* stabbed him and he died (Judg 9:54).

Abimelech's death has parallels elsewhere in the Bible and is later referred to itself. It is ironic that the millstone which was the weapon that killed Abimelech is normally considered a means of livelihood. Deuteronomy 24:6 states that, "A handmill or an upper millstone shall not be taken in pawn, for that would be taking someone's life in pawn." Here the millstone did not provide livelihood either for its owner or Abimelech. While the circumstances are not identical, Saul too feared that he would become a source of sport for the Philistines when he was wounded at the battle of Gilboa and so asked his arms-bearer to kill him with his sword (1 Sam 31:4). This parallel is another in the David/ Saul polemic. Saul's fears and relating this episode to the David/Saul situation are grounded since Abimelech's death became a standard reference in warfare seen in the reference later in 2 Sam 11:18-21 where David orchestrates Uriah's death:

> "When you finish reporting to the king all about the battle, the king may get angry and say to you, 'Why did you come so close to the city to attack it? Didn't you know that they would shoot from the wall? Who struck down Abimelech son of Jerubbesheth? Was it not a woman who dropped an upper millstone on him from the wall at Thebez from which he died?'" (JPS).

This quote is another ironic touch since is shows that precisely what Abimelech most feared, that his death at the hand of a woman would be remembered, was the legacy he left.

As discussed earlier in the case of both Deborah and Jael, death at the hand of a woman was the worst end for a military man.[17] Yet here it is in keeping with the irony in Judges and the role women have played

---

[17] Modern scholars have as much trouble with this as Abimelech. Boling's only comment about the scene is that a woman could not have done this herself and that she must have had help (*Judges*, 182).

throughout the text as the barometer of Israelite society's religious state. In the last few massacres the text emphasizes that women died as a result of Abimelech's actions (Judg 9:49), something not noted thus far in Judges. It is fitting then that Abimelech was killed by a woman. It is another example in Judges where a woman did what was necessary because no man would. A final ironic note is that Abimelech was killed by his own *na'ar*, young boy, when in the previous story, Gideon/Jerubbaal's oldest son and Abimelech's half brother, could not even kill the captured enemy military leaders.

In the last few verses the story of Abimelech relates directly to the Israelites by noting that when the men of Israel saw that Abimelech was dead, every man went to his place (Judg 9:55). This comment appears out of context since no one of clearly defined Israelite origin or tribal affinity is mentioned throughout the story, nor are they ever rounded up to take part in any battle. It is a necessary statement to tie this episode into the larger context. It notes that every man went to his own place, not home, they did not organize, nor did they change or modify their behavior.

The episode concludes by noting that Elohim returned to Abimelech for the bad that he had done to his father by slaying his seventy brothers (Judg 9:56). The final note is that Elohim also repaid the men of Shechem for all their wickedness, thus fulfilling the curse of Jotham, son of Jerubbaal (Judg 9:57). The text reinforces notions expressed earlier that the sons of Jerubbaal were not the center of the story, nor even considered as having necessarily acted correctly. Elohim repaid Abimelech for the evil done to his father. The slaying of his brothers is considered an offense against Abimelech's father, Gideon/Jerubbaal, not the sons themselves.

Summary

Abimelech's coup is considered by most to be the first attempt at monarchy despite the fact that he follows in the footsteps of his father, or at least his brothers, rather than creates something completely new. Gideon/Jerubbaal laid the groundwork for the notion of kingship in the previous story by his interrogation of Zebah and Zalmunna (Judg 8:18), and continued with the Israelites asking him to rule over them, his many children, and his acceptance of booty. Gideon/Jerubbaal explicitly rejected the offer of kingship for himself and his descendants, but in the beginning of Judges 9 his sons were in control of the city of Shechem at least, which indicates that someone changed their mind and they accepted a governing position.

The pre-existing state of a member of Gideon/Jerubbaal's clan in a ruling capacity set the stage for the Abimelech material to investigate questions of leadership. In particular, the Abimelech story ponders the questions of who it is that decides upon a leader and whether blood ties and family dynasties are legitimate criteria for a leader. Within that context the question of which son, and of which kind of mother, is highlighted.

The Abimelech material investigates the role of a dynasty in more detail than had been the case thus far and contains the most critical evaluation of kingship yet encountered in Judges. Kingship is described as "waving over the heads" of others who are too busy producing useful materials to be bothered ruling. Jotham's only defense of his family as entitled to rule was based on his father's role in a previous battle. Ironically, the son claiming his father's heroism and self-sacrifice was countered in the chapters concerning his father which reveal that the deity almost forced his father to fight, ultimately it was an act of revenge, the sons at that time were not brave enough to carry out any of the actions of the campaign, and in the end their father benefitted financially from the encounter. The most ironic point of Jotham's comment is that Abimelech too was a son of Gideon/Jerubbaal, and according to Jotham's definition, had as legitimate a claim to rule as they did. The distinguishing characteristic was the role and status of the unnamed mother of Abimelech.

Kingship is criticized by the total lack of control and disinterest Abimelech portrayed in the city over which he was king. He was never in the city. Following roles seen previously in Judges, his second in command was the one who was involved in the day-to-day running of the city and ultimately its defense. A further insult to Abimelech, and quite probably to the idea of monarchy as well, was the utter disregard that Abimelech exhibited towards his constituents, leading to their, and ultimately his own, death. Abimelech's death at the hand of a woman is the ultimate commentary on Abimelech and possibly kingship, especially since Saul died in a similar way, and David caused a death for which this episode provided the paradigm.

The role of the judge has changed significantly from the model set by Othniel. Abimelech was not legitimate either in the words of the narrator or Jotham. He did not rise to be a hero as a response to a crisis in Israel but caused the crisis. He did not fight for the people or because of a call from the deity. The deity played no role in his life or actions. Abimelech did not fight a particular battle, instead he ruled both for the sake of being in control and for revenge upon his brothers. The land was not tranquil upon his death. While the following minor judges are not as crisis-oriented as Abimelech, they highlight themes initiated in this story concerning the erosion of the military role of the hero, the role of the hero as a response to a crisis, issues of family as controlling the hero, the continuation of that family's rule, and the role of the Israelite deity in the life and actions of the judge.

Chapter 9

SOME MINOR JUDGES

Judges 10:1-5

This unit contains accounts of the "minor judges," so designated because the book does not contain stories of their accomplishments but only gives brief information describing an aspect of the character. The inclusion of minor judges brings the number of leaders in Judges to twelve, the number of tribes in Israel. This may explain why five minor judges are included in the text but does not address their placement in the story. They appear before and after the Jephthah story. Their reigns as judges are not reported in round numbers, which causes many to assume some historical authenticity to these numbers, or at least to assume an earlier source for those data.[1] This first unit describes two judges, focusing the narrative on the Israelites following the Abimelech episode, during which Israel had not appeared in the story.

Tola Son of Puah: Judges 10:1-2

Tola is introduced by placing his time as, "after Abimelech" (Judg 10:1). Tola's full name is Tola, son of Puah, son of Dodo, a man of Issachar. The text states that he "arose to save Israel." The only personal information given about him is that he lived at Shamir in the hill country. The next verse awards him status as judge, recounting that he judged Israel for twenty-three years. Immediately following this the text refers to his death and burial at Shamir (Judg 10:2).

---

[1] Boling, "Tola," *ABD* 6.596.

The reference ties Tola into the period of Abimelech. Whereas the book had viewed the period of Abimelech negatively, this reference almost seems to legitimate Abimelech's period of rule as a reign. Abimelech's reign at Shechem is treated as a historical reality upon which other events are dated. At the same time, the reference provides no information as to what happened to Israel following that episode. The text does not comment that the Israelites continued to do or returned to doing "the bad thing." There may be a hint that there were problems because Israel needed to be saved, but in previous cases there was a description of Israel's actions following major disasters. None is included here.

According to Boling the term "saved" usually implies a military form of judging. Boling is wary of awarding any military accomplishments to Tola and retreats from his interpretation because, "Perhaps it means here that in the chaos that remained after 'Abimelech' (Judg 10:1) Tola saved Israel by presiding over a peaceful interlude in the northern hill country and central Jezreel."[2] There is no evidence to support his understanding and it rejects his own interpretation of the meaning of the term "to save" in Judges, but it highlights the problems in understanding this text. The reference continues to confuse the reader who was not informed about the effects of the Abimelech incident on Israel. The introduction is rather jarring following the tension of the previous story.

Tola's name and patronymic provide little information. The name itself means "worm."[3] There are a number of references in the Bible to a Tola who was the first of the four sons of Issachar, according to biblical genealogy (Gen 46:13; Num 26:23; 1 Chr 7:1-2). The name Puah is not far from Puvah and many view it as another tribal name in Issachar.[4] Tola's grandfather is included in this context. Dodo comes from the Hebrew root *d-w-d* meaning, "beloved," or, "uncle."[5] It is the same root as the name David, and two other Dodos appear in relationship to King David's warriors, reinforcing the idea that Tola may have had some military responsibilities.[6]

There is little discussion about the role and meaning of the patronymics assigned to Tola, even though Tola is the only judge whose

---

[2] Ibid.

[3] *BDB*, 1069.

[4] C. Marittini, "Puvah," *ABD* 5. 562

[5] *BDB*, 187.

[6] The two Tolas are: the father of Eleazar, the second of "the three" most renowned warriors of David (2 Sam 23:9=1 Chr 11:12), and the father of Elhanan of Bethlehem, who immediately follows Asahel, brother of Joab, in the list of David's warriors (2 Sam 23:24). D. G. Schley, "Dodo," *ABD* 2.220.

grandfather's name is included in his patronymic. The names are understood as the standard treatment or introduction to any judge in this book. But the role of parentage, both paternal and maternal, are raised as key factors in deciding leadership in the previous story. Both Gideon/Jerubbaal's legitimate sons, as well as Abimelech, used their parentage as the basis for their claim to the right to control Shechem. The Abimelech episode is, in fact, a discussion of inherited leadership which is not ultimately viewed favorably as a paradigm. The text is explicit in asserting that Abimelech's control was not legitimate, but the final verses note that this was because of how he treated his brothers. The text does not condone the actions of Gideon/Jerubbaal's children. The narrator states that the deity took action because of what Abimelech did to Gideon/Jerubbaal, which resulted in the death of his sons, but the deity did not act on behalf of the sons.

The paucity of information pertaining to Tola's relatives makes interpretation difficult. The practice of taking control from ancestors may have continued with Tola, indicated by the inclusion of the names of an ancestor because he was a leader. Since no information is provided concerning his grandfather, it is more likely that his name is included to clarify that, since Tola was from Issachar, and even his grandfather's name is provided, he was in no way related to Abimelech/Gideon/Jerubbaal and broke with the dynasty attempted by Abimelech.

The only information regarding Tola's rise to power is that he rose. The deity was not involved in his choice nor was he granted any special powers. While the narrator provides information which legitimated his status, the deity played no role and is not part of the story. In distinction from Abimelech, Tola rose to deliver Israel. While the minor judges are considered legitimate leaders in the text, they were not explicitly deity-sanctioned. Tola held the status of judge but there is no account of how he gained that power or privilege.

Though the text contains no negative statements concerning Tola, in comparison to the way in which Abimelech is represented, his role still indicates that Israel's standards have slipped. The distance between Gideon/Jerubbaal, who had regular personal guidance from the deity, to Tola and the other minor judges is great. With Gideon/Jerubbaal the Israelites crossed the divide from deity-appointed rulers to leaders about whom little is known. The later judges Jephthah and Samson have some guidance from the deity, but its nature is very different from the type of connection enjoyed by Gideon/Jerubbaal. With the mistakes of Gideon/Jerubbaal, the way for Abimelech was paved and Israel reached a point from which it would not recover for the rest of the book.

Jair the Gileadite: Judges 10:3-5

Tola is followed by another minor judge, Jair the Gileadite. He is introduced with no reference to Tola other than that he was "after him" (Judg 10:3). He is described as judging Israel for twenty-two years. There is no patronymic for him but the text notes that he had thirty sons who rode on thirty burros and owned thirty boroughs in the region of Gilead (Judg 10:4). The text comments that these boroughs were called Havvoth Jair "to this day" (Judg 10:4). The section concludes with Jair's death and burial at Kamon (Judg 10:5).

The information regarding Jair raises questions similar to those asked about Tola. Jair judged Israel but again the reader knows this information only because it is provided by the narrator and no mention is made of whether he was deity-sanctioned. Jair has no patronymics, though the name is known from earlier biblical texts as a descendant of Manasseh (Num 32:41). His relatives are not included but the large number of sons, thirty, is reminiscent of Gideon/Jerubbaal, though the number is not quite as large (Judg 8:29).[7] Jair may be seen not as continuing a hereditary line of leadership, but having the numbers to begin one had he so desired.

Jair's sons' mode of transportation on burros reinforces the idea of creating a new ruling family. A word play appears regarding the cities and the boroughs.[8] The term for "city" ʿîr is similar to that for "burro" ʿayir and here are vocalized the same, though they should not be.[9] Scholars note that the term for the beast upon which the sons rode is different than the one which is used for the normal mode of transportation, especially in Judges.[10] This highlights the importance related to the term ḥămôr. Hamor was a family name used in Shechem, which occurs both in the story of the rape of Dinah (Gen 34:2-26) and in the previous Abimelech episode (Judg 9:28). Using either of those terms here would create an association that was not intended in this instance. Ḥămôr (donkey) is used as the transportation vehicle for Achsah (Judg 1:14) and will later be used by the raped pîlegeš (Judg 19:28). The narrator avoids those associations and it is best to follow the wordplay of the term burro/borough.

---

[7] Note that the number of sons in LXX is thirty-two, whereas 1 Chr 2:22 credits him with twenty-three cities.

[8] The translations (Boling and JPS) of "burros" and "boroughs" are quite fitting.

[9] R. G. Boling, basing his actions on haplography, follows the LXX, destroying the word play [*Judges: Introduction, Translation and Commentary*, The Anchor Bible (Garden City: Doubleday, 1981) 188].

[10] Ibid.

The intent of the word play is to show how few people are depicted as riding beasts of burden in Judges. Thus far, only Achsah (Judg 1:14), the Canaanites (in chariots; Judg 4:3, 7, 15), and the Midianites (Judg 6:5; though they have camels they are never described as actually riding them) are said to ride. All of the above-mentioned characters were powerful and part of the ruling elite. The same inference is intended here.

The cities of Jair (Hovvoth Jair) appear in a number of contexts which impact the present reference. The towns first appear in Num 32:41 where Moses assigned the land east of the Jordan to the Gadites, the Reubenites, and the half-tribe of Manasseh, son of Joseph (Num 32:33). The text continues with the descendants of Machir, son of Manasseh, going to Gilead, capturing it, and dispossessing the Amorites who were there, so that Moses gave Gilead to Machir, son of Manasseh, who settled there (Num 32:39-40). Jair, son of Manasseh, captured "their" (it is not clear to whom the pronoun refers) villages, presumably in Transjordan, which he renamed Havvoth Jair (Num 32:41).The book of Joshua reiterates that Moses assigned all of Havvoth Jair to the half-tribe of Manasseh, though Jair's name is not included (Josh 13:29).

In the context of the book of Judges, Jair is described as a judge and the information provided about him concerns his sons, their travel preferences, and the towns they occupy. The irony is that these cities were to be Jair's, or at least the half-tribe of Manasseh's, according to the commands of Moses, recognized as recently as the book of Joshua. Suddenly in the period of Judges the same information is presented as though it were something special, even defining of Jair. Following the Gideon/Jerubbaal incident where the issue of hereditary leadership was just raised, the relationship between Jair and these towns takes on a new significance. While his inheritance of them was legitimate, was his role as leader? Once again incidents that were clearly defined in the period prior to Judges are no longer so definitive.

Another reference to Havvoth Jair appears in 1 Kgs 4:13, also in relationship to kingship. This text describes Solomon's twelve prefects who governed all of Israel, and provided food for the king and his household. Each had to provide food for one month of the year. The villages are described as those of Jair, son of Manasseh. Thus the reference to Havvoth Jair is not unique. What is different in Judges is that they have been disassociated from their usual context. The villages are described as though they began with the present Jair, not that they were so designated by Moses.

Both Tola and Jair were from the region of Gilead which is on the eastern side of the Jordan, the area that is the focus of the following narrative. It is no accident that stories about these individuals appear at this point of the narrative, bringing the reader to this geographic place before the next battle. The gifted writer of Judges worked in details about these two characters that were relevant, ignored other pieces of information concerning them recounted elsewhere, and in so doing tied these two vignettes into the themes addressed in the previous narrative, some of which continue in the following episode.

Summary

These minor judges are included at this point in the story in order to provide a link to the previous episode concerning Gideon/Jerubbaal/Abimelech in terms of the theme of dynastic monarchy which remained an issue into the following episode, to provide some relief for some of the tension built up during the previous four chapters, and also to move the attention of the reader to the geographic location of the following story. The accounts of these two minor judges continue to reflect a decline in the role of the judge by these characters because they do not change any of the previous problems but maintain the status quo.

Chapter 10

JEPHTHAH

Judges 10:6–12:7

The Jephthah episode is surrounded by references to minor Judges. A transition from the first set of minor judges is facilitated by focusing on those who were from the same general area which would be important in the Jephthah narrative. The transition concerning Israel's present crisis is included in this chapter because it follows the pattern seen previously where the notice of the Israelites' reversion to negative ways relates to the enlistment and attributes of the following judge. This is the case with Jephthah as well. He is the answer to the question about leadership that is raised in the transitional material (Judg 10:18), although he does not come forward willingly.

The story of Jephthah combines a number of themes noted previously in a way which implies that his intentions may have been legitimate. However, Jephthah, as was possibly the case with the Israelites in general, no longer knew how to behave correctly concerning his deity. Jephthah is similar to Abimelech in that both stem from dubious ancestors. Jephthah also had a mercenary force and was chosen for this military ability. Jephthah turned his military skills to his advantage, as Abimelech had done, seeking more than merely military control. Jephthah recognized the Israelite deity, and the deity helped him, but the direct connection between the two was minimal. The episodes with Jephthah's daughter and the other tribes provide a preview of what will turn into a full-blown civil war at the end of the book. Israel's decline continues to the point that by the end of the episode Israel has become its own enemy.

Background for Jephthah: Judges 10:6-17

Following Jair's death the children of Israel once again did "the bad thing" in the eyes of their deity. The text explicitly describes what this "bad thing" was; they served the Baals, the Ashtaroth, the gods of Aram, the gods of the Philistines, forsook their deity, and did not serve him (Judg 10:6). In the earlier instances where this phrase appeared, "the bad thing" was interpreted in this commentary as referring to intermarriage which led to neglect of the deity. Here the aspect of intermarriage is not raised. In fact, this is the first case since Judges 3 where "the bad thing" is defined.

The result of the Israelites' actions was that they angered their deity, who sold them to the Philistines and the Ammonites (Judg 10:7) as a result. The Amorites battered and shattered the children of Israel for eighteen years (Judg 10:8). The text includes in the abuse all the Israelites beyond the Jordan, in what had been the land of the Amorites in Gilead. The Ammonites crossed the Jordan to make war on Judah, Benjamin, and the house of Ephraim, causing Israel great distress (Judg 10:9). For the first time both sides of the Jordan and most of the tribes of Israel were explicitly involved.

The children of Israel cried out to their deity, admitting their guilt and stating the source of their guilt; that they had forsaken their deity and served the Baals (Judg 10:10). The deity reiterated the nature of their history (Judg 10:11), that the Egyptians, Amorites, Ammonites, Philistines, Sidonians, Amalek, and Moan had all oppressed them, that they had cried out and that the deity had saved them (Judg 10:12).[1] The deity reminded them that despite this they forsook the deity and served other gods, so the deity refused to deliver them again (Judg 10:13). The deity continued saying that they should go to the other gods whom they had chosen and have them deliver the Israelites in their time of distress (Judg 10:14). The Israelites stood firm and implored their deity, continuing to confess their guilt, stating that while the deity should act as was fit, Israel should be saved that day (Judg 10:15). The Israelites took the initiative and removed the alien gods from their midst and served their deity, who, as a result, could no longer bear the miseries of Israel (Judg 10:16).

The story shifts at this point and turns to the military situation. The Ammonites mustered and encamped in Gilead, and the children of Israel came together and encamped at Mizpeh (Judg 10:17). While the Israelites managed to gather and arrive at the meeting place, they were again without a leader. The officers of Gilead said to each other that the

---

[1] The LXX has Moab.

man who was the first to fight the Ammonites would be "chieftain" *rō'š* over all the inhabitants of Gilead (Judg 10:18).

This last line shows how the story of Judges is being continued and places this particular episode within the broader context of the David/Saul story. The first judge had won his wife, Achsah, because he was the first to capture Kiriath Sepher/Debir (Judg 1:12). Here again the Israelites were without a leader but rather than offer a marriage to the winner the people were prepared to offer the hero rule over all of them. The two situations are similar and employ almost the same terminology but at this point in the history of Israel the stakes were higher and the people were prepared to make an offer which was not necessarily theirs to make. The irony is that in the previous few sentences the people were asking forgiveness, but either they did not wait long enough, the deity's intentions were not expressed to them in a way they understood, or in a timely enough fashion.

To win a prize for leading a battle parallels the offer of Achsah to Othniel. The question about who would go first is the same one with which the book began, which continues to pester the Israelites and which is without any resolution thus far. This is also tied into the larger context of the history of Israel since Saul too was the first to go up against the Ammonites (1 Sam 11:1-11). Their question was answered on two levels. On the one hand the leaders sought someone to lead the army, while, Saul, the only person to do this with the deity's approval, would only come much later. Not only did Saul also fight a battle with the Ammonites but it was in preparation for that battle that Saul cut a yoke of oxen into pieces to gather the troops, an act which will appear in a few chapters (Judg 19:29).

Choosing Jephthah: Judges 11:1-3

Jephthah is introduced by highlighting two of his main personal characteristics; that he was a military man and illegitimate. These two factors are the keys to his role in the story, his motivations, and possibly also provide a commentary on both his society and his actions. The first sentence about Jephthah says he was a Gileadite, an able warrior *gibbôr ḥayil* and, probably, the son of a prostitute *zônâ* (Judg 11:1). According to the text, his father was Gilead.

The description of him as a *gibbôr ḥayil* is open to various interpretations. The LXX takes it to mean he was a "mighty man," though this too is open to different meanings, which range from its being a comment on his personal strength to the power he wielded either militarily or politically. Boling likens him in this regard to Gideon, translating the term as "knight" and understanding the reference to indicate one who has been trained in upper-class combat, who furnished his own equipment and a squire or a unit of soldiers.[2] Jephthah, however, is depicted as the opposite of Gideon. Gideon had a father who was well-known and fairly well-to-do. There is little discussion concerning Gideon's mother, there is no indication that she was anything like a prostitute and, as noted previously, there are hints that she may have been a Canaanite.[3]

The difference in fathers between Gideon and Jephthah, and Jephthah and Abimelech is extreme. The actions of Gideon/Jerubbaal's and Abimelech's fathers play an important role in both their lives. So too Jephthah's father, but more because of what is not known about him than anything he did in the story. The information concerning Jephthah's father is vague. It is not clear if Gilead was a person, whether the name refers to the whole tribe, or possibly means any and every man in Gilead. The first thing mentioned about Jephthah is that he was a Gileadite, not that he was the son of anyone in particular. His mother's occupation as a prostitute is inserted where normally one finds the patronymic, which leaves the second Gilead reference open for interpretation.

Understanding who sired Jephthah is related to his mother, who is called a *zônâ*. While all terms relating to women's status in the MT are somewhat vague, this term appears more straightforward, at least on the surface. The term *zônāh* is understood to mean a professional prostitute who accepts payment for her services, but it could also apply to a woman who had sex before or outside the confines of marriage.[4] Priests were not allowed to marry prostitutes and daughters of priests were burned for plying this trade (Lev 21:7, 9, 14). However, these rules did not apply to lay Israelites, indicating that prostitution was tolerated.[5] David's ancestress Tamar acted as a prostitute in order to bring about a judgment and to create sons who would be David's ancestors (Gen 38:29-30). This is not to say that there was not contempt for prostitutes. According to Bird, the stories concerning Tamar and Rahab presuppose their low repute.[6] Dinah's brothers destroyed an entire town for one person having treated their sister like a prostitute (Gen 34:31).[7]

[2] R. G. Boling, *Judges: Introduction, Translation and Commentary,* The Anchor Bible (Garden City: Doubleday, 1981) 197.

[3] See above Chapter 7.

[4] E. A. Goodfriend, "Prostitution (OT)," *ABD* 5. 505.

[5] Ibid.

[6] P. Bird, "Images of Women in the OT," *Religion and Sexism,* ed. R. Ruether (New York: Simon and Schuster, 1974) 41–88.

[7] Note that some translations insert "whore" or "harlot" here instead of "prostitute," though the same Hebrew word is used (JPS, KJV, RSV). According to *The*

Tamar is the only woman in the Hebrew Bible who shamelessly had sexual intercourse for payment, yet the point of that story is that she was not doing it for the money but for progeny since she had not been given the husband to whom she was by right entitled (Genesis 38).

The evidence that this term refers to a woman who had sexual intercourse for financial remuneration is circumstantial. Oftentimes the noun and its associated verbal forms relate to fornication outside the boundaries established by cultic law. When used as a verb, the root is often used to describe Israel's actions when she follows other deities (e.g. Judg 2:17; 8:27). Here the term could mean either that she was a professional prostitute or that she had sex outside traditional Israelite marriage.

The reference to Jephthah's mother is a point of clarification by the narrator, it is not an insult heaped upon him by a character trying to make a point. Whether she was Canaanite or Israelite is not mentioned. Were she Canaanite, Jephthah would be another Israelite leader of mixed lineage. His relationship to Israel would be even more peripheral than the previous cases since his father's identity is so clouded. The information about his mother is noted before anything is said about his father, raising the question of whether Gilead here refers to a person, a town, or any man in the town. The question is never answered definitively but the treatment of Jephthah by other Gileadites later indicates both that Jephthah's mother was not highly regarded and that her reputation was passed on to her child.

The text next notes that the woman/wife of Gilead had sons and when they grew up they drove Jephthah out, saying that he was the son of "another woman" and that he would not share in the inheritance (Judg 11:2).[8] The other sons of Gilead do not refer to the woman's occupation or apply other degrading names to her (such as had been used by Jotham about Abimelech's mother [Judg 9:18]), but refer to her as a woman/wife. Some translations use the terminology "strange" (KJV) or "outsider" (JPS) for the phrase. No version translates, "another wife," or "wife from outside," although this is a possibility. Translators assume that the woman had no legal status. They do this despite the appearance of the phrase in the mouths of the sons of legitimate wives in the context of questions concerning inheritance. There is no statement concerning the rules of inheritance but it seems likely that if the

---

American Heritage Dictionary of the English Language (New York: Houghton Mifflin, 1969) a prostitute is "one who solicits and accepts payment for sexual intercourse," but the definition for both a "harlot" and a "whore" is prostitute. Thus all three words mean the same thing in English.

[8] The LXX has concubine here.

paternity of the father were unknown it would be difficult for the child to be considered for any inheritance. The legitimate sons' comments raise questions concerning the translation of zônâ as, "a woman whose profession is to have sexual intercourse for financial remuneration." Following stories in which the last few leaders had had numerous wives, it is not clear why this woman just being an additional wife would make her offspring illegitimate.

The text states that the woman/wife of Gilead bore him sons, setting up a comparison between the two women. The reference to a single wife of Gilead implies that Gilead was one specific person. Further support for this notion is that when the sons expel Jephthah he is called the son of "another woman," including nothing derogatory about the woman or her occupation. The sons' refusal to share the inheritance with Jephthah is not related, at least in their statements, to Jephthah's mother's profession. Ironically the situation is similar to that of Abimelech and his brothers and again, the legitimacy of the brothers' actions is questionable.

The parallels with the Abimelech story are significant at this point. Abimelech and Jephthah were both sons of a father who had an additional woman/wife who was unacceptable. How much lower in class Abimelech's mother was than Jephthah's is not clear. Ostensibly Abimelech was accepted by his mother's family but both situations have a similar result; the son was not accepted by the half-brothers on the father's side. In Abimelech's case he acted to avenge what he viewed as mistreatment on the part of his brothers, though the text provides no evidence of this mistreatment. In Jephthah's parallel situation, Jephthah responded by leaving (Judg 11:3). His departure necessitated his brothers' searching for him. Ironically the situations parallel each other, but in Jephthah's case the modern scholars' sympathies are with the ousted brother whereas in the earlier case scholars are sympathetic towards Abimelech's brothers.

The text continues with Jephthah fleeing from his brothers and settling in the Tob country (Judg 11:3). There he gathered "empty" men about him and went raiding with them. The country to which Jephthah fled may be a Syrian town later subject to Maacah in alliance with Beth-rehob, Zobah, and the Ammonites against David (2 Sam 10:6-8).[9] In later sources the name was taken to be that of a Gileadite city whose Jewish population was slaughtered by the gentiles around them.[10] Geographically speaking, Jephthah did not travel far.

---

[9] Boling, Judges, 197; B. Mazar, "The Tobiads," IEJ 7(1957) 137–45, 229–38.
[10] P. L. Redditt, "Tob," ABD 6.583.

According to Boling, the reference to Tob is important because it is a technical term of covenantal "amity."[11] He suggests that a man like Jephthah would not have spent all his time in one place and that the place name was probably selected because of its covenantal nuance.[12] In terms of irony in Judges and Jephthah's story thus far, the nuance of Tob may be much simpler. The name of the place means "good" *ṭôb*[13] The concept of going to a good land does not need such an elaborate explanation. Jephthah was in Gilead where he was not accepted because of his mother, regardless of what her precise occupation may have been. He went to a good land but gathered bad followers.

The text states that Jephthah had to "flee" *b-r-ḥ* his hometown. The text had previously noted only that he would not share in the inheritance of his brothers, but having to flee implies a more dire situation. Whatever the reason for his flight, when he left he built his own mercenary army. The people gathered to him are referred to as "empty," taken to mean "vain," "idle," "worthless."[14] This is the same term used to describe the people whom Abimelech hired with his seventy shekels, who followed him and functioned as his army when he controlled Shechem (Judg 9:4). Again Abimelech's and Jephthah's lives parallel. The difference is that the text states explicitly that Abimelech hired his men (Judg 9:4) whereas the narrative is careful to note that these men gathered around Jephthah (Judg 11:3).

Jephthah's Enlistment: Judges 11:4-11

The text continues saying that "some time later" the Ammonites went to war against Israel (Judg 11:4). Judges 10 describes the hostilities between the Ammonites and Gilead and ends with Gilead prepared to give leadership to whomever would go up first to fight the Ammonites (Judg 10:17-18). Jephthah is introduced so that when the wider story resumes the reader has the necessary background, a pattern seen earlier with the introduction of Heber the Kenite (Judg 4:11). The Gileadites' actions in the following verse imply that no Gileadite had arisen to fight the Ammonites (Judg 11:5).

While the question in Judges 10 is not formulated in precisely the same way as the question with which the book began was (Judg 1:1), its phraseology and meaning are not dissimilar. The differences highlight

[11] Boling, *Judges*, 197.
[12] Ibid.
[13] *BDB*, 373.
[14] Ibid., 938.

the changes that have occurred in the interim. At the beginning of the book the Israelites, as a body, inquired of their deity who should go up first. Here the Gileadites alone decided that whoever went up first would be rewarded, and still no one responded. This is an example of the decline in Judges, since the wrong people asked the wrong questions and offered the wrong rewards.

The Ammonites attacked Israel and the elders of Gilead attempted to bring Jephthah back from the Tob/good country (Judg 11:5). They asked Jephthah to be their "chief" *qāṣîn* and were explicit that the reason why they wanted him was to fight the Ammonites (Judg 11:6). In Jephthah's response to the elders of Gilead, he reminded them that they were the very same people who had rejected him and driven him out of his father's house. He questioned their motives for approaching him now when they were in trouble (Judg 11:7).

At this point serious negotiations began. The elders of Gilead did not answer Jephthah's question. Instead they confessed that they were honestly turning to him, and did not bother to explain their previous actions (Judg 11:8). They used the lure of an offer of command, stating that if he fought the children of Ammon he would be the "head" *rōʾš* of all the inhabitants of Gilead (Judg 11:8). Jephthah was not convinced and repeated their offer; if they brought him back to fight the children of Ammon, and the deity delivered them to him he would be their "head" *rōʾš*. He seems to have been ensuring that he had heard them correctly (Judg 11:9). The elders, using the Israelite deity as a witness between Jephthah and themselves, agreed that they would do as they said (Judg 11:10). The deal was finalized when Jephthah went with the elders of Gilead, the people made him their commander and chief, and Jephthah repeated all the terms before the deity at Mizpah (Judg 11:11).

Jephthah's recruitment, the ensuing negotiations, and the terminology used in the process raise many issues. The first issue concerns the elders of Gilead. These are the people who approached Jephthah with the offer and the text refers to them throughout the negotiating process. The group had enough power within the structure of Gilead to offer leadership of all of Gilead to Jephthah. They were not the people who had made the original decision to promote whoever led and won the battle to be head of Gilead (Judg 10:18). In the first instance, before Jephthah's introduction, the body making the decision was "the people, the second in commands of Gilead" *hāʿām śārê gilʿād* (Judg 10:18). At that point they spoke "each to his companion" *rēʿēhû* (Judg 10:18). The term *śar* is used again. In this case they were leaders but no one of them had complete authority. They made the decision among themselves, among their companions. The text already depicted companions in the Gideon/Jerubbaal story in both camaraderie (Judg 7:13), and shortly thereafter turning on each other (Judg 7:22) because of the Israelite deity and the term will carry the same connotation again in the Samson story.

There is no introduction to the elders, who simply appear in Jephthah's presence (Judg 11:5). Jephthah's response to the elders, "You are the very people who rejected me and drove me out of my father's house. How can you come to me now when you are in trouble?" (Judg 11:7, JPS), indicates that he considered them personally responsible for his having to flee his hometown in the first place. The only reason stated thus far for Jephthah's departure was his brothers' refusal to give him a share of their father's inheritance. Here Jephthah treated the elders of Gilead as though they were his brothers. The solution may go back to the identity of Jephthah's father, Gilead. If Gilead was not a specific person but was a term which implied that any man in Gilead could be his father, given his mother's occupation or actions, then it is possible that those referred to as his brothers in Judg 11:2-3 were Gilead in general, or its ruling elite.

The legitimacy of the elders' offer to Jephthah is questionable. In the preceding section the Israelites repented to their deity, rid themselves of their idols, and were prepared to accept their punishment as long as their deity rescued them (Judg 10:10-16). The text provides no indication that the deity told them to make an offer, or that they consulted the deity. In the negotiating process the first one to raise the issue of the Israelite deity was Jephthah (Judg 11:9). The elders made no apologies to Jephthah for their previous actions, actually avoiding Jephthah's question completely. They were interested only in saving themselves in this battle and were prepared to offer leadership, something that prior to Abimelech was awarded only by the deity.

The manner in which the elders made Jephthah the offer recalls Jotham's fable in the Abimelech episode. Jotham's prophetic statement appears in the explanation he offered at the end of his fable. He interpreted the bramble's response to the offer to mean that if the Shechemites were honestly offering leadership to Abimelech it would go well for them, but that if they had not examined his previous actions concerning his brothers, or if they found them legitimate, then things would not go well with them (Judg 9:16-20). As the end of the Abimelech story indicates, Jotham's statement came true, because they had not treated Gideon/Jerubbaal well through his children (Judg 9:49). In Jephthah's case, the elders of Gilead were determined to act honestly, and when they made the final offer to Jephthah they invoked the deity as the arbiter. The irony is that in this case it was not Jephthah, to whom leadership was offered, whose actions needed to be examined, but rather the elders, although they still did not acknowledge this.

The elders did not answer Jephthah's question but they changed the offer. The original offer to anyone who would lead the campaign against the Ammonites was to make him "head" *rō'š* of all Gilead. When no one took up the offer, and they had to go to Jephthah, they offered him to become "general," using the word, *qāṣîn*. The term means "chief" or "ruler" and is not common in the MT.[15] In the book of Joshua it carries the sense of "army general" since the context in which it appears has Joshua as the main military leader and these people as his aids (Josh 10:24). Their original offer to Jephthah was not as high as that originally offered to any Gileadite. When Jephthah did not accept the elders made their second offer. This time they made the original offer using the term "head" *rō'š* and clarified it by noting that it would be, "of all the inhabitants of Gilead" (Judg 11:8). In the finalization of the agreement the text is explicit that the people made him both "head" *rō'š* and "general" *qāṣîn* (Judg 11:11).

Although they made Jephthah a better offer, they exempted themselves from participation in the battle. In the original offer, as they looked for someone to lead the battle, they invited the person to go with them so that, "we may fight" (Judg 11:6). In the final negotiations the terminology became, "you may fight" (Judg 11:8).[16] At this point they had found a leader, were prepared to reward him for a victory, but were no longer willing to participate in the battle. As had been the case with Baraq and Gideon/Jerubbaal, the leadership of Israel no longer willingly fought on behalf of Israel or their deity.

The role of the deity is introduced in this section. The elders did not introduce the deity's name but Jephthah referred to the Israelite deity when he reiterated his understanding of the deal, noting that if he defeated the Ammonites with the help of the deity he would be made ruler. At this point in the narrative, though the Israelites proclaimed their guilt and mended their ways, only the reader knows that the deity could not bear their misery. There is no reference indicating that the Israelites knew that the deity was involved in this transaction. Jephthah introduced the deity's role into the forthcoming battle. The elders did not comment on the role that the deity would play in the battle but raised the deity's name only as arbiter in the negotiations between Jephthah and the elders of Gilead. Even at the conclusion of the negotiations, the deity had not taken a stand on the elders' choice of Jephthah as military or community political leader.

---

[15] Ibid., 892.

[16] J. C. Exum, *Tragedy and Biblical Narrative: Arrows of the Almighty* (New York: Cambridge University Press, 1992) 48.

Boling considers the phrase referring to the deity as arbiter as tying the story to the previous story of Jotham and Abimelech because Jotham demanded that the leaders listen to him, and here the elders asked the deity to decide.[17] The phrase also ties it to later events in Jephthah's life. The elders' formulation, using the name of the deity in the negotiating process, is not far from what Jephthah offers later in the story, which leads to the loss of his daughter's life.

The signing of the agreement occurred at Mizpah (Judg 11:11). The use of this site has many possible ramifications. Mizpah was the site in the Benjaminite town-list when Joshua allotted cities captured in the conquest to the various tribes (Josh 18:26). It was also the site where the Israelites would gather after they received the brutalized and raped *pîlegeš* as an invitation to battle the tribe of Benjamin at the end of the book (Judg 20:1). The site relates to Saul because it was there that Samuel would choose him as the first king over Israel in a lottery held at Mizpah (1 Sam 10:17). The site is significant later in Jephthah's own story, and its role in the David/Saul polemic may be related to this use, because, despite his living in the land of Tob, he returned after the battle to his home in Mizpah (Judg 11:34). The site appears as a place where important proclamations were made and meetings held which governed the fate of Israel.

Jephthah as Negotiator: Judges 11:12-29

Jephthah began his career as commander by trying to strike a deal with the Ammonites. He sent messengers to the king of the Ammonites asking what they had against him that they came to make war on his country (Judg 11:12). The formulation of his question, "What is to me and to you?" is not common in the MT, occurring only five other times, four of them in the Deuteronomistic History (2 Sam 16:10; 2 Sam 19:23; 1 Kgs 17:18; 2 Kgs 3:13; 2 Chr 35:21). The contexts of some of these are relevant to this passage since four of them focus on the region of Gilead, the crossing of the Jordan, and oaths impacting the life of children.

After the instance being examined at present, the next two contexts for this question appear in 2 Samuel and concern the same trip of David, one instance appearing at the beginning and the other the end of his trip across the Jordan during the Absalom incident. In the first, 2 Sam 16:10, Shimei son of Gera from the house of Saul approached

---

[17] Boling, *Judges*, 198.

during his crossing of the Jordan at the beginning of the Abshalom incident.[18] Shimei insulted King David. Abishai son of Zeruiah wanted to cut off Shimei's head (2 Sam 16:9), but King David responded with calm asking Zeruiah, "What is between me and you . . . ?" He elaborated, noting that at this point even his own son wanted to kill him, so how much more might a Benjaminite desire to do so, and the incident ended. The question appears again between the same characters but this time on King David's return following Abshalom's death (2 Sam 19:22). Again Shimei appeared with many Benjaminites, this time repentant since King David had secured his throne. Again Abishai son of Zeruiah wanted to put Shimei to death and again David asked "What has this to do with you?" He decided that there had been enough death that day and gave Shimei his oath that he would not die (2 Sam 19:24).

The passages from 1 and 2 Kings relate in more distant and yet still relevant ways. 1 Kings 17:18 is in the midst of an incident concerning Elijah, the Tisbite, who was also from Gilead. He told Ahab that there would be no rain because of the deity of Israel whom he served (1 Kgs 17:1). Elijah then fled to Zarrephath and was taken in by a woman whose son fell sick (1 Kgs 17:7-17). The woman of the house responded to her son's sickness by saying to the prophet, "What is between me and you?" noting that he recalled her sin and was causing the death of her son (1 Kgs 17:18). Elijah took action and the child's life returned to his body (1 Kgs 17:19-23). The woman accepted this as proof that Elijah was a man of Elohim (1 Kgs 17:24).

The final occurrence appears in 2 Kgs 3:13. This case also deals with the eastern side of the Jordan, in this case with King Mesha of Moab. According to the text Mesha used to pay tribute to the King of Israel, but when Ahab died the king of Moab rebelled against the King of Israel, so King Jehoram set out from Samaria and mustered all Israel (which at this point means the northern kingdom of Israel) and even invited the king of Judah to join him (2 Kgs 3:4-8). The troops of all Israel (i.e. Israel and Judah) found themselves at the Dead Sea with no water. They sought Elisha, who said to the kings, "What is between me and you?" (2 Kgs 3:13). Because the king of Judah was with the King of Israel Elisha relented and water was made available (2 Kgs 3:14-26).

When the king of Moab and his troops were in trouble, he resorted to a desperate measure, offering up his first-born son, who was to succeed him as king, on the wall as a burnt offering (2 Kgs 3:27).

The five passages containing the identical question in the Deuteronomistic History all share common elements. All the references concern

---

[18] Note that Ehud is referred to as "son of Gera" and was also a Benjaminite (Judg 3:15), discussed above in Chapter 4.

the death or near-death of a beloved child (this is not yet evident in Judges but will be shortly). Four of the five passages occurred on the eastern side of the Jordan, all but the incident in which Elijah took part. All of the passages involve an upstart in some way: Jephthah, in Judges, who has been an outsider until this case, both Shimei and Abishai in the David episodes, and the prophets Elijah and Elisha. All of the contexts in which the question appears surround a change in the power structure: Jephthah who had been exiled gaining control and fighting the new overlords, David fighting Abshalom and being questioned by a supporter of the house of Saul, Elijah fighting the Omrides, and Israel and Judah together fighting Moab.

Through this phrase and similarities in the content of the stories in which it appears Jephthah is identified with David, Elijah, and Elisha. While there are many parallels among the stories, two themes stand out particularly in relation to the Judges scenario: the role of the ruler and leadership, and the leader's actions in relation to the death of a child. The question of leadership and the evaluation of their actions ties in beautifully with that theme so important to Judges. It is no accident that Jephthah's child, who died as a result of her father's role as a leader, is the only case among the five where the child is a daughter. In the verse currently under discussion, even though the issue of Jephthah's daughter has not been raised explicitly, the issue is broached implicitly by the choice of phrase. Again, the treatment of females provides both a barometer of society and the evaluation of the ruler in Judges. The king of Ammon provided his version of the conflict's historical background (Judg 11:13). According to his message to Jephthah's messengers, when Israel came from Egypt they seized his land from the Arnon to the Jabbok as far as the Jordan. He added that it should be restored peaceably (Judg 11:13). Jephthah responded by again sending messengers to the king of the Ammonites (Judg 11:14), this time providing Jephthah's historical background of the same conflict (Judg 11:22).

Jephthah's rendition of the conflict began with the Israelites' departure from Egypt. He noted that Israel traveled through the wilderness to the Sea of Reeds and went to Kadesh (Judg 11:16). At this point the conflict began with areas to the east of the Jordan. He noted that Israel sent messengers to the king of Edom asking his permission to cross his country, but the king of Edom would not consent so they sent a message to the king of Moab and he refused (Judg 11:17). After Israel's stay at Kadesh they traveled through the wilderness, skirting the land of Edom and Moab, keeping to the east of Moab, until they encamped on the other side of the Arnon. He noted that since Moab ends at the Arnon, the Israelites never entered Moabite territory (Judg 11:18). In his version Israel then sent messengers to Sihon, king of the Amorites, king of Heshbon, asking him for permission to cross through his country to their homeland (Judg 11:19). He also did not trust that Israel would simply pass through his land and instead of giving the permission which had been requested mustered his troops and engaged Israel at Jahaz (Judg 11:20). The story continues to say that the Israelite deity delivered Sihon and all his troops to Israel, which defeated them, whereupon Israel took possession of all the land of the Amorites, the inhabitants of that land (Judg 11:21). As a result the Israelites possessed all the territory of the Amorites from the Arnon to the Jabbok and from the wilderness to the Jordan (Judg 11:22).

This concludes Jephthah's messenger's historical survey of the conflict. While Jephthah's messenger left out many details included in the original narration of these events (Num 21:22-35; 23-24; Deut 1:4), it does not deviate from those other references regarding Israel's relations with Moab and her neighbors. Jephthah detailed the history of the conflict, which is ironic since he has been depicted as an outsider, exiled from his home, and yet was well versed in the history and tradition of Israel. This makes Jephthah the only leader in Judges who exhibited any knowledge of Israelite history or their conflicts.

At this point the present conflict was contextualized. The messenger noted that the deity of Israel had dispossessed the Amorites in favor of his people Israel and asked if they were now trying to repossess their land (Judg 11:23). He asked rhetorically whether he held on to whatever his god Chemosh gave him and noted that so too the Israelites would hold on to everything that their deity gave them to possess (Judg 11:24). Finally he asked whether he, the king of the Ammonites, was better than Balak son of Zippor, king of Moab, asking whether he had ever started a quarrel with Israel or gone to war with them (Judg 11:25). This recalls the story of Balaam who could not curse Israel despite his efforts to the contrary (Num 22:2–24:25). This is imbedded in the same passages in the book of Numbers that recount the travels of the Israelites which had been summarized earlier by Jephthah's messenger.

The text continues with Jephthah's interpretation of Moab's actions, or inaction, insinuating that Moab's statute of limitations had expired. He stated, through his messenger, that while Israel was dwelling in Heshbon and Aroer and their dependencies along the Arnon for three hundred years the Moabites never tried to recover their territory (Judg 11:26). He claimed that he had done them no wrong yet they were harming him and making war on him. He declared that the Israelite deity would judge between the Israelites and Ammonites (Judg 11:27), again bringing in the Israelite deity as arbiter. Despite Jephthah's plea the king of the Ammonites disregarded his message (Judg 11:28).

Many scholars have trouble understanding the point of Jephthah's messenger's entire recitation. It is long, repeats information found in more detail in other books, and does not have any impact on the enemy ruler. This understanding assumes that the Judges story reflects a historical scenario. There would be no need to repeat the entire recitation if the story were intended, either in its present form or even within the narrative, for the Moabites. The only benefit of recounting the story to the Moabites is to depict Jephthah as part of the Israelites and their history. What is more likely is that this recitation was for the Israelites. Since Jephthah was leading the Israelite troops it is unlikely that he would have to prove to the enemy leader that he was the legitimate leader of Israel. In light of his background, he may have had that need for the Israelites whom he commanded.

The speech failed and Israel continued to prepare for the ensuing battle. The deity became actively involved by descending upon Jephthah as he marched through Gilead and Manasseh, passing Mizpah of Gilead, and crossing over to the children of Ammon (Judg 11:29). If one considers the speech to have been only partially for the stated audience (the king of Ammon), but primarily for the readers or the others in the text who would have heard Jephthah give the speech, then the text has new meaning. Jephthah was originally depicted as an outsider, gathering the wrong crowd, the son of a prostitute or woman of low status. Suddenly he was a devoted Yahwist (i.e., he worshiped Israel's deity), knew his people's history, was prepared to negotiate before fighting, and pled his people's innocence while glorifying his deity, a completely different character.

Jephthah's messenger's speech reflects the Israelites' relationship with their deity, which was at a crossroads. They recently admitted their guilt regarding their behavior towards their deity (Judg 10:14-15). The recitation of the Israelites' history following the Exodus from Egypt is a radically different approach than Gideon/Jerubbaal's encounter with the deity. The difference is highlighted further because Gideon/Jerubbaal had been hand-picked by the deity. It is possible that Jephthah's memory of the history, recounted on the surface for the enemy king's benefit, caused the deity to finally acknowledge the elders' choice of Jephthah, because it was only after he made this attempt that the deity descended upon him.

Jephthah's Vow: Judges 11:30-31

At this point in the story Jephthah made the vow which would prove fatal for his daughter. Jephthah vowed to the Israelite deity that if the deity delivered the children of Ammon into his hand (Judg 11:30) whatever came out of the door of his house to meet him on his safe return from the Ammonites would belong to the Israelite deity and he would offer it as a burnt offering (Judg 11:31). His vow and the object which met him have become the most memorable aspects of Jephthah's career and a topic of much recent scholarly attention.[19] The preparation to his vow and his personality, as well as what the reader already knows about returning heroes, makes his vow even more dramatic.

Recently Reis has offered the suggestion that the vow was not an offer to sacrifice what came out of the house but reflected the idea of Lev 27:1-8 concerning redemption of a sacrificed object.[20] She emphasizes that Jephthah had just shown detailed knowledge of Israelite history and as a result would know that human sacrifice was only acceptable in cases of self-defense, deity-sanctioned warfare, and capital punishment. She posits that Jephthah intended to dedicate and redeem a slave, i.e. that if one vowed to the deity a male between the ages of twenty and sixty, that person was not slaughtered but rather a gift of fifty shekels of silver was given to the priests and the human being was redeemed.[21] In her thesis the vow mentioned here was not to sacrifice a person, but to redeem them for what could be a fair amount of money.

While the argument is tantalizing there are aspects of it which do not fit into the climate of Judges. Thus far no organized priesthood was operating. Jephthah expressed knowledge concerning the history of Israel, especially as it related to the eastern side of the Jordan river, but there are no indications in the book that any of the cultic laws of Israel were remembered, in place, imposed, or practiced in any way. Even if Jephthah made his vow with this act of redemption in mind it is doubtful that anyone hearing it would have understood the implications or the reference and acted accordingly. Levenson points out that despite many claims that there is no evidence of child sacrifice in Israel in the Bible, there are places where child sacrifice, especially of the eldest son, is not only acceptable but required.[22]

The timing of the vow is odd. In the sequence of the story, Jephthah was surprised when the elders of Gilead initially came to him, since he

---

[19] See the bibliography for more extensive discussions of this episode.

[20] P. Reis, "Spoiled Child: A Fresh Look at Jephthah's Daughter," a paper delivered at the Annual Meeting of the Society of Biblical Literature, 1997. I would like to thank Dr. Reis for providing me with a copy of her fascinating paper.

[21] Reis, "Spoiled Child," 7.

[22] J. D. Levenson, *The Death and Resurrection of the Beloved Son: The Transformation of Child Sacrifice in Judaism and Christianity* (New Haven: Yale University Press, 1993) 14.

considered them to be the ones who had originally ejected him from his home. At the conclusion of the negotiations he made a vow with the deity as arbiter. He then repeated the terms in front of the Israelite deity at Mizpah. Despite the attempts to make the appointment in front of the deity, the deity did not respond. Jephthah negotiated with the Ammonite king in order to avoid hostilities and when that did not work the deity descended upon him. Since the deity descended upon Jephthah after he made the vow, it could appear that the vow was what lured the deity to Jephthah's side. In that case the deity would condone and accept child sacrifice as the final element legitimating Jephthah as leader.[23]

The reason for a vow is noteworthy. Gideon/Jerubbaal tested the deity repeatedly before committing to involvement in the campaign. He did not make a deal with the people he was leading but, once convinced of the deity's power, accepted the offer. Though Gideon/Jerubbaal was offered leadership from the deity he was not offered any kind of rule prior to the battle either by the deity or his countrymen. When he was offered some form of leadership he rejected it (Judg 8:22), though as discussed above it is possible that he, or more likely his children, accepted it. The contrast here is that Gideon/Jerubbaal was chosen by the deity and after he proved himself to his people was offered rule by them. Jephthah was offered rule as the lure to involve him, he accepted, the deity accepted him, and only then did he feel the need to make a deal with the deity rather than verify his other deals in front of the deity. Rather than focus so exclusively on what Jephthah might have meant by this vow, it would be better to try to understand why Jephthah, at this point in his career, felt the need to make any sort of a vow.

The legitimacy of the vow concerns whether Jephthah had an idea about what was going to come out of the house or whether he had no sense of what would exit. At this point in the story the reader still does not know who or what will exit, though a vow like this is so rare and worded in such a way as to establish the possibility that someone he loved would, quite likely, be the first to come out. Sisera's mother reveals that, at least among the Canaanites, or the Canaanite nobility, women waited anxiously for the men to return. This has not changed considerably throughout the last three thousand years. Thus it is likely that a person who loved the military man would be as apt as an animal to come out of the house upon his return.

Caleb's offer of Achsah at the beginning of the book has many parallels with this situation, but again, the order and results of the oath

---

[23] Levenson does not say that the deity required it or that the positive result of the battle was a result of the vow, but does not see any indications in the story that child sacrifice was considered unacceptable to the deity. Ibid.

differ, indicating the downward spiral. Caleb, like the men of Gilead, offered something to the person who was originally unidentified. In Caleb's case he was lucky and a man of Judah, his own brother, won the battle and the hand of his daughter (Judg 1:13). Even here there are indications that the offer was only semi-legitimate as can be seen in Achsah's response to the marriage when she speaks accusingly to her father, saying "you have given me away" (Judg 1:15). In the continuing spiral downward Jephthah made a vow which also led to a status change for his daughter, though in a more destructive way. The final vow made in the book will lead to the destruction of a town and the rape/marriage of its virgin women (Judges 21).

The text does not state what the status of the vow was or who observed it but instead returns to the battle at hand. Jephthah crossed over to the Ammonites, attacked them, the deity delivered them into his hands, the Israelites utterly routed the Ammonites (Judg 11:32), and the Ammonites submitted to them (Judg 11:33). This is one of the shortest battle accounts in Judges. The brevity of the battle's description is emphasized by the extensive negotiations which lead up to it. Three verses introduce Jephthah, seven verses are needed for the negotiations to recruit Jephthah as leader, and sixteen verses are given to the negotiation with the Ammonite king. The entire battle is recounted, however, in a mere two verses. Jephthah was not even concerned with following and capturing the enemy ruler. Clearly the book of Judges is not interested in the details of battle but in the story about the leader, how they were hired, their actions while in charge, and what they did with their power.

The text, and most readers, are focused on what exits Jephthah's house first. When he arrived at his home in Mizpah his daughter came out to meet him with timbrel and dance. The text elaborates that she was an only child, and that he had no other son or daughter (Judg 11:34). Up to this point in the story the text has not mentioned anything about Jephthah's family other than his mother and possible fathers. From the parallel situation in the Deborah narrative the reader expects the mother to have waited for her son to return from battle, and she presumably would have been the one to greet him.

The scenario, especially the introduction to the daughter, recalls the sacrifice of Isaac (Gen 22:2). In that case Abraham was put to the test and was told to take, "your son, your only one, Isaac, whom you love" and sacrifice him to the deity. At the last minute the deity kept Abraham from going through with the task. There are many similarities here, even in phrasing, but the differences are extreme.

The verse introducing the daughter refers to her as, "his daughter, coming out to meet him with timbrel and dance, only she was his one, he did not have from him either a son or daughter" (Judg 11:34). As in Isaac's case the text uses four different descriptions to introduce her. In both cases the offspring were only children.[24] In both cases the child was going to be sacrificed by their father. Both parents were known negotiators, Jephthah with the elders of Gideon and the Ammonites and Abraham repeatedly with the Israelite deity and other people in his life (Gen 12:11-13; 13:8-12; 15:2-6; 17:17-22; 18:20-32; 23:4-16). Both parents had military troops and fought battles (Gen 14:13-16). The similarities set up the comparison but the significant differences, such as who the child was, how the child was classified, the role of the parent in the scene, and the parent's relationship to the deity highlight the contrast and final outcome.

In the Genesis case Isaac was the long awaited offspring of both Abraham and Sarah (Gen 21:1-3). He was the one promised to Abraham, the one to carry on the family line, who would receive the deity's promise in turn, father the nation, and inherit the land (Gen 17:15-22). His father had a special relationship with the deity and his mother was chosen specifically by the deity to bear the line (Gen 17:19). The contrast with Jephthah's daughter is severe.

Jephthah's daughter has no name. Her grandmother was a prostitute or woman of low social standing. Her grandfather either chose not to recognize her father or was unknown. Her mother is not mentioned or referred to in any way. Her father had originally been forced to flee from his home as a result of his parentage. In sharp contrast to the reference that Isaac was the beloved son, the reader of Judges knows nothing about this father's feelings towards his daughter, though it is clear that Jephthah was not the beloved son of his father.[25] All the reader knows about Jephthah's daughter is that she met her father, after his victory, with song and dance.

The two fathers differ in how they reached this point of having to sacrifice their children. Abraham was chosen by the deity to leave his homeland for the promise of a future. While there were difficult moments in his life and he did not receive his gift of children until late in life, the deity provided well for him. He was wealthy (Gen 12:16; 13:5; 20:14),

---

[24] In Isaac's situation in Genesis the reference to his being an only child carries special weight since the reader knows this to be not completely true since Abraham has a son older than Isaac, Ishmael, the son of Hagar. Isaac was the only child only for his mother, Sarah.

[25] Levenson notes the similarity in the terminology of "his only" to the concept of the other beloved sons. Thus the terminology may have a special referent beyond simply numbers of children and relationship to the parent (*Death and Resurrection*, 14).

apparently respected, and eventually received his children. The deity's request for him to sacrifice his son is referred to as a test indicating that it was too easy for Abraham to trust the deity since things had been so good for him.

Jephthah's life was very different. His life began with rejection. He was asked to return to his home only because of what those who had once rejected him felt he could offer them. In many ways Jephthah appears more like Isaac's brother Ishmael, son of Hagar and Abraham. Hagar once fled (Gen 16:6) and was later forced to leave (Gen 21: 9-14) Abaraham's home. Ishmael was the son of a handmaid, therefore a woman with less status than a wife. She fulfilled a narrowly procreative role, similar to Jephthah's mother's apparent sexual role. Sarah, Abraham's legitimate wife, resented Hagar as a rival when she could do the one thing Sarah could not, bear a child. Once Sarah had a child of her own, Hagar's child became a rival in inheritance issues and was banished.

Jephthah's career differed considerably from Abraham's. There is no mention of what would happen if Jephthah did not win his battle against the Ammonites. Jephthah was the one to raise the issue of the deity in the first place, and apparently won the deity over to his side in the negotiating process. Rather than the deity requesting anything of him, he made a vow to the deity before the battle. The text is silent concerning the deity's reaction to the vow. Since the deity joined Jephthah prior to the vow, there is no implication that the deity fought with him only because of the vow. Whether the deity wanted Jephthah to make the vow, or that once the vow was made, would actually desire that Jephthah carry it out, is not clear. In Abraham's case, the deity sent an angel to keep Isaac's sacrifice from happening. Such did not happen here.

The relationship of the fathers to the deity differs considerably. Abraham was chosen by the deity to create a great nation (Gen 12:2). They conversed with each other periodically. Abraham was allowed to question the deity's judgment on such issues as the fate of the inhabitants of Sodom and Gemorrah, and convinced the deity of his own position (Gen 18:23-32). Such was not the case with Jephthah. The deity never called out or spoke to him. He received no direction from the deity, nor is it indicated whether he even knew the deity was with him until he won the battle. Without direct communication to the contrary, Jephthah believed his vow to have been legitimate, successful, and, therefore, one that must be fulfilled.

Both the reader and Jephthah know what would result from fulfilling the vow, but his daughter did not until he saw her, rent his clothes, cried that she had brought him low, and said that she had become his trouble, explaining that he had uttered a vow to the deity and could not retract it (Judg 11:35). He did not state what the vow was, nor what he would do. After he mentioned the sacrifice he would offer to the deity in Judg 11:31 the vow is referred to but never described. When Jephthah told his daughter about the vow he blamed her, because she had come out to greet him, not himself for having made the vow in the first place.

His daughter was dutiful and did not complain. She called him "my father," and stated that he uttered a vow to the Israelite deity and that he must do to her as he vowed since the deity vindicated him against his enemies the Ammonites (Judg 11:36). Her wording is reminiscent of the vow itself. The vow states that Jephthah would sacrifice the first thing that came out of his house to meet him and a literal translation of her words is, "my father, you have opened your mouth to the deity, do to me as came out of your mouth."

While not contesting or even questioning her father's actions she made one final request. She asked for two months to lament upon the hills and bewail her virginity, she and her companions (Judg 11:37). He agreed, using the imperative "Go." The text repeats that he let her go and that she and her "companions" went and bewailed her virginity for two months (Judg 11:38). After two months she returned and he carried out his vow. The text reminds the reader that she had never known a man and finishes by noting that as a result it became a custom for the virgins of Israel to chant dirges for four days in memory of the daughter of Jephthah the Gileadite (Judg 11:39-40).

There has been much discussion concerning what Jephthah's daughter bewailed, what her father did to her, and why. The bottom line is that scholars have difficulty with the daughter lamenting her virginity and her father sacrificing her. In most discussions Jephthah's daughter is said not to be mourning her virginity but the fact that she had no children, and Jephthah is said not to have made the vow in haste but that there was a greater emergency than the text seems to indicate. The need to legitimate Jephthah's actions may be rooted in the New Testament where Jephthah appears in a list as one of the faithful, possibly because he went through with his vow (Hebrews 11:32). Any discussion of the legitimacy of his vow causes trouble with that text.

Jephthah's daughter stated that she was going to the mountains with her "companions" (feminine plural) to bewail "my virginity" *bĕtûlay* (Judg 11:37). The full sense of this term "virgin" must be examined. This is the only form in which the Semitic root, from which the Hebrew word derives, appears except for the plural which refers to "virginity" in the abstract.[26] Its Akkadian cognate means "young

[26] J. Schmitt, "Virginity," *ABD* 6.853.

(unmarried) girl."[27] The term is used in a number of different passages indicating that it is not always precisely synonymous with the modern English idea of the word referring to one who has not experienced sexual intercourse.[28] Many times the term is qualified by a phrase such as "who has never known a man" (Gen 24:16; Num 31:18, and to a certain extent our case). In Joel 1:8 the woman called "a virgin" appears to have had a husband.

Bal suggests that the term means she was a pubescent woman, meaning that she had entered an age when she could be married, and so was no longer a girl.[29] The reference revolves around her role as a marriageable object.[30] Bal connects the scene to that of Achsah, so that in her interpretation Jephthah's daughter was also offered to the victor of the battle, namely the Israelite deity.[31] But one should bear in mind, when evaluating Bal's treatment, that the biblical text never records the females' ages nor what their bodies were or were not doing at any time. The implication is also that she was of an age where she could bear children.

Others connect her bewailing of her (undefined) virginity as a lament for her childlessness. Boling claims, "virginity is presumably a shorthand for childlessness."[32] When the text later notes that she never knew a man Boling again states that the reference is not addressing her knowing a man but her childlessness.[33] The problem with this interpretation is that there is no evidence to support it and it goes against what is happening in the story. The Bible has examples of women who were barren and wanted children and there is terminology available to the biblical writer to express that (Gen 11:20; 16:1; 25:21; 30:1; 1 Sam 1:2). If children were the issue there were a number of ways for the text to say so.

What is somewhat unique about Judges is that the role of women is not the same as in other biblical books. In other biblical books the women's main role revolves around their reproductive status and, if they produce children, how they play a role in the lives of their off-

---

[27] Ibid.

[28] Ibid.

[29] M. Bal, *Death and Dissymmetry: The Politics of Coherence in the Book of Judges*, Chicago Studies in the History of Judaism (Chicago: University of Chicago Press, 1988) 46–52. Also P. Day, "From the Child is Born the Woman: The Story of Jephthah's Daughter," *Gender and Difference in Ancient Israel*, ed. P. Day (Minneapolis: Fortress Press, 1989) 58–74.

[30] Bal, *Death and Dissymmetry*, 51.

[31] Ibid., 63.

[32] Boling, *Judges*, 209.

[33] Ibid.

spring. Such is not the case in Judges. Judges contains few cases of women with their children (Samson's mother appears in Judges 13–14, Michah's mother in Judg 17:2-3). This is the second case where the status of the mother made the son unacceptable to some important ruling group despite the absence of the mothers in the story. The assumption that Jephthah's daughter's distress is rooted in her lack of children is unfounded and goes against the pattern of women in the book thus far.

There are some relevant factors in the daughter's life which are seldom emphasized. She was the granddaughter of a prostitute or woman of low status. There is no reference to who or what her mother was. The only time the daughter is shown she is depicted leaving the house singing and dancing to celebrate her father's return. Her request was to go to the mountains with her "companions" (all women as evidenced by the use of the feminine plural). She bewailed her virginity or possibly her non-married state. The emphasis on what she was missing lies not with what she could have created but those aspects of life that she would never have a chance to experience. The stress repeatedly on what she was missing emphasizes sexual experience.

She asked to mourn her virginity with her companions, not alone. Only when she returned from her trip does the text state that she "never knew a man." The reference to her not knowing a man may not define her status of not having been sexually active, which is not conveyed by the Hebrew term virgin, but stresses that even after her trip to the mountains she still had not known a man, destroying the possibility that she had taken actions to change that status in her two month mountain visit.

Arguing that the daughter feels amiss because she would be missing life or sexual relations may seem extreme, but it is not when one examines the story of Judges thus far, and looks forward to what follows. In the first story of the book, Achsah used sexual relations with her husband to convince him to gain better land, though to no avail (Judg 1:14).[34] Jael may have used her sexuality to lure Sisera into a comfort zone allowing her to kill him (Judg 4:18-21). The previous story described two women who bore children, and therefore were sexually active, although outside some traditional marriage known in Israel (Judg 8:31). In this story a woman was possibly a prostitute and her child's paternal lineage was questioned causing problems in his life (Judg 11:1-3). In the story following Jephthah, the hero Samson visited both a prostitute (Judg 16:1) and a woman. Most assume that there was a sexual relationship between Samson and Delilah and there are no indications that a marriage

[34] Note that Achsah's mother is not listed. Both 1 Chr 2:46 and 1 Chr 2:48 mention Caleb's sons by his various *pîlegeš* but she is not listed as the wife of either.

occurred (Judg 16:4-20). Following Samson there are stories leading to the civil war which involve a *pîlegeš*, a type of woman already seen to carry less than fully wifely status (Judges 19). This *pîlegeš* "prostituted" herself and was raped to death. In the aftermath of the civil war there was a search for "virgins" to marry the Benjaminites (Judges 21). It is clear that it is the sexuality, not the reproductive capabilities of these women (with the possible exception of the wives for Benjamin), that is highlighted. There is no reason to assume anything different about Jephthah's daughter.

The text notes that all the virgins of Israel participated in a festival, though the text does not state where it was held. The tradition of the virgins honoring Jephthah's daughter is significant in light of the end of the book when there is a search for virgin wives for Benjamin (Judges 21). One of their solutions was to take the girls from Shiloh (Judg 21:21). While the text does not state anything explicitly, in all the other cases they were searching for "virgin" wives for Benjamin. In Shiloh the women go out to the fields to celebrate an annual feast of the deity, leaving open the possibility that it may be a reference to the festival initiated in honor of Jephthah's daughter.

There is discussion concerning whether Jephthah carried out the original vow because it is never repeated after its first utterance. This leads some to state that the reason for the discussion of virginity is that she was not sacrificed, in the sense of being killed, but was not allowed to marry.[35] There is little evidence for this. The text states that he carried out the vow. The daughters of Israel commemorated the sacrifice with an event carried out by the virgins of Israel. Throughout the episode the daughter was faithful to her father, he felt sorry for himself, the daughters of Israel remembered Jephthah's daughter with a festival, and the New Testament describes Jephthah as one of the faithful (Heb 11:32).

The question of whether Jephthah carried out his vow has parallels both to the Abraham and Isaac episode mentioned earlier, and the later scene involving Saul and Jonathan. Saul too made a vow, "Cursed be the man who eats any food before night falls and I take revenge on my enemies" (1 Sam 14:24, JPS). Unfortunately for Saul, at that time Jonathan slipped across the Jordan and did not hear the vow. He initiated the attack that ended in a great victory for Israel (1 Sam 14:23-30). A number of problems ensue as a result of the following acts by the famished Israelites, who eat in defiance of the vow of which they were unaware, and Saul notes that even if it was his son Jonathan who de-

---

[35] D. Marcus, *Jephthah and His Vow* (Lubbock, TX: Texas Tech University Press, 1986).

fied the vow he was to be put to death (1 Sam 14:39). Saul learned that Jonathan was the source of the problem and ordered him to be put to death (1 Sam 14:44). In Jonathan's case no angel of the deity saved the son, as in Isaac's case, but the troops declared that because of their great victory, which they had achieved as a result of Jonathan's actions, he was not to be hurt, not so much as a hair on his head (1 Sam 14:45).

The power of this second example is that it again raises the issue of Saul. Saul lost the respect, advice, and counsel of Samuel the prophet shortly after this battle, something from which he never recovered (1 Sam 15:26). While this was not as a result of Saul not carrying out his vow, it was the beginning of the end for him. This case too raises the question of whether Saul's order was legitimate or not. Even his son Jonathan noted that it was not a wise choice since it left the troops famished before an important battle when they would have fought better had they been better fed. This is another example of the sacrifice of a child which was rooted in a vow of dubious legitimacy.

The event which caused Saul's dismissal by his deity also involved an inappropriate sacrifice. The deity commanded the Israelites to proscribe the city, destroying everything. Saul decided to do what he thought was right and took the best sheep and oxen to offer a sacrifice for the Israelite deity (1 Sam 15:21). Samuel and the deity were both explicit that the deity would rather be obeyed than receive illegitimate sacrifices. How powerful a concept in light of the Israelites' initial claim to having repented when they chose Jephthah and offered him rule over them, and his response, making what was apparently an inappropriate vow. Of the three possible human sacrifices which might have been carried out by Israelites, two were not because of intervention. It is no accident that the only time the sacrifice of a child to the Israelite deity was carried out, the victim was a woman who was sacrificed by her father who, despite his victory over the Ammonites, did not usher in a time of rest, nor rule for the traditional forty years, and whose sacrifice took place during this period in Judges which was marked by Israel's downward spiral.

Negotiating a Way Out of a Civil War: Judges 12:1-6

The text immediately turns to the next crisis. The men of Ephraim gathered and crossed the Jordan to Zaphon asking Jephthah why he had marched to fight the Ammonites without calling them (Judg 12:1). Without waiting for an answer, they threatened to burn down the houses of the Gileadites on top of them (Judg 12:1). This is the second time in Judges that the Ephraimites missed a call to fight and appeared afterwards to complain about their treatment (the first time was in Judg 8:1).[36]

The text reintroduces a motif seen earlier, that of burning peoples' houses upon them. This appeared earlier in Jotham's prophecy (Judg 9:20) as a threat from someone whose family had been destroyed by Abimelech, and came true at Shechem (Judg 11:49). This same threat will appear later (Judg 14:15) and be carried out against Samson's intended Philistine wife (Judg 15:6).

Jephthah was again prepared to negotiate, and recounted the history of the conflict by reminding them that he and his people had been in a bitter conflict with the Ammonites, and that he had summoned them but that they had not saved him from them (Judg 12:2). He continued that when he saw that they were no "saviors," he risked his life, advanced against the Ammonites, and the Israelite deity delivered them into his hand. He concluded by asking them why they came to fight him (Judg 12:3).

It is not possible to corroborate Jephthah's portrayal since the text provides no details as to what happened when Israel mustered troops prior to the battle with the Ammonites. The order represented in the text indicates that when the troops were mustered no one was prepared to take a leadership role, which caused the elders of Gilead to enlist Jephthah. After his failed diplomatic appeal he marched through Gilead and Manasseh, but to what end is not recorded. Regardless of the veracity of Jephthah's claims, his attempt at negotiating a way out of this battle was as unsuccessful as his previous effort had been.

One of Jephthah's comments in this speech reveals his attitude toward his mission and role in the victory. Like Gideon/Jerubbaal's children before him, Jephthah viewed his having risked his life as calling for some special treatment. Jotham said since his father risked his life the people owed him and his brothers something (Judg 9:17). Both made this comment despite the Israelite deity's role in their victories. Jephthah's comment is ironic since his life was saved and preserved while in the previous lines he sacrificed his daughter to fulfill his vow and preserve his life, win the battle, and rule over Gilead.

The breakdown in diplomacy caused Jephthah to gather all the men of Gilead, to fight and to defeat the Ephraimites (Judg 12:4). The text

---

[36] There was conflict between the tribes on the eastern and western sides of the Jordan as early as the book of Joshua. Ironically, it was the tribes on the western side of the Jordan who interpreted actions of the eastern Jordan tribes as treasonous and gathered at Shiloh to fight them. The Joshua conflict was settled peacefully by the priest Phinehas, son of Eleazar (Josh 22:7-33).

states that a motivating factor was that Ephraim had called the Gilead-ites nothing but fugitives from Ephraim, because being in Manasseh is like being in Ephraim (Judg 12:4). Boling claims that this was an ob-scure taunt, obscure because we no longer understand the precise im-plications.[37] However, after two stories about men who were considered illegitimate by their brothers, the ramifications of such name-calling is not obscure. What is important for the downward spiral of Judges is that the taunt was along tribal lines, which emphasizes Israel's increas-ing lack of unity and fragmentation into tribes. Yet another leader was motivated by the taunts of an enemy (Gideon/Jerubbaal Judg 8:15).

The Gileadites did not settle for winning. They held the fords of the Jordan against the Ephraimites and tested anyone from Jordan who asked to cross. The Gileadites would ask if they were from Ephraim and if they said no (Judg 12:5), they would ask them to say *"Shibboleth."* According to the text, this is because Ephraimites would not pronounce it correctly, saying *"Sibboleth"* instead. The Gileadites beat the Ephraim-ites in battle and in the war of name-calling actualized their own taunt against Ephraim. The cost of mispronouncing the word was that the Gileadites would seize them and slay them by the fords of the Jordan, felling forty-two thousand Ephraimites in this way (Judg 12:6).

The episode concerning Jephthah ends when Gideon fought and won his battle against Ephraim, but there was no conclusion to their argument. Despite civil war in Israel, the text notes that Jephthah judged Israel for six years (Judg 12:7). This might provide insight into what could happen in Israel while a judge is judging, or it might serve as a commentary on the level to which Israel and her leaders had fallen.

The text notes that Jephthah the Gileadite died and was buried in one of the towns of Gilead (Judg 12:7). Boling follows the LXX, which states that he was buried in his city, but the text never states which city that was. He was born in Gilead, moved to Tob, and had a house in Mizpah, making it unclear which city would be considered his. As with Abimelech (Judg 9:56), there is no mention that the land had rest.

Summary

With Jephthah's story the Israelites continue following the negative characteristics of the previous heroes while neglecting to follow the positive traits modeled by Othniel. The hero no longer fought on behalf of his people but to gain power and seek revenge on those who rejected

---

[37] Boling, *Judges*, 212.

him or called him names. Despite the deity's help in the victory the
hero claimed responsibility. The hero made vows whose end result was
more of an aberration than the failure to fulfill them would have been.
Even worse, the hero initiated the first civil war so that Israel was already fighting itself.

The story picks up on many of the themes seen thus far, though
showing what negative consequences they have when taken to their
extreme. Such is the case with the vow. A vow of dubious legitimacy
was uttered by Caleb, leading to marriage; here, with Jephthah, it led to
child sacrifice. Women were the source of many of Jephthah's problems, through no fault of their own, and were sacrificed by him rather
than protected. Women's sexuality is highlighted, not their role as
mothers. Revenge was the motivating factor. Elements of the David/
Saul polemic are evident.

The following narratives concern minor judges who relate to some
of these issues and provide a slight reprieve from the tension of the
story before the book moves to its conclusion.

Chapter 11

MORE MINOR JUDGES

Judges 12:8-15

The next three judges are similar to the minor judges introduced prior to Jephthah, i.e. they are called minor not because their actions were insignificant but because of the amount of information provided about them and, to a certain extent as well, the types of activities in which they engaged. There is little information concerning any of them. Two of the stories focus on the judge's children, just as in the previous group. However, whereas following the Abimelech episode the focus was on the minor judges' sons, after the Jephthah episode Israelite daughters are included.

Ibzan of Bethlehem: Judges 12:8-10

The text leads into this unit by noting that "after him," Ibzan of Bethlehem judged Israel (Judg 12:8). Since the previous ruler was Jephthah it is likely that he is the "him" to which the text refers. The connection is not strong. There is no reference to rest in the land nor any report of negative actions carried out by the Israelites nor problems that she was having with her neighbors. Israel had a leader when there was no immediate threat necessitating one. As with the earlier minor judges, it is difficult to ascertain if this individual was deity-approved.

While the text states that Ibzan was from Bethlehem, the one in Judah/Benjamin, many scholars have difficulty viewing him as a Benjaminite. According to Boling, the structure of Judges is, at least in part, defined by the idea that each of the tribes at one time or another produced a leader who judged. Since Elon of Zebulun follows, Ibzan was possibly from Asher.[1] According to Soggin there were two Bethlehems in the story; one of Judah and another in the north near Nazareth (also mentioned in Josh 19:15).[2] Both may be correct. Bethlehem, which is specifically not defined by tribal affiliation, plays an important role in the final story and so may be mentioned here to introduce problems concerning that city which would arise in following episodes.

The biblical description of Ibzan causes a theological problem from the Deuteronomistic standpoint. The MT states that he had thirty sons, and he sent outside thirty daughters and he brought for his sons thirty daughters from outside (Judg 12:9). Regarding these children and their in-laws, the text does not state either where they came from or went to. Most versions and commentaries say something like "outside the clan," rather than outside Israel.[3] There is no noun in the text which could be translated "clan," so such a translation is pure speculation.

The use of the term "outside" brings the problem of intermarriage to the text. Ibzan married his daughters "outside," possibly meaning outside of Israel, and brought foreign wives into Israel, or at least into his tribe. Prior to the Jephthah story when judges had many sons, as was the case with both Gideon/Jerubbaal and Jair the Gileadite, the problem of finding wives for them was not raised. Suddenly, after stories about two judges, Abimelech and Jephthah, whose mothers possibly came from outside of Israel, the subject of a source of wives is explicitly raised. The issue of finding a wife for the first time, a theme which plays an important role in the upcoming Samson episode and is the major goal of the final story, also appears here.

Ibzan's pericope ends by noting that he died and was buried in Bethlehem (Judg 12:10).

Elon the Zebulunite: Judges 12:11-12

The text continues to connect the stories of the judges by using the clause "after him." The next judge is Elon, the Zebulonite. He ruled Israel for ten years. About him nothing is known other than that he died and was buried in Aijalon in the territory of Zebulon. The only information provided about this judge is that the name of the location of his burial has the same consonantal spelling as his name.

---

[1] Boling, "Ibzan," *ABD* 3.356.

[2] J. A. Soggin, *Judges: A Commentary,* Old Testament Library (Philadelphia: Westminster, 1981) 223.

[3] Boling, "Ibzan," 356; Soggin, *Judges,* 223; JPS, and RSV.

Problems surrounding him, in light of the limited amount of information, concern the issue of what is happening inside Israel. There is no mention of how or why Israel needed a judge in the time of Ibzan, nor does the text mention that the land had rest as a result of his leadership. The same holds true for Elon. The reader does not know what Israel's status was. All the reader is told is that he was from Zebulun.

At this point the reader is forced to question what qualifications both Ibzan and Elon had to be leaders. They were not designated by the deity, they were not picked by the people, they did not do anything (at least nothing which has been recorded) that benefitted Israel in any way. Even though Elon did not carry out any negative actions, reference to him judging Israel indicates a decline in the office. These minor judges needed no qualifications, did not do anything, nor did they hold the office in response to any crisis.

Abdon, Son of Hillel: Judges 12:13-15

Abdon is connected to the previous judge by the use of the same recurring phrase, "after him." He is introduced as Abdon, son of Hillel, the Pirathonite (Judg 12:13). The text says that he had forty sons and thirty grandsons who rode on seventy burros. The term used for the beast of burden is the same as the one that was used to describe what Jair's children rode (Judg 10:3). As in that previous case, this is remarkable because the number of people traveling on animals in Judges is limited. The reference to grandchildren raises the issue of dynastic plans. He too died and was buried in Pirathon, which is in the territory of Ephraim on the hill of the Amalekites (Judg 12:15).

Summary

The minor judges serve a number of functions in the story. These brief mentions, if nothing else, change the the overall narrative pace of the story and offer further clarifications about leadership in Israel. These stories break the tension following two disquieting episodes. Israel had just witnessed the sacrifice of its leader's daughter and had experienced civil war. Israel's most recent leader had been picked because the times necessitated a ruler, and had a background which, according to his contemporaries, was questionable. The Israelites were in a crisis situation which worsened. The introduction of these three judges breaks the tension. Nothing major happened, there were no major crises. Readers have a chance to find their ground and readjust to the situation before the story hurtles forward again.

These judges reveal to the reader where Israel stands at this point in the narrative, especially important since the stage is constantly being set for what happens at the end of the book. The narrator gives the reader a chance to evaluate what has happened and changed before the final trajectory of the story is revealed.

Where Israel is at this point in the story is not where she was prior to Jephthah. Most scholars consider the paucity of information about the minor judges to be a problem in understanding them. The minor judges are not considered as creating a break with previous circumstances, nor is the lack of information about them, despite the text's reference to them as judging, considered relevant to the discussion about Israel's leadership during the narrative period of Judges.

These stories follow a civil war. The Gileadites fought with their brother tribe of Ephraim. The final resolution to this was the slaughter of forty-two thousand Ephraimites (Judg 12:6). Jephthah judged Israel, but for only six years and the land did not have rest. Jephthah was a leader but not a completely successful one, according to the narrator. This means that while the Ammonites were no longer a threat the land was not at rest, and Israel did not have a leader. There is no reference to the status of Israel's loyalty to their deity.

Three men who judged Israel are introduced next. Up until this point the only judges who were not discussed in the context of an immediate crisis were those who preceded the Jephthah crisis with the Ammonites (Tola son of Puah in Judg 10:1-2 and Jair the Gileadite in Judg 10:3-4). In their cases no specific conflict was mentioned. The minor judges introduce a new theme to the book because now Israel had a leader despite there being no specific crisis at hand. From the beginning of the book until the introduction of the first minor judge, the judges were introduced in response to a specific crisis. The implication is that Israel would go into crisis mode because of the lack of leadership and needed a leader to deal with whatever the crisis was. With the people's request to Gideon/Jerubbaal to rule over them, a new idea is introduced, that Israel needed constant leadership, someone to be in charge at all times. The minor judges introduce that theme in a non-dynastic way. Leaders are introduced without a specific incident necessitating them, leading eventually to the situation where Israel would need a leader regardless of their predicament.

Who the leader should be and what qualities they had is not addressed by the text. These leaders were not deity-appointed, so the reader recognizes them as such simply because of the narrator's statement. No leadership qualities are listed. They do not respond to any specific crisis. The reader is not informed in what capacity they judged nor how they did so. The question of what sort of leadership Israel should have is raised implicitly, because the text seems to imply that anyone can judge, that no special qualities were required. These questions concerning leadership are raised in an indirect way by showing that Israel did not think about addressing who chose their leaders, nor what characteristics they had or should have, nor what their responsibilities should be.

These questions prepare the reader for Samson who, despite being deity chosen, showed no signs of leadership, nor any consideration for his people. It is not even clear that the deity who chose him did so at a time when the Israelites clearly needed leadership.

Chapter 12

SAMSON

Judges 13:1–16:31

Samson is the last major judge in this book and was leader at the lowest end of the scale, just before Israel plunged to its absolute nadir in Judges. In Samson the Israelite deity made a last attempt at temporary leadership, engaging the leader from before his birth. Samson abused almost every aspect of the office of judge. He began the pattern of Israelites doing what was right in their eyes, an action with negative results. His actions set the stage for the ensuing civil war. He chased women who were expressly forbidden by the deity. He engaged the enemy only for purposes of personal revenge.

Samson's story is another example where modern scholarship is particularly sexist with scholars describing Samson as, for example, "a helpless hero in the power of a woman."[1] Soggin claims, "The erotic adventures of the hero are simply the exemplification of the theme of the foreign woman who brings shame, deception and death."[2] The idea of Samson as a virtuous hero appears as early as Josephus who declares (exempting his sexual weaknesses), ". . . in all other respects he was one of extraordinary virtue" (*Ant.* 5.8.12). Parallels between Samson and the New Testament further keep the text from being interpreted on its own merit or even allowing it to function within the context of the MT.[3] Yet Samson's story is in line with what has happened thus far in

---

[1] James A. Crenshaw, "Samson," *ABD* 5.952.

[2] J. A. Soggin, *Judges: A Commentary,* Old Testament Library (Philadelphia: Westminster, 1981) 237.

[3] The text relates particularly with that of Matt 1:21 where Jesus' pending birth is announced. Crenshaw, "Samson," 951–4, and Soggin, *Judges,* 234.

Judges. Questions surrounding leadership are raised, the relationship between Israel and the deity is examined, intermarriage is denigrated, and women are fundamental to the way the leader is evaluated.

Samson's Birth Announcement: Judges 13:1-23

The Samson story begins with the notice that the children of Israel did "the bad thing" in the eyes of the deity who gave them to the hand of the Philistines (Judg 13:1). "The bad thing" has played an important role in the lives of most of the heroes thus far but in no other case has the text been so explicit about the judge's interest in marrying a foreign woman and having other liaisons, in this case two of them, probably with foreign women. The announcement of the Israelites' return to doing "the bad thing" is particularly relevant preceding this final judge.

The Israelites did not cry out to the deity for help. In the stories about the minor judges, they seem to have judged without cause since no case of oppression was introduced into the text. The situation is the opposite in the Samson story; the Israelites were in distress but did nothing about it. It is not clear if this is a commentary on the previous minor judges, which would indicate that even having a judge had not helped them, or on the Israelites, that they did not notice that they were in distress, or that they no longer knew what to do or to whom they should turn in a crisis.

The period of time since the previous ruler was an even forty years, a generation. As with the other judges, this contextualizes the following information tying it into the ongoing story of Israel. Up to this point the Philistines were one of the peoples left as a test of the Israelites, but with whom the Israelites had had direct contact on only two occasions. In the first case (Judg 3:31) Shamgar slew six hundred. In Judg 10:6-7 Israel served the Philistine deities, among others, which resulted in the Israelite deity selling them to the Philistines and Ammonites. Neither here nor in the previous cases has much information been provided about this enemy.

The present story continues by focusing on what happened to Manoah, from Zorah from the family of Dan, the man who became Samson's father (Judg 13:2). Zorah was a town originally assigned to Dan on the border with Judah (Josh 19:41). Later in Judges it will be used as the point of departure for the migration of the Danites (Judg 18:2, 8, 11). Samson's mother is introduced, as are most barren women in the biblical text, by focusing on her as an unlikely source of procreation, the first thing noted about her is that she was barren (as was Sarah in Gen 11:20 and as Hannah will be in 1 Sam 1:2). In this case the absence of children and her barren state are more important than her name which, as was the case with Jephthah's daughter, mother, and wife, is not included.

A messenger of the Israelite deity appeared to the woman informing her that she was barren, and had not borne children, but that she would bear a son (Judg 13:3). He warned her to be careful and not to drink any wine or other intoxicant or to eat anything unclean because she was going to conceive and bear a son (Judg 13:4).[4] She should let no razor touch his head because he was going to be a Nazirite to the deity from the womb. The messenger continued that the child would be the first to begin to deliver the Israelites from the Philistines (Judg 13:5). The messenger does not state that he would deliver the Israelites, only that he would begin that battle. Note that the stakes have changed. The deity-chosen leaders, even when designated before their conception, can now only hope to begin the process of redemption. The statement is reminiscent of the Israelites' original question to the deity, "Who will go up for us in the beginning to lead us?" (Judg 1:1).

The status of Samson's mother is slightly difficult to understand because of the tenses employed in her description. Originally the text notes that the woman was barren and had borne no children. Here the messenger declared, "you are already pregnant and bearing a son" (Judg 13:5).[5] According to Boling this is not a problem because the same pattern is found with Hagar in Gen 16:11. Both appear in discussions between a woman and a messenger of the deity concerning an impending birth of a son. The difference is that in the case of Hagar, intercourse between her and the father of the conceived child had already taken place prior to the messenger's announcement and Hagar was fleeing because she already knew she was pregnant (Gen 16:4). In Judges, a barren woman suddenly became pregnant with no apparent interceding sexual experience.

The divine messenger delivering news of the impending birth of a child to a barren wife is similar to the Sarah episode where messengers

---

[4] R. G. Boling translates this term as beer. He sees no evidence for distilled liquors in ancient times, and states that since wine was mixed with water, beer was stronger in alcoholic content. He continues that the Philistines must have used an enormous amount of beer as indicated by so many "beer strainer jugs" found at Philistine sites. His assumption is that what archaeologists refer to as, "beer strainer jugs," definitively held beer, something for which there is no evidence. *Judges: Introduction, Translation and Commentary*, The Anchor Bible (Garden City: Doubleday, 1981) 219.

[5] Boling's translation (*Judges*, 217).

of the Israelite deity visited Abraham and told him that Sarah would bear a child (Gen 18:10). Crenshaw notes the comparison and the contrast by stating that, "Like her predecessor Sarah, Manoah's wife received a divine visitor who communicated news of a forthcoming birth. Unlike Sarah, she was still capable of giving birth, hence her response was thoughtful silence rather than disbelieving laughter."[6]

Crenshaw notes that the messengers visited Sarah and told her that she was going to bear a child, though this is not exactly what happened, according to the text. The messengers visited Abraham who, upon their arrival, sent Sarah to cook (Gen 18:1-6). The men asked where his wife Sarah was, using her name specifically and intentionally to indicate which of his women/wives was intended, so that there would be no confusion (Gen 18:9).[7] The messengers never spoke to Sarah directly but she listened at the entrance to the tent (Gen 18:10). The narrator informs the reader that both Abraham and Sarah were old, and that Sarah was no longer having her period (Gen 18:11).

All other assertions to the contrary, according to the MT Sarah spoke to herself. The reason she provided for her own laughter was, "Now that I am withered am I to have enjoyment—with my husband so old?" (Gen 18:12, JPS). There is no mention of a child. Her laughter was not in disbelief but excitement. It is not clear if her excitement was from the prospect that she would have enjoyment from the joy of being a mother or that she was about to have a sexual encounter with her husband. The term "enjoyment" 'ednâ is from the root meaning "languor."[8] This is the only case where the root appears in this form and is treated as having a sexual connotation.[9] The implication is that the reason for Sarah's laughter was not rooted in the reproductive aspect of the messenger's claim but the sexual. The two scenes must be compared in light of the way the text is written.[10]

The first key difference is that in both stories a messenger delivered the information about the impending birth, but differ in whom they ad-

---

[6] Crenshaw, "Samson," 952.

[7] Identifying which wife/woman is important since Hagar had already borne Abraham a son and she is referred to as his wife/woman "Sarai. . . . gave her to her husband Abram as a wife" ʾiššāh lô lĕ ʾiššâ in the episode when he first took Hagar sexually and she conceived Ishmael (Gen 16:3).

[8] BDB, 726.

[9] Ibid.

[10] It is true that later in the text Sarah was reprimanded by the deity for laughing (Gen 18:13), and the implication is that she laughed about having a child. The truth, according to the text, is that Sarah did not laugh about having a child, but Abraham laughed at that thought earlier, when he first heard about Sarah's possible pregnancy (Gen 17:17). The deity reprimanded Sarah for something Abraham did.

dress. Sarah's messenger did not visit Sarah, nor did he speak to her. She was not invited to the discussion and, had she not been listening at the door, would never have heard his words. The contact was between Abraham and the messenger. In the Judges case the messenger sought out Samson's mother specifically. As the story unfolds, it becomes clear that she was the one who had been singled out and that the messenger only spoke to the father Manoah as a last act, primarily for the mother's sake. Samson's mother was the one who had direct contact with the messengers in contrast to Sarah. The fathers also play a role in this comparison. Abraham regularly had contact with the deity, either directly or in the form of messengers. The strangers appeared directly after the incident in which the deity changed both Abram's and Sarai's names and stated explicitly that Sarah would be the mother of the great nation that would descend from Abraham's seed (Gen 17:15). In this section Abraham did not believe that Sarah could give birth and laughed at the idea (Gen 17:17), informing his deity that he was prepared to accept Ishmael as his son and successor (Gen 17:18). The deity assured Abraham that Ishmael would fare well, but nonetheless designated Sarah as the mother of the child of promise (Gen 17:20). Despite this the deity did not appear to her, either in person or through a messenger, but only to her husband. Such is not the case with Samson. As the text continues it becomes even more apparent that Samson's mother was the person for whom the message is intended.[11]

One reason for the message being given directly to Samson's mother is rooted in the messenger's intention that Samson be a Nazirite from the womb. The Nazirite reference makes a connection to the following story about Samuel. He was also the son of a previously barren mother and went on to lead Israel in the transition from judges, rulers who arose only in times of crisis, to a king and a stable monarchy, but did so as priest. Elements from the transition between Judges and the books of Samuel are introduced here.

The term *nāzîr* comes from the root *n-z-r* which refers to dedication and consecration.[12] The laws of the Nazirite are found in Num 6:1-21. A Nazirite may be either a man or a woman (Num 6:2). The salient feature is that the person utter a vow setting themselves apart for the Israelite deity (Num 6:2). There are a number of specific details which are

---

[11] There are also parallels with the birth of Samuel story (1 Sam 1:1–2:11), but the situations are very different because the point of parallel here concerns not the birth of a child to a barren woman but, more importantly, the messenger of the Israelite deity announcing the pregnancy and birth and there are no such characters in the Samuel/Hannah story.

[12] *BDB*, 634.

important in understanding the relationship of the term to Samson. A Nazirite must abstain from wine and any other intoxicant, not drinking anything in which grapes have been steeped or even eating grapes at all, whether fresh or dried (Num 6:3). Throughout the term of their vow no razor shall touch their head (Num 6:5), indicating that one was considered a Nazirite for a period of time, a term. During the term a Nazirite shall not go where there is a dead person, even if it is a close relative (Num 6:7). If a person dies suddenly near the Nazirite it defiles their consecrated hair and they have to shave their head on the same day to make themselves clean (Num 6:9).

These laws indicate that being a Nazirite is a temporary state, not a life-long one. There are extensive instructions concerning how to make the Nazirite clean again after their hair has been defiled by someone near them dying suddenly. The Nazirite must be reconsecrated and re-dedicated to the deity for the remainder of their term as Nazirite, stressing again the temporary nature of the status (Num 6:9-12). The reconsecration includes shaving off the consecrated hair and putting the locks of hair to the fire. As is evident in the Samson episode, the hair of the Nazirite is a major element in defining their distinctiveness.

The woman returned to her husband and told him that a man of the Israelite deity came to see her and that he looked like a messenger of the deity. She called it "frightening" (Judg 13:6). She relayed what the messenger had told her; she was going to conceive and bear a son and she could drink no wine or other intoxicant and eat nothing unclean for the boy was to be a Nazirite to the deity from the womb to the day of his death (Judg 13:7). The woman is described as knowing who the messenger was.

Samson's mother added in her account, "until the day of his death." Some note that since the term of the Nazirite is limited, her addition placed too large a burden on Samson. Related to this problem is that she did not tell Samson's father that he would become the first to save Israel from the Philistines, the act which ultimately cost him his life. She was either prophetic in her words, through her interpretation of what the messenger said to her, or responsible for later problems in the hero's life, as were the mothers of Abimelech and Jephthah.

Manoah's first action was to plead with the deity asking that the man of Elohim whom he had sent earlier should come again and instruct them how to act with the child who was to be born (Judg 13:8). He expressed no joy or thanks about the child that was to be born, nor did Samson's mother. Neither parent expressed dismay at the lack of a child in their lives.[13] Manoah used the first person plural pronoun "we"

[13] Crenshaw, "Samson," 952.

in his question when asking, what should "we" do concerning the child. The man of whom he spoke had already told the mother how to act and she was the only one who could do anything for the child at that point. The man was not willing to accept her words or account of the incident. According to Boling this shows that in the Hebrew Bible caution about the testimony of women is a recurring phenomenon.[14] He goes on to say, "The woman doesn't really know what she is saying, though she is dropping hints all along the way."[15]

Boling's sexism clouds his understanding of the text since his statement assumes that Manoah's questioning of his wife is legitimated by the text. He never contemplates the possibility that Manoah's disbelief concerning his wife is indicative of some of the problems of the period. Throughout the book the role of women, and the way men have treated them, has been haphazard and often dangerous for the women. The examples are numerous: Achsah, who had to ask her father for land rather than her husband; Jael, whom Sisera assumed would protect him and instead protected Israel; Abimelech's mother, who was not considered equal to the others; the women Abimelech killed in the tower, the one who ultimately caused his death, and most recently Jephthah's daughter, who was killed by her father for meeting him in joy over his victory. Throughout the book, women's situations have been becoming more desperate. A request for better land from a father who gave her away has led ultimately to a father killing his own daughter. It is possible that in the Samson case, especially in light of what follows, Manoah should have believed Samson's mother since the text goes on to prove that she was correct. This may be ironic foreshadowing since Samson had the opposite problem of trusting women at the wrong times.

In the following verse the deity heeded Manoah's plea and the messenger of the deity visited the woman again when she was sitting in the field (Judg 13:9). While it is clear that the messenger's appearance was in response to Manoah's request, the text also states explicitly that the woman's husband Manoah was not with her. This reemphasizes the role of the woman, showing that her messages should be trusted (Judg 13:9). The woman, either knowing that she would not be believed or that her husband wanted to see the messenger for himself, hastily ran to tell her husband that the man who came to her before had just appeared to her again (Judg 13:10).

---

[14] Boling, *Judges*, 221.

[15] Ibid. So too Soggin who claims that she anticipates something that she cannot yet know (*Judges*, 234).

Manoah followed his woman/wife and when he came to the man he immediately asked him if he was the man who had spoken to his woman/wife (Judg 13:11), again showing that he gave no credence to his woman/wife. The messenger answered in the affirmative. The text phrases Manoah's question in this way, "are you the man who spoke to the woman/wife." This is a case where traditionally the word for "wife" is translated as "woman" because "woman" would not make sense in this context. For example, Boling claims that the definite article has demonstrative force, understanding it as "this woman." Yet knowing that the term also means wife, combined with the first reference to her as the woman/wife of Manoah in this same verse, could mean that Manoah was making a statement of ownership.

Manoah continued with the wish that the man/messenger's words should come true. He asked what rules should be observed for the boy (Judg 13:12). The messenger, who here is identified as belonging to the deity, told Manoah that the woman must abstain from all the things of which he warned her (Judg 13:13), repeating them almost verbatim: she must not eat anything that comes from the grapevine, nor drink wine or other intoxicant, nor eat anything unclean. He concluded that she must observe all that he commanded her to do (Judg 13:14).

Most commentators note that the emphasis in this case is on the mother, but do not connect the messenger's address with statements made previously. Earlier Manoah either did not believe his wife, or wanted to be involved in the prophecy himself. When he finally received the opportunity it was because his wife took the time to find him when the messenger appeared again. When he had a chance to determine his role he was almost rebuffed by the messenger. He has no role in the preparations for the child's birth, everything was the responsibility of the mother.

Manoah spoke again to the messenger asking if he could detain him so that he could prepare a kid for him (Judg 13:15). The messenger told him that if he detained him he would not eat his food, and if he wanted to present an offering he should offer it to the Israelite deity (Judg 13:16). Manoah persisted by asking the man his name, explaining that they would like to honor him when his words came true (Judg 13:17). The narrative makes very clear that Manoah said this to a messenger of the Israelite deity, highlighting that the reader, and to a certain extent Manoah's wife, know this, but that Manoah either still does not understand or refused to believe.

Some emphasize that Manoah asked the question incorrectly, stating, "who is your name" rather than, "what is your name."[16] Boling

---

[16] Boling, *Judges*, 222.

says that this was a stutter resulting from nervous excitement. He notes that Manoah, like Gideon, needed evidence. He ties this to Jacob's question following his struggle with the deity's messenger (Gen 32:28) and Moses' question at the burning bush (Exod 3:13). While both ask the deity's name, Jacob had just had a battle with the messenger and felt he deserved to know with whom he had fought, and Moses had to carry out a mission on behalf of the deity and did not know how to address the source of his mission. The contexts are significantly different. In the cases of Jacob and Moses, the deity had already proved to the humans that the character with whom they were dealing was divine. Manoah still did not realize who or even what the messenger was.

What is not discussed is that the wife/mother needed no proof. She understood who the man was upon her first meeting with him and unlike Gideon and her husband she did not need a name or proof. This might mean simply that, because she was a woman, she lacked the ability to question. If her gender were different this would be evidence of her great faith in the deity. The messenger's response to Manoah, that he must not ask his name, for it is unknowable, highlights her act and its legitimacy. The lack of a name for the deity's messenger likens the messenger to Manoah's wife, who also has no name. Those who are named continue the trend, since the story of Deborah and Jael, where none of the women have names, a trend that with the exception of Delilah continues until the end of the book.

Manoah took the kid and meal and, rather than offer them to the messenger, offered them upon the rock to the Israelite deity. While he did so, according to the text, a wonderful thing happened (Judg 13:19). As Manoah and his wife watched, the flames leapt from the altar toward the sky and the deity's messenger ascended in the flames of the altar. While Manoah and his woman/wife continued to look on they flung themselves upon the ground (Judg 13:20).

The text's next comment is that the messenger of the deity never appeared to Manoah and his wife again (Judg 13:21). How long it took is not clear but Manoah eventually realized that the man was a messenger of the deity (13:21). Manoah said to his wife that they would surely die for having seen a divine being (Judg 13:22). His wife, having figured out who the messenger was the first time she saw him, added that had the deity intended to take their lives he would not have accepted their burnt offering and meal offering nor let them see such things. She added that he would not have made such an announcement (Judg 13:23). The next verse actualizes her analysis by noting that the woman bore a son and named him Samson (Judg 13:24).

Boling points out that this unit (Judg 13:21-24) displays a skillful antithesis to the preceding one, where the unnamed wife was shown to be on the brink of an identification that would require a miracle to convince her husband.[17] The woman immediately identified the deity's messenger and required no proof of who he was. It would not be an antithesis had it been acknowledged earlier that she was correct. It was the husband who could not believe her because he was not immediately involved. It was also the husband who, like Baraq, Gideon, and Jephthah, needed proof of the deity's word and presence, often at the expense of others. The woman understood that the deity would not promise them a child, especially a consecrated child, only to kill them.

Samson's Early Years: Judges 13:24-25

The woman/wife bore a son, and she named him Samson (Judg 13:24). The text states explicitly that the woman named the son. The messenger had not hinted at a name, nor is there any explanation of the name in the text. The name is related to the Semitic word for sun *šemeš*.[18] There are a number of plays on words with sun and night, lightness and darkness, in this cycle; fire plays an important role also, and Samson's name introduces those themes initially.

No narrative is dedicated to Samson's birth or childhood other than the mere mention that he grew and that the Israelite deity blessed him (Judg 13:24). When Samson next appears the spirit of the deity moved him in the camp of Dan between Zorah and Eshtaol (Judg 13:25). Geographically speaking this is the region of the tribe of Dan prior to their northern migration and is in keeping with what the text provided about Samson's father. The text is vague about what is entailed in being "moved by the spirit of the deity." As observed in the Jephthah episode, it is not always apparent to the character that the deity was with him since Jephthah only made his vow after the deity's spirit had invaded him. In this case Samson was moved, but to do what is not explained.

Samson's Attempt at Marriage: Judges 14:1-20

Samson's age when the deity moved him is as unclear as his age when, in the next scene, he went down to Timnah and saw a woman from the daughters of the Philistines (Judg 14:1). The text is silent as to

---

[17] Ibid., 225.
[18] *BDB*, 1039.

the reason for Samson's trip to Timnah. Philistines have played only a minor role in the book of Judges thus far, and what cities were considered "Philistine" or "Israelite" has not been specified. Timnah is associated with the site of Tel Batash, which has recently been excavated to reveal a Philistine city dating to the Iron I period.[19] The text adds that the daughter of the Philistines was a woman/wife. Here the term carries the connotation of woman rather than wife, although its use here is unique since this description usually is not used for younger single women. Samson is apparently of marriageable age because when he returned he told his father and mother that he had seen a woman in Timnah from among the Philistines and he desired that they should take her for him as a woman/wife. The phrase that Samson used, "to take," usually contains a sexual connotation, especially in the phrase, "to take a wife." The exact phrase is used by Sarah when she suggested Abraham have sexual relations with Hagar (Gen 16:2). The interpretation that Samson wanted her as a wife is legitimate but there could also be sexual allusions in his request.

Samson's mother was still involved. She played an important role in learning about his impending birth and was the parent who understood the situation better and earlier than the father concerning the messenger heralding Samson's birth. Her presence is distinct from that of the other women in the book, who either did not have children (Achsah, Deborah, Jael, and Jephthah's daughter), or who are mentioned only in passing, without names (the mothers of Abimelech and his half brothers, and Jephthah's mother). Samson's parents' displeasure with his choice is revealed by their asking whether there was no one among the daughters of his brothers or among all their people that he had to go to the uncircumcised Philistines (Judg 14:3). Samson answered his father with the command, "Get me that one," adding that she was the one that was right in his eyes (Judg 14:3). The text states that he answered his father and the command is in the masculine singular. In Samson's eyes the mother apparently no longer played a role. As seen above, his mother had been the one to understand situations more quickly than the father and interpret them more appropriately. Samson's dismissal of his mother may be an early sign of the beginning of his trusting the wrong women, leading to his personal ruin.

Rejecting his mother's advice Samson chose what was, "right in his eyes," introducing a problem that will escalate and continue to be used until the end of the book, which says, "every man did what was right in his own eyes" (Judg 21:25). The phrase is not used as a laudatory description of the people's freedom but rather as a sign of the anarchy

---

[19] A. Mazar and G. Kelm, "Batash, Tel," *NEAEHL* 1.152-7.

which followed the civil war. A hint of the idea was introduced in the Abimelech story when Zebul commanded Abimelech to do, "as your hand finds" (Judg 9:33). The Samson story adds the idea of doing what is right, although it focuses not on one's hands, but on one's eyes. Samson's choice led to disaster for the woman, her family, a number of Philistines, and the Israelites.

The use of eyes also plays up the light and dark aspects of the Samson story. Samson followed his eyes, not his parents or the deity. His choice led to fire and destruction. It is ironic since at the end of the story it is his eyes, which caused the initial tragic series of events, that were destroyed, leaving him in total darkness.

This is also the first time that the uncircumcised state of the Philistines is mentioned. Although all translations use the term "uncircumcised," a better translation of the term is, "the foreskinned ones." This is fitting since what was different about the Philistines, in the eyes of the Israelites, was not that they were missing something but that they possessed something that the Israelites did not. One reason for the use of "uncircumcised" may be because "foreskinned ones" sounds somewhat crude. Yet the crudeness of the term is quite possibly the intention. The Philistines were the enemy and what better way to depict them as dirty and barbaric than by referring so vividly to something that the writer's group disdains.

The narrator emphasizes that Samson's father and mother did not know that this choice, apparently Samson's alone, was in fact the deity's doing. In so doing, the narrator allows the reader to identify with the parents, sharing their discomfort. The narrative continues to explain that the deity was seeking a pretext against the Philistines, for they were ruling over Israel at that time (Judg 14:4). The term for rule used here is the same that the Israelites had used earlier in their request of Gideon/Jerubbaal (Judg 8:22), the last deity-appointed ruler. The situation is that since no one was leading the Israelites the deity created Samson. The deity needed to seek a pretext because the Israelites no longer fought Philistine control nor did they cry out to their deity.

Despite his parents' protest, Samson, accompanied by his father and mother went down to Timnah. When "he," the pronoun apparently refers to Samson, came to the vineyards of Timnah a full-grown lion came roaring at him (Judg 14:5). The spirit of the deity gripped him and he tore the lion apart with his bare hands, as one might a kid, but he did not tell his father and mother (Judg 14:6). This episode is crucial for understanding many aspects in Samson's life. This incident will be used for Samson's riddle. It is the first demonstration of Samson's strength, which the text says was from the deity, that the reader is aware of.

Samson continued his journey, spoke to the woman, and again, she was still right in his eyes (Judg 14:7). When Samson returned some time later to take her he turned aside to look at the remains of the lion, and in the lion's skeleton he found a swarm of bees and honey (Judg 14:8). Samson scooped the honey into his palms and ate it as he went along. When he rejoined his father and mother he gave them some and they ate it, but he did not tell them he had taken the honey from the lion's skeleton (Judg 14:9).

These verses raise serious questions about Samson. On his first trip to Timnah he went through the vineyard to kill the lion, apparently without his parents. Both his mother and father, who joined him on the trip to Timnah, were with him, but when he went through the vineyard he was apparently alone. The vineyard is a place that he, as a Nazirite, should not have been. Theoretically, there could be a time of year when there were no grapes on the vine, and if the owners of the vineyard had been careful and there were absolutely no leftover grapes of any kind remaining in the vineyard Samson may not have transgressed the prohibition which forbade Nazirites from coming into contact with grapes. The text's stress on the rules for the Nazirite prior to his birth, elaborating on precisely what the mother could not consume, along with the stress of the specific type of field he was traversing make this highly unlikely. The reference to Samson not telling his parents reinforces that he knew they would be displeased with his actions. The text here highlights Samson's possible trespass of the Nazirite vows.

The story continues once the family arrived in Timnah, with Samson's father coming down to the woman and Samson making a feast there, in the words of the text, "as the young men do" (Judg 14:10). Soggin notes that all the ancient manuscripts have the absurd reference to "his father" carrying out these actions.[20] The prime motivation in his analysis is the idea that Samson must emerge a hero. In his interpretation Samson alone arranged the marriage, the feast, and the companions indicating that he "took matters into his own hands."[21]

Soggin's interpretation ignores the fact that the very thing which Samson pursued was what the deity had explicitly forbidden the Israelites throughout the text, intermarriage. This pursuit of the forbidden highlights many issues raised throughout Judges thus far. Samson asked for something from his parents which he should not have requested (reminiscent of Achsah?), his parents noted why this should not take place, and offered other options. Samson stated that this option was the one which appeared right (straight) in his eyes. This sets the

---

[20] Soggin, *Judges*, 241.
[21] Ibid., 240.

reader up for the final statement in the book (Judg 21:25) where the phrase is used in a non-praiseworthy fashion. What indicates a further decline in Israel's standards is that like Caleb, the parents followed their child's command. In Achsah's case it is not clear whether she was disregarding a request of her father, as Samson clearly did not listen to his parents. Samson is depicted as an uncontrollable child whose parents followed his command to break the deity's commandments and were not able to persuade him to follow their suggestions.[22]

The lack of parental control is in keeping with other gender issues in the book. Samson's father lacked control over Samson. Manoah was not the one who understood the identity of the messenger or his task. When Samson asked something of his parents that he knew they would not like he spoke directly to his father and to his father only (Judg 14:3). The present reference reemphasizes the father's lack of control over his child. The placement is important since in the following stories the relationships between the father of the *pîlegeš* to her and her man/husband are crucial, and this text provides another look at relationships and the role of in-laws. It is possible, in light of what happens later on in the story, that it was the father-in-law-to-be who watched over the new wife while the husband participated in the feasting ritual.

The term for the feast which Samson hosts comes from the word for drinking and translates as an "occasion for drinking" or even, "drinking bout" *mišteh*.[23] In many instances where the term is used, the people partaking in the event became very drunk, indicating that alcoholic beverages were served (1 Sam 25:36-37). Samson as a Nazirite was prohibited from drinking alcohol. In this case he not only did not avoid it but promoted it. The text states that the reason for doing this was that this was what the young men did. In other words, Samson was following a custom, possibly of the Philistines since he was marrying one.[24] The repeated fear in the book of Judges is that intermarriage leads to carrying out the traditions of other people, which then leads to the worship of other gods. Here, even before the marriage was finalized, Samson carried out Philistine rituals defying both his Israelite and Nazirite obligations.

---

[22] According to Deut 21:18, Samson should be stoned for his defiance and disobedience to his parents.

[23] *BDB*, 1059.

[24] The concept of a *mišteh* is not Philistine, since Abraham threw one for the weaning of Issac (Gen 21:8). In light of the Philistine bride, the Philistine location of the event, the Philistine guests, the custom is either a Philistine practice or Samson

The text continues that an undefined "they" saw "him" (referring to Samson) and as a result designated thirty companions to be with him (Judg 14:11). Rather than, "upon their seeing him," Boling translates, "because they were afraid of him."[25] He bases his change on a private communication with David Noel Freedman where he states that the difference between "see" and "fear" were often confused. The change seems an extreme position considering what Samson must have looked like and what the Israelites knew he was capable of physically. If his hair was as long as most picture it, he was a foreigner in Timnah, and had he shown any of his strength in a public setting, then the mere sight of him could cause fear. The idea of seeing and judging by sight alludes to the ongoing theme that people were doing what was right in their eyes, a practice the text does not legitimate.

The thirty people are designated as the "companions." The term appears in a number of other places in Judges. There were "comrades" in the Amalekite camp discussing dreams (Judg 7:13), and only a few lines later they turned on each other (Judg 7:22). In Jephthah's story the daughter went off for two months with her female "companions" (Judg 11:37-8). The idea of friendship is included in the term. Yet in the Gideon/Jerubbaal story the companions were described as turning on one another as soon as confusion erupted in the camp (Judg 7:22). In keeping with the later reference, the actions of these people toward Samson appear less than friendly, and the reason they were appointed in the first place was because of their discomfort with his looks.

Much discussion concerning the companions surrounds the reference that "this was the custom."[26] Since Samson was a Nazirite, who was not supposed to be drinking, the reference to a custom legitimates why he would go so far as to provide a drinking festival. The argument continues that if this were not an Israelite, but Philistine custom, it would explain why the companions were provided by the Philistines. What both these aspects highlight is that Samson was doing precisely what the Israelites were repeatedly told not to do; take on the customs of those people left surrounding them by the deity as a snare. Samson, the final judge, sought out foreign customs. Having companions provided for him indicates that he had none of his own. Samson had no Israelite companions, other than his parents and those Israelites with whom he is depicted in moments of conflict. He chose to marry, live

---

is imposing an Israelite practice on the Philistines at the moment when he chooses to spend his life with Philistines.

[25] Boling, *Judges*, 231.

[26] J. Gray, *Joshua, Judges, Ruth*, The New Century Bible Commentary (Grand Rapids: Eerdmans, 1986) 329.

with, fight, and die with the Philistines. His love of Philistines was precisely what the deity feared and why the Israelites were tested; to see if the Israelites would follow the nations surrounding them. This is the beginning of Samson failing the test miserably.

Samson's Riddle: Judges 14:12-18

Samson propounded a riddle to his guests. He stated that if they, presumably the companions, could give him the right answer during the seven days of the feast then he would give them thirty linen tunics and thirty sets of clothing (Judg 14:12). The other side of the bargain was that if they could not tell him the answer they had to give him thirty linen tunics and thirty sets of clothing. They agreed, telling him to ask his riddle and saying that they would listen (Judg 14:13). Samson told them this riddle: "Out of the eater came something to eat. Out of the strong came something sweet." For three days they could not answer (Judg 14:14). It is most likely that Samson made his bet about the riddle with the thirty companions.

Samson's riddle was not really a riddle since it was based on his personal experience and could not be solved by anyone who was not in the vineyard with him when he encountered the lion.[27] According to the information provided by the text, no one was with Samson in the vineyard. The text states explicitly that even Samson's parents were not in the vineyard when the lion attacked, nor later when he found the honey. It also states that he did not tell his parents, thus Samson was the only person in the world who could solve the riddle. Samson's addition of a hefty bet to the riddle indicates that he knew he would win. What his intentions were and how he thought this situation would be received by his new in-laws and their friends is not clear.

The text is confused concerning the timing of the next few events. It originally states that the marriage feast was to last seven days and that they had until the seventh day to solve the riddle. The previous verse stated that on the third day they still had not solved the riddle, which leads the reader to believe that the following event would happen either on the evening of the third day or on the fourth day. Instead the text states that the next event occurred on the seventh day, which would be the last possible day, which cannot be. The LXX, Syr, and OL all read "fourth day."

---

[27] A riddle is defined as, "A puzzling question stated as a problem to be solved by clever ingenuity: a conundrum." *Funk and Wagnalls Standard Dictionary*, s.v. "riddle."

While the timing in the text is confused, as it stands now it says that on the seventh day they told Samson's woman/wife to coax her man to provide them with the answer to the riddle or else they would put her and her father's house to the fire. Their reason is rooted in the following question where they asked her if she had invited them in order to impoverish them (Judg 14:15). The relationship of all the characters to each other is not clear in this verse, though the main theme is. The people who agreed to the bet, presumably the companions, threatened Samson's woman/wife if she did not learn the answer to the riddle and tell them.

One of the relationships that is not clear at this point is that of Samson to his intended bride. As mentioned earlier it is not clear at what point in the arrangements the woman officially became a wife. The terminology used in this sentence is ambiguous since she is called a woman/wife using the same noun applied to her when Samson first saw her (Judg 14:1). Its use here does not require that she was officially his wife yet. Boling claims that the status of betrothed women is almost identical to that of married women, but even he admits that they are not identical.[28] The difference between the two is crucial here, especially in the eyes of Samson and the woman/wife's father. Boling uses Gen 29:23-27 to show that a marriage was consummated on the first day of the seven day feast.[29] The passage cited involves Jabob's accidental marriage to Leah rather than Rachel. While it is true that he cohabited with Leah on the first night of the marriage week, he was not allowed to marry the other wife until the end of the week, which may mean that mere cohabitation was not the final consummating feature of a marriage. Here the text refers to Samson as her "man." When the term *îš* is used for husband it is often in unusual circumstances where the term seems to be intentionally open to multiple interpretations.[30]

They asked Samson's woman/wife to coax him to give her the answer. The term used is *p-t-ḥ* from the root relating to being wide open and carrying a verbal meaning, "to entice, seduce or deceive."[31] It appears in the law in Exod 22:15 concerning the seduction of virgins, "If a

[28] Boling, *Judges*, 231.

[29] Ibid.

[30] For example, when Eve was punished for the apple episode she was told that she would cling to her "man." While the implication is that Adam and Eve were "married," none of the legalities of marriage were yet developed in the story and the term "husband" would be anachronistic, at that point in the story. It is no accident that the *pîlegeš'* Levite is called, "her man," leaving their precise relationship obscure (Judges 19).

[31] *BDB*, 834.

man seduces a virgin for whom the bride-price has not been paid, and lies with her, he must make her his wife by payment of a bride-price. If her father refuses to give her to him, he must still weigh out silver in accordance with the bride-price for virgins" (JPS). Judges has not mentioned a bride price, nor is it clear if Israelite law or marriage practices were relevant in this situation since Samson was marrying a Philistine woman. What is clear is that the companions suggested she use her sexual powers to gain information from him, the first time this theme occurs in Samson's life, though not the first time that a woman used this method on a man in Judges. Later the same term will be used on Samson by Delilah with the same success (Judg 16:5).

The companions did not ask her to do this but threatened her; if she did not do what they asked they would destroy her family. They questioned her reasoning for inviting them. Earlier the peculiarity of the family inviting them to watch the groom was noted and it is implied again here. They asked rhetorically if they were invited to, literally, "take possession of us." The verb *y-r-š* is precisely what the Israelites were trying to do throughout the book, take possession of the land (Judg 2:6).

Commentators often discuss the threatening foreign women in Samson's life, who led to Samson's destruction. In this first case, the foreign woman did not seek him out but he sought her. Samson's riddle placed his in-laws in a position where their guests would suffer severe financial ruin on his account. His wife and her family were threatened because of Samson's actions. In the threat to her she was told to seduce Samson in order to save herself and her family. The depiction of her as a foreign temptress luring Samson is completely unfounded. Samson was the aggressor and she was threatened by the action of her own people and her future, possibly present, husband.

Samson's woman/wife followed their orders and harassed Samson with tears saying that he really hated her and did not love her (Judg 14:16). She supported this by stating that he asked her countrymen a riddle and did not tell her the answer. He attempted to reassure her by saying that he did not even tell his parents the answer. The chronology is slightly off again since it is noted that during the rest of the seven days of the feast she continued to harass him with her tears.[32] On the seventh day Samson told her the answer to the riddle because she bothered him so much, and she then explained the riddle to her countrymen (Judg 14:17).

---

[32] The problem is that the text reads, "for seven days," but if she was threatened on the fourth day she could only pester him for three more days, or until the seventh day when they needed the answer.

On the seventh day, before sunset, thus apparently making the deadline, they said to him (Samson), "What is sweeter than honey and what is stronger than a lion?" Samson responded by noting that had they not "ploughed with his heifer" they would not have guessed his riddle (Judg 14:18). His phrase is a crude way of making his point and indicates that he understood what transpired though, like his father, this realization came a little late. While noting that they learned the answer through his woman/wife, he blamed the companions rather than the woman.

Another word play referring to the sun is at work in this passage. The term used for sun, as in sunset, is an unusual word, *ḥaḥarsâ*. As noted earlier, Samson's name and other elements of the story play with the role of the sun and sun names. Here a less traditional name for the sun is used in the story where the sun and light play such a dominant role. One reason for the use of this term, especially following a riddle, is that almost the same letters, only reading the final letter as a *ś* rather than a *š*, is the word, "to cut in/plough."[33] Since only a few stories earlier in the Jephthah story the difference between a *shin* and a *sin* meant life or death for an Ephraimite, this may be a word play that the audience would notice. The term *ḥ-r-š* also has a meaning, "to be silent, dumb, and deaf," and may also be a subtle word play since by Samson's not being deaf he was dumb in this story.[34] The word for heifer, *ʿeglâ*, refers to the type of beast used for ploughing and threshing, as implied by Samson.

The companions won this round, but the result was that the spirit of the deity gripped Samson and he went down to Ashqelon and killed thirty of its men (Judg 14:19). He stripped them, gave the sets of clothing to those who answered his riddle and left in a rage for his father's house. The action is described as one of revenge and anger on the part of Samson for having lost the bet, but the type of equipment he took is described as *ḥălîṣâ*, what is stripped off a person as plunder in war (2 Sam 2:21). Samson's actions were intended to settle a personal vendetta but now included soldiers, raising it to a military situation.

The result of Samson's leaving his woman and going to his father's house is that Samson's woman was given "to his companion who had companioned him" (Judg 14:20). The problem with this verse is that it is missing verbs. Traditionally it is translated as though it had a verb, and that it means that she was married to this other man (RSV, JPS, KJV). According to most, Samson's wife became the wife of his best man whom he had befriended. There are a number of laws from the

---

[33] *BDB*, 360.
[34] Ibid., 361.

ancient Near East governing the role of the friend in the marriage process, yet whether they would apply and which elements were the same
is difficult to determine.[35] As noted earlier, the text refers to Samson's
woman/wife always as a woman/wife rather than a young girl or virgin. Unfortunately it is never clear what Samson's relationship was
with his companions nor is it ever established whether the marriage
was officially consummated, by whatever means marriage was finalized. The father's actions and those of his companion are not clear.
What seems to be the case, from the following episode, was that Samson thought he had rights to the woman.

Samson's Attempt to Retrieve His Woman/Wife: Judges 15:1-20

Some time later, in the season of the wheat harvest, Samson returned to his woman/wife bringing a kid as a gift (Judg 15:1). He asked
to be let into the room of his woman/wife but her father did not let him
enter. The text is not clear about how long after the wedding week this
event occurred. The reference to the wheat season indicates that there
was something flammable and economically viable nearby for later
events in the story. The wheat reference also reveals something about
Samson's character. Thus far the text has not depicted Samson engaged
in any form of work, even as a professional military person. The wheat
harvest would be a time when there was plenty of work and yet Samson
took this time to visit the wife from whom he had estranged himself
earlier. His continued interest in this woman seems to imply that he no
longer held the woman responsible for the riddle revelation.

The father explained that the reason for not letting him in was that
he had been sure that Samson hated her, he had given her to his companion (Judg 15:2). He continued by offering her younger sister who,
he claimed, was more beautiful than her elder sister, and said that he
should let her become his woman/wife instead. Boling translates the
phrase, "I thought you hated her," as, "you in fact divorced her."[36] He
likens the situation to that described in Deut 24:1.

---

[35] For example, law 25 in the Laws of Eshnunna state that, "If a man calls at the
house of (his) father-in-law, and his father-in-law *accepts* him *in servitude*, but (never-
theless) gives his daughter to [another man], the father of the girl shall refund the
bride-money which he received twofold" (*ANET*, 162). See also laws 159–61 in the
Laws of Hammurabi, *ANET*, 173.

[36] Boling, *Judges*, 235.

A man takes a wife and possesses her. She fails to please him because he finds something obnoxious about her and he writes her a bill of divorcement, hands it to her and sends her away from his house. She leaves his household and becomes the wife of another man, then this latter man rejects her, writes her a bill of divorcement, hands it to her and sends her away from his house. It may also be that the man who married her last dies. The first husband who divorced her shall not take her to wife again for she has been defiled and that would be abhorrent to the LORD (JPS).

Using the Deuteronomy passage as a guide to this situation is problematic on two levels. It assumes that the practices portrayed are those of the Israelites when the text makes clear that the wife in this case was a Philistine. The book of Judges as a whole treats intermarriage between Israelites and anyone else as a destructive force for the future of the nation. The complications and different or unpleasant practices expressed by the Philistines in this episode should not be read as reflecting Israelite practice but problems concerning the Philistines. What better way to present the problems of intermarriage than with a story where different cultural practices collide resulting in disaster for both parties.

The second problem with Boling's comparison is that it assumes that the two were officially divorced. It is not even clear that the two were considered formally married by both sides. Since the text disapproves of intermarriage it is not known if the Israelites considered a mixed marriage legitimate at all. It is evident from Samson's return that he did not consider his departure as indicative of divorce. His reaction reveals a complete lack of forethought or analysis concerning how his actions were perceived.

The official divorce comparison breaks down completely since they were clearly not divorced in Samson's understanding. In the eyes of the Israelites in order to be officially divorced the husband had to take some action which Samson did not think he had. In the eyes of the Israelites they were either never married or the woman was now an adulteress. In any case the woman never left her home and was still under the control of her father, since Samson abandoned her, allowing her father to take whatever actions he deemed appropriate.

Apparently Samson was not interested in the younger sister and declared that the Philistines now had no claim against him for the harm he would do to them (Judg 15:3). Samson actualized the deity's earlier desire of seeking a pretext against the Philistines (Judg 14:4). Samson carried out his revenge by catching three hundred foxes (Judg 15:4). He took torches and, turning the foxes tail to tail, placed a torch between each pair of tails. He lit the torches and turned them loose among the standing grain of the Philistines, setting fire to the stacked grain, standing grain, vineyards, and olive trees (Judg 15:5). At this point, in contrast to the Gideon/Jerubbaal situation, the Israelites destroyed the crops of their enemy.

The Philistines asked who did this act and were told that it was Samson, the son-in-law of the Timnite who had taken Samson's woman/wife and given her to his wedding companion (Judg 15:6). Their reaction to hearing this news was to put the woman and her father to the fire. The irony is that this was what the woman had tried to avoid by learning the secret of the riddle in the first place (Judg 14:15). In the words of the people in town Samson was the son-in-law of the man in Timnah. They were questioned by Philistines about a serious loss and it was in their best interests to implicate someone else. If those asked were those who threatened the woman in the first place, i.e. some of the companions, they would be interested in clearing their own names. There is little information on either side, but it was an easy case to make and the father of the woman/wife became the guilty party.

A major theme of this unit is the actions and practices of the Philistines. Samson stated that if this was how they acted then he would not rest until he took revenge on them (Judg 15:7). His revenge was expressed when he smote them leg on thigh, a great strike, and then went down and stayed in the cave of the rock to Etam (Judg 15:8). Samson's governing motivation was revenge. This was a motivating factor for another judge, Gideon/Jerubbaal (Judg 8:19), and possibly drove Jephthah for legitimacy (Judg 11:6-9), but with Samson it is the primary driving force. The irony is that Samson sought revenge not for what happened to his people, or even what happened to him personally, but for this woman/wife.

A subtle theme in this story relates to the concept of intermarriage and the practices and customs of non-Israelites. Originally Samson's parents attempted to dissuade him from marrying the woman because she was a Philistine and they had foreskins (though presumably his wife did not), highlighting a practice that was not customary among the Philistines, a lack that caused them to be abhorrent to the Israelites. The companions then threatened the bride, leading to financial loss for the groom, which Samson turned into death for more Philistines. The Philistines, or at least the woman's father, then gave away an already married or possibly betrothed woman to another man. While Samson had a great deal to do with the shift of husbands for the woman, if Samson and the woman were officially married the Philistine father turned his daughter into an adulteress. If they were not officially married then the rest of the town lied about Samson's status to save their own lives.

Again, none of these practices or customs were acceptable in the eyes of Israelite law. It provides a platform to describe the illegitimate practices of the Philistines, thereby describing what the Israelites should not be doing.

The Philistines' reaction to Samson's destruction was to come up and pitch camp in Judah and spread out over Lehi (Judg 15:9). The Philistines' strength is made evident by the ease with which they make an incursion into Judah. It reintroduces Judah, about whom little has been written in the last few stories. The place where they encamped was Lehi, meaning "jawbone," a possible allusion to what follows.

The men of Judah, who were suddenly involved, asked why they came up against them (Judg 15:10). They responded that they came to take Samson prisoner and do to him what he did to them. Judah took the lead by going down to the cave of Etam with three thousand men, telling Samson that he knew that the Philistines ruled over them, and asking him why he had done this to them (Judg 15:11). He replied that as they did to him so he did to them. The Judites informed Samson that they had come down to take him prisoner and to hand him over to the Philistines (Judg 15:12). Samson asked them to swear to him that they themselves would not attack him. They replied that they would not because they were only interested in handing him over as prisoner (Judg 15:13). They reiterated that they would not slay him, and they bound him with two new ropes and brought him up from the rock.

This situation describes what the text will later state explicitly, that everyone did what was right in their own eyes. Samson decided he wanted a Timnite woman and did not consider the problems involved. Problems resulted, Samson was a sore loser, burned a village, and the Philistines took revenge on who they thought was the source of the difficulty. Samson decided that the Philistines were wrong, followed with his own counteractions, and left. His source of refuge caused trouble for Judah, who were not prepared to throw off Philistine rule. Judah was interested only in Judah's status and did not consider the larger issues. They were prepared to turn over their own countryman to help themselves. Samson worried what his own people would do to him. His own people did not trust him enough to turn him over to the enemy without ropes. The whole situation descended to a petty game of revenge and mistrust with each acting on what they saw as best for themselves at any particular moment.

The text continues that when Samson approached Lehi and the Philistines came shouting to meet him, the spirit of the deity gripped him again, causing the ropes on his arms to become like flax that catches fire, and the bonds melted off his hands (Judg 15:14). He came upon a jawbone of an ass, picked it up, and killed a thousand men with it (Judg 15:15). Samson concluded, "With the jaw of an ass, mass upon mass. With the jaw of an ass I have slain a thousand men" (Judg 15:16). When he finished speaking he threw the jawbone away, thus giving the name Ramoth-Lehi (high place of the jaw) to the place (Judg 15:17).

There is another word play in this unit in reference to both the heap and the ass. The root *ḥ-m-r* can mean "heap" or, "to make a ruin heap," and a similar root is the word for "ass," the same word used in reference to the tool he used to kill these people in Judg 15:15.[37] The text states explicitly that Samson's strength, and even some of his actions, were the work of the Israelite deity, but Samson did not recognize the deity and took full credit for the event.

Samson was thirsty at this point and called to the deity, finally admitting the deity's role by stating, "You yourself have granted this great victory through your servant and must I now die of thirst and fall into the hands of the foreskinned ones?" (Judg 15:18). At this point he recognized the deity but still claimed some of the responsibility for his victory. He claimed the event as a great victory even though the victory over the Philistines was an act of revenge on behalf of a Philistine family and was protested by his own people, or at least Judah. Samson appears to be less enamored of the Philistines at this point, referring to them as "the foreskinned ones" for the first time.

This incident recalls some of Gideon/Jerubbaal's actions and claims. He too had hungry troops and asked for food and water, though not of the deity but of local towns which he later destroyed because of their refusal. After his death Gideon/Jerubbaal's sons claimed that the people of Israel owed Gideon/Jerubbaal's memory, or possibly his sons, some special honor because they put their lives at stake for the people. Only later in the book did the idea surface that if the heroes put themselves at risk they deserved something special. This idea appears with the two characters who wanted credit for fighting for Israel, though both did it for personal reasons.

The Israelite deity reacted favorably to Samson's request and split open the hollow at Lehi. Water gushed out of it, he drank, and his spirit returned to him, reviving him, and thus the place was named *ʿên haqqôrēʾ* of Lehi (Judg 15:19). Most translations note that his strength returned to him. The term is the same as that used to refer to the deity descending upon him. On the surface it makes sense that after drinking his strength revived. It is also possible that on another level he returned to his regular self.

Only after this military victory was Samson called a judge. The text states that he judged in the days of the Philistines for twenty years

---

[37] *BDB*, 331.

(Judg 15:20). This differs from the description of the careers of the other judges. None of the other judges judged at a time when a foreign enemy was in control. The reference to the Philistines implies that they still existed, presumably were still a threat, and, from the rest of the episode, had power in the region. The strength of the judge has lessened considerably. The narrative has a new definition of judging for Samson.

The timing of the judging highlights the difference between Samson and the other judges. In previous cases the reference to the length of time for which the judge held that position in Israel is the last comment prior to the judge's death. In this case, though the next episode ultimately leads to his death, there is still much to happen before that event occurs.

Samson's First Trip to Gaza: Judges 16:1-3

The text turns again to Samson's personal life which, as before, involved him in military events. He went to Gaza where he met a *zônâ* and came to her (Judg 16:1). Here the text does not state that Gaza was a Philistine city, though later it is the place of his Philistine captivity (Judg 16:21). One cannot assume that the woman was a Philistine, nor can one state that Israelite women were not prostitutes since the same term is used in reference to a mother of a judge, though Jephthah's mother is never explicitly described as an Israelite either (Judg 11:1).

The woman he visited is an *ʾiššâ zônâ*, the same term used to describe Jephthah's mother (Judg 11:1). Again the question arises as to how the term *ʾišāh* is used and functions. Does it indicate age, that she was a mature woman, or that she was married, since it is the same word used for "wife"? It is not clear how it functions when next to the term for prostitute *zônâ*. Gaza was a place filled with many Philistines later in the story, it is not designated as a Philistine city here or even later in the text. The text is explicit in designating Samson's first woman as a Philistine, though this woman is not so defined. This woman did not notify the authorities about Samson's presence indicating that the text does not hold this woman responsible for the following raid.

The Gazites were told that Samson had come there and so they laid an ambush for him at the town gate (Judg 16:2). They waited, whispering to each other that when daylight came they would kill him. The text is vague about who learned of Samson's whereabouts but it is clear that people, probably Philistines, were looking for him, making it even more unclear why Samson chose Gaza of all places. While there were people looking for him, and others waiting to be informed of his whereabouts, they too are not designated as Philistines. The reference to waiting all night and attempting to kill him at daylight continues playing with the concepts of darkness and light seen in his name and the many episodes concerning Samson and fire.

Samson destroyed their plan by laying in bed only until midnight, at which point he arose, grasped the doors of the town gate together with the gateposts, and pulled them out along with the bar (Judg 16:3). He then placed them, the gates and the posts, on his shoulders and carried them to the top of the hill that was near Hebron. In this scene Samson fought no battles, did no judging, faced no attackers, and had no dealings with the deity. Why he traveled all the way to Hebron is curious. Since no battles took place the function of this unit must be to define other aspects of the story and its plot.

The focus of this unit is solely on Samson and to a large extent lays some of the groundwork for the following situation. Samson was still interested in women, though apparently not for marriage. The woman in this scene is not described at all meaning she could be either Philistine or Israelite. She is another nameless woman, though very different from Samson's previous and following women. What is important is Samson's interest in women. All the major episodes involving him contain women as his main objective. Other judges in the book had many women/wives, but references to these women were always noted in connection to children and inheritance or power, never in the context of a character's sexual appetite. In this story the role of women and their sexuality is a major governing characteristic of the Judge which leads to his death.

Samson is depicted as a hunted man. In the previous episode his own people captured him and turned him over to his enemy. After that episode and Samson's victory he was suddenly judging. The next event describes people watching Samson's every move, even, or especially, a visit to a prostitute. Some unknown people relayed this information to even more important people who designed an ambush to capture him. Neither Israelites nor the Israelite deity were involved. These themes, Samson's search for women, his hunted state, and the way he acted on his own, are all major themes in the following section. This unit sets up Samson's personality in such a way that the following events are not out of character for Samson or his relationship with the Philistines.

Samson and Delilah: Judges 16:4-21

The story of Samson and Delilah has captured readers' imaginations for centuries and as a result songs, poems, Hollywood movies, even miniseries are rooted in this story. With poetic license, all these productions reflect someone's interpretation of the story. Yet these popular creations are so powerful that it makes the task of understanding the characters in the biblical text more difficult, especially as they fit into the Samson saga and the book of Judges. The task is complicated further by the many folkloristic themes and motifs in the text.

The previous episode is connected to the Delilah story by the phrase, "after that." The sentence continues to say that Samson loved a woman in the Wadi Sorek named Delilah (Judg 16:4). The reference could be a chronological indicator noting that the Delilah event occurred following the incident with the prostitute in Gaza. Mentioning that Samson loved Delilah ties it to what has gone before by noting that the two situations were different because Samson loved this woman.

Delilah has not fared well in most analyses of this text until more recently.[38] She is depicted in popular culture as the treacherous Philistine temptress who betrayed her lover for money.[39] Many seek to understand her personality and role by examining her name. The name Delilah is a good Hebrew name often assumed to have something to do with "night," *laylâ*. The two are not really related linguistically but the biblical text often creates meanings out of less than precise etymological similarities. It is possible that even though the source of the name does not deal with "night," it may be intended as a pun,[40] in opposition to the sun of Samson's name. Exum understands the name as relating to "loose hair" or "small, slight," in both cases reinforcing the common folklore theme of the strong man overcome by a woman who learned the secret of his strength and betrayed it to his enemies.[41] Boling takes it from the Aramaic *dallatum*, "flirt," yielding a sense quite congenial to his understanding of the narrative structure.[42] The numerous name possibilities illuminate how even her name provides many varying portrayals of Delilah.

The text is explicit about a number of aspects in their relationship but is silent about many others. Samson loved Delilah. The text does not describe her feelings toward him nor does it define the nature of

---

[38] J. C. Exum, "Why, Why, Why, Delilah?" *Plotted, Shot, and Painted, Cultural Representations of Biblical Women*, JSOT Supplement Series 25 (Sheffield: Sheffield Academic Press, 1996) 175–237. J. C. Exum, "Aspects of Symmetry and Balance in the Samson Saga," *JSOT* 19 (1981) 3–29.

[39] J. C. Exum, "Delilah," *ABD* 2.134. Not that this is Exum's approach to Delilah but her summary of the traditional depictions is here.

[40] Ibid., 133.

[41] Ibid.

[42] Boling, *Judges*, 248.

their relationship to each other. The text never refers to Delilah as a prostitute, but Samson was recently seen in the company of one and the connection is not far from many depictions of her. The text states that she was from the Wadi Sorek. This site is in the region of Timnah and the northern area of Philistine control but is not far from Zorah, Samson's Danite birthplace. The book of Judges never defines the precise borders of Philistia and thus neither Delilah's abode nor her name define her ethnicity or occupation.

After her introduction and the establishment of Samson's feelings toward her, the text continues with the lords of the Philistines visiting her and telling her to coax him, find out what makes him so strong, how they can overpower him, tie him up, and humble him. The Philistine lords used the same word, *p-t-ḥ*, to describe what Delilah should do to him as was suggested to Samson's first wife (Judg 14:15). They offered her eleven hundred shekels of silver each (Judg 16:5). Boling revises the amount that each promised to give to "each man's unit, one hundred."[43] He bases this translation on a redivision of the MT.[44] He assumes five tyrants, because later books stress five cities of the Philistine Pentapolis, and notes that it is too much money to be offered. He sees it as having been confused because of the eleven hundred that Michah's mother had in the following chapter.[45] This is another example where it is easier to assume a mistake in the text than determine how these elements may strengthen the story. The similarity in the number of shekels that Delilah was offered and Michah's mother had is significant and will be addressed below in the Michah discussion.

Much is said about the lords of the Philistines who made the offer to Delilah, especially in terms of trying to understand the Philistines. There is clearly more than one Philistine lord since the plural is used, and each would provide Delilah eleven hundred shekels of silver, but the text never states how many lords existed. These lords claimed they wanted to overpower Samson only to capture and humble him, never stating that they were going to injure or kill him. What they asked of her is similar to what the Judites attempted to do with Samson: capture him, tie him up, and hand him over to the Philistines (Judg 15:12). The difference is that the Judites carried out these acts to improve their relationship with the Philistines, though the text never states that the Philistines demanded it.

The offer to Delilah was money, presumably a great deal of money. The situation between the Philistines and Delilah was similar to the

---

[43] Ibid.
[44] Ibid., 249.
[45] Ibid., 248–9.

previous case with Samson's first wife. The difference is that in the first case it was not the leaders who were interested in Samson but those who suffered from losing the riddle bet. Rather than offer her money her and her family's lives were threatened. Delilah was offered money directly following an episode involving a prostitute, presumably a woman who accepted money to be with Samson. Delilah is between depictions of a wife, which she clearly was not, and a prostitute, raising serious questions about who she was and what she did for a living. These questions are important in light of the role women held in society, who did and did not protect them, and how they threatened society when they were not controlled. Her liminal status between wife and prostitute is similar to the raped *pîlegeš* whose story follows shortly.

Delilah must have accepted the deal because in the next verse she seeks the source of Samson's strength. Her first attempt was straight-forward, asking directly, "Tell me what makes you so strong and how could you be tied up and made helpless?" (Judg 16:6). She was honest in her words. Samson replied that if he were tied with seven fresh ten-dons that had not been dried he would become as weak as an ordinary man (Judg 16:7). Apparently Delilah informed the lords of the Philis-tines of this information for they brought her seven fresh tendons that had not been dried and she bound him with them while they waited in the next room (Judg 16:8). She called out to Samson that the Philistines were upon him, at which point he pulled the tendons apart as a strand of tow comes apart at the touch of fire, and the source of his strength remained a secret (Judg 16:9).

Samson was playing with Delilah at this point by creating a story to tell her. Some scholars see in the tendon reference an obscure reference that has been lost over time.[46] It is possible that Samson created some-thing that sounded magical when it was not since he involved a number of people in a bet on a riddle that was not really a riddle. Apparently he thought he was funny, not realizing the ramifications of his actions. Even now he did not realize that he should question Delilah's query.

Delilah did not give up and now had ammunition against him. She said to Samson that he deceived and lied to her and asked again how he could be tied up (Judg 16:10). This time Samson told her that if he were bound with new ropes that had never been used he would be-come as weak as an ordinary man (Judg 16:11). The reader already knows that new ropes will be useless on Samson since they were used on him by the Israelites when they handed him over to the Philistines (Judg 15:14-15). Delilah clearly did not have this knowledge and took

[46] Ibid., 249.

new ropes and bound him with them while an ambush waited in the next room. Again she cried to Samson that the Philistines were upon him (Judg 16:12).

Samson had no problems because next Delilah cried to him that he had been deceiving and lying to her and again asked how he could be tied (Judg 16:13). This time he answered that she must weave seven locks of his head into a web. She followed his instructions and pinned his hair with a peg and cried out to him that the Philistines were upon him (Judg 16:14). When he awoke from his sleep he pulled out the peg, loom, and the web. The Philistines were no longer laying an ambush in the next room.

A few things are noteworthy at this point. Samson repeatedly told Delilah fanciful explanations about the source of his strength, though moving closer to the secret with each new version as they progressed. Each time he told her something she managed to lull him to sleep, revealing something about their living arrangement or his physical exhaustion at some point in his visit to her. He was not surprised to find the Philistines were still looking for him, and was on the lookout for them, though at the same time complacent in his knowledge that his strength would protect him. After each request Delilah carried out the task Samson claimed would weaken him, and tested it to see if what he said was true, and yet he never questioned her motives. Samson was either so naive as not to see what was happening, or so arrogant and confident in his strength that he had no fear.

Delilah pulled out the final tool and said to him that he said he loved her but his heart was not with her (Judg 16:15). She reminded him that three times he had deceived her and not told her the source of his strength. She nagged and pressed him until he was wearied to death (Judg 16:16). He finally confided everything to her, telling her that no razor had ever touched his head since he had been a Nazirite to the Israelite deity since he was in his mother's womb (Judg 16:17). He concluded that if his hair were cut his strength would leave him and he would be as weak as an ordinary man.

Popular images of Samson depict a long-haired strong man. Yet this is the first time that the text states the source of his strength, and the first time since Samson has been alive, not in utero, that reference is made to his Nazirite status. From stories told thus far, there is no indication that Samson was aware of or recognized his Nazirite state. When his Nazirite status was discussed by his mother and the messenger of the deity, reference was made to abstaining from alcohol but nothing was included concerning his hair. This is the first reference to it and his confession was to a woman who was interested in making money from weakening him.

The phrase indicating that he confessed is, "he told her all his heart," a phrase that was important in the Achsah story at the beginning of the book and that will be crucial and used against women in the *pîlegeš*'s story (Judg 19:3). Boling takes this to mean that he told her everything that was in his mind because heart, in Hebrew at this time, meant the mind.[47] From the circumstances where the term appears it is difficult to ascertain if the heart was connected to emotional wishes, in the way that heart is the seat of emotions today, or whether it was a source of intellect. In the Judges cases the differences between the two are minor. Regardless of whether it was the heart or mind the outcome was the same. In Achsah's case she received land from her father as a result of his giving, "according to heart" (Judg 1:15). In this case the term brought disaster upon Samson. In the final case the use of this term destroyed a woman leading to a civil war.

The text states that Delilah sensed that he had told her everything and again sent for the lords of the Philistines with a message that they should come up once more for he had confided everything (Judg 16:18). The lords of the Philistines brought the money with them this time. The woman knew when she heard the truth, like Samson's mother. This time she was more careful and lulled him to sleep on her lap. Only then did she call in a man, who cut off the seven locks of his head, weakening Samson and making him helpless.[48] As he said would happen, his strength slipped away from him (Judg 16:19).

The parallels here are with Jael. A strong military man sought a woman whom he thought would provide a safe haven, she lulled him to sleep in her lap (with possible sexual allusions, especially since in this case Samson was asleep in her presence three times already), and she turned on him. Both men thought they were safe because of who they thought they were with at the time, but ironically their sense of security was what allowed the women to accomplish their goals. The difference is that earlier the defeat of Sisera saved the Israelites, whereas ironically in this case it destroyed Israel's judge.

How could Samson not have known? Delilah repeatedly asked him the source of his strength and then carried out what he said would limit it. Once before he gave a woman information that destroyed his plans and was burned (as were the woman and her family) as a result of it, and he knew that the Philistines were after him. It is difficult to believe that the depiction of Samson as judge could possibly be used as an

---

[47] Ibid., 250.

[48] According to J. Sasson the man to whom she calls is actually Samson. ("Who Cut Samson's Hair? [And Other Trifling Issues Raised by Judges 16]," *Prooftexts* 8 (1988) 333–9).

example of Israel's finest. As emphasized thus far, each judge had a weak spot which grew progressively larger as the narrative time of Judges progresses. If these weak spots are indicative of problems the Israelites must consider when choosing a leader, and who that leader should be, then Samson is a perfect example. It relates to the David/ Saul discussion since David too committed acts unbecoming a king because of a woman, such as in his relationship with Bathsheba where he ordered an innocent man (Uriah) killed (2 Sam 11:2–12:23). Samson's lack of judgment in affairs of the heart led to his own destruction.

Following the previous pattern Delilah cried to Samson that the Philistines were upon him (Judg 16:20). This time he awoke from sleep thinking he would free himself, as the other times, but did not know that the Israelite deity had departed from him. This is the third time in Judges that a woman captured the enemy ruler. The first time Jael, possibly a foreign woman, saved Israel. The second time an unnamed woman of unknown origins killed Abimelech, who, while an Israelite, was not legitimate either as a son of Gideon/Jerubbaal or ruler of Israel. This last example brings the book full circle with a foreign woman destroying an enemy leader but this time the enemy was Israel. Samson claimed the source of his strength was his hair when it was the Israelite deity; the symbol of the bond between them was Samson's hair. When Samson's hair was cut, so too was the bond and the deity was no longer with him. This functions, to a large extent, as a metaphor of Israel and her deity's relationship. Throughout the book the deity tried to maintain the bond while Israel slowly snipped away the threads of that bond.

Samson's Return to Gaza: Judges 16:21-31

The Philistines seized Samson and gouged out his eyes. They brought him to Gaza, shackled him in bronze fetters, and he became a mill slave in the prison (Judg 16:21). The gouging of the eyes continues the theme of light and dark. Samson, the little sun, was now in perpetual darkness by the woman night. Rather than kill Samson, when they had the chance, they decided to humiliate and torture him. What the Philistines did not consider was that after Samson's hair was cut off, it grew back (Judg 16:22), emphasizing to the readers what will happen shortly.

The lords of the Philistines were unaware of the potential danger and gathered to offer a great sacrifice to their deity Dagon and to make merry (Judg 16:23). They chanted that their deity had delivered into their hands the enemy Samson. The biblical author set this up well.

This is a case where the author could prove the Israelite case that other deities were non-deities. The Philistines were crediting their deity with the capture of Samson while the reader knows that it was a woman who captured Samson and then only because Samson was not true to his deity-ordained status. Once Delilah cut his hair the Israelite deity was no longer involved. The reader also knows that the situation was changing and the Philistines were unaware of the ensuing danger.

When the people saw Samson they sang praises to their own deity, chanting that their deity had delivered into their hands the enemy who devastated their land and who slew so many (Judg 16:24). There is a play on words here because the term used for "praise" is *h-l-l* and the term for "slay" is the near homonym *ḥ-l-l*. Again the text plays with the notion that the people praised Dagon for the acts of a woman.

The text states that "it was good in their hearts" and that they wanted Samson to dance for them. Samson was brought from the prison and he danced for them. They put him between two pillars (Judg 16:25). The phrase, "it was good in their hearts," is usually translated as, "their spirits rose" (JPS), or, "their hearts were merry" (RSV, KJV), implying that this happened when the people were in a good mood. While that is the sense on one level, the wording conveys other notions as well. The phrase that, "she was right in his eyes," as noted above, is later used to show the low state of affairs in Israel and its use with Samson's choice of a wife emphasized that. Just a few sentences earlier Samson revealed his heart to Delilah leading to his present predicament. The phrase combines the ideas that the Philistines were doing what seemed good in their hearts and, as it did for Samson and later will for the Israelites, it will cause their destruction.

Samson told the young man *naʿar*, who was leading him by the hand, to let go of him and let him feel the pillars that the temple rested upon so that he could lean upon them (Judg 16:26). The text momentarily digresses to set the stage describing the temple full of men and women. All the lords of the Philistines were there and there were three thousand men and women on the roof watching blind Samson (Judg 16:27), humiliated by a roaring crowd of Philistines, forced to dance before them. The reader knows that Samson has regained his strength and the repeated references to the pillars provides a good idea of what is to come. The digression builds the suspense by noting the great number of people, even on the roof. The lords of the Philistines are referred to repeatedly and their importance to such a large crowd elevates their status prior to their destruction.

Samson called out to the Israelite deity asking the deity to remember him and give him strength, just this once, to take revenge on the Philistines if only for one of his two eyes (Judg 16:28). Even at his worst hour Samson was motivated by revenge and thought only of himself in the form of his eyes. There is no indication that he saw his present predicament as his own doing and expected the deity to come to his aid.

Samson embraced the two middle pillars upon which the temple rested and, with one arm around each pillar, he leaned against them (Judg 16:29). Samson cried that he wanted to die with the Philistines and pulled with all his might (Judg 16:30). The temple crashed down on the lords and all those people in it. The text summarizes that those who were slain by him as he died outnumbered those slain by him when he lived.

In Samson's final words he asked to die with the Philistines. This is fitting since most of the text dedicated to Samson involved him with Philistines. There is only one interaction with Samson and Israelites, other than his parents, and at that moment the Israelites turned him over to the enemy Philistines. Samson was the last judge of Israel and the difference between the first judge and their relationship to their countrymen is striking. Othniel married an Israelite woman, the daughter of a war hero, and fought on behalf of all of Israel. He fought with the troops in a preordained battle. He completed his mission resulting in the land resting following his tenure. In contrast, Samson, who was picked in the womb, did not follow the laws of the Nazirites to which he was bound, married a nameless Philistine woman, and fought on behalf of himself and his problems alone. Rather than receive reward from his countrymen he was turned over to the enemy by them. The text's judgment is severe; Samson was the only judge to die in battle with the enemy.

The episode ends with Samson's brothers and all his father's household coming down, carrying him up, and burying him in the tomb of his father Manoah, between Zorah and Eshtaol. The text repeats that he judged Israel for twenty years.

Summary

Samson is the last judge in the book. How far Israel transgressed concerning her deity is emphasized through the main themes designated already at the beginning of the book concerning leadership, the David/Saul polemic, intermarriage, and the role of women to reflect Israel's state. Samson was hand-picked by the deity prior to his birth, apparently because there was no longer anyone whom the deity could persuade to fight on behalf of Israel. Despite Samson's Nazirite birth he followed none of the rules associated with such a status, in some places going out of his way to be in circumstances where a Nazirite should not be. He did not fight on behalf of Israel or the deity but for his own personal revenge.

Samson was not a paradigm for a leader of Israel. He never led the Israelites, instead he picked battles with the Philistines with no concern about the effect it would have on the Israelites or himself. The only persons of definite Israelite origin with whom he interacted were his parents. His mother disappeared from the story as soon as she questioned his choices and he did not listen to his father. The narrator condemns his decision making processes with the terminology used (things being right in his eyes), and the results of those decisions.

Women played a major role in his career and its evaluation. Samson descended from a woman whose ability to recognize a messenger of the deity was superior to her husband's. Samson's nameless mother disappeared as soon as Samson overrode his family's suggestion for a wife. He chose a Philistine wife, Israel's enemy at the time, over his parents objections. His Philistine wife was forced to betray him because of her compatriots' threats, though to no avail since she and her father were destroyed anyway. The prostitute in Gaza functioned in the story to characterize Samson. Delilah is an ironic twist on the Jael story, leading this time not to Israel's victory but Samson's destruction. Her character brings the story back to the evaluation of leaders by revealing Samson's weaknesses that other important leaders, following the period of Judges, had regarding women. The emphasis upon women, combined with what men did for and because of them, prepares the reader for the following stories in which these factors rise to such a pitch that Israel almost destroyed itself over them.

Chapter 13

THE DANITE MIGRATION

Judges 17:1–18:31

The focus of the next unit is the tribe of Dan as it seeks a new home, finds it, and takes it. In the process they come into contact with an Ephraimite, a Levitical priest, and a statue of dubious legitimacy in the eyes of the Israelite cult, which has been made from money from an unknown, possibly tainted, source. The story is filled with intrigue made more complicated by passages of difficult Hebrew prose.

This chapter is part of what is traditionally considered an addition by the Deuteronomistic Historian to Judges, thought to have been added at the same time as the beginning chapters. The reasoning is that in the final chapters there are no judges or heroic actions. The thesis continues that on thematic grounds these chapters are better tied to the following stories rather than the previous.[1] The events and themes are considered so theologically motivated as to be useless in terms of historical reconstruction.[2] In a new move to understand the motivation of this episode, Brettler ties this story into the David/Saul, north/south polemic and focuses on it as an allegory.[3]

More recently Sweeney clarifies how this unit is tied to the previous section syntactically providing a perfect bridge from the previous stories, focused on individual tribes, to the major catastrophe at the end.[4] Thematically, the episode continues the pattern of topics from the pre-

[1] R. G. Boling, *Judges: Introduction, Translation and Commentary*, The Anchor Bible (Garden City: Doubleday, 1981) 258.
[2] M. Brettler, "Literature as Politics," *JBL* 108 (1989) 412.
[3] Ibid.
[4] Sweeney, "Davidic Polemics in the Book of Judges," *VT* 47 (1997) 517–29.

vious story, the Danites, the role of women, and money, and then moves into themes that will explode in the raped *pîlegeš*'s story which culminates in Israel's civil war. The story also continues themes seen throughout the whole book such as the David/Saul, north/south polemic, the question of how to choose a leader and who should do it, and the role of women. The two portions are tightly woven together both in language and content, but this episode introduces a slightly different approach to the situation Israel faced because there is no individual judge.

Michah's Ephod: *Judges 17:1-13*

This unit is not tied into the previous story with the connecting phrases used thus far such as, "after that," or "the Israelites did the bad thing in the eyes of the deity." Instead it begins what appears to be a completely new story by introducing a man in the hill country of Ephraim whose name was Michah (Judg 17:1). The last story was not in Ephraim, there is no notice that the Israelites were doing anything wrong, and no new enemy entered. The reason for this new introduction is that, based on the progression of events, Israel's enemy was now itself. "The bad thing" that the Israelites did in their deity's eyes has been intermarriage leading to worship of other deities and in the last story the supposed hero was himself the one who transgressed that command. No new enemy was necessary and the Israelites did not even realize their need of the deity's help.

The story is tied syntactically to the previous story, as described by Sweeney, by the *waw* consecutive formulation indicating that this is a continuation of the previous story.[5] The stories are also connected through the focus on the tribe of Dan. Samson was a Danite, born in Danite territory, Samson's relationships with various Philistines reflect the problems that the tribe of Dan suffered from such proximity to the Philistines, and how they corrupted even an Israelite consecrated in the womb to the deity. The introduction to this unit ties it into the previous story but at the same time signals that the narrative, and the Israelites it depicts, have entered a new era.

Michah's name is indicative of the irony of the book, this story, and Michah's actions. The name shifts between Michah (Judg 17:5, 9, 12, 13) and Michayahu (Judg 17:1, 4). The variation between long and short forms of a single name is well attested.[6] The name in its long form

---

[5] Ibid.

[6] Brettler, "Micah," *ABD* 4.806.

means, "who is like YH(WH)," which expresses the notion of the deity's incomparability.[7] This story, and the book as a whole, have strong ideological interests and Michah's name serves ironic purposes since the person whose name glorifies the deity, by suggesting the deity's incomparability, was a thief who helped establish what was in the eyes of the later cult, illegitimate worship of the Israelite deity.

The Hebrew of the next sentence is difficult but it is possible to understand the general sense of what happened. Michah admitted to his mother that the eleven hundred shekels of silver that were taken from her, about which she had uttered a curse which she repeated in his hearing, were taken by him, and that he had the silver (Judg 17:2). Her response was to praise her son in the name of the Israelite deity. What happened was that money was stolen, the mother swore an oath against whoever stole it in the hearing of the son, and he, the son and thief, confessed his crime. His mother's reaction was to praise her son.

Scholars often comment on the amount of money involved. Boling notes that it is extravagant, but not incredibly so, especially as the amount was budgeted by a prosperous woman for contribution to a Yahwist sanctuary in the form of religious art, though at this point the destination of the money has not been determined.[8] Scholars note that this amount, eleven hundred shekels, influenced the description of individual contributions to Delilah's fund.[9] What is not considered is the possibility that the numbers influence each other intentionally, raising questions about the money's original source.

Boling notes that the amount would not be excessive for a prosperous woman. Yet at this point in Judges women's relation to wealth is complicated at best. One gained land by asking her father, the war hero (Judg 1:15). Another by working as a prostitute, though as discussed before the implication of financial remuneration for services rendered is not necessarily inherent in the Hebrew word *zônâ*, despite the standard translation of the word as prostitute in English. The only other woman to receive financial remuneration was Delilah, who was paid for turning Samson over to the Philistines. Delilah's ethnicity is never described, the reader only knows that she lived in the Wadi Sorek, which could easily be Israelite or Philistine. The stories concerning Delilah indicate that the Philistines had as easy access to her as Samson did. Her character was such that she sold her lover/boyfriend/client to the Philistines for a price, a very high price. Michah's mother is de-

---

[7] Ibid.

[8] Boling, *Judges*, 255.

[9] Boling, *Judges*, 255; J. Gray, *Joshua, Judges, Ruth*, The New Century Bible Commentary (Grand Rapids: Eerdmans, 1986) 339.

picted as so upset by the loss of the money that she uttered a curse, something not out of character with a woman who gained money in the manner Delilah did.

There are other circumstantial elements indicating that Michah's mother could have been Delilah. The Michah incident appears directly following Samson's death. The money is exactly the amount as the payment from one of the Philistine lords. The text does not state that all of Michah's mother's money was stolen, only one batch that happened to be in that amount. Michah, the woman's son, has no named father. While many male character's mothers are nameless, this would be the first case in Judges where a main male character did not have a named father, even if his mother was a prostitute. A final link is that in the story Michah has dealings with Dan, Samson's tribe. The finishing ironic touch is that Michah ultimately lost to the tribe of Dan.

If the text implies that Delilah was the mother of Michah there must be a reason why it does not state this, especially since Delilah figures so prominently in the previous chapter. Yet the book of Judges regularly plays with themes by hinting at them without stating them. Heber's woman/wife Jael is not mentioned when he is first introduced and his relationship with Moses is highlighted (Judg 4:11), whereas when Sisera approached Jael's tent the relationship between Heber and the Canaanites was emphasized (Judg 4:17). Jael's relationship to the situation is defined by her actions, her motivations are never stated. So too when Gideon/Jerubbaal was originally approached by the deity's messenger there was no mention of the fact that the enemy Gideon/Jerubbaal was recruited to fight killed his brothers. It is not out of the pattern established thus far in Judges for the narrative to hint at situations that impact the motivation of the various characters without stating them explicitly. As this story progresses, scholars claim that it concerns the establishment of the northern sanctuary, though it is never defined as such in the text. While the text never states the mother's identity, it drops hints about it, while at the same time raising questions designed to denigrate the origins of the northern cult site.

The son returned the eleven hundred shekels of silver to his mother who then consecrated the silver to the Israelite deity, transferring it to the son to make a sculptured image and a molten image, and returned it to him (Judg 17:3). In this verse the irony continues. The amount, and probably the same money, had been paid in the previous story to destroy the previous Judge. The money was stolen. The mother gave the money back to the thief, and asked that it be made holy by making an unholy object. The text repeatedly stresses the amount of money, either because it was a great amount, or to remind the reader of the possible connection to its origin in the previous story. The mother then told the son that she wanted the money used to be consecrated to the Israelite deity (using the deity's name), but the manner in which she did it, by creating a *pesel* and a *massēkâ*, is expressly forbidden by that same Israelite deity.

When the son returned the silver to his mother she gave two hundred shekels of silver to a smith who made a *pesel* and a *massēkâ* from it which, the text notes, was kept in the house of Michah (Judg 17:4). The mother did not give all of the money to the son for these objects but only a small fraction of it and two images were created from that sum. The only information in the text concerning these objects is that they could be made by a smith. Questions about who made these objects are raised in the literature on this passage because slightly later, according to internal biblical chronology, the text states that there were no smiths in Israel because the Philistines feared the Hebrews would make swords and spears (1 Sam 13:19). The characters provide no indication as to what these objects were nor how they thought they would function.

The text continues with Michah, noting that he had a house of Elohim, made an *ʾēpôd* and *tĕrapîm*, and inducted one of his sons to be his priest (Judg 17:5).[10] It is unlikely that these objects were legitimate in the Israelite cult because they were not set up by those designated to do so, nor was his son of the right clan or group to have functioned as a legitimate priest. The relation of these actions on the part of Michah to his mother's actions is not clear. The text uses different terminology to refer to the cult items that Michah's mother wanted made and those which are in Michah's possession. It indicates that Michah had quite a collection of cultic objects of dubious legitimacy, and that his mother added to them.

The text continues with a summary of the situation in Israel, a point to which the text has been building, by stating, "In those days there was no king in Israel; each man did what was straight/right in his eyes" (Judg 17:6). This line follows immediately upon the reference to a sanctuary filled with idolatrous objects consecrated in the name of a deity, presumably the Israelite deity, though Elohim is used rather than

---

[10]The text does not qualify Michah's as a house of the Israelite deity by name, but uses the more generic term Elohim for the title of this structure. An *ʾēpôd* was a golden garment which had special status in the elaborate series of priestly apparel. C. Meyers, "Ephod," *ABD* 2.550. *tĕrapîm* are more difficult to define. Y. Kaufman does not define them but categorizes them as, "figurines of foreign manufacture that archaeological excavations have discovered in abundance in Israelite Palestine." *The Religion of Israel: From Its Beginnings to the Babylonian Exile*, trans. M. Greenberg (Chicago: University of Chicago Press, 1960) 142.

YHWH in this verse. The entire book of Judges has been a search for a leader, yet each leader was problematic because of their actions, motivations, or what they did with their power. The text slowly introduced modifications of this verse, such as Samson's statement that the woman was "right in his eyes." The Samson episode also proves that what appeared right in his eyes was not as it seemed. The way is paved for the following scenes where there is only anarchy in Israel, no one ruled, and no one could differentiate between right and wrong.

While most understand this to reflect a later period when there was a proper king or even after the period of kingship, Talmon proposes that the term *melek* and *šōpēṭ* are in parallel structure and interchangeable.[11] The focus of the phrase is a positive evaluation of the advantage of monarchy, but a negative evaluation of the interim period of Judges in which no ruler maintained order. Klein points out that this equation underscores a shift in the relationship between the deity and Israel.[12] Both arguments are at work here. The phrase does reveal a negative evaluation. At the same time, regardless of one's evaluation of Samson, he had been designated by the deity. Israel now enters a period when even a bad deity-designated leader no longer existed.

The timing of this statement is particularly relevant in light of the David/Saul, north/south polemic in the book. A northerner establishing his idolatrous sanctuary was the final proof given that Israel had strayed significantly from their deity. The sentence indicates a clear need for leadership. The introduction to the title "king" foreshadows the path that will follow. The phrasing of the verse implies that the root of the problem was the lack of proper leadership and it introduces the term "king." Up to this point Israel had not had a king and different solutions were tested. The end result was a slow decline until Israel reached this point. The phrasing reveals Israel's problem now was a lack of a substantive leadership and the solution was kingship. This sentence sets up the remaining stories which reveal that it was the southern Judite king that was legitimate, not the northern kingdom of Israel.

The text shifts focus to introduce another character, a young man from Bethlehem of Judah, from the family of Judah, who was a Levite and resided there as a sojourner (Judg 17:7). This verse introduces this character and a number of elements that will be continued in the fol-

---

[11] S. Talmon, "In Those Days There Was No King in Israel," *Proceedings of the 5th World Congress of Jewish Studies*, ed. Pinchas Peli et al. (Jerusalem: Hacohen, 1969) 242–3.

[12] L. R. Klein, *The Triumph of Irony in the Book of Judges*, JSOTS/Bible and Literature Series 14 (Sheffield: The Almond Press, 1989) 141.

lowing chapter. The man was from Bethlehem and, more specifically, Bethlehem of Judah, possibly to distinguish him from Ibzan of Bethlehem who had judged Israel earlier (Judg 12:8). Ibzan was famous for marrying his sons and daughters outside the group. The stress here is on the Judite locale. This man was from Judah, from the family of Judah. In this case he was a Levite and thus only resided in Judah.

The term for "reside" is *g-w-r*, whose nominal form is used to refer to one who is a resident alien, and thus the verb denotes someone whose status is only temporary, in keeping with the role of all Levites, who at this time, were not allotted land. The reference contains a play on words. The name of the Levite is revealed after the establishment of the northern shrine in Dan (Judg 18:30). There he is named Jonathan, son of Gershom, son of Manasseh (Judg 18:30). The words for, "he resides," are *gār šām* not far removed in sound from Gershom.

The story continues with the man leaving Bethlehem of Judah to reside wherever he could find a place (Judg 17:8). In this fashion, the story returns to Michah because, on the Levite's way, he came to the house of Michah in the hill country of Ephraim (Judg 17:8). Michah asked him where he was from and the man replied that he was a Levite. Again, the text notes that he was from Bethlehem of Judah. The Levite added that he was traveling to take up residence wherever he could find a place (Judg 17:9). In the last three verses the man's origin in Bethlehem of Judah is noted three times, that he was a Levite twice, and twice that he was seeking a place. This sets him up for his departure, later in the story, since the tribe of Dan had the same goal; to go anywhere they could find a place.

Michah asked the man to stay with him and noted that he could be a father and a priest to him and that he would pay him ten shekels of silver a year, an allowance of clothing, and his food (Judg 17:10). The Levite agreed to stay with the man and the youth *naʕar* became like one of his own sons (Judg 17:11). Michah then installed the Levite and the young man *naʕar* became his priest and remained in the house of Michah (Judg 17:12). Michah then commented to himself that the Israelite deity, who is named specifically, would make him prosper because he made the Levite his priest (Judg 17:13).

On the surface the key issue is the legitimacy, or illegitimacy, of this cult and its priest, both of which later go on to service in the northern kingdom. The reader already knows what is inside this sanctuary: *těrāpîm*, an *ʔēpôd*, and a *pesel* and *massēkâ* made with money that originated from a dubious source and was once stolen by the keeper of the sanctuary. The Levite took the job for the money. It is not clear if he knew what was inside the sanctuary, its origins, or if his role as a Levite meant he was not authoritative enough to become a legitimate priest.

There are many strange elements to the story. Michah first made his own son a priest at the sanctuary and was quick to fire him and hire the Levite. He viewed the Levite as more prestigious, especially concerning the Israelite deity, as is made clear by his later statement (Judg 17:13). His motivation was to find favor with the deity so that he would prosper, apparently financially.

Michah originally asked the man to serve as priest and father to him. Yet the Levite is repeatedly described as a *naʿar*. Since there is no listed father for Michah (could his father have been Samson?), this reference is particularly striking. When the Levite agreed to the job, the text notes that he was like a son to Michah. Michah already had a son who was fired as soon as the Levite appeared. The differences between the role of a priest as father versus a son are quite striking. A father sets the rules and is in a teaching role whereas a son is subject to the father. In the previous story the roles were reversed where Samson dictated to his father. Michah may have originally sought direction from a priest but the reference to his being like a son implies that Michah determined the rules of the sanctuary, emphasized by Michah's installing him into the priesthood rather than the Levite establishing the rules himself.

The Danite Search: Judges 18:1-29

This next unit is often separated as a different episode since the text reiterates that, "in those days there was no king in Israel" (Judg 18:1). The notation of each man doing right in his eyes is not restated. Instead the text continues by referring to what else happened in those days, namely that the tribe of Dan sought a territory in which to settle. Up until that point, no territory had fallen to them (Judg 18:1). The juxtaposition of the reference to the lack of a king in Israel implies that the absence of a king was responsible for the lack of territory for the tribe of Dan. The king reference follows the case of Michah who hired a Levite priest but prior to meeting Michah had nowhere to be and was also looking for a place. The storyline connects Michah and the Levite priest, as well as the homeless status of the Levite and the Danites. This story ties into the Samson episode since Samson too was a Danite and the results of his not having a place were made very clear.

The Danites were ready to change their situation and sent out five from their family at Zorah and Eshtaol to spy out the land and explore it (Judg 18:2). The text repeats that the men were told to go and explore the land. When they arrived at the hill country of Ephraim, at the house of Michah, they stopped for the night. Near Michah's house they recognized the speech of the young *na'ar* Levite and they asked him who had brought him to these parts and what he was doing there (Judg 18:3). As opposed to the Sibboleth/Shibboleth incident, the text does not state which aspects of his speech were identifiable nor did the fact that his speech was distinctive cost him his life.

The movement of Danites at this time may be more closely tied to the Samson cycle than is regularly noted. While historically speaking there is little connection between the two, the placement of Samson's story prior to the movement of Dan ties the stories together in the narrative sense. During Samson's life the text makes no references to any association between him and his tribe members. The only obvious Israelites with whom he interacted, other than his parents, were the Judites who turned him over to the Philistines. Samson's life ended destroying the city of Gaza, but that event may have been the straw that broke the camel's back for the Danites, necessitating their movement in the following story.

The Levite did not repeat the whole scenario but states, "thus and thus Michah did for me, he hired me and I became his priest" (Judg 18:4, JPS). His credentials were well enough established for them to ask him to inquire of Elohim, since they wanted to know if the mission they were on would be successful (Judg 18:5). The text does not relate any actions on the priest's part other than his response for them to go in peace and that the Israelite deity viewed with favor their mission (Judg 18:6). The priest offered no prayer, did nothing with the cult paraphernalia, nor did he investigate the project.

The Danites were happy with the response and continued on to Laish (Judg 18:7). They observed the people there but the Hebrew describing what they observed is difficult to understand. A rather inelegant but literal translation is, "the people dwelling carefree, dwelling safely, like the family of the Sidonians, quiet and safe, and there was nothing against them in the land, possessor of restraint, and they are far from Sidonians, they had nothing with man." Translations vary considerably because of the difficulty of understanding this passage: "They observed the people in it dwelling carefree, after the manner of the Sidonians, a tranquil and unsuspecting people, with no one in the land to molest them and no hereditary ruler" (JPS). In this case the translators redo some of the Masoretic pointing and translate terms loosely. This translation plays up the theme of leadership and provides a new version, but there is a great deal of interpretation involved. Boling interprets even further, translating, "Living securely according to 'Sidonian's rule,' calm and confident, without anyone perverting anything in the territory or using coercive power. They were far from the

Sidonians, however, they had no treaty with Aram."[13] In his understanding there is a switch from a *d* to a *r* providing the reading Aram,
and he views most of the sentence as referring to treaties. The text later
repeats the same terminology (Judg 18:28) and translating it this way
demands modification of the later reference as well.

While it is difficult to deduce precisely what is referred to here,
there was a connection with Sidon. It is not clear what the connection
was, but it is not surprising since the site of Laish/Dan is in the north
which was often influenced by the Phoenician area in different time
periods. The reference is not out of place. Regardless of whether the
people of Laish lacked a treaty with Aram, or had nothing to do with
anybody, most scholars would agree that one of the appealing aspects
of the site, for the Danites, was that they were not part of any coalition
nor were they prepared for an attack.

The scouts returned and their brothers at Zorah and Eshtaol asked
them how they fared (Judg 18:8). Their reply was that they should go at
once and attack them. Their enthusiasm is revealed in their response
that the land was good and their brothers were sitting around idle.
They pressured them not to delay, but to go and invade the land and
take possession of it (Judg 18:9). They continue by noting that the deity
had delivered it into their hand. When they came they would find an
unsuspecting people and spacious land; nothing on earth was lacking
there (Judg 18:10). Their recommendation was enough and they departed from there, from the family of the Danites, from Zorah and
Eshtaol, six hundred men ready for war (Judg 18:11). Zorah and Eshtaol
are named each time the text refers to the Danites in this chapter.

The Danites encamped at Kiriath Jearim in Judah (Judg 18:12). The
text explains that this is why the place was called "the camp of Dan" to
this day, placing it west of Kiriath-Jearim. The Danites continued from
there to the hill country of Ephraim, arriving at the house of Michah
(Judg 18:12). The five men who spied out the region earlier commented
to their brothers, the Danites, rather conversationally, that there was an
ʾēpôd in these houses, *tĕrāpîm*, a *pesel*, and a *massēkâ*, ending by reminding them that they knew what they had to do (Judg 18:14). The other
Danites knew exactly what to do which was to turn off, enter the house
of the young Levite at Michah's house, and greet him (Judg 18:15).
Their greeting was tempered by the six hundred Danite men girded
with weapons of war standing at the entrance to the gate (Judg 18:16).
While the army guarded the house, the five men who were on the original scouting mission went inside and took the *pesel*, *ʾēpôd*, the *tĕrāpîm*,
and the *massēkâ* (Judg 18:17). The priest was standing at the entrance to

---

[13] Boling, *Judges*, 260.

the gate along with the six hundred men with their weapons of war (Judg 18:17) and thus fully aware of what happened, and what he faced.

This scene vividly depicts and repeats a number of aspects, with the repetitions driving home the point. Each move included reference to the six hundred armed men waiting at the gate, and thus constantly reminds the reader of the military pressure. The Levite priest is always referred to as young *na'ar* and thus either inexperienced, threatened, or small and no match for Danite warriors. The entire list of cultic objects in Michah's house is listed three times. The scene is clear; there were six hundred armed warriors surrounding the house, a place of worship with cultic artifacts inside, protected by nothing more than a young priest. The scene dramatizes what will be commented upon again shortly; there were no rules, people did whatever was right in their eyes.

The men entered Michah's house and took the cultic objects, listing them all again, and the priest asked them what they were doing (Judg 18:18). Their response was a command, "Be quiet, put your hand on your mouth!" (Judg 18:19). They also made him an offer to come with them and be their father and priest. In a question reminiscent of Abimelech's of his brothers in Shechem, they asked, "Would you rather be priest to one man's household or be priest of a tribe and family in Israel?" (Judg 18:19). The ironic difference between this and the earlier situation with Abimelech is that Abimelech asked his brethren whether it would not be better to be ruled by one relative rather than seventy sons of a stranger, and here the priest was offered a promotion, making the question whether it would not be better to minister to many people rather than one.

The priest had no problem with the Danites' offer, stealing the idolatrous objects, and luring away the officiating priest. The text notes that it was good in his heart (Judg 18:20). He took the *ʾēpôd*, the *tĕrāpîm*, and the *pesel* and joined the Danites. Since all four categories of objects in Michah's house were listed in each rendition of what the Danites were doing, the absence here of the *massēkâ* is quite obvious. Boling interprets this as a mistake on the part of the MT, and uses its presence in the LXX as proof that it simply fell out of the MT by accident.[14] Another possibility is that this was left out intentionally. The Danites had just stolen Michah's priest and his cultic objects, maybe the priest left something behind for Michah.

The Danites set out again, placing the children, cattle, and their household goods in front (Judg 18:21). This reference introduces new elements because when the Danites first left they only referred to the six hundred fighting men and their weaponry. No reference was made

---

[14] Ibid., 264.

to children and household goods (Judg 18:11). It is unusual that these items, considered the most in need of protection, should go first when they should be last to be most protected.[15] The implication is that they were expecting trouble from behind, possibly Michah, from whom they had stolen so much.

The Danites were correct to be nervous because they had gone some distance from Michah's house when the men in the houses near mustered and caught up with the Danites (Judg 18:22). They called out to the Danites who turned around and asked Michah what the matter was and why he had mustered, thus feigning ignorance (Judg 18:23). He reminded them that they had taken his priest and the gods that he had made and walked off. How could they ask what the matter was (Judg 18:24)?

The issue in the book of Judges, the very thing the Israelite deity feared, was that through intermarriage the people would worship other non-gods. Ironically, this was exactly what happened to Michah and he did not realize what an abomination his shrine was with its idols, made with stolen money, served by a Levite priest. His comment, a few lines earlier, that since he now had a priest the Israelite deity would surely favor him reveals he believed he was doing something that would be favored by the deity. The reference to walking off with his gods highlights the biblical notion that these idols were nothing more than mere idols. They were manufactured. They could be carried off as easily by one person, their owner, as someone else.

The Danites' response was not sympathetic. They threatened him telling him not to shout at them, because some desperate men might attack him and he and his family would lose their lives (Judg 18:25). Michah, realizing that they were stronger than he, turned back and went home while the Danites continued on their way (Judg 18:26). Even though the Danites stole from him they could do what was right in their eyes. The bottom line was that whoever was militarily stronger prevailed.

Taking Michah's idols and priest the Danites proceeded to Laish (Judg 18:27). The people of Laish are again described as peaceful and unsuspecting. The importance of this repeated description is that the end of the verse notes that the Danites put them to the sword and burned the town. Since the people of Laish are never described in terms of ethnicity they are not Canaanites, Amorites, or Perrizites. It is

---

[15] When Jacob was about to meet Essau, who had been ready to kill him at their last encounter, he placed the children he loved the most closest to him and farthest back, while those of the least loved wives were in front, in the least protected position (Gen 33:1-7).

not clear how the Danites' action should be interpreted. It could be a legitimate action because the Danites needed and deserved territory of their own. On the other hand the Danites had just done what was right in their own eyes regarding Michah. While Michah himself is not portrayed favorably by the text, it is not clear that his negative characterization legitimates the Danites' actions towards him, or the items they stole from him. The Danites' action toward the people of Laish is of questionable legitimacy.

The depiction used earlier as their description is now repeated as the explanation for why the Danites could so easily capture the town; there was no one to come to their rescue for it was distant from Sidon and they had no dealings with anyone (Judg 18:28). The text adds here that the town lay in the valley of Beth-rehob. The Danites rebuilt the town and settled there. The text explains that they named the town Dan after their ancestral father who was Israel's son (Judg 18:29). The text reminds the reader that the name of the town was Laish. This last line accomplishes two things. It reinforces Dan's tie to Israel by reminding the reader that Dan too was a son of Israel and that therefore the Danites were as well. It does not let the reader forget that the Danites destroyed the people of Laish and that the city had a previous identity. By not labeling the people of Laish with an ethnic affiliation the legitimacy of Dan's actions remains questionable.

The Origins of the Northern Cult: Judges 18:30-31

The final portion concerning the Danites addresses the stolen cult objects. The Danites set up the sculptured image for themselves. The name of the Levite is finally mentioned; he was Jonathan, son of Gershom, son of Manasseh (Judg 18:30). The text says that his descendants served as priests to the Danite tribe until the land went into exile (Judg 18:30). The discussion ends by noting that they maintained the sculptured image that Michah made throughout the time that the House of Elohim stood at Shiloh (Judg 18:31).

These final references address problems of the David/Saul, north/south dichotomy and prepare the reader for the final chapters. The establishment of the northern sanctuary was rooted in goods stolen numerous times. Michah originally stole the money for the *pesel* from his mother. The *pesel* was stolen from Michah. The priest in charge of the stolen objects legitimated the robbery for career advancement. No one in this entire episode acted faithfully to anyone else in the story, questioning how anything legitimate could stem from this place.

The text blatantly discounts the legitimacy of the cult by reminding the reader of the destruction of the northern kingdom which, in narrative time, has not yet occurred. Since, according to 2 Kgs 17:7-12, the reasons for the destruction of the northern kingdom were its illegitimate northern sanctuary, sacrifices, intermarriage, and practicing of the customs of others, referring to its destruction in the same line as its inception is less than subtle. The text makes the statement that the northern cult was illegitimate in the means by which it was established, proved by its destruction and the sending of its people into exile.

The Levite priest was active for two chapters but only at the end of the second chapter does the narrator introduce his name, Jonathan, son of Gershom, son of Moses/Manasseh. He is reported to be a direct descendant of Moses through Gershom, but the MT alters the name of Moses to that of Manasseh through the addition of the letter *nun* to the name of Moses.[16] These two different options change the status and role of Jonathan rather dramatically.

The first option is that Jonathan was a descendant of Moses. References to Moses appear throughout the text. He is mentioned regarding the descendants of the Kenites in Judg 1:16, where the reference highlights the transitional nature of Judges 1. There are a number of places in the MT where Moses and his descendants are considered the legitimate priests and heirs to the priesthood (Exod 32:25-29). The inclusion of Moses and all that he stood for might be seen as another example in Judges where positive terms, people, and actions at the end of the book are turned around so that they become the thing against which the deity warned.

The other possibility is to follow the MT and read this person as the son of Manasseh, Judah's apostate king.[17] There is much in favor for this understanding as well. Manasseh ruled after Hezekiah and, according to 2 Kgs 21:2, carried out the abominable practices of the nations who lived in the land before the Israelites. His sins included rebuilding the "shrines" *bāmôt*, that Hezekiah destroyed, setting up altars for *Baal*, making an *Asherah*, worshiping all the host of heaven, causing his son to pass through the fire (possibly referring to child sacrifice), all things, with the exception of child sacrifice, that Judge's Jonathan also did. Even child sacrifice had been carried out only a few chapters earlier by Jephthah. Relating the northern cult's origins to Judah's worst and most irreligious king, furthers the point, made ear-

---

[16] This is done by suspending the letter *nun* above the line, inserting it between the first two consonants of the name of Moses.

[17] J. Berridge, "Jonathan," *ABD* 3.943.

lier, by reminding the reader that the northern sanctuary was active until the exile.

Both readings make sense in terms of the themes of Judges and deciding which reading is to be preferred is difficult. Most scholars treat the insertion of the *nun* as an intrusive element to protect the name of Moses.[18] The Masoretic system is, relatively speaking, fairly recent and this reading is not preserved in the other ancient versions. This would be the only place thus far in Judges where the Masoretic reading appears less legitimate. Yet even the Masoretes questioned their reading by including the *nun* as a superscription rather than as a regular letter. This makes the name stand out on the page, possibly indicating that the Masoretes were troubled, not so much by the reference to Moses, but that they were emphasizing the comparison with the actions of the later king Manasseh.

The historicity of the entire account is dubious, but its appearance as the main description of the northern sanctuary is crucial. The verb "to place" for what happened to the objects does not clarify what the objects did or how they functioned, but the text stresses certain elements about the objects. Michah made the objects. Since the reader knows that Michah no longer had the objects, this verse diminishes their authority. They were made by a thief. They were stolen. They are referred to as gods by Michah but the nature of what happened to them mocks their divine status.

The reference to Shiloh is also significant. The text states that they used the image, which Michah made, all the days that the house of Elohim was at Shiloh. According to 1 Sam 3:3 and 4:3, prior to the establishment of the Temple in Jerusalem, Shiloh housed the ark of the covenant and was the main religious center for the Israelites. Even though both Laish and Shiloh are located in what was considered northern territory, the establishment of the northern cult is not associated with the site but is in distinction from it. The reference denigrates the legitimacy of the northern shrine by placing its origins in a period when the legitimate cult was already housed in northern territory.

Reasons for the transference of the central site and home of the ark are laid in the book of Judges. In a later chapter women will be stolen and forced into marriages with Benjaminites while at a celebration in Shiloh. Saul was a descendant of one of these marriages. Saul was crowned king in Shiloh. This episode concerns the establishment of the northern shrine but also connects, in its impacts on the idea of leader-

---

[18] Boling, *Judges*, 266, J. Gray, *Joshua, Judges, Ruth* The New Century Bible Commentary (Grand Rapids: Eerdmans, 1986) 347; J. A. Soggin, *Judges: A Commentary*, Old Testament Library (Philadelphia: Westminster Press, 1981) 268.

ship and kingship, to central themes in the book. It is clear, from this passage, that anarchy reigned and that Israel needed a strong centralized ruler.

Summary

The story of the Danite migration functions as transitional material. It bridges the stories of the individual judges and leads to anarchy and civil war, the note on which the book ends. This is done through the Danites, the tribe of the last judge examined, through the actions of the characters, and the terminology employed. The text introduces references to much later events, further tying the themes about the role of the north into the story and preparing the reader for the following story when this becomes the predominant message.

The episode takes many of the themes which have slowly evolved throughout the book to their more destructive end. The Israelites no longer had leaders. In the previous Samson episode a woman could be bought, here a Levite can be purchased. A son steals from his mother. People coveted the favor of the Israelite deity with objects which the deity rejected, and which had been incorporated from the surrounding people. Israel's enemy was itself. Each man did what was right in his own eyes, and his own eyes only. These practices led to the situation where a civil war exploded, turning Israel militarily against itself.

Chapter 14

THE RAPED *PÎLEGEŠ*

Judges 19:1–20:7

Chapter 19 of the book of Judges presents what is, for the modern reader, one of the most distressing stories in the entire Bible. A woman was thrown to a gang of thugs and raped, possibly to death. Neither her husband, her father, nor the person who brought them into his home, protected her.[1] The aftermath of the episode escalates into a civil war with the tribes of Israel finally gathered together as a group but only to fight the tribe of Benjamin. The dramatic portrayal of the woman's ordeal is chilling. This episode is what the preceding stories in Judges have led up to and is itself the catalyst for what is to come. Despite the importance of this story for understanding Judges, scholarship in general has not focused attention on this chapter. Perhaps the absence of a judge makes it uninteresting. Perhaps it is too painful. Perhaps it does not fit well with the military hero worship of many commentaries on this book.

The episode of the rape has recently been discovered by feminist scholars who have worked on the text as a self-contained story and as part of literature dealing with women in the biblical text. Because of the nature of these new studies they have not tied this story into the larger narrative of Judges. It is apparent when viewing the entire book of Judges that the events in the book lead to this chapter which is the catalyst for the final civil war. Literary motifs and references made throughout the book culminate in this episode.

---

[1] See below for a detailed discussion of the way in which the text defines the relationship between the woman and man.

This story contains most of the main questions raised thus far in the book: what happens when there is no leadership, what is the role of Judah versus Benjamin, what is the relationship between Israelites and non-Israelites, and more frightening, the relationships between the different Israelite tribes. The image of Israel as reflected by the treatment of their women is of paramount importance in this episode. The use of women as a barometer of how the Israelites are faring is most obvious when the way the *pîlegeš* is treated is compared to Achsah, the first woman introduced in the book following the first major episode. The two stand as book ends encompassing the text that leads the Israelites from the point of Achsah to that of a gang-raped woman.

Introductions: Judges 19:1-20

This section begins with the comment, "In those days there was no king in Israel" (Judg 19:1). As noted above (Judg 18:1), this phrase is a comment both on what has just happened as well as what is to come. The phrase "in those days" is an implication on the part of the narrator that the situation described here no longer obtains. The differences between this occurrence of the phrase and its earlier variants are significant. In the first case the phrase is followed by the comment that, "every man did what was right in his eyes" (Judg 17:6). In the second case it is followed by a reference to the tribe of Dan seeking territory (Judg 18:1). As noted above, Dan's search for a new home indicates that "every man did right in his own eyes." Although phrased differently in this instance in Judges 19, the latter half of the sentence performs the same function as did its earlier variants. In other words, the sentence describes yet again what happens in Israel when, lacking the authority of a king, each man does what seems right to him.

In Judges 19, the continuation of the verse is, "a Levite residing at the other end of the hill country of Ephraim took to himself a woman/ wife, a *pîlegeš* from Bethlehem in Judah" (Judg 19:1).[2] In light of what the reader has already learned in Judg 17:5, the second half of the sentence forewarns the reader that anarchy will somehow result from the actions of the characters described in this sentence. By including references to a Levite, Ephraim, Bethlehem, and Judah, all of which have just been encountered in the previous story, the reader is signaled at the

---

[2] For a discussion of this text with a different approach to the beginning and ending of the story see P. Trible, "An Unnamed Woman: The Extravagance of Violence," *Texts of Terror: Literary-Feminist Readings of Biblical Narratives* (Philadelphia: Fortress, 1984) 65–91.

beginning of this fresh episode that issues similar to those just seen in the previous episode will be revisited.

The first person introduced is the Levite. He is not a youth *nāʿar*, as was the Levite in the previous story, but is an adult man *ʾîš*. Similar to the earlier Levite, the verb referring to his place of residence is *g-w-r*, a term that is used for temporary abodes, not long term residence. Trible says that referring to the man as a Levite indicates that he had status in his society.[3] While Levites are generally considered persons of status and rank, the previous story portrays a Levite, with an ill-defined status, carrying out actions which are probably to be considered idolatrous by setting up a shrine of dubious legitimacy (Judg 18:30-31), filled with stolen graven images (Judg 18:14-20), which had been manufactured with stolen money (Judg 17:1-4). Calling this new character a Levite, does less to provide him with status, than it raises questions about his character and intentions.

This Levite too was dwelling in Ephraim. Precisely where in Ephraim depends on the understanding of the term *yarkâ* which means "flank, side, extreme part."[4] Exactly what it means to speak of the "flank" of Ephraim is not clear. JPS translates the terms as "at the other end" of Ephraim, and understands it to refer to the previous story, parts of which took place in Ephraim. Since the previous story also contained a Levite, comparison of the two is natural. Boling translates the term as, "in the remote hills of Ephraim."[5] In his interpretation the term is used to indicate that the man was from a remote area. Since the first part of the verse connects this story with the one preceding, as does the appearance of another Levite, a translation such as, "other side," separates it from the previous location while bringing them together because of the comparison.

The final part of the verse introduces the woman. The text states literally that, "he took to himself a woman/ wife *pîlegeš* from Bethlehem Judah." The phrase "to take a woman/wife" is complex. The official status of the relationship of the two protagonists to each other is crucial for understanding the rest of the story and for evaluating their actions appropriately. The phrase can mean that one person married the other, i.e. he took her to wife. No translations use this understanding of the verb in this instance; instead, all state that he took the woman as a concubine (JPS, RSV, KJV). The question then becomes, what is a concubine/ *pîlegeš*?

---

[3] Trible, *Texts of Terror*, 66.

[4] *BDB*, 438.

[5] R. G. Boling, *Judges: Introduction, Translation and Commentary*, The Anchor Bible (Garden City: Doubleday, 1981) 271.

The English term was defined earlier as, "a woman who cohabits with a man without being his wife."[6] The term can also mean secondary wife in certain societies but, as will become apparent, there is no evidence here of the existence of a primary wife to whom this woman would be second. Neither translation addresses what is implied in terms of marriage, rank, status, legal rights, or inheritance procedures. Even if "concubine" accurately reflects the meaning of the Hebrew term *pîlegeš*, the ramifications of a woman cohabiting with a man not her husband are different in the 1990s, the 1950s, and 1611 c.e.[7]

Simply to apply the contemporary understanding of the term is problematic here because later the father of the *pîlegeš* is called a "father-in-law" (Judg 19:6). The English definition of concubine implies that the decision for the arrangement is on the part of the woman, which probably does not apply here. There are few references to this type of woman in the biblical text making it difficult to determine their status in Israel and the degree of power they had in their relationships with other people in their lives.[8]

There are two major issues concerning *pîlegeš* that are regularly highlighted in the biblical stories: what the status of their children is when compared to the children of the women/wives, what a *pîlegeš* of a ruler means politically. Often the two are related, especially when determining who inherits power. In Genesis the children of Abraham's *pîlegeš* received gifts but were sent away (Gen 25:6). However, in Gen 36:12 the children belonging to Esau's *pîlegeš* are not treated as less important than his other children. Then again, only a few chapters earlier in Judges, Abimelech was not considered a true son of Jerubbaal by the sons of Jerubbaal's women/wives (Judg 8:31).

The consequences of sons sleeping with their father's *pîlegeš* is an issue a number of times: when Reuben slept with Bilhah (Gen 35:22), when Abner slept with Saul's *pîlegeš* (2 Sam 3:7), and when Absalom slept with David's *pîlagšîm* (2 Sam 16:21-22 and 2 Sam 20:3).[9] Other references show that they were counted when numbering the size of a king's harem, but that these women do not share the same status as women/wives since they are listed after them (2 Sam 19:6, 1 Kgs 11:3). None of the references explicitly define their status.

---

[6] *Funk and Wagnall's Standard Dictionary*, s.v. "concubine."

[7] 1611 is the date of the publication of the King James Version of the Bible.

[8] Trible states that the woman in this situation has no power, especially when compared to her Levite man, and claims that she has an inferior status even regarding other women. Trible, *Texts of Terror*, 66.

[9] This is noted in the text. No action was taken at the time, but this action was regarded as illegitimate according to the final blessing from Jacob (Gen 49:3-4).

The question of how this particular woman in Judges 19 became his *pîlegeš* is not addressed. The text notes simply that he "took her." The reader does not know who made the arrangements, what they were, how they found each other, and what role the woman's father played. The man does not appear to have other women/wives, making the woman's status even more baffling. The only other *pîlegeš* in Judges is the mother of Abimelech. Her man/husband had other women/wives who, according to the text, had status. The *pîlegeš* and her status arises as a problem only when the question of her child's status regarding inheritance with his half-siblings became an issue (Judg 8:31). Jotham refers to her as an *ʾāmâ*, as discussed above. This is a way for him to insult Abimelech, but such an insult would be meaningless if there were no question about her status.[10] If the major difference between a women/wives and a concubine concerned inheritance there would be no reason for the Levite to take a *pîlegeš* as opposed to an official woman/wife at this stage of his life. This will become important in trying to understand many of the character's later actions.

The woman is said to be from Bethlehem of Judah. The focus again returns to Judah. Another Bethlehem is mentioned regarding Ibzan (Judg 12:8) but which Bethlehem is intended is not included in the text. It is important in the David/Saul polemic to raise the role of Judah, and more specifically, Bethlehem of Judah, David's home, at this point in the story. The outrage committed against this woman can be personalized by Judah and used as a symbol of what they must protect, their women. It also brings the cycle full circle. The first woman to whom one must compare the nameless woman of this story is Achsah. The two stand as bookends and their introductions already indicate their similarities and differences. Achsah was from the tribe of her father Caleb, the Kenites, who were absorbed into Judah, making both women Judites.

The next verse says, "his *pîlegeš* fornicated against him, leaving him for her father's house in Bethlehem in Judah, and staying there for four months" (Judg 19:2). The woman's actions, fornicating or prostituting herself and then leaving, are details that have received much attention. As with Achsah's actions in the first chapter, the difficulty in understanding this episode has less to do with precisely what translation is selected for the Hebrew verb than it does with interpreters' problems with the ramifications of the verb as they attempt to reconstruct what the text must mean.

Soggin is adamant, in discussing whether the verb in question here is *z-n-h*, and says that, "in no way can this be zanah, 'practice prostitution'

[10] See Chapter 8 concerning Abimelech.

in the sense of 'betrayed him,'" but he provides no reason why this cannot be.[11] He continues that,

> "The responsibility for the matrimonial crisis, on which the text gives us no information, must have lain with the husband, at least in view of his later behavior; however the case of the quarrel cannot have been very serious if the wife and the father-in-law are so glad to be reconciled."[12]

He provides no proof that the woman was considered a wife, nor any reason why this must mean what he states.

Boling agrees that the term cannot possibly mean "prostitute," translating it instead as "was unfaithful against him," wondering why, if she had practiced prostitution or fornicated against him, she would go home to her father.[13] Despite his shifting translation of the term he still rejects that verb and follows the LXXa which reads, "she became angry with him."[14] He brings in Israelite law which does not allow for divorce by the wife, interpreting that the woman became an adulteress by walking out on him.[15] He notes how this situation is the opposite of the Samson situation where Samson left the woman.[16] Trible's problem with the terminology concerns who initiated the action.[17] Jungling emphasizes that the woman initiated the separation, something he finds reminiscent of Hagar.[18]

Most scholars simply cannot believe that an Israelite woman would do things that they do not expect her to do, in this case that a Judite woman would prostitute herself. It is interesting that the term *z-n-h* means both "fornicate" and "prostitute," though most assume if they are following the MT that the implication is that she prostituted herself rather than that she merely committed fornication.[19] One basic reason for this is that even if she only fornicated, in their minds, she prostituted herself. But while most would translate the previous verse as, "he took to himself a concubine," meaning that she was never a wife, in this verse they assume she was a legitimate wife.

---

[11] J. A. Soggin, *Judges: A Commentary*, Old Testament Library (Philadelphia: Westminster, 1981) 284.

[12] Ibid.

[13] Boling, *Judges*, 273.

[14] Ibid. Note that RSV and NEB also follow the LXXa.

[15] Boling, *Judges*, 274.

[16] Ibid.

[17] Trible, *Texts of Terror*, 67.

[18] H. W. Jungling, *Pladoyer für das Königtum; eine stilistische Analyse der Tendenzerzählung Ri. 19,1-30a; 21.25* (Rome: Pontificio Instituto Biblico, 1976) 87–90.

[19] *BDB*, 275.

The rules governing the status of a *pîlegeš* concerning inheritance are poorly understood. It is that much harder to discern the Israelite laws governing concubinage. For example, if she were officially a wife and committed adultery, according to Deut 22:21 the woman should have been stoned to death. There are no rules in the MT governing what is considered adultery or unlawful procedures for a *pîlegeš* because it is not a state that the laws recognize or regulate.

The use of the term *z-n-h* must be placed within the context of Judges as a whole. The verb is used three times in the context of Israel going after foreign gods (Judg 2:17; 8:27, 33). The reader has been reminded repeatedly in the preceding three chapters that the result of Israelites prostituting themselves after foreign gods is the situation in Israel where every man did what right in his own eyes. Whether the *pîlegeš* physically fornicated against him or metaphorically fornicated against him is not clear but that, at this point in Judges, is almost irrelevant. Throughout most of the book, and especially in the last few episodes, all Israelites metaphorically fornicated against the deity and the *pîlegeš*'s doing what was right in her eyes was no different than what the deity-appointed leaders did. Ironically, the previous generation of Judges scholars tried to exonerate the woman of prostitution, while many feminist scholars are not clear that changing the meaning of the word helps her cause.[20]

Regardless of her reasons, the *pîlegeš* left her man, creating a parallel with the story of Achsah. Achsah left her husband in order to speak to her father. Her travel on a beast of burden indicates either privilege, because she had such transportation available to her, or, more likely, distance. The parallel is that both women left their men and returned to their fathers. This similarity is key to understanding the text, the differences in the outcomes, how each was received by her father, and what they received for their return.

Many of the above mentioned interpretations imply that the woman could not have committed an act such as fornication or prostitution and then returned home, yet no alternative place for her to have gone is suggested. The book of Judges thus far indicates that women's fate, especially in the second part of the book, was controlled by men, either their own or others. The two mothers who were not wives are recorded without names and their children (Abimelech and Jephthah) suffered because of their status. Jephthah's daughter was killed by her father to advance his career. Samson's mother was not believed by her husband.

---

[20] Boling feels she could not have prostituted herself, but that she became an adulteress by walking out on him (*Judges*, 273–74). Soggin feels that the situation must be the husband's fault (*Judges*, 284).

Samson's wife was married to whomever her father selected. Michah stole from his mother. The only woman with any control was Delilah and, in light of what happened to Samson's woman/wife and her family, it is not clear how much choice she had. Where else, and to whom, would this woman go other than her father?

The implication throughout the book is that it is because of the men, usually the fathers, that the women were in their predicaments. Achsah accused her father by claiming, "You have given me away" (Judg 1:15). A similar situation concerns Jephthah's daughter when she agreed, "you have uttered a vow to the LORD; do to me as you have vowed" (Judg 11:36).

After four months he set out with a young man *na'ar* and a pair of donkeys and went after her to speak to her heart and win her back. The Hebrew text, in distinction from the various English translations which, in agreement with the LXX, alter the verb in question to an action on the part of the Levite, notes that she admitted him into her father's house. The text claims that when the girl's father saw him he received him warmly (Judg 19:3). Many of the points raised earlier by previous scholars use aspects of this verse as evidence for their interpretation. Yet the components of this verse, the words and what they mean, must be examined in the context of the book as a whole, before this particular sentence can be understood.

The first aspect concerns the length of time the man waited until following her, which is included in the previous sentence (Judg 19:3). The *pîlegeš*'s stay at her father's house is described as lasting four months. This information is included in the same verse which describes serious actions on the part of the woman: she fornicated against the man, she left, and went to her father's house. The stay ends only because of the arrival of the man, thus the four months is determined to a large extent not by verse 2, where the woman was active, but verse 3 where the man took action, but only after four months had passed.

Four months is an unusual number for the biblical text. Common lengths of time are in the form of three days, seven days, a month, year, or numbers of years. Later in the book the Benjaminites stay in hiding for four months though there is little discussion describing the reason for that. Scholars discuss this time lapse in terms either of it indicating how committed the man was to her by going after her, or that he waited quite a while before going after her.[21] However, there might be

---

[21] Boling even states that the Levite's concern to recover her suggests that she, not he, was the offended party (*Judges*, 274). J. Gray sees the reference to "four months" as a corruption of "many days" (*Joshua, Judges, Ruth*, The New Century Bible Commentary [Grand Rapids: Eerdmans, 1986] 348).

other reasons for the specificity of this number. If the woman had sexual relations with another man, four months would be the amount of time to determine for certain, at least for those without modern medicine, whether the woman was pregnant.[22] His return, after four months, may not have been because he missed her but because it was only after that period of time that he could see what he wanted to see. In other words, the length of her stay was a function of her previous behavior. The only action that needed a four month period to be fully revealed is in keeping with the verb's meaning of fornicate.

The text states that his reason for going was to "speak to her heart," a phrase with a number of interpretations. The phrase has been interpreted to refer to an appeal to her mind, not her emotions, since, according to both Boling and Soggin, in the Bible the heart was the seat of the reason, not emotions.[23] Trible has studied the use of the term in other biblical contexts centering on the actions of a man toward a woman and found that it is used either by the offended or the guilty party.[24] In this case the phrase is used to explain why the man goes after her but says nothing about what he intended to do after winning her back.

Regardless of whether he was speaking to her heart or her mind, the phrase incorporates the word "heart." Since this is used in other key passages in Judges some comparison is in order. Achsah's father Caleb first used it when referring to giving her land. In that case he "gave according to the heart" (Judg 1:15). More recently Samson told Delilah "all of his heart" (Judg 16:18), which meant he told her the secret of his strength. In the episode just prior to the one currently under consideration, the heart was made good in the Levite priest, meaning the priest was delighted to serve a whole tribe rather than one man (Judg 18:20). Here, in Judges 19, the drama begins by the man's going to "speak to her heart," which will eventually lead to someone's destruction. Again Achsah and the *pîlegeš* carry out the same actions and their stories incorporate similar terminology but the ramifications of the words and actions are different.

The continuation of the verse describes the man's arrival and acceptance by the woman's father. The text highlights the relationships by using different terminology to refer to the female, male protagonist, and the secondary character of the father. In the first verse the male protagonist is referred to as both a man *îš* and a Levite (Judg 19:1). In

---

[22] I would like to thank the women of the Woman's Institute for Continuing Jewish Education in San Diego for this insight.

[23] Boling, *Judges*, 110; Soggin, *Judges*, 285.

[24] Trible notes Shechem speaking to Dinah after raping her (Gen 34:3), and the prophecy of Hosea (Hos 2:14). *Texts of Terror*, 67.

the second verse he is referred to only as "him," and by the third verse he is called merely a "man." When that term was applied to him earlier in combination with his title as Levite, it has been interpreted in the literature either as indicating his age, or is simply not mentioned in the translation.[25] All of a sudden, when the same word appears in verse 3 it is translated "husband" (JPS, KJV, RSV, Boling). This is most likely because of the reference in that verse to her being his *pîlegeš*. He is referred to as "her man," but to assume that this means "her husband" is not standard translation technique. The problem is that for the man to be a husband at this point he must have a wife, and that has not been established by the narrative.

The female protagonist is first called an *ʾiššâ pîlegeš*, leading Bal to equate the status of a *pîlegeš* with a type of marriage rather than some other sort of relationship.[26] The problem is similar to the term for virgin, why would one need to call her both a virgin and emphasize that she had never known a man (as is the case in Judg 11:36-40). Here, why would she need to be called both a woman/wife and a concubine if marriage were involved in the definition of *pîlegeš?* In the next verse, when the woman carried out some action against him, she is his *pîlegeš*. When she was home with her father she is a girl *naʿărâ*. Each term carries with it different connotations making it difficult to determine who she was. This is intentional on the part of the writer since with anarchy comes confusion of status and people's roles in society.

The final aspect of the verse concerns the *pîlegeš*'s father and his reception of the man. The father is referred to as her father, or the girl's father. Like the rest of the characters in this episode, he has no name and is referred to only by his relations with the other characters in the scene. The text notes that the father greeted him warmly (Judg 19:3). This is used as evidence to indicate that both the man and the woman were happy to see him. All it really indicates is that the men greeted each other warmly. It may mean that the father was hospitable. It may mean that he wanted his daughter out of the house since he gave her away in the first place. It may mean that he was expecting him to appear and wanted to make him comfortable and discover what his side of the story was. Only a few chapters earlier a similar occurrence happened where an Israelite man left his woman/wife and returned, pos-

---

[25] Note Boling's comment that using both man and Levite is a conscious contrast to the preceding story of a "young Levite" (*Judges,* 273). JPS does not translate it, and RSV and KJV translate, "a certain Levite."

[26] M. Bal, *Death and Dissymmetry: The Politics of Coherence in the Book of Judges.* Chicago Studies in the History of Judaism (Chicago: University of Chicago Press, 1988) 84–86.

sibly months later (Judg 15:1). There are so many explanations for the father's warm greeting that it is difficult to use the greeting as evidence for a particular interpretation of the story.

The next line begins the account of a series of evenings of eating and lodging. The father-in-law, described immediately thereafter as the girl's father, pressed him (the Levite) and he stayed with him for three days; they ate and drank and lodged there (Judg 19:4). Early on the morning of the fourth day the Levite started to leave but the girl's father said to the man, here called his son-in-law, to eat something to give him strength before he left (Judg 19:5). The text states that the two of them sat down and feasted together. Then the girl's father said to the man that he should stay the night and make his heart good (Judg 19:6), using the same terminology as that used in the previous chapter to refer to the earlier Levite's pleasure at serving a larger community (Judg 18:20). The man started to leave but his father-in-law kept urging him until he turned back and spent the night there (Judg 19:7). Early on the morning of the fifth day, he was about to leave when the girl's father suggested that he have a bite, and again the two of them ate, dawdling until past noon (Judg 19:8).

Throughout these lines the narrative employs a number of different terms to express the various relationships of the protagonists to each other. In verse 3 the Levite is called "her man/husband," and the father is referred to as, "the girl's father," while she is called "young girl" naʿărâ. The next verse calls the father both "the girl's father" and "his (the man/husband's) father-in-law," stressing the father's relationship to each of the individuals in this pair. In verse 6 the characters are described as "the girl's father" and "the man/husband." In verse 7 they are "man/husband" and "father-in-law" again. Critical scholarship sees this is a sign of different sources.[27] The references to "his father-in-law, the father of the young woman," in verses 4 and 9 are seen as forming a neat inclusio around the story of the visit.[28] The double identification at the outset is considered necessary because of the ambiguity of unpointed ḥōtēn which may be either "father-in-law" or "son-in-law."[29]

The term ḥōtēn appears three times in Judges and in every circumstance it is confused, or as in this case, it has to be qualified lest it be confused. The first appearance, in 1:16 of the MT, uses "father-in-law" when, according to many, it should really be "son-in-law."[30] Hobab is a

[27] Boling, *Judges*, 274.
[28] Ibid.
[29] Ibid.
[30] Ibid, 57; Gray, *Joshua, Judges*, 237; Soggin, *Judges*, 22–3.

difficult character to understand because the text refers to him as both "father-in-law" and "brother-in-law" of Moses.[31] The second appearance of the term again relates to Moses and describes the Kenites. They are referred to as coming from the area of Hobab, Moses' father-in-law. It is clear that, at least in reference to Moses' in-laws, the terminology is not straightforward. It is difficult to know whether this term, when used in relationship to a *pîlegeš*, was clearly understood. If the usage was clear then the shift in terminology must be a stylistic addition by an author to ensure that, because of the absence of names, it was clear who was being addressed. Another option is that the author was trying to establish that even though the woman character was a *pîlegeš*, she was considered a wife in this case. A final option is that a number of terms are used intentionally to show how problematic these relationships were, especially at this time in Israel's history.

The present episode reveals how complicated relationships became. The greatest contrast is with the Achsah narrative where all the parties are named and their status and relationship to each other was consistent and clearly defined. By the time of Gideon/Jerubbaal things were not as straightforward; wives, concubines/*pîlegeš*, and their children fought over what those differences in status meant. These issues continue with the story of Jephthah, whose mother had a different status, forcing upon him an even lower status among his peers. While Samson's parents are clearly identified, though no name is recorded for the mother, the status of his various women impacted him, especially since even their ethnicity is not always specified. By the time of the *pîlegeš* none of the protagonists have names, each is referred to by changing definitions of who they were, thereby confusing, for the reader, all of their relationships to each other.

Most discussions surrounding the length of the days of feasting view them as indicative of ancient hospitality.[32] In terms of what will happen later, these passages establish a standard of hospitality by which the later events might be viewed. Boling entitles this entire episode "Hospitality."[33] There is no contact with the *pîlegeš* throughout the feasting days (Judg 19:4-9). She did not speak, nor act, nor was she involved in any of the feasting or decisions concerning their departure.

After the last meal the man, his *pîlegeš*, and his young boy *naʿar* tried to leave. His father-in-law, called the "girl's father" for the final

---

[31] D. Launderville, "Hobab," *ABD* 3.234.

[32] L. R. Klein, *The Triumph of Irony in the Book of Judges*, JSOTS/Bible and Literature Series 14 (Sheffield: The Almond Press, 1989) 163; R. Patai, *Sex and Marriage in the Bible and the Middle East* (Garden City: Doubleday, 1959) 541.

[33] Boling, *Judges*, 271.

time, said to him that the day was waning toward evening and that he should stay for the night (Judg 19:9). He repeated that the day was declining and that he should spend the night with him and enjoy. He added that they could start early the next day and head for home. This time the man refused to stay the night, set out, and traveled as far as the vicinity of Jebus, that is Jerusalem (Judg 19:10). The narrator reminds the reader that he had with him a pair of laden donkeys and that his *pîlegeš* was with him as well. Since they were close to Jebus and it was late in the day the *naʿar* suggested that they turn aside to the town of the Jebusites and spend the night in Jerusalem (Judg 19:11).

These sentences set the scene for what follows. The man had had enough hospitality and set out even though it was late. The father had already stated twice that it was already late when they set out. The arrival near Jerusalem is important because the first battle in Judges included Jerusalem. In that case it was where they brought Adoni Bezek. Adoni Bezek was physically mutilated by the Israelites and Bezek was the place where Saul disarticulated a yoke of oxen. Thus the reference here to Jerusalem reminds the reader of other events there.

It is ironic and prophetic that the *naʿar* suggested they stay in Jerusalem. The man, at this point called "his master," told him, "We will not turn aside to a town of aliens who are not of Israel but will continue to Gibeah" (Judg 19:12). The narrator refers to the man here as the young man's master, *ʾădôn*, another term used more often for husband than *ʾîš*. Ironically the narrator uses the term for husband to refer to the relationship between the *naʿar* and the man, but not for the man with his woman/wife/concubine. Another ironic comment is that they would be safer with Israelites rather than the residents of Jerusalem, especially since the last time Jerusalem was mentioned in Judges it was not taken over by Benjaminites, rather they were living there together with the original inhabitants. The woman was silent and not involved in the discussion.

With his first idea rejected, the *naʿar* suggested that they approach one of these places and spend the night either in Gibeah or Ramah (Judg 19:13). The master took the *naʿar*'s advice, they traveled on, and the sun set when they were near Gibeah of Benjamin (Judg 19:14). They turned off there and went in to spend the night and their problems began. The man went and sat down in the town square but nobody took them indoors to spend the night (Judg 19:15). The last three verses are in the voice of the narrator and do not depict what the characters thought. It is described in such a way as to reflect what was apparently common practice. It appears that when needing lodging in a strange town one sat in the town square and waited to be invited into someone's home. This is reflected in a number of cases where the people were messengers of the deity (Gen 18:1; 19:1). No one in the town taking them indoors indicates that something was not right in this town.

It is no accident that the town in question is Gibeah, a town closely associated with Saul. Saul was sent on a mysterious mission to Gibeah (1 Sam 10:5), established a base against the Philistines near there, and it served as his base camp for his campaigns against surrounding enemies (1 Sam 22:6; 23:19). It remained the home of Saul's progeny after his death, evidenced by seven members of the house of Saul being executed there by Gibeonites at the behest of David (2 Sam 21:6). The town was so cemented to Saul that it eventually gained the name Gibeah of Saul (1 Sam 11:4; 15:34; 2 Sam 21:6; Isa 10:29). Thus the north/south, David/Saul battle becomes more prominent as the idea of kingship in Israel becomes more imminent.

In the evening, an old man came along from his property outside the town (Judg 19:16). Since the previous verse noted that the sun had already set it is not clear how much longer they waited. By noting that the old man arrived only in the evening implies they waited long enough for someone to have invited them in before the old man arrived. The text digresses to note that the man was from the hill country of Ephraim and resided at Gibeah where the people were Benjaminites (Judg 19:16). This information creates a tie with the Levite who was a resident alien in Ephraim. It also establishes that the old man was not from the town, exonerating him before any crimes were committed.

The man saw the wayfarer in the town square and asked where he was going and where he came from (Judg 19:17). A more literal translation of the Hebrew term translated here as "wayfarer" (JPS and RSV) is "the wandering man" (KJV). While the two words have the same general meaning, the Levite is called a man *îš* and is then qualified, similar to what was done when referring to him as a Levite. Since the term *îš* has regularly been applied to him, but has sometimes been translated "husband," it must be noted that this person is regularly called a man, and that term is periodically qualified.

On one level the Levite must be qualified because the new character entering the scene is also called a man *îš* but is further described as being old. On a number of levels the reference to him as a wanderer differentiates him from the newest character in the scene. But there may be more to the reference. The Levite was in the town square with his *pîlegeš* and the *nā'ar*, yet the old man spoke to the Levite in the singular, as though he were there alone. The scene is between the two men.

The old man questioned the man concerning his destination and origin. The man replied that they were traveling from Bethlehem in Judah to the end of the hill country of Ephraim, adding that it was where he lived. He elaborated by noting that he had made a journey to

Bethlehem of Judah and now was on his way to the house of the Israelite deity. He informed him that no one had taken him indoors (Judg
19:18). While the Levite did not lie, he deleted information that the
reader knows and added information that had not been included previously, raising the reader's suspicion after having read about situations like this previously (Heber the Kenite in Judges 4, Samson's
mother in Judges 14–16, the Levite priest's name in Judges 17–18).

Prior to the old man's question there had been no reference to the
Levite visiting the house of the Israelite deity. Scholars easily explain
this away as a scribal misunderstanding and follow the LXX.[34] Yet explaining this away ignores this character's similar actions later in the
story in his effort to initiate a civil war, where he provided only part of
the story and deleted his role in the situation (Judg 20:4-6). The slant on
his story highlights his status as a Levite. To the old man, hearing that
this Levite was traveling to the house of the deity presented him more
sympathetically than would have been the case if he had spoken of
himself as chasing after a *pîlegeš* who cheated on and ran away from
him.

The man did not state the primary reason for his trip, according to
the information provided by the text, to regain his *pîlegeš* once he could
determine whether or not she was pregnant. The reference to the house
of the deity was not a mistake but certainly presents the man, a Levite,
in a more religious and righteous light than has been the case in the
earlier part of the story. His statement was not necessarily a lie. The text
never notes where the Levite was taking the *pîlegeš* or what his intentions were when they arrived at their destination. The reader knows
that the Levite could be stating the truth but leaves open the possibility
that the man was grandstanding.

The Levite man continued to be the ideal guest by telling the old
man that he had straw and feed for the donkeys, and bread and wine for
himself, the female slave, and for the young man *na'ar* with his servant.
He added for emphasis that they lacked nothing (Judg 19:19). The man
used the plural "our" donkeys. The man employed the most polite and
deferential terminology, referring to himself as the old man's servant.

While he referred to himself as the old man's servant, he also referred to the woman separately. She was not a "female servant," but an
ʾāmâ, the same term used by Jotham to refer to Abimelech's mother in a
negative context (Judg 19:18); it is often translated, "handmaid." The
translation, "female slave," places the *pîlegeš* in the same context as the
man, showing deference in the hopes that he would take them into his
home, but the noun used to refer to her is not the feminine of the term

---

[34] Boling, *Judges*, 275; Soggin, *Judges*, 287.

used to refer to the man. The narrator uses it in an ironic sense since the two will spend the night in different accommodations.

The old man told the man to rest easy because he would take care of all his needs and he should not, on any account, spend the night in the square (Judg 19:20). He took him into his house, mixed fodder for the donkeys, bathed their feet, and then they ate, and drank (Judg 19:21). The old man spoke directly to the Levite man. He stated that he took him into his house. When referring to the food and drink the text switches to the plural, but it could as easily refer to the two men as to the Levite man, his *pîlegeš*, and his *naʿar*.

The Rape: Judges 19:22-25

The continuation of the narrative sets the tone of the group in the house by stating that they were enjoying themselves, literally, "making good their hearts" (Judg 19:20). This is the same terminology used for the previous Levite's attitude toward his Danite promotion and this Levite's time with the woman's father (Judg 19:6). In the continuation of the verse the men of the town, qualified as a "depraved lot," gathered about the house and pounded on the door (Judg 19:27). They called to the elderly owner of the house to bring out the man who had come into his house so that they could be intimate with him (Judg 19:22). These men are described as "without worth" by the narrator, a definitive if general description.[35] The term they used to refer to what they wanted to do with the man is "to know," a clearly sexual term.

There have already been parallels with the story of Lot in Sodom, and the reference to knowing the man sexually firmly ties the two stories together. In the Genesis account the messengers were prepared to wait in the town square to be taken in for the night (Gen 19:12). Just as in Judges, Lot, the person who took them in was not from that area but elsewhere (Gen 19:3). In both cases the male residents of the town wanted to know the male visitors sexually (Gen 19:5). There are also differences that become more pronounced in the next few verses. Here it is relevant to note that in the Genesis account the visitors were no mere travelers but messengers of the Israelite deity, as opposed to a Levite of questionable character. The Levite man also had a woman, to whom he was connected in some way, and a young man *naʿar*.

The Judges account continues with the owner of the house asking them politely (he used a Hebrew form which may be translated as "please") not to commit such a wrong (Judg 19:23), and calling them

[35] BDB, 116.

friends. He stated his feeling of responsibility toward the Levite, noting that since the man had entered his house as a guest they should not perpetrate this outrage. Again the text parallels, almost exactly, Lot's words to the men of Sodom where he states, "I beg you, my friends, do not commit such a wrong" (Gen 19:7, JPS).

The owner of the house continued his speech by making an offer (Judg 19:24). He told them that his virgin daughter and the *pîlegeš* were available. He told them that he would bring them out to them. He even offered them ideas, telling them to have their pleasure with them and do what they liked with them, but not to do this outrageous thing to this man (Judg 19:8). The parallels with the Sodom episode continue. Lot, too, offered his two daughters who had not known a man. He, too, offered to bring them out to the townspeople of Sodom. He, too, suggested that they may do to them as they pleased. He, too, noted that they should not do anything to the men since they were under the shelter of his roof (Gen 19:8-9).

The similarities and differences between the Genesis and Judges accounts are striking, yet each episode functions in the context of its book and the larger story line found there. The translation that they should, "do what they want with them," masks the literal translation, "do to them what is right in your eyes," which carries such force in Judges where variations of that phrase have appeared as markers of Israel's state. The reference to his daughter as a virgin is also important here. In the Genesis context they are referred to as never having known a man, but the daughter of the old man is referred to as a virgin. As noted earlier, it is not clear if there is a difference between the two or if when they both appear it is for emphasis. In the Judges context, the aftermath of the civil war concerned a search for virgins for the Benjaminites and the inclusion of the term here is prophetic. Here the Benjaminites rejected what all Israel must find for them later.

"The men would not listen to him, so the man seized his *pîlegeš* and pushed her out to them. They raped her and abused her all night long until morning, and they let her go when dawn broke" (Judg 19:25).

This verse is one of the most powerful and frightening in the book. The book no longer recounts quaint folk tales. A woman was thrown to a pack of men to be raped and abused for an entire night. While the men surrounded the house there was no indication that they were about to enter the house or that the man was in imminent danger. The original offer was two women which, awful as it was, at least meant the burden would be shared by two rather than one suffering alone. The man had a young boy *naʿar* who was not considered in the offer. The man who carried out these actions was the very person who was responsible for the *pîlegeš*'s safety.

The passage is so painful that many commentaries do not address the issues involved. Since the Hebrew is rather straightforward there are no philological issues to discuss, no way to avoid what happened. Most commentaries place the rape in the context of the military event that follows.[36] They do not refer to it as the abandonment and rape but the "Outrage of the Gibeonites."[37] Soggin attempts to exonerate the man by stating that the reference to the *pîlegeš*'s presence in verse 24 is a mistake and thus the Levite was continuing to be polite and threw his own woman out rather than his host's.[38] He attempts to minimize her plight by stating that the term "ravish/abuse" *ʿ-n-h* does not mean ravish/abuse but is a euphemism for "humiliate."[39]

Difficult as the reality of this verse is, the MT makes no attempt to hide the events.[40] He, quite clearly the Levite man, pushed his *pîlegeš* out to the depraved mob. The text does not attempt to minimize or sanitize what happened to her. She was raped and abused all night long. In case the reader did not now how long "all night long" was, the text emphasizes that she was raped and abused until morning. The text rephrases the idea again stating that they let her go when dawn broke. The *pîlegeš*'s nightmare is more poignant because the Levite had just taken her from her home, her father, and apparent security to ultimate horror.

The comparisons with the Genesis story are chilling. While Lot made the offer of his daughters, the messengers of the deity prevented it. In this case not only did the Levite man not refuse but he offered only his woman. As in Lot's case, the visitors he sheltered protected him. The difference is that in this case the man being sheltered protected himself by sacrificing his woman. There were no messengers protecting the women of Israel in Judges.

The Morning After: Judges 19:26-28

The woman's final scene is possibly more powerful than the previous. Toward morning she returned and it was growing light (Judg

---

[36] Boling, *Judges*, 276–77; Gray, *Joshua, Judges*, 352; Soggin, *Judges*, 288.

[37] Soggin, *Judges*, 287.

[38] Ibid., 288.

[39] Ibid., 288.

[40] For a fuller discussion of the horror of the episode see Trible. Trible's analysis of this chapter stands on its own scholarly merits, it is that much more impressive when viewed in light of the previous scholarship surrounding this episode. She brought forth the terror and abuse of this passage which had been ignored for so long (*Texts of Terror*, 65–91).

19:26). She collapsed at the entrance to the man's house where her man was. This is the first time that the girl/*pîlegeš* is called a woman *ʾiššâ*. Up to this point she was either an *ʾiššâ pîlegeš*, a daughter, or a young girl, without qualifiers. Only now was she a woman.

The text continues that she collapsed at the entrance to the house. It is a poignant scene. She had reached the gate, she was almost safe but collapsed before ever reaching it. This is yet another comment on the lack of protection for the women in Israel once they left the home. Jephthah's daughter was only safe when she was inside the home. As soon as she came out of the entrance she was sacrificed. So too this woman; as soon as she was pushed out the gate she lost all security and was sacrificed.

The text indicts the Levite man. The text draws the picture of an abused raped woman collapsing on the doorstep of the house just as the sun was rising. The narrator then notes that it is the house where her man was. On one level the reference simply defines which house was intended, but it reminds the reader that while the woman was suffering gang rape and abuse the man was safe inside the house.

The narrator emphasizes the security the man enjoyed inside the house all night by noting, in the next verse, when he arose in the morning he opened the doors of the house and went out to continue his journey (Judg 19:27). He is not called a man or a Levite but, "her lord" *ʾădōnêhā*. The text recounts that he had to open the door to get out, the door which protected him but which she could not reach. His way was hampered because there was the woman, his *pîlegeš*, lying at the entrance of the house, with her hands on the threshold (Judg 19:27). The use of the verb "he arose" *(q-w-m)* implies that he had lain down, probably sleeping throughout the night while his *pîlegeš* was raped and abused. The quick succession of verbs conveys a sense that he was simply going about his morning business. The text informs the reader that he was planning on continuing his journey. It does not note whether he was planning on looking for the woman or was simply prepared to make a quick departure. Her abused body blocking the way kept him from his flight. Her hand on the threshold, as Trible notes, functions as a finger pointing at him, one could almost imagine in accusation.[41]

The text continues to emphasize the man's insensitivity by his reaction to her abused body. He gave the command seen so many times thus far in Judges, "Get up" (Judg 19:28). In the other cases the command ignited a military battle and was a way to muster the troops (Judg 4:14, 7:15). In this case there was no reply. The man placed her on the donkey, got up, and set out for home. Most translations do not include the

[41] Ibid., 79.

verb following his placing her on the donkey, "he got up." In the MT the Levite did the thing his *pîlegeš* could no longer do.

The point that is clear by the way this verse is narrated is that the man did not express any remorse nor did he feel responsible for her plight. He made no attempt to save her from the fate to which he threw her. There is no indication that he would have sought her out had she not been lying there. He felt no need to "talk to her heart," or even ask her how she was. It is difficult to assume that he had intended to find her to woo her back for the joy of her company all along. In fact, the quickness with which he threw her to the mob almost seems to indicate that it was an opportunity he was seeking.

Sending a Message: Judges 19:29–20:7

This next scene uses the rape as the link between a personal outrage and civil war in Israel. There were minor skirmishes between tribes throughout the book as seen among the sons of Gideon/Jerubbaal, the Ephraimites at the end of the Jephthah episode, and the Danites and Michah in Ephraim. All those cases were either within a single tribe (Abimelech) or between two tribes. The Levite man enjoined all of Israel against Benjamin by mutilating his raped *pîlegeš*.

The story continues that when he came home he picked up the knife, took hold of the *pîlegeš*, cut her up limb by limb into twelve parts which he sent throughout Israel (Judg 19:29). The most difficult problem with this verse concerns whether the *pîlegeš* was already dead or whether the Levite killed her with this action. Most discussions include analysis of the various words used as well as some previous additions in other translations of the text.

Most traditional commentators follow the LXX which adds at the end of verse 28 that "there was no answer from her for she was dead." The omission is then easily explained as lost through haplography due to homoioteleuton in the MT.[42] Yet this is another case where the LXX may be correcting a passage that was too difficult for its readers to bear. The absence of the phrase creates a more ambiguous situation, as the book of Judges does repeatedly. Many issues can be read in two ways and the ambiguity provides depth to the story. In this case the woman was not explicitly identified as already dead. She then traveled by donkey for some unknown distance and was cut up into twelve pieces. The reader is left to question who was responsible for her ultimate death.

[42] Boling, *Judges*, 276.

This is particularly important in evaluating the Levite's statements about his actions in the following chapter.

Trible has reflected on the relation to the sacrifice of Isaac through the reference to the knife.[43] The man does not take "a" knife but "the" knife. The same terminology is used of the knife that Abraham intended to use in his sacrifice of Isaac (Gen 22:10). Once again the difference between a story in Genesis and that in Judges is that in Genesis the heinous acts were stopped by the deity. In Judges the acts were initiated by men against women and carried through to their completion.

The narrator notes that everyone who saw it, presumably the body parts, cried out that never had such a thing happened or been seen from the day the Israelites came out of the land of Egypt to this day (Judg 19:30). They then commanded each other to put their mind to it and take counsel.

The placement of the first seven verses of Judges 20 are difficult. They are traditionally treated with the rest of Judges 20 since they are considered to mark the beginning of the civil war against Benjamin. At the same time they are the last verses concerning the *pîlegeš* directly and contain the Levite's explanation for his actions and his account to Israel of his story. Separating his comments on the story from the actual events allows commentators to focus on what is to come and not examine the Levite's account of his actions. Since the rape and the reasons it was allowed to occur are central to the entire book of Judges, it is necessary to view the Levite's words in light of the events he was recounting, thus the first seven verses will be examined in this chapter. The difficulty in placing these verses highlights the smooth transitions in language, story line, and plot in Judges.

The last line of Judges 19 has the children of Israel taking counsel. In 20:1 the children of Israel from Dan to Beersheba and from Gilead marched forth and assembled at Mizpah. This statement is ironic because it is not true since, according to verse 3, Benjamin was not there. Boling notes that elsewhere in the book of Judges this expression occurs only in the Deuteronomistic indictment (Judg 2:1-5), and in Judg 8:27 where Gideon used the federal militia in pursuit of private vengeance and all Israel prostituted themselves.[44] This is another case where a phrase and situation originally appear as minor and in the final three chapters are twisted to lead Israel to carry out some of its worst acts.

The following verse continues, referring to all the tribes of Israel with the exception of Benjamin, when it notes that all the leaders of the people and all the tribes presented themselves in the assembly of

---

[43] Trible, *Texts of Terror*, 80.
[44] Boling, *Judges*, 283.

Elohim's people, and places the number at 400,000 (Judg 20:2). The text
does not state that they gathered before the deity, or requested the deity's advice, or even prayed to the deity. To a certain extent this defines
the community differently at the end of Judges than at the beginning.
At the beginning of the book the Israelites were defined as a people
with a shared history and their relationship to the deity was based on
acts the deity had carried out on their behalf. Throughout the book
each tribe, or affiliation of tribes, experienced different settlement patterns with greater and lesser success in establishing themselves and associating with their neighbors. At this juncture they were united
through the deity, but not necessarily through recent history.

The word translated here as "leader" literally means "corners"
pinnôt.[45] The use of the term is rare. Of the two other examples of this
usage, one concerns the incident of Saul attempting to find who broke
the prohibition against eating (1 Sam 14:38).[46] Again the irony here is
that the one tribe missing in this context is the tribe that was leading in
the following instance. It is fitting that another term is found to refer to
a leader in Judges since so many different titles and forms of leadership
were examined already.

Only in verse 3 does the text clarify that Benjamin was not included
by noting that the children of Benjamin heard that the Israelites had
come up to Mizpah. The children of Israel gathered but only now that
they were gathered, and after Benjamin heard about it, did they want
to know, "how did this bad thing happen?" (Judg 20:3) The question is
intentionally open-ended, not stating to which specific act they referred. On the basic level they asked how a woman's body came to be
cut up and sent around. The reader knows the events leading up to the
present situation but it is clear from the progression of the story that
the question could be applied to the whole situation in which Israel
was enmeshed.

The Levite responded to the question with his version of the story.
In his response he is referred to by the narrator as the man/husband of
the murdered woman (Judg 20:4). The term used to refer to her is "murdered" from the root *r-ṣ-ḥ*. Up to this point even the narrator had not
qualified the nature of the woman's death. The reference to her as murdered does not clear the Levite man of wrongdoing. If one follows the
LXX which notes that the woman was dead when the man put her on
the donkey, then the reference to the woman as murdered means the
narrator here is indicting the rapists. By not stating in the MT at what
point the woman died her murderer is not specified. In this reference

---

[45] *BDB*, 819.
[46] The third use of the term in this way is in Isa 19:13.

the narrator does not state who murdered her, simply that she was murdered. Using the term raises the issue, in the mind of the reader, concerning who was ultimately responsible for her death. This reference raises the tension and irony in the story since an entire nation was called to war on behalf of one of the murder suspects.

The Levite man's version of the story deletes a number of elements which had been narrated in the text, and couches some of the events in different ways. According to the Levite man, he and his *pîlegeš* went to Gibeah of Benjamin to spend the night (Judg 20:4). He provided no commentary about where they had been, where they were going, or what the nature of their business was. He continued by stating that the citizens of Gibeah set out to harm him, that they gathered against him all around the house in the night with the intention of killing him, and humbled his *pîlegeš* until she died (Judg 20:5). He explained that only then did he take hold of his concubine, cut her into pieces, and send her to all of Israel. He concluded that his reason was because an outrageous act of depravity had been committed in Israel (Judg 20:6).

On a number of levels the man gave a fairly accurate report of the events, yet some important details were left out and other details changed just enough to shift any blame from himself. While not necessarily relevant to the issue at hand, the question of the relationship between the man and the *pîlegeš*, especially after the time at the woman's father's house, is never settled. As a result the reason for the couple traveling at all, why they were out late at night, and how they chose Gibeah could be considered relevant in determining the extent of the outrage and his role in it.

The Levite did not accurately describe the incident outside the house. The men of Gibeah did not want to kill him, they wanted to use him sexually. It may be understandable why the man did not want to broadcast this, yet it is relevant to this story which the Levite used to begin a civil war. He did not explain how the woman arrived in the clutches of the mob because it implicates himself. It is not accidental that the reader knows more about the situation than the characters in the narrative world of the story. This is a means for the narrator to further highlight what happened in Israel. Depraved events led to civil war and people were prepared to go to war based on a story which was not based on the information provided to the reader.

The man also stated that they humbled his *pîlegeš* until she died. The implication of this is that they continued raping her until she died, which the reader knows to be untrue since she managed to arrive at the door of the house where the man was sheltered. One could interpret this as a general statement concerning the cause of death, though not necessarily the time of death. As noted previously, the time, and possibly the reason for the woman's death are not stated. When the woman managed to crawl to the man's shelter, the Levite was not waiting for her return and only noticed her when he was on his way to leave. Whether she was alive at that point is not stated in the MT. It is not even clear that she was dead when the knife cut her into pieces.

While it is not surprising that the man would hide any culpability he had in the rape and murder of this woman, it is important for the sake of the cause. The Levite instigated a civil war. The cause of this is usually said to be the rape and death of the woman. Another interpretation is that this is yet another revenge killing, though this time not on behalf of a military leader but by a man who felt he was wronged. While the other leaders also led battles of significant import as a result of their own personal feuds (Gideon/Jerubbaal, Jephthah, and Samson), it was never on this scale.

The final verse of this unit has the Levite man challenging the children of Israel to produce a plan of action immediately (Judg 20:7). The irony surrounding the reference to the woman's time of death earlier was clearly intentional, leaving open the possibility of thinking about motives for the man's actions and the reasons for the civil war. This Levite man manipulated the woman's personal situation, turning it into a major national conflict and demanding action from the entire nation against a tribe on his own behalf. The irony is that the Levite man demanded that the Israelites go to war on account of the woman whom he had done nothing to help and whose situation he had caused in the first place. The real issue at stake for the man was that he had been threatened sexually, and yet that reason was obscured by the man in order to help himself to achieve his revenge. The reality is that the children of Israel, so shocked by the chopped woman's body, immediately rallied and followed on behalf of the man's modified version of the story.

According to Judges the cause of the civil war was the rape of the woman, yet it is clear that the root issue did not really concern the wider community of Israel. Neither protagonists' name was important enough to record, the Levite man's account of the story deleted enough important details and cast the other facts in a different enough way to make it obvious that it is no longer the same story but a modification of it. The narrator casts doubt on the trustworthiness of the man and the reason for the war. Israel claimed to fight a just war on behalf of this woman, but it is clear that this was not what was at stake. They were quick to believe a man who had carried out a horrendous act, cutting up the woman's body and sending it around, regardless of his reasons for doing it. That they acted quickly, because of one man and his strange account shows how far they had descended. The actions of the

Israelites in the final chapter, in their effort to find wives for Benjamin, indicate that the rape of the woman was not of any interest to them. The only possibility left is that the Israelites were looking for a war. There was no order and each man did what was right in his eyes.

The text at this point barely cloaks its interests in the larger issues. The narrative focuses on cities and tribes, not people and characters. The text depicts the Israelites fighting over a specific incident when their actions could not possibly be rooted in those events. At this point the narrative is barely still rooted in the period of Judges and its narrative world, but rather addresses, as directly as possible, the issues between David and Saul.

Summary

The rape of the *pîlegeš* in this chapter is used as the catalyst for the civil war which follows in the next two chapters. The account of the story parallels a number of incidents which occurred in the first chapter of the book in its use of terminology and themes. The characters in the *pîlegeš* story are nameless, with relationships to each other which are confused and difficult to understand with any precision, thus forming a contrast to the story of Achsah when everyone's role and responsibilities were clear. The narrator recounts the time in the *pîlegeš's* father's house very carefully in order to emphasize the confused relationships. The comparison of the two stories highlights Israel's debased state because, rather than the actions in the *pîlegeš* story leading to a positive resolution for Israel, as it did in Achsah's situation, it led to gang rape, murder, and civil war.

The text does not sanitize or lighten the horror of the rape, the unprotected state of the woman, her complete abandonment, or her murder. The text carefully phrases the relevant questions leaving room for numerous interpretations concerning who was the real culprit in the episode. The text accuses the depraved men in Gibeah, the whole town for not taking the travelers in, the man for throwing her out in the first place, leaving open the possibility that he actually murdered her eventually, and ultimately all of Israel for so quickly rushing to violence although knowing only a part of the story. All the elements are in place for the final battle where Israel goes to war with itself.

Chapter 15

CIVIL WAR

Judges 20:8–21:25

This chapter concerns the civil war between the tribe of Benjamin and the rest of the Israelites. The apparent cause has already been stated by the Levite in the previous chapter. As noted there, his account to the Israelites was not precisely what had been narrated in the previous chapter. The Israelites did not evaluate the man's story, nor did they consult with Benjamin other than asking for the guilty, as Jephthah did with the Ammonites (Judg 11:12-27), but immediately rushed to the conclusion of war. One reading of the text is that the Israelites were seeking a pretext for a war, or at least a war with Benjamin. It cannot be a coincidence that, directly preceding the account of the institution of monarchy in Israel, at least according to the version of the Deuteronomistic Historian which has been canonized in the Bible, there is an account of a war between Benjamin, the tribe to which the first king belonged, and the rest of Israel. The defeat of Benjamin here prefigures Saul's loss of the kingship to his Judite rival David.

This civil war stands out in Judges because it was not sanctioned by the deity, was based on the testimony of a man whose actions in the whole episode have been dubious, was decided on by a group acting in the absence of a leader, whose decisions repeatedly caused larger problems. All of this is tied to the question of leadership, which is fitting since the whole book focuses on the search for a leader, the relationship of the leaders to the deity, and the reasons and motivations of leaders. Here there was no leader and the entire nation rallied together and made a decision as a group. Their motives were immediate and personal, not based on the commandments of their deity or on Israel's relationship to their deity. How the Israelites carried out their task and the role of the deity in these events is central both to the chapter and to the role of the chapter in Judges, especially since the book ends on this note. The final judgment of the book is clarified in this episode; while a system of government dependent on the judges did not work for Israel, the concept of group leadership was even worse.

This episode, as was the case with the one preceding, uses themes and phrases which appeared earlier in the book and brings them to a final conclusion. The treatment of women in the book continues to be the barometer by which Israel and her actions are evaluated. This episode follows the horrific abandonment of a woman to brutal gang rape and will see Israel descend even further into moral decay, whether judged by contemporary standards, those of ancient Israel, or the standards which are set up in the chapter itself. In this final chapter Israel is described as completely bereft of any leadership. The Israelites had no plan and, as a result, simply reacted. As Boling notes, they acted first and thought later. The difference between Boling's view of the situation and that emphasized here is that he sees a "comedy of correctness," in relation to the women of Shiloh, while the present analysis sees this episode as depicting the situation as nothing but horrific.[1]

Boling views this chapter lightly because he does not see it as central to the ongoing development of the book's argument, in contrast to the present author. Since he considers the civil war a comedic finale, viewing it in comparison to the previous righteous heroic judges, the book ends on a note not as important to the theology of Israel as the previous examples had been. The classification of the unit as a later Deuteronomistic addition gives added reason for ignoring or de-emphasizing its importance. But with a different perspective, one that views the judges not only negatively on the whole, but becoming progressively worse over the narrative time of the book, then the final episodes concerning the rape of the *pîlegeš*, the civil war, and rape of the virgins of Israel are anything but humorous. The end of the book highlights how horrendous the situation had become for all Israel, but especially for the women of Israel.

Preparing for War: Judges 20:8-18

The previous chapter ends with the Levite challenging the Israelites to produce a plan of action. The Israelites' response was to rise as one

---

[1] R. G. Boling, *Judges: Introduction, Translation and Commentary*, The Anchor Bible (Garden City: Doubleday, 1981) 294.

man and declare that they would not go back to their homes nor enter their houses (Judg 20:8), but instead that they would do to Gibeah against it according to lot (Judg 20:9). The verb is missing. The LXX has "we will go up against it by lot," which fits the context well. The people were filled with righteous indignation and roused themselves for their mission.

The text continues with the scheme by which they decided how many they would take to fight and how many would be required to supply provisions for the troops to prepare for their going to Gibeah in Benjamin (Judg 20:10). The verse notes that this was all because of the outrage which had been committed in Israel. It is ironic that they repeated the reason, the outrage, but did not define what was meant by it. On the surface it could be the rape of the woman, but since the Israelites have shown no concern for the woman and the reader knows the story the man told is problematic, the outrage to which the text refers could be many different things. Irony abounds because by the end of the chapter the Israelites, who were righting this outrage, inflicted the same outrage on more women.

Before beginning to fight any battles the Israelites attempted to convince the Benjaminites to hand over the guilty. The tribes of Israel sent men through Benjamin asking what was "the bad thing" that happened among them (Judg 20:11-12). They asked the Benjaminites to hand over the scoundrels in Gibeah so that they could be put to death, thereby stamping out "the bad thing" in Israel. The Benjaminites, however, would not listen to the voice of their brothers, the children of Israel (Judg 20:13).

Throughout the book "the bad thing" has been intermarriage leading to worship of other gods. In this case intermarriage was clearly not implied. Does this mean that the previous interpretation is incorrect, or might something else be happening in this case? According to the deity, the other peoples were left behind to test Israel on the issue of intermarriage. In the chapters of the book focusing on internal events leading to civil war, intermarriage was not the issue. The problem may be the Israelites' misuse of the term. The last judge interacted only with foreign women (Judges 14–16), whom he chose because they were good in his eyes (Judg 14:3). The rape is not referred to as the "bad thing" by the narrator or the deity but the people of Israel. The Israelites were the people described as living in a time when each man did what was right in his own eyes (Judg 17:6; 21:25). The Israelites are described as going to war over an outrage which, while offensive, could have been averted, according to the theology of the book, if the Israelites had not evaluated with their own eyes but followed their deity.

The Israelites were careful and specific in their language. The Israelites differentiated between Benjamin and the scoundrels therein. They claimed they were trying to root out "the bad thing" in Benjamin, indicating that at this point they did not view all Benjamin as guilty. The scoundrels to whom they referred were "worthless ones," using the same term applied to the group that raped the *pîlegeš* in the preceding chapter (Judg 19:22).[2] The Israelites were not asking for all of Benjamin but referred to specific individuals.

The result of the Benjaminites not listening was that they were prepared to go to war to protect the scoundrels of Gibeah. Israel may not have had the whole story, may have reacted quickly, and the Levite was not completely blameless, but the men of Gibeah were not above reproach. However, the Benjaminites gathered from their towns in Gibeah in order to take the field against the children of Israel (Judg 20:14).

Benjamin is described as mustering twenty-six thousand fighting men, noting that this number does not take into account the inhabitants of Gibeah (Judg 20:15). Of this force there were seven hundred handpicked men who were left-handed, who according to the text could all sling a stone at a hair and not miss (Judg 20:16). This hearkens back to Ehud, the first charismatic judge whose left-handedness was his secret device (Judg 3:15-21). Earlier left-handedness was used to save Israel, now it is used against Israel. The slingshot was not mentioned earlier and may be an ironic twist considering the later story when David used this weapon despite Saul's offer of his own armor to fight Goliath (1 Sam 17:40-50).

With the Benjaminite soldiers mustered the text returns to Israel where the men of Israel, excluding Benjamin, numbered four-hundred thousand fighting men (Judg 20:17). The text is careful to note that this is the number of men of Israel without Benjamin. The group went to Bethel to inquire of the deity (Judg 20:18). This is the first time the deity was involved in the proceedings. The Israelites never questioned the legitimacy of their actions but instead asked the question posed in the first sentence of the book, modified for this situation, "Who shall go up first to fight against Benjamin?" The deity's response was the same as at the beginning, "Judah first" (Judg 20:18). Thus Judah was in conflict with Benjamin before Saul or David ever appear.

The Battles: Judges 20:19-48

The children of Israel accepted the deity's response, arose in the morning, encamped against Benjamin at Gibeah (Judg 20:19), took the

[2] *BDB,* 117.

field, and drew up in battle against them at Gibeah (Judg 20:20). Contrary to Israel's plan the Benjaminites came forth from Gibeah and struck down twenty-two thousand men of Israel (Judg 20:21). The end of the verse states that Benjamin struck the Israelites down "earthward" *ʾārṣâ* (Judg 20:21). The use of the phrase, "towards the ground," is unusual. Boling sees it is as similar to what Onan did in Gen 38:9 when he wasted his seed, in that here too many lives were wasted. A closer parallel is with Jael who drove the pin through Sisera's temple into the ground (Judg 4:21). In that case the mention of the ground was interpreted as describing the force with which Jael drove the pin through his skull. Jael was a non-Israelite woman, praised by the text, who killed Israel's enemy leader, thereby saving Israel when Israel's male hero could not (Judg 4:8). The ironic twist here is that Israelite men died on behalf of an Israelite woman, yet in both cases the episode was a result of the men not providing the necessary protection.

The army of the men of Israel rallied and drew up in battle order at the same place as they had on the previous day (Judg 20:22). Israel repeated their battle tactics because they had gone up and wept before the deity the previous evening (Judg 20:23). When they again inquired of their deity whether they should again join battle with their brothers, the children of Benjamin, the response was positive. The Israelites took the positive response to be about their strategy and advanced against the children of Benjamin on the second day (Judg 20:24). Again Benjamin came out from Gibeah and this time struck down eighteen thousand more Israelites (Judg 20:25). All of the men are called fighting men.

The Israelites were not planning on losing again, so all the children of Israel, all the army, went up to Bethel and sat there weeping before their deity (Judg 20:26). They fasted until evening, presented burnt offerings and offerings of well-being to their deity and inquired of the deity again (Judg 20:27). The narrator notes that this was done at Bethel because the ark of the deity's covenant was there in those days, and that Phinehas son of Eleazar, son of Aaron, the priest ministered before the deity (Judg 20:28). This is new information, since there had so far been no mention of which place was considered the major cult site. An entire episode (Judges 17–18) explained the development of a different place, with cult personnel and accouterments that were stolen (Judges 18–19). Bethel was legitimated because of the presence there of both the ark and a priest who was a descendant of Aaron, rather than the previously mentioned priest who stemmed from the line of Moses/Manasseh (Judg 18:30).

The deity provided no answer but the Israelites' next move placed men in ambush against Gibeah on all sides (Judg 20:29). On the third day the children of Israel went up as they had earlier (Judg 20:30). Benjamin responded as earlier by dashing out to meet the army (Judg 20:31). By so doing they were drawn away from the town onto the roads, one of which ran to Bethlehem, the other to Gibeah. As before, they started out by striking some of the men dead in the open field. The Benjaminites assumed that the Israelites had not learned from the previous incidents. However, this time the Israelites intended to draw the Benjaminites away from the town to the roads (Judg 20:32). While the main body of the men of Israel moved away from their positions and drew up in battle, other Israelites, waiting in ambush, rushed out from their position (Judg 20:33). Ten thousand men of Israel came to a point south of Gibeah in a furious battle before the Benjaminites realized that disaster was approaching. So the deity routed Benjamin before Israel (Judg 20:34). That day Israel slew 25,100 fighting men of Benjamin (Judg 20:35).

These are the most detailed battle descriptions in the entire book of Judges. Some stories provided specifics concerning how the leader was designated, the soldiers chosen, and locations of battles, but this is a detailed day-by-day account supported by daily casualty reports. The narrator notes that the deity routed the Benjaminites, not the Israelites. This is the first time in the book when the deity fought a battle without a specific Israelite leader. The situation had reached the point where the deity had to lead the battle as military commander.

The Benjaminites realized they were routed because the men of Israel, relying on the ambush against Gibeah (Judg 20:36), yielded ground to Benjamin. One group deployed against Gibeah and the other advanced and put the whole town to sword (Judg 20:37). A time had been agreed upon by the Israelites and those laying the ambush and a huge column of smoke was sent up from the town (Judg 20:38). At that time the men of Israel were to turn about in battle (Judg 20:39). Benjamin had the upper hand by striking about thirty men of Israel dead and they assumed they were routing the Israelites as they had previously. When the smoke began to rise Benjamin saw the whole town going up in smoke to the sky (Judg 20:40). This is another ironic use of terminology since earlier in the story the Benjaminites beat the Israelites into the ground, whereas when Benjamin was destroyed the terminology draws the image skyward.

The men of Israel turned, and the Benjaminites were thrown into panic for they realized that disaster had overtaken them (Judg 20:41). They retreated along the road to the wilderness where the fighting caught up with them, while those in the towns were massacred (Judg 20:42). "They," presumably the Israelites, encircled Benjamin, pursued them, and trod them down to Menuhah to a point opposite Gibeah on the east (Judg 20:43). That day eighteen thousand men of Benjamin fell, all of them called brave men (Judg 20:44). The Benjaminites turned and fled to the wilderness, to the rock of Rimmon, the Israelites picked off another five thousand on the roads, continuing in hot pursuit of them to Gidom, where they slew two thousand more (Judg 20:45).

The text ends the battle by noting that twenty-five thousand Benjaminite fighting men fell that day, all of them brave (Judg 20:46). The narrator's description implies a certain amount of respect for the fallen Benjaminites, preparing the reader for the Israelites' feeling of regret which will follow shortly. The final note is that six hundred men turned and fled to the wilderness to the rock of Rimmon and remained there for four months (Judg 20:47). In the meantime, the men of Israel turned back to the rest of the Benjaminites and put them to the sword, towns, people, cattle, everything that remained, and then set fire to all the towns that were left (Judg 20:48).

This section recounting the final battle with the Benjaminites and their defeat is usually considered to be a poorly written unit. It is repetitive and not as well focused as other portions. It has the longest amount of text dedicated to any battle in Judges. As seen in previous cases, the text elaborates on the concerns most relevant to the issue at hand, seldom the battle itself. In most encounters it is not the battle which is detailed in the text but how the leader was picked, what led to the battle (as seen in the stories about Gideon and Jephthah), and the attempt to capture the enemy leaders (as seen in the stories about Ehud, Deborah, Gideon). Here the stress on recounting the battle, even if poorly executed, is significant.

In this case the day-by-day account of the battles, in particular the third day when Benjamin was routed, is crucial because this was a civil war. This is the end of the book when Israel reached its absolute bottom. The people gathered without a leader. They did not ask the deity whether they should fight, but who should lead, so repeating the question with which the whole book had opened. They were fighting one of their own tribes based, not on the word of the deity, but on the word of a suspect source. The battle itself is important because it was a culmination of events.

Resolving the Situation: Judges 21:1-24

Chapter 21 of the book of Judges focuses on the aftermath of the Benjaminites' destruction. It follows the war and addresses how the tribe of Benjamin will continue. Because it is the last chapter of the book it sets up the situation in which the Israelites find themselves, at least according to the present arrangement by the Masoretes, when the books of Samuel begin. In this chapter themes from the rest of the book are woven together and a final statement about the period and how Israel should be governed is made.

Benjamin's Future: Judges 21:1-23

The Israelites were quickly roused to battle to root out "the bad thing" in Benjamin. Once the Benjaminites decided to protect the men of Gibeah the focus was on the battle and destroying them. Only after all the towns of Benjamin were destroyed and only a few Benjaminites remained does the text reveal that the Israelites had taken an oath at Mizpah, that none of them would give their daughter to Benjamin as a woman/wife (Judg 21:1).

The people were almost surprised by what happened. They congregated at Bethel and sat before the deity until evening, weeping again (Judg 21:2). The cause of their distress is contained in the following verse where they asked the deity of Israel why it should be that one of Israel's tribes must now be missing (Judg 21:3). Their query was accompanied by building an altar, burnt offerings, and offerings of well-being (Judg 21:4).

The question is ironic and yet fitting for the book. The Israelites, like Jephthah, took an oath whose ramifications were not considered beforehand. Previously the Israelites would request help from the deity before taking any action, and asked the deity's help to save them from their enemies. In this case, the enemy was one of their own and the legitimacy of their cause was never determined. They did not ask advice from the deity before the war but only afterwards, when they had to deal with the results of their actions.

This event occurred at Bethel. At the beginning of the book the people gathered at Bochim for their first reprimand by the deity in the narrative time recounted by the book of Judges (Judg 2:4). That place was named for the people's weeping (Judg 2:5). At that point in the story the Israelites were first grappling with not having a direct line of communication with the deity. A new site was used highlighting the new situation and the lack of a tradition. The people were reprimanded for having made covenants with the local inhabitants and not having torn down their altars.

As noted in the earlier discussion, many scholars follow the LXX and replace Bochim with Bethel because of its reference here. There are significant differences between the two cases. In the Bochim instance, the tests of leaders and sorts of leadership fundamental to Judges were just beginning to appear, and the enemy was the non-Israelites left in the land that the Israelites did not destroy. By Chapter 21 the results are evident; Israel did what was right in its eyes, not the eyes of the deity. A new cult site with unauthorized priestly personnel had been established recently (Judges 17–18). The enemy was no longer outside, but was Israel itself. The practices carried on throughout Judges led to the near destruction of a tribe. Only then did Israel return to a more traditional site with the correct personnel and equipment. The book establishes a future for Israel tied to its past, though the Israelites will not actualize the option appropriately until later books.

There was no response from the deity because the children of Israel continued asking if there was anyone from all the tribes of Israel who had failed to come up to the assembly before the deity. The text refers to yet another oath taken concerning anyone who did not go up to the deity at Mizpah, saying that they should be put to death (Judg 21:5). This is another oath, not mentioned earlier in the text, made hastily, without forethought or consideration of its potential ramifications.

The text repeats Israel's distress that a tribe had been cut off from Israel (Judg 21:6). Israel thought out loud, asking what they could do to provide wives for those who were left, since they had sworn by the deity not to give any of their daughters to them as women/wives (Judg 21:7). This is the third time in seven verses the text states that the tribes of Israel agreed not to give their daughters to Benjamin as women/wives. Again the Israelites turned to the deity and inquired whether there was anyone from the tribes of Israel who had not gone up to the deity at Mizpah (Judg 21:8). The text reads almost as an aside to the reader providing them with background information concerning a town that was not present. The deity still did not respond to the question, but the Israelites determined the answer themselves. The following verse confirms the narrator's previous remark that when the roll of the troops was taken not one of the inhabitants of Jabesh-Gilead was present (Judg 21:9).

Jabesh-Gilead's absence for the oath is an ironic twist packed with significance for later stories concerning Saul. There are so many similar elements between the story in 1 Sam 11:1-11 and this that it is necessary to summarize here what happened later.

Nahash, the Ammonite, threatened the people of Jabesh-Gilead (1 Sam 11:1). They were prepared to surrender when they learned that the cost of surrender was that the right eye of all the men had to be gouged out (1 Sam 11:2). The Jabesh-Gileadites sent word throughout all Israel (1 Sam 11:3). When Saul heard what was happening the spirit of the deity gripped him in anger, he took the yoke of oxen he was driving, cut them into pieces, and sent them throughout Israel saying that he would do the same to anyone who did not appear to help him do battle on behalf of the Jabesh-Gileadites (1 Sam 11:6-7). Saul then mustered them all at Bezek and from there proceeded to rout the Ammonites on behalf of the Israelite deity (1 Sam 11:9-11).

There are numerous parallels both to the immediate story, the larger unit within which this story fits, and to the whole book of Judges. The discussion began because Jabesh-Gilead was the one place that did not send people to fight the battle against Benjamin. The Israelites would later muster on their behalf through an invitation which would be similar to that which had been issued before the fight with Benjamin, i.e. a mutilated living thing was passed through Israel as the call to arms. In 1 Samuel the invitation was not human, as in Judges, but the parallel holds nonetheless. The source of the conflict in Judges was an event in Gibeah, precisely where Saul was when he received the message about the plight of the Jabesh-Gileadites. The place Saul mustered the troops was Bezek. Adoni Bezek was the first enemy that Israel fought in the book of Judges and the final fight of the Israelites occurs in a place with a relationship to Bezek.

All of this is open to a number of interpretations. It is clear that Saul will have a special relationship with this town, especially for reasons that become clear after the fate of the town was sealed. According to Boling their inclusion here elicits sympathy for this city later so friendly and faithful to Saul and here alone the only segment of Israel not guilty of overreacting.[3] Yet it is not clear that any sympathy for the city is elicited. The battle with Benjamin, while problematic, was the one battle in which all the rest of Israel fought together. How Jabesh-Gilead's absence was originally marked is not raised by the book, but when discovered, the missing tribe was appreciated on some levels since it provided a solution to the predicament. This is not to say that Jabesh-Gilead's absence was viewed positively, especially in light of the next verse. Considering what happened to the city in the following verses it is more likely that this explains Saul's later relationship to the city and the reason for his intense reaction upon hearing the city's predicament.

The assemblage proceeded to dispatch twelve thousand warriors with instructions to put the inhabitants of Jabesh-Gilead to the sword, women and children included (Judg 21:10). One reads in detail how they were to proscribe every man and every woman who had known a man (Judg 21:11). The Israelites were prepared to carry out the oath to

---

[3] Boling, *Judges*, 292.

kill those who had not attended the battle, yet would make exceptions to the oath in order to carry out their plan. Again the irony is that they were prepared to kill all the people of Jabesh-Gilead in order to repopulate the people of Benjamin whom they just destroyed. None of these actions were done in consultation with the Israelite deity.

The text continues that they found among the inhabitants of Jabesh-Gilead four hundred young maidens who had not known a man and brought them to the camp at Shiloh, which, the text notes, was in the land of Canaan (Judg 21:12). A number of issues concerning the women can be raised. They are referred to as "young girls" who had not known men. The terminology used to refer to these women is different from that used for Jephthah's daughter. She was called a "virgin" *bĕtûlâ*, whereas the term *naʿărâ* is employed here. Ironically the raped *pîlegeš* was called a *naʿărâ* when she was in her father's house. Both terms are qualified to indicate that these women had not known men. As mentioned earlier (Judg 11:39-40), if the term *bĕtûlāh* referred to a virgin, i.e. one who had not known a man, what would be the reason for including the phrase following it? One possibility is that it adds emphasis, which in this case is fitting. Oblique ironic references to Jephthah's daughter and her plight are evident in this because she lamented having to die before knowing a man, whereas the women of Jabesh-Gilead were saved only because they had not known a man. Shiloh stands out here because the oath was taken at Mizpah, the people were gathered at Bethel, and there had been no reference to Shiloh until the issue of the women was raised. This is significant because the rest of the women gathered for Benjamin were taken from Shiloh.

While the text hints that the women were taken as wives for the Benjaminites, this has not been stated explicitly. Retaining the women and not killing them with the rest of the residents of Jabesh-Gilead is in direct violation of the oath. Again, an oath was taken which was difficult to carry out and was fulfilled only partially.

The "whole community" *kol-haʿēdâ* sent word to the children of Benjamin who were at the Rock of Rimmon offering them terms of peace (Judg 21:13). The terms are not defined (Judg 21:13). However, since the offer follows directly upon the preservation of the women from Jabesh-Gilead it appears that they offered women/wives with no demands on the Benjaminites. The Benjaminites returned and the Israelites gave them the girls who had been spared from the women of Jabesh-Gilead, but there were not enough for all the remaining Benjaminites (Judg 21:14).

The narrator notes that the people relented toward Benjamin because the deity had made a breach in the tribes of Israel. The fault is laid on the Israelite deity by the narrator although the Israelites had not consulted the deity throughout the major part of the proceedings, at least according to the information provided by the narrator. In the previous stories in Judges the deity was responsible for Israelite victories although the commanders took the credit. Here the deity was held responsible by the narrator but the positive outcome of the battle was of limited benefit.

The elders of the community now asked what to do about the wives for those who were left since the women of Benjamin had been killed (Judg 21:16). They declared that there must be a saving remnant for Benjamin lest a tribe may be blotted out of Israel (Judg 21:17). Though the raid on Jabesh-Gilead was completed and the women from there taken for the Benjaminites, this is the first explicit statement that such was the case. They were now in the awkward position of not being able to give them their daughters since the children of Israel had taken an oath that anyone who gave a woman to Benjamin was cursed (Judg 21:18). Earlier the statement was that they had sworn not to marry their daughters to the Benjaminites (Judg 21:1, 7). This has now been altered to say that anyone who would do so was cursed.

The answer to the problem again revolves around Shiloh. An undefined "they" said that the annual feast of the deity was being held at Shiloh, and the rest of the verse places Shiloh north of Bethel and east of the highway that runs from Bethel to Shechem and south of Lebanon (Judg 21:19). The women from Jabesh-Gilead were brought to Shiloh, another sudden decision on the part of the Israelites. They instructed the Benjaminites to go and lie in wait in the vineyards (Judg 21:20) and when they saw the women of Shiloh coming out to join in the festivities to seize a woman from Shiloh and hurry back to Benjamin (Judg 21:21). The final recommendation to the Benjaminites was that if their fathers or brothers complained they should tell them to be generous to the Benjaminites because they could not provide themselves with women/ wives because of the war and if their fathers had given them they would have incurred guilt (Judg 21:22).

On a basic level the Israelites offered kidnap and rape as a viable method for obtaining a wife. Many issues are raised by this method. One is the role of Shiloh. If the Israelites were encamped there why did they need to give the Benjaminites directions. If Shiloh was not Israelite then the Israelites were demanding intermarriage, the bad thing, to resolve the Benjaminite problem. If Israelites could not give their daughters to the Benjaminites, and Shiloh was Israelite, how could the Shiloh women be available for the Benjaminites? Since the women were celebrating a festival to the Israelite deity, they were depicted as Israelites. Later the shrine of Shiloh becomes the training ground for Samuel and thus plays a very important role in later books. The conclusion must be that the women were Israelite. However, had their fathers and brothers given them to the Benjaminites they would have incurred guilt. It was fine, however, to kidnap them.

A comparison with Achsah and Othniel, the first couple of the book, can provide a bracket for this discussion, highlighting the role of group decisions and lack of leadership, how the demise of leadership impacts the least protected group, women, and how far from the deity the Israelites had strayed. Both Othniel and the Benjaminites gained their women/wives through battle, Othniel's as a prize for winning, the Benjaminites because they lost. In both cases vows were made. Caleb's oath was somewhat legitimated because he had authority through being a deity-designated leader. In the final case no one had the authority to make the oath (as seen in other difficult vows made throughout Judges such as Jephthah, and Samson), and the vow was only partially kept. The vow could be broken to support Israel's bad decisions, regardless of its impact on the women. In Achsah's case, despite her personal distress at being married off in such a manner, at least she had leverage with her father to gain land out of it. In the final case the women were kidnaped and the Israelites kept the women's fathers and brothers from protecting them.

Thus far in the story there have been a number of reminders of the Jephthah episode, such as the prominence of oaths which would be difficult to fulfill and the interest in virginity or "not having known a man." After Jephthah's daughter's death the text concluded that there was a festival in her honor every year, though no time of year or name for the festival is provided. Here is another festival of women, since no men are mentioned, and it is described as the ideal time to kidnap a virgin woman for a wife. The irony is that Jephthah's daughter was killed never having known a man because she came out of her house dancing. In this situation, women left their homes in dance leading to rape/marriage, the opposite of not knowing a man and death. The other twist in the story is that the civil war was carried out, according to the Levite man's story, because his woman was raped to death. As a result of that one rape six hundred more women were raped, the difference being that these women were made "wives" in a fashion that was condoned, in fact recommended, by Israel.

The text confirms that the children of Benjamin followed the instructions and took to wife from the dancers, whom they carried off, a number equal to their own, went back to their own territory, rebuilt their towns and settled in them (Judg 21:23). According to the text therefore, all the descendants after this time had on their paternal side an inhabitant of Benjamin, but their maternal side descended either from someone who had dwelled in Shiloh, or Jabesh-Gilead. Saul's ancestress must either have been from Shiloh or Jabesh-Gilead. Saul's extreme anger at the treatment of the residents of Jabesh-Gilead could easily be rooted in the fact that an ancestress of his was kidnaped from Jabesh-Gilead.

The End: Judges 21:24-5

Once Israel found wives for Benjamin, ensuring the continuation of that tribe, they dispersed, each to his own tribe and clan, everyone for his own territory (Judg 21:24). While everyone went home, according to the last verse, problems persisted because, "In those days there was no king in Israel and everyone did as he pleased" (Judg 21:25, JPS).

What is the effect of the book ending on this note? Soggin claims that the end is a note of suspense, since only the last situation has been resolved and thus there is the anticipation of what is to come.[4] This is true to a large extent. Nothing has been resolved. No leader or form of leadership has been found. There were problems both within and outside of Israel. Israel almost destroyed one of its own tribes. Its solution was to modify its vows and institutionalize the very situation which had caused the civil war to be begun in the first place, the rape of women.

The theme of the last four chapters, although hinted at earlier, is highlighted in the last verse, "each man did what was right in his own eyes." The last story emphasizes how dangerous Israel's situation was. The addition of this comment after the resolution of the Benjaminite crisis implies that the narrator did not condone the resolution of that conflict, that this was another case of solving a problem by judging what was right in their own eyes alone. The deity was not consulted concerning whether or how to provide wives for the Benjaminites. The Benjaminites did as they were told without questioning the legitimacy of the proposal.

Despite the many unsolved issues leaving a sense of suspense, the final line also conveys an idea about the direction Israel must take. "In those days there was no king," implies that part of the problem was the lack of a king. The notion that when there is a king people do not do as they please but rather as the king pleases is inherent in that statement, thereby promoting the idea that kingship is preferred.

[4] J. A. Soggin, *Judges: A Commentary*, Old Testament Library (Philadelphia: Westminster, 1981) 305.

Summary

The book of Judges ends with an episode that could be comical if its results were not so horrific. The Israelites fought a civil war because of the rape of one woman, and almost destroyed an entire tribe as a result. That was prevented from happening only by the death of an entire town from which six hundred women were sent to rape/marriage. The Israelites made vows which they only partially kept, and even then kept only in a way that was to their advantage though it led to death and rape/marriage for many others. Israel consulted with the deity only on peripheral issues, but never about the fundamental questions concerning the motivation for their actions.

The chapter reveals what happens when the themes highlighted throughout the book come to full fruition. There was no leader, leading to anarchy. People were intermarrying and thereby taking on practices opposed by their deity. Women were no longer protected by anyone. Fathers were no longer allowed to protect their daughters. Everything was upside down and ironic. Israel was in total anarchy and, according to the narrator, the only solution was kingship.

CONCLUSIONS

This study argues that the book of Judges stresses the theological message that during the narrative period of Judges the Israelites strayed from their deity. The deity repeatedly responded by appointing temporary leaders or judges. Each judge acted progressively worse than the predecessor had, leading Israel finally to anarchy and civil war. In the eyes of the narrator of Judges, Israel reached a point where kingship was Israel's only option, so laying the groundwork for the following books of Samuel through Kings. As the book progresses the north/south, David/Saul issues rise more to the surface of the text so that, just as Israel is about to enter the stage of history when dynastic issues are more relevant, the themes are addressed most directly in the text.

The theological message of the Deuteronomistic Historian has been recognized in the past in the book's beginning, ending, and in periodic refrains. This study has revealed that the Deuteronomistic theology is not only in the opening and closing chapters and in the periodic notices throughout the text that the Israelites did "the bad thing" in the eyes of the deity, but that the Deuteronomistic message is inherent in the structure of the narrative, the ordering of events, the information provided about them, the role of Jerusalem, and the terminology used in the narrative.

The narrator wove together a series of stories, whose origin will continue to be discussed by scholars, to emphasize the theme of Israel's degeneration. In the process, other themes and issues were introduced into the narrative. The most obvious is the issue of leadership. On one level the question of leadership is integral to the thesis that the Israelites strayed from their deity, since it was often the leaders who led them astray. On another level questions surrounding leadership exist as a sub-theme. The book examines many different forms of leadership, employing a large range of terminology to refer to those positions of control. Judges examines how leaders are chosen, attributes they need to be successful, personality and character flaws which cause trouble, and how all of these features impact the leaders and their ability to rule.

The focus on leadership repeatedly foreshadows Israel's monarchy. Many of the leaders' flaws are found in the later leaders of Israel. Israel's kings in later books repeat many of the failures and defeats presented here. The aspect that most repeats itself between the various judges and Israel's later kings is that the Israelites' leaders forget that in the biblical world the deity is the ultimate ruler. Israel's kings forget their deity, leading them to stray, not following the commandments, but intermarrying, incorporating customs and practices of the surrounding communities.

The evaluation of monarchy in Judges is both good and bad. The first line asks a question about the locus of rightful leadership. The answer is that Judah should lead. This foreshadows the books of Samuel through Kings which will follow. Despite the gradually building idea that kingship is the answer to Israel's predicament, monarchy is not condoned by Judges. Monarchy is the answer when the alternative is anarchy, but monarchy is not described in glowing terms. In Jotham's fable, during the first attempt at kingship, monarchy is described as "waving over the others," when the others are carrying out productive actions. Those who will exercise kingship will levy taxes (Judg 8:24), and destroy their own subjects (Judg 9:45-55). Foreign kings described in Judges are unattractive in all senses, being overweight (Judg 3:17), or doing nothing in the story (Judges 4–5).

The foreign communities surrounding Israel are another snare for both Israel and her leaders. The customs and religious practices of the foreign nations were incorporated into Israel, in the book of Judges, through intermarriage, most often through marriage of Israelite men to foreign women. Intermarriage is clearly among the things forbidden to the Israelites in Judges 3, in Samson's first marriage, and more subtly in stories such as Gideon/Jerubbaal's, and the minor judges. While not all the women appearing in Judges are foreign, most of the women who appear in the book serve as a foil to the judges in some way. The most obvious way is the one which has been emphasized traditionally, the foreign woman leading the hero astray, as both Samson's first wife and also Delilah did. It is not the case that all the women in Judges are necessarily a threat to men. However, a negative evaluation of a judge will stem from the way they treat and respond to women.

Men in Judges often receive a negative evaluation because of the women in their lives, and the role those women take, though the characters of the women themselves are not always seen negatively. Achsah was a means to legitimate her husband's succession to power. Her relationship to power led to success for her husband, who is viewed positively in the text. Achsah could be considered a vehicle for a slightly negative evaluation of Othniel because of the questionable legitimacy of her father's actions in offering her as a prize and in using marriage as a means of succession of power. Similarly Deborah receives a positive evaluation because she fought on behalf of the deity, but caused a negative evaluation for Baraq, who was compared and contrasted to women and shown to be lacking in many qualities.

In Judges the focus is not on the women as characters evaluated in their own right but as foils through whom the men, especially the judges, are tested. This is reflected not only in the minimal narrative time devoted to them, but also by the absence of most of their names. Their role as benchmarks for the judge's evaluation is most obvious in the case of Gideon/Jerubbaal. Women are not part of the stories concerning his military abilities, but serve to evaluate him by providing his reasons for fighting (seeking revenge for the sons of his mother), and in leaving a descendant of a non-legitimate (in the eyes of the children of his other wives) son (Judg 8:31). There is too little information in the text to evaluate the women themselves, but the impact they had on the actions of male protagonists is of crucial importance in Judges.

Women also serve to reveal the impact of Israel's actions on the nation of Israel at large. The stories in general focus on particular individuals, yet the women reveal the personal impact of such practices. Most obvious in this regard are the women of Jabesh-Gilead and Shiloh. None of them are named, in fact they were not even involved in the oaths or situations leading to the battles, or the way in which those battles destroyed their lives. Instead they were used as pawns. While the tragedy of Jabesh-Gilead is extreme, one could argue that the men decided not to join in the fight and therefore made a decision and bore the consequences. But the women of Shiloh were not only forced into rape/marriages, but their fathers and brothers were kept from protecting them. The Shiloh women's tragic plight demonstrates how Israelite society strayed so that women were institutionally raped and the system of protection was intentionally destroyed.

The narrative of Judges recounts a period in Israel to which the only response could be monarchy. Since dynastic monarchy is not legitimated in the Pentateuch, the biblical text needed a reason to legitimate the creation of a monarchy, and especially to legitimate the Davidic line. In light of the following books the degeneration of Israel's leaders should be expected. The beauty of Judges is that it describes the situation through a series of stories, each raising different issues inherent in monarchy. Israel's decline is subtle but steady. The text is so elegantly narrated that the decline is portrayed in the actions of the characters, the terminology used to describe their actions, and the outcome of their actions. The end result of the narrative time of Judges is anarchy so that Israel is ready and waiting for the following books to address Israel's monarchic period.

FOR FURTHER READING

This is not intended to be a comprehensive bibliography for Judges, but rather a record of the reference works, monographs and articles that were most influential in the research for this book. Since so many of them cover a number of topics they have not been categorized according to chapters or themes.

Aharoni, Yohanan. *The Land of the Bible: A Historical Geography.* Rev. ed. Trans. Anson Rainey. Philadelphia: Westminister, 1969.

Alter, Robert. *The Art of Biblical Narrative.* New York: Basic Books, 1981.

Amit, Yairah. "'Manoah Promptly Followed His Wife' (Judges 13:11): On the Place of the Woman in Birth Narratives." *A Feminist Companion to Judges.* Ed. Athalya Brenner, 146–56. Feminist Companion to the Bible 4. Sheffield: Sheffield Academic Press, 1993.

Anchor Bible Dictionary Vol. 1–6. *(ABD)* Ed. David N. Freedman. New York: Doubleday, 1992.

Bal, Mieke. "A Body of Writing: Judges 19." *A Feminist Companion to Judges.* Ed. Athalya Brenner, 208–30. Feminist Companion to the Bible 4. Sheffield: Sheffield Academic Press, 1993.

____. *Murder and Difference: Gender, Genre, and Scholarship on Sisera's Death.* Indiana Studies in Biblical Literature. Bloomington: Indiana University Press, 1988.

____. *Death and Dissymmetry: The Politics of Coherence in the Book of Judges.* Chicago Studies in the History of Judaism. Chicago: The University of Chicago Press, 1988.

Bar-Efrat, Shimon. *Narrative Art in the Bible.* Bible and Literature Series 17. Sheffield: The Almond Press, 1989.

Bartlett, J. R. "Cushan-rishathaim." *ABD* 1.1220.

Ben-Tor, Amnon. "Hazor." *New Encyclopedia of Archaeological Excavations in the Holy Land.* Ed. Ephraim Stern, 2:594–605. Jerusalem: The Israel Exploration Society and Carta., 1993.

Benjamin, Paul. "Jabin." *ABD* 3.595–6.

Berlin, Adele. *Poetics and Interpretation of Biblical Narrative*. Bible and Literature Series 9. Sheffield: The Almond Press, 1983.

Berridge, John. "Jonathan." *ABD* 3.943.

Bird, Phyllis. "Images of Women in the OT." *Religion and Sexism*. Ed. Rosemary Ruether, 41–88. New York: Simon and Schuster, 1974.

Blenkinsopp, Joseph. "Ballad Style and Psalm Style in the Song of Deborah." *Biblica* 42 (1961) 61–76.

Bledstein, Adrien J. "Is Judges a Woman's Satire on Men who Play God?" *A Feminist Companion to Judges*. Ed. Athalya Brenner, 34–54. Feminist Companion to the Bible 4. Sheffield: Sheffield Academic Press, 1993.

Boling, Robert. "Judges, Book of." *ABD* 3.1107–17.

_____. "Othniel." *ABD* 5.51.

_____. "Tola." *ABD* 6.595–6.

_____. "Ibzan." *ABD* 3.356.

_____. "Shamgar." *ABD* 5.1155–6.

_____. *Judges: Introduction, Translation and Commentary*. The Anchor Bible. Garden City: Doubleday and Company, 1981.

Bowman, Richard G. "Narrative Criticism of Judges: Human Purpose in Conflict with Divine Presence." *Judges and Method: New Approaches in Biblical Studies*. Ed. Gale A. Yee, 17–44. Minneapolis: Fortress Press, 1995.

Brenner, Athalya. *A Feminist Companion to Judges*. Feminist Companion to the Bible 4. Sheffield: Sheffield Academic Press, 1993.

_____. "Introduction." *A Feminist Companion to Judges*. Ed. Athalya Brenner, 9–22. Feminist Companion to the Bible 4. Sheffield: Sheffield Academic Press, 1993.

_____. "A Triangle and a Rhombus in Narrative Structure: A Proposed Integrative Reading of Judges 4 and 5." *A Feminist Companion to Judges*. Ed. Athalya Brenner, 98–109. A Feminist Companion to the Bible 4. Sheffield: Sheffield Academic Press, 1993.

Brettler, Marc. "Micah." *ABD* 4.806.

_____. "Literature as Politics." *Journal of Biblical Literature* 108 (1989) 405–28.

Bronner, Leila L. "Valorized or Vilified?" *A Feminist Companion to Judges*. Ed. Athalya Brenner, 79–97. Feminist Companion to the Bible 4. Sheffield: Sheffield Academic Press, 1993.

Brown, Cheryl A. "Deborah." *No Longer Be Silent: First Century Jewish Portraits of Biblical Women. Gender and the Biblical Tradition*, 39–92. Louisville: Westminster/John Knox Press, 1992.

Crenshaw, James A. "Samson." *ABD* 5.950–4.

_____. *Samson: A Secret Betrayed, A Vow Ignored.* Atlanta: John Knox Press, 1978.

Cross, Frank M. "Newly found inscriptions in Old Canaanite and Early Phoenician Scripts." *Bulletin of the American Schools of Oriental Research* 238 (1980) 1–20.

Dandamayev, Muhammad. "Slavery (OT)." *ABD* 6.63–5.

Day, Peggy. "From the Child is Born the Woman: The Story of Jephthah's Daughter." *Gender and Difference in Ancient Israel.* Ed. Peggy Day, 58–74. Minneapolis: Fortress Press, 1989.

Dothan, M. "Ashdod." *New Encyclopedia of Archaeological Excavations in the Holy Land.* Ed. Ephraim Stern. 1.93–100. Jerusalem: The Israel Exploration Society and Carta., 1993.

Dothan, Trude, and Seymour Gitin. "Miqne, Tel (Ekron)." *New Encyclopedia of Archaeological Excavations in the Holy Land.* Ed. Ephraim Stern 3.1051–9. Jerusalem: The Israel Exploration Society and Carta., 1993.

Driver, G. R. "Problems in Judges Newly Discussed." *Annual of the Leeds University Oriental Society* 4 (1964) 6–25.

Exum, J. Cheryl. "Why, Why, Why, Delilah." *Plotted, Shot, and Painted: Cultural Representations of Biblical Women,* 175–237. Gender, Culture and Theory 3. JSOT Supplement Series 25. Sheffield: Sheffield Academic Press, 1996.

_____. "Feminist Criticism: Whose Interests Are Being Served?" *Judges and Method: New Approaches in Biblical Studies.* Ed. Gale A. Yee, 65–90. Minneapolis: Fortress Press, 1995.

_____. "Samson's Women." *Fragmented Women: Feminist (Sub) Versions of Biblical Narratives,* 61–93. Valley Forge: Trinity Press International, 1993.

_____. "On Judges 11." *A Feminist Companion to Judges.* Ed. Athalya Brenner, 9–22. The Feminist Companion to the Bible 4. Sheffield: Sheffield Academic Press, 1993.

_____. *Tragedy and Biblical Narrative: Arrows of the Almighty.* New York: Cambridge University Press, 1992.

_____. "Delilah." *ABD* 2.133–4.

_____. "Deborah." *HBD,* 214.

_____. "The Centre Cannot Hold: Thematic and Textual Instabilities in Judges." *Catholic Biblical Quarterly* 52 (1990) 410–31.

_____. "Aspects of Symmetry and Balance in the Samson Saga." *Journal for the Study of the Old Testament* 19 (1990) 3–29.

Fewell, Danna N. "Deconstructive Criticism: Achsah and the (E)razed City of Writing." *Judges and Method: New Approaches in Biblical Studies.* Ed. Gale A. Yee, 119–45. Minneapolis: Fortress Press, 1995.

_____. "Judges." *Women's Bible Commentary*. Ed. C. A. Newsom and S. H. Ringe, 67–77. Louisville: Westminster/John Knox Press, 1992.

Fretz, Mark J. "Achsah." *ABD* 1.56–7.

Frymer-Kensky, Tikvah. *In the Wake of the Goddesses: Women, Culture, and the Biblical Transformation of Pagan Myth*, 63–67. New York: The Free Press, 1992.

Fuchs, Esther. "Marginalization, Ambiguity, Silencing: The Story of Jephthah's Daughter." *A Feminist Companion to Judges*. Ed. Athalya Brenner, 116–30. The Feminist Companion to the Bible 4. Sheffield: Sheffield Academic Press, 1993.

Gaster, H. *Myth, Legend, and Custom in the Old Testament*. New York: Harper, 1969.

Goodfriend, Elaine A. "Prostitution (OT)." *ABD* 5.505–10.

Gray, John. *Joshua, Judges, Ruth*. The New Century Bible Commentary. Grand Rapids: Eerdmans, 1986.

Halpern, Baruch. "Kenites." *ABD* 4.17–22.

_____. *The First Historians: The Hebrew Bible and History*. San Francisco: Harper & Row, 1988.

Hamilton, Jeffries. "Ophrah [Place]." *ABD* 5.27-28.

Hamlin, E. John. *Judges: At Risk in the Promised Land*. International Theological Commentary. Grand Rapids: Eerdmans, 1990.

Hunt, Melvin. "Harosheth-Hagoiim." *ABD* 3.62–3.

Jobling, David. "Structuralist Criticism: The Text's World of Meaning." *Judges and Method: New Approaches in Biblical Studies*. Ed. Gale A. Yee, 91–118. Minneapolis: Fortress Press, 1995.

Jones-Warsaw, Koala. "Toward a Womanist Hermeneutic: A Reading of Judges 19–21." *A Feminist Companion to Judges*. Ed. Athalya Brenner, 172–86. The Feminist Companion to the Bible 4. Sheffield: Sheffield Academic Press, 1993.

Jungling, Hans-Winfried. *Richter 19 — Ein Plädoyer für das Königtum*. Analecta Biblica 84. Rome: Biblical Institute Press, 1981.

Kamuf, Peggy. "Author of a Crime." *A Feminist Companion to Judges*. Ed. Athalya Brenner, 187–207. The Feminist Companion to the Bible 4. Sheffield: Sheffield Academic Press, 1993.

Kaufman, Yehezkel. *The Religion of Israel: From Its Beginnings to the Babylonian Exile*. Trans. Moshe Greenberg. Chicago: University of Chicago Press, 1960.

Klein, Lillian R. "A Spectrum of Female Characters." *A Feminist Companion to Judges*. Ed. Athalya Brenner, 24–33. The Feminist Companion to the Bible 4. Sheffield: Sheffield Academic Press, 1993.

_____. "The Book of Judges: Paradigm and Deviation in Images of Women." *A Feminist Companion to Judges*. Ed. Athalya Brenner,

55–71. The Feminist Companion to the Bible 4. Sheffield: Sheffield Academic Press, 1993.

_____. *The Triumph of Irony in the Book of Judges.* JSOTS/Bible and Literature Series 14. Sheffield: The Almond Press, 1989.

Kobayashi, Yoshitaka. "City of Palm Trees." *ABD* 1.1052-3.

Kuntz, J. Kenneth. "Jotham." *ABD* 3.1022.

Launderville, Dale. "Hobab." *ABD* 3.234-5.

Levenson, John D. *The Death and Resurrection of the Beloved Son: The Transformation of Child Sacrifice in Judaism and Christianity.* New Haven: Yale University Press, 1993.

Lindars, B. "Jotham's Fable-A New Form-Critical Analysis." *Journal of Theological Studies* 24 (1973) 355–66.

Lowery, Kirk. "Jael." *ABD* 3.610-611.

_____. "Lappidoth." *ABD* 4. 233.

Maier, Walter A., III. "Anath." *ABD* 1.226.

Malamat, Abraham. "The Danite Migration and the Pan-Israelite Exodus-Conquest: A Biblical Narrative Pattern." *Biblica* 51 (1970) 1–16.

_____. "Origins of Statecraft in the Israelite Monarchy." *Biblical Archaeologist* 28 (1965) 34–50.

Marcus, David. *Jephthah and His Vow.* Lubbock Texas: Texas Tech University Press, 1986.

Marittini, Claude. "Puvah." *ABD* 5.562-3.

Mayes, A.D.H. *Judges.* Sheffield: JSOT Press, 1985.

Mazar, Amihai. "Beth-Shean." *New Encyclopedia of Archaeological Excavations in the Holy Land.* Ed. Ephraim Stern, 1:214-23. Jerusalem: The Israel Exploration Society and Carta., 1993.

Mazar, Amihai, and George Kelm. "Batash, Tel." *New Encyclopedia of Archaeological Excavations in the Holy Land.* Ed. Ephraim Stern, 1:152–7. Jerusalem: The Israel Exploration Society and Carta., 1993.

Mazar, Benjamin. "The Tobiads." *Israel Exploration Journal* 7 (1957) 137–45, 229–38.

McGovern, Patrick. "Beth Shean." *ABD* 1.693–6.

Mendenhall, George. "Zebah." *ABD* 6.1055.

_____. "The Census Lists of Numbers 1 and 26." *Journal of Biblical Literature* 77 (1958) 61–64.

Meyers, Carol. "Ephod." *ABD* 2.550.

Moore, George. *Judges.* The International Critical Commentary. New York: Harper, 1969.

Moran, William. *The Amarna Letters.* Baltimore: The Johns Hopkins University Press, 1992.

Morrison, Martha. "Hurrians." *ABD* 3.335–338.

Mosca, P. G. "Who Seduced Whom? A Note on Joshua 15:18//Judges 1:14." *Catholic Biblical Quarterly* 46 (1984) 18–22.

Niditch, Susan. "Eroticism and Death in the Tale of Jael." *Gender and Difference in Ancient Israel*. Ed. Peggy Day, 43–57. Minneapolis: Fortress Press, 1989.

O'Connell, Robert H. *The Rhetoric of the Book of Judges*. Supplements to Vetus Testamentum 63. Leiden, E.J. Brill, 1996.

Ovadiah, Asher. "Gaza." *New Encyclopedia of Archaeological Excavations in the Holy Land*. Ed. Ephraim Stern, 2:464–7. Jerusalem: The Israel Exploration Society and Carta., 1993.

Patai, R. *Sex and Marriage in the Bible and the Middle East*. Garden City: Doubleday, 1959.

Pitard, Wayne. "Aram-Naharaim." *ABD* 1.341.

Polzin, Robert. *Moses and the Deuteronomist: A Literary Study of the Deuteronomic History: Part One. Deuteronomy, Joshua, Judges*. Bloomington: Indiana University Press, 1980.

Rainey, Anson. "The Identification of Philistine Gath: A Problem in Source Analysis for Historical Geography." *Eretz Israel* 12 (1975) 63*–76*.

Redditt, Paul L., "Tob." *ABD* 6.583.

Reinhartz, Adele. "Samson's Mother: An Unnamed Protagonist." *A Feminist Companion to Judges*. Ed. Athalya Brenner, 157–70. Feminist Companion to the Bible 4. Sheffield: Sheffield Academic Press, 1993.

Reis, P. "Spoiled Child: A Fresh Look at Jephthah's Daughter." Paper presented at the Annual Meeting of the Society of Biblical Literature, San Francisco, CA, November 1997.

Revell, E. J. "Masoretes." *ABD* 4.593–4.

_____. "Masoretic Studies." *ABD* 4.596–7.

_____. "Masoretic Text." *ABD* 4.597–9.

Richter, Wolfgang. *Traditionsgeschichtliche Untersuchungen zum Richterbuch*. Bonner Biblische Beiträge 18. Bonn: P. Hanstein, 1963.

_____. *Die Bearbeitung des 'Retterbuches' in der deuteronomistishen Epoche*. Bonner Biblische Beiträge 21. Bonn: P. Hanstein, 1964.

Sasson, Jack. "Who Cut Samson's Hair? (And Other Trifling Issues Raised by Judges 16)." *Prooftexts* 8 (1988) 333–39.

Schley, D. G. "Abiezer." *ABD* 1.15.

_____. "Adoni-Bezek." *ABD* 1.74.

_____. "Dodo." *ABD* 2.220.

Schmitt, John J. "Prophecy (Pre-exilic Hebrew)." *ABD* 5.482–9.

_____. "Virginity." *ABD* 6.853–4.

Schneider, Tammi J. "Rethinking Jehu." *Biblica* 77 (1996) 100–7.

Schniedewind, William. "The Geo-Political History of Philistine Gath." *Bulletin of the American Schools of Oriental Research* 309 (1998) 69–78.

Seely, Jo Ann H. "Succoth." *ABD* 6.217–8.

Smith, David C. "Penuel." *ABD* 5.223.

Soggin, J. Alberto. *Judges: A Commentary.* Old Testament Library. Philadelphia: The Westminster Press, 1981.

Spina, F. "The Dan Story Historically Reconsidered." *Journal for the Study of the Old Testament* 4 (1977) 60–71.

Stager, Larry. "Ashkelon." *New Encyclopedia of Archaeological Excavations in the Holy Land.* Ed. Ephraim Stern. 1:103–12. Jerusalem: The Israel Exploration Society and Carta., 1993.

Steinberg, Naomi. "Social Scientific Criticism: Judges 9 and Issues of Kinship." *Judges and Method: New Approaches in Biblical Studies.* Ed. Gale Yee, 45–64. Minneapolis: Fortress Press, 1995.

Stern, Ephraim. "Zafi, Tel." *New Encyclopedia of Archaeological Excavations in the Holy Land.* Ed. Ephraim Stern, 4:1521–4. Jerusalem: The Israel Exploration Society and Carta., 1993.

Sweeney, Marvin. "David Polemics in the Book of Judges." *Vetus Testamentum* 47 (1997) 517–29.

Talmon, Shemaryahu. "In Those Days There Was No King in Israel." *Proceedings of the 5th World Congress of Jewish Studies.* Ed. Pinchas Peli, 242–3. Jerusalem: World Union of Jewish Studies, 1972.

Trible, Phylis. "An Unnamed Woman: The Extravagance of Violence." *Texts of Terror: Literary-Feminist Readings of Biblical Narratives,* 65–91. Philadelphia: Fortress Press, 1984.

____. "The Daughter of Jephthah: An Inhuman Sacrifice." *Texts of Terror: Literary-Feminist Readings of Biblical Narratives,* 93–116. Overtures to Biblical Theology 13. Philadelphia: Fortress Press, 1984.

Van Dijk-Hemmes, Fokkelien. "Mothers and a Mediator in the Song of Deborah." *A Feminist Companion to Judges.* Ed. Athalya Brenner, 110–14. The Feminist Companion to the Bible 4. Sheffield: Sheffield Academic Press, 1993.

Wallis, G. "Die Geschichte der Jakobtradition," *Wissenschaftliche Zeitschrift der Martin-Luther-Universität* 13 (1964) 436–38.

Walls, Neal H. *The Goddess Anat in Ugaritic Myth.* SBL Dissertation Series 135. Atlanta: Scholars Press, 1992.

Webb, Barry. *The Book of Judges: An Integrated Reading.* JSOT Supplement Series 46. Sheffield: Sheffield Academic Press, 1987.

Wright, G. Ernest. "The Literary and Historical Problem of Joshua 10 and Judges 1." *Journal of Near Eastern Studies* 5 (1946) 105–14.

Yadin, Yigal. "And Dan, Why Did he Remain with the Ships?" *Australian Journal of Biblical Archaeology* 1 (1968) 8–23.

Yee, Gale A. *Judges and Method: New Approaches in Biblical Studies.* Minneapolis: Fortress Press, 1995.

_____. "Ideological Criticism: Judges 17–21 and the Dismembered Body." *Judges and Method: New Approaches in Biblical Studies,* 146–70. Minneapolis: Fortress Press, 1995.

_____. "By the Hand of a Woman: The Metaphor of the Woman Warrior in Judges 4." *Semeia* 61 (1993) 111–12.

_____. "Introduction: Why Judges." *Judges and Method: New Approaches in Biblical Studies,* 1–16. Minneapolis: Fortress Press, 1995.

Zertal, Adam. "Bezek." *ABD* 1.717–8.

SUBJECT INDEX

INDEX OF BIBLICAL REFERENCES